WISCONSIN Real Estate PRACTICE & LAW

Lawrence Sager

ELEVENTH EDITION UPDATE

This publication is designed to provide accurate and authoritative information in regard to the subject matter covered. It is sold with the understanding that the publisher is not engaged in rendering legal, accounting, or other professional service. If legal advice or other expert assistance is required, the services of a competent professional should be sought.

President: Mehul Patel
Executive Director of Product Development: Kate DeVivo
Managing Editor: Anne Huston
Managing Editor: Tony Peregrin
Director of Production: Daniel Frey
Production Editor: Bill Guerriero
Senior Production Artist: Virginia Byrne
Creative Director: Lucy Jenkins
Vice President of Product Management: Dave Dufresne
Director of Product Management: Melissa Kleeman

Published by Dearborn™ Real Estate Education
30 South Wacker Drive
Chicago, IL 60606-7481
(312) 836-4400
www.dearbornRE.com

Printed in the United States of America

08 09 10 10 9 8 7 6 5 4 3 2 1

The Library of Congress has cataloged the 11th edition as follows:

Sager, Lawrence.
Wisconsin real estate : practice & law / Lawrence C. Sager—11th ed.
p. cm.
Includes index.
ISBN 0-7931-8872-5
1. Real estate agents—Licenses—Wisconsin. 2. Real estate business—Law and legislation—Wisconsin. 3. vendors and purchasers—Wisconsin I. Title

KFW2682.R4S24 2004
346.77504'37—dc22 2004016299

11th edition, update ISBN-13: 978-1-4277-7943-4
11th edition, update ISBN-10: 1-4277-7943-0

This book is dedicated to my wonderful wife, Adrienne, for all of her support and encouragement.

Contents

Preface

Although real estate activity in the state of Wisconsin is subject to federal laws and regulations, it is controlled primarily by Wisconsin's laws, rules, regulations, and case law, and by state customs that prevail where no law covers a practice.

The real estate salesperson and broker licensing exams in Wisconsin are administered by Promissor. The curriculum for both salesperson and broker exams is primarily state-specific and transaction-based. The sales exam no longer contains a state and national portion; it is now just a 140-question, state-specific exam, plus five to ten pretest questions.

To help you prepare for the exam, each chapter in this book is followed by a practice quiz. These quizzes serve as both learning and teaching devices. As you finish each chapter, and before going on to the next, be sure that you can answer each question and that you understand all the material covered. An Answer Key for the chapter quizzes is included at the end of the book.

Changes in forms approved by the Department of Regulation and Licensing are being made as this book is being published. You can refer to the instructor resource site at *www.dearborn.com* to get an update on newly approved forms, as well as an explanation of the new forms.

REAL ESTATE LAW COVERED IN THE EXAM

The salesperson exam covers the following statutes and administrative rules:

- S. 66.1011 Equal Opportunity Law
- S. 77 Taxation and Transfer Fee
- S. 106.50 Equal Rights
- S. 240.10 Real Estate Agency Contracts
- S. 254 Environmental Health
- S. 406 Bulk Transfers
- S. 452 Real Estate Practice
- S. 703 Condominiums
- S. 706 Conveyances of Real Property
- S. 709 Disclosures by Owners of Residential Property
- S. RL15 Documents and Records
- S. RL16 Contractual Forms and Legal Advice
- S. RL17 Licensure and Supervision of Employees
- S. RL18 Trust Accounts
- S. RL23 Change of License
- S. RL24 Ethical Practices
- S. AG134 Residential Rental Practices

For further information refer to the *Promissor Real Estate Candidate Handbook*. The Web site for Promissor/Wisconsin real estate is:

WEB LINK

http://www.promissor.com.

The salesperson exam will contain one story problem with questions based on the real estate forms that are provided with the exam.

The broker's exam contains 100 questions with a focus on state law; it no longer has a general broker management section. The content emphasizes drafting of contracts as well as supervision of licensees.

REAL ESTATE FORMS EMPHASIZED IN THE EXAM

The salesperson exam focuses on the following Wisconsin real estate forms:

- WB-1 Residential Listing Contract
- WB-4 Residential Condominium Listing Contract
- WB-36 Buyer Agency/Tenant Representation Agreement
- WB-11 Residential Offer to Purchase
- WB-13 Vacant Land Offer to Purchase
- WB-14 Residential Condominium Offer to Purchase
- WB-40 Amendment to Offer to Purchase
- WB-41 Notice Relating to Offer to Purchase
- WB-44 Counter-Offer
- WB-46 Multiple Counter-Proposal

TESTING LOCATIONS AND FEES

The salesperson and broker exams are administered at the following Promissor Assessment Centers:

	Location	Schedule
1.	Elm Grove/Milwaukee	Tuesday through Saturday
2.	Madison	Monday, Tuesday, Wednesday, and Saturday
3.	Green Bay	Tuesday, Wednesday, and Saturday
4.	Eau Claire	Saturday
5.	Wausau	Saturday
6.	Edina, Minn.	Monday through Saturday
7.	Duluth, Minn.	Saturday
8.	Chicago, Ill.	Tuesday through Saturday

The testing fee is $69 for both the salesperson and broker examinations. There is an additional fee of $50 to test outside Wisconsin.

ABOUT THE AUTHOR

Lawrence Sager is a licensed real estate broker, certified residential appraiser, AQB-certified USPAP instructor, and REALTOR®. He holds a master's degree in urban land economics from the University of Illinois and was Real Estate Coordinator at Madison Area Technical College (MATC). His writings have appeared in numerous publications on real estate and related fields. Larry has served as a research consultant for MATC, the University of Wisconsin, and other public and private organizations. He is a certified fair housing trainer and has served as president of the Community Reinvestment Alliance. He has worked with the Wisconsin Real Estate Examining Board as a course writer and as the assistant executive secretary in the certification of educational programs for real estate licensure. He is a member of both the Professional Standards Committee of the REALTORS® Association of South Central Wisconsin and the Governor's Council on Real Estate Curriculum and Examinations. Previously, he has held membership on the Appraiser Application Advisory Committee of the Wisconsin Department of Regulation and Licensing, and on the Advisory Committee on Continuing Assessor Education of the Wisconsin Department of Revenue. For many years, he has served as an expert witness in the areas of real estate practice and law, as well as competency of real estate licensees.

In addition to *Wisconsin Real Estate: Practice & Law*, he is also the author of *Guide to Passing the PSI Real Estate Exam.*

ACKNOWLEDGMENTS

I wish to thank Sue Lanham, owner of Lanham Realty, and Anne Blood, Instructor in both the real estate and paralegal programs at Madison Area Technical College, for their insightful reviews of the previous edition, which helped to guide the changes that appear in this edition. Your help has been invaluable!

I would also like to acknowledge Wisconsin Legal Blank Co., Inc., Milwaukee, Wisconsin, for the use of their forms in this book and the Wisconsin Department of Regulation and Licensing for its continued cooperation.

Wisconsin Real Estate: Practice & Law may also be used with other tools from Dearborn™ Real Estate Education. The conversion chart on page x indicates the chapter, or chapters, in the Dearborn™ national publications that correspond with your Wisconsin-specific text. We hope this conversion chart will help you as you study for your real estate exam.

CHAPTER CONVERSION TABLE

Wisconsin Real Estate: Practice & Law, 11th Edition		*Modern Real Estate Practice,* 16th Ed.	*Mastering Real Estate Principles,* 3rd Ed.	National Real Estate Principles Software, Ver. 2.0	*Guide to Passing the PSI Real Estate Exam,* 5th Ed.
1.	Real Estate Agency and Brokerage	4, 5	13	4, 5	7
2.	Listing Agreements	6	15	6	9
3.	Interests in Real Estate	7	7	7	3
4.	How Ownership Is Held	8	9	8	3
5.	Legal Descriptions	9	6	9	3
6.	Real Estate Taxes and Other Liens	10	5, 25	10	4
7.	Real Estate Contracts	11	14	11	9
8.	Transfer of Title	12	10	12	10
9.	Title Records	13	11	13	10
10.	Real Estate License Laws	—	16	—	—
11.	Real Estate Financing	14, 15	Unit VII	14, 15	5, 6
12.	Leases	16	8	16	13
13.	Land-Use Controls and Property Development	19	3	19	4
14.	Fair Housing and Ethical Practices	20	17	20	11
15.	Closing the Real Estate Transaction	22	12	22	6, 12 (Math Review)

CHAPTER 1

Real Estate Agency and Brokerage

In Wisconsin, a person must be a licensed real estate broker in order to perform, negotiate, or attempt to perform or negotiate "for others for a fee or anything of value" any of the following activities involving real property or a business opportunity: listing, selling, buying, exchanging, leasing, renting, or dealing in options to buy. In other words, a person must have a broker's license in order to operate a real estate brokerage and collect commissions.

REAL ESTATE LICENSE LAW

Wisconsin real estate licenses are granted and regulated by the Wisconsin Department of Regulation and Licensing under the provisions of Chapter 452 of the Wisconsin Statutes. This law and the department's rules and regulations also regulate and restrict the activities of real estate brokers and salespeople. Many of the provisions of this law are discussed in Chapter 10 of this text and are covered on the salesperson's licensing exam.

CREATING AN AGENCY

In Wisconsin, an agency between a broker and seller generally is created by a listing contract. The listing contract establishes the relationship between the broker and the seller and defines the broker's right to a commission. According to Wisconsin law, the listing contract must be in writing, describe the real estate involved, state the price and terms of the sale, state the commission, establish the expiration date, name the broker involved, and be signed by the person paying the commission. If a real estate broker and his or her associates wish to act as agents of the buyer in a real estate transaction, they must use Form WB-36, Buyer Agency/Tenant Representation Agreement, or they must permit the buyer's attorney to draft the contract.

Dual Agency and Designated Agency

The Wisconsin Supreme Court has ruled that a broker "cannot sacrifice the interests of either party in order to further his or her own individual interests by attempting to procure double commissions . . ." Therefore, dual agency is prohibited in Wisconsin unless: (1) the agent acts as a middle person, introduces the parties, and leaves further negotiations to them and (2) the broker acts as agent for both parties after he or she has made full disclosure to each of the parties. Dual agency consent must be in writing. The broker agency law refers to multiple representation rather than dual agency. Section 452.134 (3) states that a broker in a multiple representation relationship may not engage in designated agency, unless all of the broker's clients in the relationship have consented to designated agency in writing. It states further that a client may withdraw consent to designated agency by written notice to the broker at any time.

THE BROKER'S COMMISSION

In order for a broker to collect his or her commission, the amount or rate of the commission must be clearly stated in the listing agreement as a percentage of selling price or dollar amount or as a percentage of the list price if the property is exchanged. The listing contract also must meet the requirements of a valid listing as detailed in Chapter 2 of this book.

In any Wisconsin real estate transaction, the amount of a broker's commission is determined by mutual agreement between the broker and the seller. The commission usually is based on a percentage of the final sales price. However, the parties may agree on a fixed dollar amount of commission as opposed to a percentage. Either of these provisions, if clearly stated, satisfies the legal requirements for a listing contract in Wisconsin.

Generally, brokers earn a commission by accomplishing what they were employed to do. Under most listing agreements, the broker must procure a buyer who is ready and willing to enter into a binding offer-to-purchase contract and financially able to carry out the terms of that contract and complete the sale. According to the listing contract, the broker's "commission is due and payable in full at the earlier of closing or the date set for closing" (i.e., earned earlier, but not payable until closing).

BROKER-SALESPERSON RELATIONSHIP

The nature of a real estate salesperson's relationship with an employing broker is determined by mutual agreement. The actual form of the employment contract between a broker and salesperson will depend on whether the salesperson is to operate as the broker's employee or as an independent contractor.

Most real estate salespeople in Wisconsin are affiliated with their brokers as independent contractors. A sample contract creating a broker-independent contractor relationship has been developed by the Wisconsin REALTORS® Association. It contains seven provisions:

1. The independent contractor must work *exclusively for the real estate company.*
2. The independent contractor must *abide* by the applicable *state laws* and the *rules and regulations* of the Wisconsin Real Estate Board and the Wisconsin Department of Regulation and Licensing, as well as by the *Code of Ethics* of the National Association of REALTORS® and its local affiliates. Some contracts specify that the contractor must abide by the *company policy manual.* This provision, which is optional, tends to limit contractors' control over the details of their work and may call into question their status as independent contractors. Caution should be exercised by both sides in establishing this provision.
3. The independent contractor will be *compensated on a commission basis according to a schedule attached to the contract.* The division of commission set out in the schedule may be altered in special cases by mutual agreement. Commissions are held by the real estate company in the independent contractor's name and paid in accordance with the commission schedule. The company broker may not hold the commissions in the trust account used for clients' deposits. Federal law dictates that no more than 10 percent of an independent contractor's income can be from wages or salary and at least 90 percent must come from commission.
4. *Expenses charged against commissions will be paid before a commission is divided.* Expenses, therefore, will be shared between the contractor or employee and the company (i.e., the broker or employer).
5. The independent contractor *is not a servant, an employee, or a partner* and is solely responsible for reporting and paying taxes on commissions received.
6. The contract *may be terminated at any time* by either party upon notice. Termination does not affect accrued commissions due the independent contractor.
7. The *contract* and the *commission schedule* must be *signed* by both parties and *dated.* Independent contractors should have an attorney review the contract before they sign it so that it can be properly modified according to their particular situations. The broker-independent contractor relationship does not release brokers from responsibility for the actions of their salespeople.

ETHICAL RESPONSIBILITIES OF THE BROKER

Broker's Responsibility for Own Statements (Chapter RL24 of Wisconsin Statutes)

Licensees (brokers and salespersons) make many statements and representations regarding the condition of a property being offered for sale or rent. Because employing brokers are held liable for such statements, licensees must be very careful not to make statements that misrepresent or are not true. To help licensees avoid problems in this area, at least four rules of practice have been suggested for use by licensees:

1. Brokers should *make full disclosure* of all material adverse facts known to them without violating the basic duty of the agent-principal relationship. They must also provide confidentiality to all parties.

2. Licensees should *obtain as much information* as possible from the seller. The law has been requiring more disclosure and requires the seller to acquire facts for the purpose of disclosure, as evidenced by the Seller Disclosure Law and the Real Estate Condition Report.
3. Licensees should *not knowingly make false representations*, nor should they state an opinion without disclosing all the facts that may affect that statement.
4. When dealing with inexperienced buyers, licensees must *exercise extra care in making full and complete disclosures* and must refrain from making statements that generally might be considered to be "puffing" or sales psychology.

REAL ESTATE BROKER AGENCY LAW

The real estate broker agency law identifies specific duties that licensees have to all parties in a transaction as well as the duties to clients only. Ten major points regarding agency law are:

1. Licensees must disclose as an adverse fact information that indicates that a party to a transaction is not able or does not intend to meet his or her obligations under a contract or agreement made concerning the transaction such as either the buyer or seller has no intention of completing the contract.
2. Licensees must keep confidential any information given to them in confidence or any information they obtain that they know a reasonable party would want to keep confidential, unless the information is an adverse fact that must be disclosed or the party specifically authorizes the licensee to disclose it. Licensees must continue to keep the information confidential after the transaction is complete and after their firm is no longer providing brokerage services to the party and must keep such information confidential forever.
3. Agency law in Wisconsin requires two types of agency disclosure forms. One form is for "customers" and the other form is for "clients." Any buyer or seller who is not in a contract with an agent (such as a for sale by owner (FSBO) or a buyer who does not want a buyer agency agreement) would be considered a "customer." Any buyer or seller who has signed a listing contract or entered into a buyer agency agreement would be considered a "client."
4. In Wisconsin, an agent may present an agency disclosure form at any time, but the form must be disclosed prior to any negotiations. "Negotiate" means to provide assistance to a party in the development of a proposal or agreement relating to a transaction. Although an agent can go over the agency forms sooner and have a buyer enter into a Buyer Agency Agreement, it is not required. It is also important to stress that an agent showing a property to a customer in the "pre-agency" stage will not be able to give any advice that would have a negative impact on the seller, unless he or she is acting as an agent for the buyer.
5. You should also be aware that an agent is the subagent of the broker/listing agent. An agent's duties are to the broker and not to the seller. Subagents cannot place their own interests ahead of the interests of the other broker's client and cannot provide advice and opinions to the parties in a transaction that are contrary to the interests of the other broker's client, unless otherwise required by law.

FIGURE 1.1

Sample Confidentiality Statement

NOTICE TO CLIENTS AND CUSTOMERS

A BROKER IS REQUIRED TO MAINTAIN THE CONFIDENTIALITY OF ALL INFORMATION OBTAINED BY THE BROKER IN CONFIDENCE AND OF ALL INFORMATION OBTAINED BY THE BROKER THAT HE OR SHE KNOWS A REASONABLE PARTY WOULD WANT TO BE KEPT CONFIDENTIAL, UNLESS THE INFORMATION IS REQUIRED TO BE DISCLOSED BY LAW. THE FOLLOWING INFORMATION IS REQUIRED TO BE DISCLOSED BY LAW:

1. MATERIAL ADVERSE FACTS, AS DEFINED IN SECTION 452.01(5G) OF THE WISCONSIN STATUTES.
2. ANY FACTS KNOWN BY THE BROKER THAT CONTRADICT ANY INFORMATION INCLUDED IN A WRITTEN INSPECTION REPORT ON THE PROPERTY OR REAL ESTATE THAT IS THE SUBJECT OF THE TRANSACTION.

TO ENSURE THAT THE BROKER IS AWARE OF SPECIFIC INFORMATION YOU CONSIDER CONFIDENTIAL, YOU MAY LIST THAT INFORMATION IN THE SPACE BELOW MARKED "CONFIDENTIAL INFORMATION." AT A LATER TIME, YOU MAY ALSO PROVIDE THE BROKER WITH OTHER WRITTEN NOTIFICATION OF THE INFORMATION YOU CONSIDER TO BE CONFIDENTIAL.

CONFIDENTIAL INFORMATION:

____

____

____

6. Agency law in Wisconsin allows for multiple representation with designated agency. This law allows a seller's agent and buyer's agent under one broker to negotiate on a property and give comprehensive advice to each party in each party's best interest.
7. You must have two agents to represent two clients in a transaction under multiple representation with designated agency. If you are the listing agent and have a buyer agency agreement with the buyer, you would have all parties agree to multiple representation or dual agency, treat all parties fairly, and remain neutral when negotiating.
8. Agency law gives the client the option of working with a broker in one of three ways. These three options pertain to how the client wants to be represented while being shown the agent's company listings or while negotiating on a company listing.
   a. Multiple representation with designated agency, which is what most sellers and buyers in a buyer agency agreement choose.
   b. Multiple representation without designated agency, called dual agency, in which the agents must remain neutral in negotiations.
   c. No multiple representation (dual agency) relationships, which means that the seller is stating that no one from the listing broker's company can show his property and the buyer is stating that she does not want to look at any of the buyer agent's company listings.
9. Agency law also deals with limited service brokers. A limited service broker, for example, might list a property but provide no service other than placing the property on the multiple listing service. The limited service broker would provide no marketing services such as negotiating with prospective buyers. Negotiation has been added as a duty, but it is a duty that the client may waive. It will require an express written waiver of negotiations by the client, which is an example of what a limited service broker would not provide.

10. Agency law also clarifies that a broker is only responsible for brokerage services provided on behalf of the broker by the broker's licensees (e.g., if a broker accidentally injures someone at a social gathering unrelated to real estate, the broker would not be liable).

Licensees must be especially aware of Chapter RL24, which covers conduct and ethical practices for real estate licensees in Wisconsin. Chapter RL24 addresses four situations:

1. *Misrepresentation.* A client is not liable for a misrepresentation made by a broker when providing brokerage services, unless the client knows or should have known of the misrepresentation or the broker is repeating a misrepresentation made to him or her by the client.
2. *Inspection.* A licensee acting as an agent in a real estate transaction involving real estate improved with a structure must make a *reasonably competent and diligent inspection* of accessible areas of the structure and immediate surrounding areas of the property to detect observable material adverse facts. A reasonably competent and diligent inspection of real estate improved with a structure does not require the operation of mechanical equipment; the opening of panels, doors, or covers for access to mechanical systems; or the moving of furniture, boxes, or other property; nor does it require a licensee to observe areas of the property for which entry presents an unreasonable risk of injury or areas accessible only by ladder, by crawling, or by other equivalent means of access. A reasonably competent and diligent inspection of vacant land requires an observation of the vacant land from at least at one point on or adjacent to the land.
3. *Disclosure.* A licensee acting as an agent in a real estate transaction must *disclose* to each party, in writing and in a timely fashion, all material adverse facts that the licensee knows and that the party does not know or cannot discover through a reasonably vigilant observation, unless the disclosure of the material adverse fact is prohibited by law. The provision is not limited to the condition of the property but includes other material adverse facts in the transaction.
4. *Recommendation*. If a licensee acting as an agent in a real estate transaction becomes aware of information suggesting the possibility of an adverse fact material to the transaction, competent practice requires the licensee to disclose such information to the parties in writing and, in a timely fashion, *recommend* that the parties obtain expert assistance to inspect or investigate for possible adverse facts material to the transaction and if directed by the parties, draft appropriate inspection or investigation contingencies. A licensee is not required to retain third-party inspectors or investigators to perform investigations of information suggesting the possibility of an adverse fact material to the transaction.

Section 452.23 of the Wisconsin Statutes makes clear certain facets of what can and cannot be disclosed by real estate licensees. Brokers and salespeople may not disclose any information that may result in unlawful discrimination under Section 106.50 of the Wisconsin Statutes or unlawful discrimination based on handicap under federal law. For example, licensees may not disclose that current or former occupants of a property suffered from acquired immune deficiency syndrome (AIDS) (S. 452.23[1]).

Stigmatized property 4 –

Section 452.23 also states that brokers and salespeople are not required to disclose the following: (1) that the property was the site where an act such as a murder occurred if such occurrence has no effect on the physical condition of the property (S. 452.23[2][a]); (2) information on the physical condition of the property if a written report that discloses the information was prepared by a qualified third party and provided to the appropriate persons (S. 452.23[2][b]); and (3) whether the property is located near any adult family home, community-based residential facility, or nursing home (S. 452.23[2][c]). In addition, a broker or salesperson must disclose any information that contradicts the written report of a qualified third party (RL24.07 (G)).

Section 452.23(4) states that "in performing an investigation or inspection and in making a disclosure in connection with a real estate transaction, a broker or salesperson shall exercise the degree of care expected to be exercised by a reasonably prudent person who has the knowledge, skills, and training required for licensure as a salesperson or broker under this chapter." In other words, if a broker or salesperson is not required to have specific knowledge, skills, or training to be licensed, he or she will not need that knowledge, skill, or training to perform a competent inspection, investigation, or disclosure.

Finally, Section 452.24 states that a real estate licensee, if asked about whether a specific person is required to register as a sex offender, the location of sex offenders in a neighborhood, or for any other information about the Sex Offender Registry, the licensee must disclose whatever actual knowledge he or she has on the subject, or provide the toll-free telephone number and Internet address for the Department of Corrections' Sex Offender Registry. The Wisconsin Department of Corrections' Sex Offender Registry (effective June 1, 2001) is available to the public via the Internet and the toll-free telephone number (see below).

A real estate licensee will have immunity relating to the disclosure of information on sex offenders if he or she provides written notice that information about registered sexual offenders and sex offender registry can be obtained by contacting the Department of Corrections via either the Internet or a toll-free number. This type of disclosure has been inserted into the disclosure language in all agency agreements, agency disclosure forms, real estate condition reports, and tenant application and disclosure forms. The incorporation of the Internet address and toll-free number for the Department of Corrections into the Real Estate Condition Report is important to the seller because it fulfills his and her separate disclosure requirements to the buyers if the sellers are asked about sex offenders and the form is provided to the buyers. The notice states that one may obtain information about the Sex Offender Registry and persons registered with the registry by contacting the Wisconsin Department of Corrections toll-free at (877) 234-0085, or via the Internet at the following Web address:

WEB LINK

http://www.widocoffenders.org.

Thus, even if the licensee is aware of information about sex offenders in the neighborhood, the licensee will have immunity if the person asking the question is referred to the Wisconsin Department of Corrections. Licensees should also be aware that disclosure is required only when someone asks questions regarding the Sex Offender Registry or sex offenders in the neighborhood. However, the risk of giving an inadequate answer makes it sound practice to refer client and customer inquires to the Wisconsin Department of Corrections by providing them with the toll-free number and Internet address above.

SELLER DISCLOSURE LAW

Chapter 709 of the Wisconsin Statutes requires most sellers of one-family to four-family residential properties to provide buyers with a copy of the Real Estate Condition Report presented in the statutes. (See Figure 1.2.) The law covers broker-assisted transactions as well as property sold by owners.

The law requires a seller to complete the condition report with information based on his or her own personal knowledge as well as on information obtained from experts, professionals, and qualified third-party inspectors as defined in Section 452.23(2)(b) of the Wisconsin Statutes. The Real Estate Condition Report requires the seller to respond to a list of 27 statements concerning the condition of the property as to whether the seller is aware of any defects. It is the seller's obligation to respond to each statement with regard to the property as "yes," "no," or "not applicable." If a defect is disclosed in the report, an explanation of the defect should be included within the report.

Upon completion of the report by the seller, the seller must sign and date the report, stating that to the best of the seller's knowledge, the information presented in the report is true and correct. Third-party inspection reports relied on by the seller to complete the condition report should be attached to the seller's real estate condition report.

Each potential buyer may receive a copy of the Real Estate Condition Report upon viewing a property for sale prior to submitting an offer to purchase. However, a copy of the report must be provided to a buyer no later than ten days after acceptance of an offer to purchase. Receipt of the report should be verified in writing. If defects are disclosed in the report and the buyer did not receive the report prior to the acceptance of the offer to purchase, the buyer has two business days to rescind the offer to purchase. However, if the buyer received a copy of the Real Estate Condition Report prior to accepting the offer to purchase, the buyer has no right of rescission via the condition report.

The seller disclosure law was amended in 1996. The amendments included Section 709.035, which states that if any time after completing a report, but before acceptance of an offer to purchase or option, an owner obtains information or becomes aware of any condition that would change a response on the completed report, the owner must amend the Real Estate Condition Report. The owner is not required to amend the condition report if the new information or condition arises after acceptance of the offer or option. The condition report may be amended by either preparing an amendment to the previously completed condition report or by completing another condition report. The amended report must be given to the buyer no later than ten days after acceptance of the offer to purchase or option.

It is important to emphasize that the seller has no statutory duty to amend the Real Estate Condition Report or representations made in the offer to purchase

FIGURE 1.2

Sample Real Estate Condition Report

Form No. 907 Real Estate Condition Report
Wis. Stats. 709.02 (09-1-02)

Wisconsin Legal Blank Co., Inc.
Milwaukee, Wis.

REAL ESTATE CONDITION REPORT

THIS CONDITION REPORT CONCERNS THE REAL PROPERTY LOCATED AT ______________________ (STREET ADDRESS) ______________________ IN THE ______________ (CITY) (VILLAGE) (TOWN) OF ______________________, COUNTY OF ______________________, STATE OF WISCONSIN. THIS REPORT IS A DISCLOSURE OF THE CONDITION OF THAT PROPERTY AS OF ______________ (MONTH) ______ (DAY), 20______, IN COMPLIANCE WITH SECTION 709.02 OF THE WISCONSIN STATUTES. IT IS NOT A WARRANTY OF ANY KIND BY THE OWNER OR ANY AGENTS REPRESENTING ANY PRINCIPAL IN THIS TRANSACTION AND IS NOT A SUBSTITUTE FOR ANY INSPECTIONS OR WARRANTIES THAT THE PRINCIPALS MAY WISH TO OBTAIN.

OWNER'S INFORMATION

B.1. In this form, "am aware" means to have notice or knowledge. In this form, "defect" means a condition that would have a significant adverse effect on the value of the property; that would significantly impair the health or safety of future occupants of the property; or that if not repaired, removed or replaced would significantly shorten or adversely affect the expected normal life of the premises.

B.2. The owner discloses the following information with the knowledge that even though this is not a warranty, prospective buyers may rely on this information in deciding whether and on what terms to purchase the property. The owner hereby authorizes any agent representing any principal in this transaction to provide a copy of this statement, and to disclose any information in the statement, to any person in connection with any actual or anticipated sale of the property.

B.3. The owner represents that to the best of his or her knowledge the responses to the following statements have been accurately noted as "yes", "no" or "not applicable" to the property being sold. If the owner responds to any statement with "yes", the owner shall provide, in the additional information area of this form, an explanation of the reason why the response to the statement is "yes".

B.4. If the transfer is of a condominium unit, the property to which this form applies is the condominium unit, the common elements of the condominium and any limited common elements that may be used only by the owner of the condominium unit being transferred.

STATEMENTS

		Yes	No	N/A	See Expert's Report*
C.1.	I am aware of defects in the roof.	____	____	____	____
C.2.	I am aware of defects in the electrical system.	____	____	____	____
C.3.	I am aware of defects in part of the plumbing system (including the water heater, water softener and swimming pool) that is included in the sale.	____	____	____	____
C.4.	I am aware of defects in the heating and air conditioning system (including the air filters and humidifiers).	____	____	____	____
C.5.	I am aware of defects in the well, including unsafe well water.	____	____	____	____
C.6.	I am aware that this property is served by a joint well.	____	____	____	____
C.7.	I am aware of defects in the septic system or other sanitary disposal system.	____	____	____	____
C.8.	I am aware of underground or aboveground fuel storage tanks on *or previously located on* the property. (If "yes", the owner, by law, may have to register the tanks with the Department of Commerce at P.O. Box 7970, Madison, Wisconsin 53707, whether the tanks are in use or not. Regulations of the Department of Commerce may require the closure or removal of unused tanks.)	____	____	____	____
C.9.	I am aware of an "LP" tank on the property. (If "yes", specify in the additional information space whether or not the owner of the property either owns or leases the tank).	____	____	____	____
C.10.	I am aware of defects in the basement or foundation (including cracks, seepage and bulges).	____	____	____	____
C.11.	I am aware that the property is located in a floodplain, wetland or shoreland zoning area.	____	____	____	____
C.12.	I am aware of defects in the structure of the property.	____	____	____	____
C.13.	I am aware of defects in mechanical equipment included in the sale either as fixtures or personal property.	____	____	____	____
C.14.	I am aware of boundary or lot line disputes, encroachments or encumbrances (including a joint driveway).	____	____	____	____
C.15.	I am aware of a defect caused by unsafe concentrations of, or unsafe conditions relating to, radon, radium in water supplies, lead in paint, lead in soil, lead in water supplies or plumbing system, or other potentially hazardous or toxic substances on the premises.	____	____	____	____
C.16.	I am aware of the presence of asbestos or asbestos-containing materials on the premises.	____	____	____	____
C.17.	I am aware of a defect caused by unsafe concentrations of, unsafe conditions relating to, or the storage of, hazardous or toxic substances on neighboring properties.	____	____	____	____
C.18.	I am aware of current or previous termite, powder-post beetle or carpenter ant infestations.	____	____	____	____
C.19.	I am aware of defects in a wood burning stove or fireplace or of defects caused by a fire in a stove or fireplace or elsewhere on the property.	____	____	____	____
C.20.	I am aware either that remodeling affecting the property's structure or mechanical systems was done or that additions to this property were made during my period of ownership without the required permits.	____	____	____	____
C.21.	I am aware of federal, state, or local regulations requiring repairs, alterations or corrections of an existing condition.	____	____	____	____
C.22.	I have received notice of property tax increases, other than normal annual increases, or am aware of a pending property reassessment.	____	____	____	____
C.23.	I am aware that remodeling that may increase the property's assessed value was done.	____	____	____	____
C.24.	I am aware of proposed or pending special assessments.	____	____	____	____

FIGURE 1.2 (CONTINUED)

Sample Real Estate Condition Report

		Yes	No	N/A	*See Expert's Report**
C.25.	I am aware of the proposed construction of a public project that may affect the use of the property.	____	____	____	____
C.26.	I am aware of subdivision homeowners' associations, common areas co-owned with others, zoning violations or nonconforming uses, rights-of-way, easements, or another use of a part of the property by nonowners, other than recorded utility easements.	____	____	____	____
C.27.	I am aware of other defects affecting the property.	____	____	____	____

ADDITIONAL INFORMATION

		Yes	No	N/A	*See Expert's Report**
D.1.	I am aware that a structure on the property is designated as a historic building or that part of the property is in a historic district.	____	____	____	____
D.2.	Land sold with the property has been valued under Stat.§70.32 (2r) (use-value assessment).	____	____	____	____
D.3.	I am aware of the presence of unsafe levels of mold, or roof,basement, window or plumbing leaks, or overflow from sinks, bathtubs or sewers, or other water or moisture intrusions or conditions that might initiate the growth of unsafe levels of mold.	____	____	____	____

D.4. The owner has lived on the property for ________ years.

D.5. Explanation of "yes" responses. (See B.3.) ____

Notice: You may obtain information about the sex offender registry and persons registered with the registry by contacting the Wisconsin Department of Corrections on the Internet at http://www.widocoffenders.org or by phone at 877-234-0085

OWNER'S CERTIFICATION

E. The owner certifies that the information in this report is true and correct to the best of the owner's knowledge as of the date on which the owner signs this report.

☐ *The undersigned owner believes he or she is not subject to Wisconsin Statutes Chapter 709, but is completing this report on a voluntary basis. Accordingly, buyer would have no rescission rights based on this report. (Check if applicable)*

NOTE: Wisconsin Statute 709.035 requires owners who, prior to acceptance, obtain information which would change a response on this report, to submit a new report or an amended report to the prospective buyer.

Owner	Date	Owner	Date
Owner	Date	Owner	Date

CERTIFICATION BY PERSON SUPPLYING INFORMATION

F. A person other than the owner certifies that he or she has supplied information on which the owner relied for this report and that information is true and correct to the best of that person's knowledge as of the date on which the person signs this report.

Person	Items	Date	Person	Items	Date
Person	Items	Date	Person	Items	Date

NOTICE REGARDING ADVICE OR INSPECTIONS

G. THE PROSPECTIVE BUYER AND THE OWNER MAY WISH TO OBTAIN PROFESSIONAL ADVICE OR INSPECTIONS OF THE PROPERTY AND TO PROVIDE FOR APPROPRIATE PROVISIONS IN A CONTRACT BETWEEN THEM WITH RESPECT TO ANY ADVICE, INSPECTIONS, DEFECTS OR WARRANTIES.

BUYER'S ACKNOWLEDGMENT

H.1. THE PROSPECTIVE BUYER ACKNOWLEDGES THAT TECHNICAL KNOWLEDGE SUCH AS THAT ACQUIRED BY PROFESSIONAL INSPECTORS MAY BE REQUIRED TO DETECT CERTAIN DEFECTS SUCH AS THE PRESENCE OF ASBESTOS, BUILDING CODE VIOLATIONS AND FLOODPLAIN STATUS.

H.2. I ACKNOWLEDGE RECEIPT OF A COPY OF THIS STATEMENT.

Prospective Buyer	Date	Prospective Buyer	Date
Prospective Buyer	Date	Prospective Buyer	Date

**NOTE: All information appearing in italics in this REAL ESTATE CONDITION REPORT is purely of a supplemental nature and is not part of the REAL ESTATE CONDITION REPORT required pursuant to Section 709.03 of the Wisconsin Statutes.*

if the seller learns of new defects after acceptance of the offer. If there is damage to the property between the acceptance and the closing, the terms found in lines 115–123 of the Residential Offer to Purchase form will determine if the seller will be required to repair the property. The seller must still disclose all material defects but should not disclose them in an amended Real Estate Condition Report that could then allow the buyer to rescind within two business days.

An additional change included in the 1996 amendment, Section 709.05(2)(b), states that a buyer may not rescind an offer to purchase or to option on the basis of a defect disclosed in a condition report, amended report, or amendment to a report if the buyer was aware or had written notice of the nature and extent of the defect at the time the offer or option was submitted to the owner or owner's agent. Section 709.05(2)(a) states that if a buyer, after submitting to the owner or owner's agent an offer to purchase or to option, receives an amendment to the previously received condition report or an amended report that discloses a new defect, the buyer may rescind the offer to purchase or to option within two business days after receipt of such information. Such rescission notice must be in writing and can be delivered to either the owner or the owner's agent, and the right to rescind is the only remedy under Wisconsin Statues. Fiduciary representatives, trustees, conservators, property exempt from real estate transfer fees, and real property (that has never been inhabited) are all exempt from the requirements of Chapter 709, which is covered on the salesperson's licensing exam.

Lead-Based Paint Disclosure

The federal laws for the disclosure of lead-based paint on all residential real estate became effective on December 6, 1996. The laws require that landlords and sellers of residential real estate built prior to 1978 disclose lead-based paint and lead-based paint information and warnings to tenants and buyers before they become obligated contractually to rent or buy. All real estate agents, with the exception of buyer's agents compensated only by the buyer, are required to inform the owners of their responsibility under the laws and to ensure compliance with the laws. Agents must inform landlords and sellers of their obligations and make sure that the required forms are completed either by the landlord or seller, or by the agent personally. (See Figure 1.3.)

Licensees should be aware of the *Antwaun v. Heritage Mutual Insurance Company* case in which the Wisconsin Supreme Court held that "a duty to test for lead paint arises whenever the landlord of a residential property constructed before 1978 either knows or in the use of ordinary care should know that there is peeling, flaking, or chipping paint on the rental property." The court concluded that if there is peeling or chipping paint present in a residential structure built before 1978, it is foreseeable that lead-based paint may be present. The court also found that if there is, in fact, lead-based paint on the premises, this would present an unreasonable risk of harm to the property occupants. Thus, real estate licensees involved in sales or rental transactions regarding residential rental property built prior to 1978 will need to interpret any observed flaking, chipping, or peeling paint in those properties as potential adverse material facts. Furthermore, if the owner fails to disclose the flaking, etc., and fails to test for deteriorating paint, the licensee must make the disclosure in writing to the parties. The *Antwaun* case could result in high liability for pre-1978 property owners, but some can be ameliorated by the following new law passed by the legislature as a response to the *Antwaun* case.

FIGURE 1.3

Lead-Based Paint Hazard Addendum

Form No. 976 Seller's Disclosure of Information on Lead-Based Paint and/or Lead-Based Paint Hazards

LEAD ADDENDUM

Wisconsin Legal Blank Co., Inc.
Milwaukee, Wis.

Disclosure of Information on Lead-Based Paint and/or Lead-Based Paint Hazards

This addendum is made part of the offer to purchase dated: ______

Property Address: ______

Seller(s): ______ /Seller's Agent: ______

Purchaser(s): ______

Lead Warning Statement

Every purchaser of any interest in residential real property on which a residential dwelling was built prior to 1978 is notified that such property may present exposure to lead from lead-based paint that may place young children at risk of developing lead poisoning. Lead poisoning in young children may produce permanent neurological damage, including learning disabilities, reduced intelligence quotient, behavorial problems and impaired memory. Lead poisoning may also pose a particular risk to pregnant women. The seller of any interest in residential real property is required to provide the buyer with any information on lead-based paint hazards from risk assessments or inspections in the seller's possession and notify the buyer of any lead-based paint hazards. A risk assessment or inspection for possible lead-based paint hazards is recommended prior to purchase.

Seller's Disclosure (Check (1) or (2) below):

(1) ☐ Seller has knowledge of lead-based paint and/or that lead-based paint hazards are present in the housing (explain).

______

______

______

(2) ☐ Seller has no knowledge of lead-based paint and/or lead-based paint hazards in the housing.

Records and reports available to the Seller (Check (1) or (2) below):

(1) ☐ Seller has provided the Purchaser with all available records and reports pertaining to lead-based paint and/or lead-based paint hazards in the housing (list documents below).

______

______

______

(2) ☐ Seller has no reports or records pertaining to lead-based paint and/or lead-based paint hazards in the housing .

Purchaser's Acknowledgment

Purchaser acknowledges receipt of copies of all information listed above. Purchaser acknowledges receipt of the pamphlet *Protect Your Family From Lead in Your Home.*

Purchaser has (Check (1) or (2) below):

(1) ☐ received a 10-day opportunity (or mutually agreed upon period) to conduct a risk assessment or inspection for the presence of lead-based paint and/or lead-based paint hazards by a federal or state certified lead inspector or lead risk assessor; or

(2) ☐ waived the opportunity to conduct a risk assessment or inspection for the presence of lead-based paint and/or lead-based paint hazards.

Agent's Acknowledgment

Agent has informed the Seller of the Seller's obligations under 42 U.S.C.4852d and is aware of Agent's responsibility to ensure compliance.

Certification of Accuracy

The following parties have reviewed the information above and certify, to the best of their knowledge, that the information they have provided is true and accurate.

Seller ______ Date

Purchaser ______ Date

Seller ______ Date

Purchaser ______ Date

Agent ______ Date

Agent ______ Date

The Lead-Based Paint Immunity Law was passed in year 2000 by the Wisconsin State Legislature. The objective of the law is to protect the occupants of properties by issuing lead-safe or lead-free certificates that warrant the property is free from lead-based paint hazards. The law creates the Lead-Based Paint Immunity program to encourage property owners to invest in long-term measures aimed at reducing lead-based paint hazards.

The Wisconsin Department of Health and Family Services created rules aimed at implementing the Lead-Based Paint Immunity Law in year 2002. The rules create the standards that must be met by a property owner in order to have his or her property certified as lead-safe or lead-free by the Department of Health and Family Services. The rules provide protection from liability for property owners who receive lead-free or lead-safe certificates from the state. This protection for liability will last as long as the property owners comply with Wisconsin Department of Health and Family Services rules for keeping the property free of lead-based paint hazards.

Chapter 254 of the Wisconsin Statutes deals with environmental health. It defines a lead hazard as any substance, surface, or object that contains lead and that, due to its condition, location, or nature, may contribute to the lead poisoning or lead exposure of a child under six years of age. The statute also states that lead poisoning or lead exposure means a level of lead in the blood of 10 or more micrograms per 100 milliliters of blood. Chapter 254 is covered on the salesperson's licensing exam.

BROKER'S LIABILITY FOR SALESPEOPLE AND OTHER BROKER STATEMENTS

Brokers bear full responsibility not only for any false statements that they may make during a transaction but also for false statements made by their sales employees and sales associates, whether or not the brokers had prior knowledge of their misstatements. Under the new broker agency law, the listing broker is not liable for a misrepresentation made by a cooperating broker, unless the listing broker knew or should have known of the other broker's misrepresentation or the other broker is repeating a misrepresentation made to him or her by the listing broker.

MOBILE HOME SALES

In Wisconsin, mobile homes may be considered personal property. Mobile-home salespeople, therefore, need not be licensed as real estate salespeople or brokers, although they must be licensed by the Division of Housing of the Wisconsin Department of Administration. This department also regulates the sale of mobile homes. Section 70.043 of the Wisconsin Statutes states that a mobile home is considered to be real property if it is connected to utilities and is set upon a foundation on land that is owned by the mobile-home owner. A mobile home is set upon a foundation if it is off its wheels and is set upon some other support. A mobile home is considered to be personal property if the land upon which it is located is not owned by the mobile-home owner or if the mobile home is not set upon a foundation or connected to utilities. As a conveyance of real property, a mobile-home sale no longer applies under Chapter 218 of the Wisconsin Statutes; in this situation, a real estate license would be needed.

FEDERAL AND STATE TELEMARKETING LAWS

Federal and state telemarketing laws, or "Do Not Call" laws, limit telephone "sales" calls. Under these laws, people register either with the Federal Trade Commission (FTC) or with the Wisconsin Department of Agriculture, Trade, and Consumer Protection (DATCP), and are placed on "Do Not Call" lists. Registration provides to brokers access to all Wisconsin telephone numbers on the federal and state lists for checking before making sales calls.

The purpose of the "Do Not Call" lists is to restrict the "cold calling" of individuals who do not want to be called and to allow potential customers to identify telephone numbers at which they do not want to be called by salespeople.

Real estate licensees are considered "telemarketers" under these laws. The "Do Not Call" regulations do not apply unless the call is intended to sell real estate, real estate services, or other products or services.

In addition, the federal law also states that a person can notify a specific company to say that he or she does not want the company to call his or her number. A "Company Do Not Call" list is a list of all those persons who have said they do not want to receive any more sales calls from a particular company.

While the "Do Not Call" lists prohibit cold calling to sell real estate or real estate services, licensees may call numbers on the lists if

1. written permission has been given by the person using that telephone number; or
2. an exception applies, such as (a) calls required in an ongoing transaction; (b) calls to persons with whom the agent has an established relationship (e.g., a customer or client from a transaction involving the agent within the last 18 months); or (c) requests for information (e.g., floor calls where the person has left his or her telephone number).

The rules are not intended to interfere with ongoing transactions or to deter calls required in the regular course of business. In other words, if the agent, in his or her professional opinion, determines that the telephone call is necessary for completion of a given transaction or to render ongoing services to a client or a customer, the agent can make the call.

For compliance purposes, agents should develop the routine of checking all numbers for sales calls to people for whom they do not have written permission to call; or for calls to people not involved in an ongoing transaction; or with whom the agent does not have an established relationship. Licensees should also be aware that because the lists are updated periodically, a number may not have been on one of the lists last month but may be on a list today. In addition, the number does not have to be on both the federal and state lists for the rules to apply.

Telemarketers are required to register. However, registration gives the company the ability only to check the federal and state lists for Wisconsin. Registration does not give permission to a company to call numbers on those lists. Those lists must still be checked by agents making sales calls to persons from whom they do not have written permission or with whom they do not have an established relationship. Licensees should also be aware that the federal list also includes cellular phones while the state list covers only residential phones.

Four other important points regarding the federal and state "Do Not Call" rules are:

1. Follow-up calls to previous customers or clients may be made within 18 months of the previous sale involving the agent.
2. Agents may not call owners who are selling their own homes (FSBOs) to offer listing services if the homeowners are on any "Do Not Call" list unless the person has given written permission or unless there is an established relationship with the seller. The exception to this rule is if the agent is calling as a "buyer's agent," representing a specific buyer under a written and signed Buyer Agency Agreement. If that is the case, the agent may call the FSBO clearly stating that he or she is representing a specific buyer with an interest in seeing the property.
3. Calls to residential phones (or cell phones) of sellers with expired listings are subject to both federal and state telemarketing rules. There is no exception in the "Do Not Call" laws allowing calls to expired listings based upon the mere fact the seller's property was at one time listed and entered in the multiple-listing service (MLS).
4. An agent may call someone who has sent an e-mail inquiry only if the e-mail sender has authorized the call.

QUESTIONS

1. A listing contract in Wisconsin must
   a. be oral.
   b. be written.
   c. name the salesperson involved.
   d. be signed by the owner of the property being listed.

2. A broker is entitled to a commission when he or she
   a. brings an offer to the seller.
   b. lists the property with a multiple-listing service.
   c. makes a good faith effort to sell the property.
   d. produces a ready, willing, and able buyer.

3. Which statement does *NOT* correctly describe the independent contractor relationship in Wisconsin?
   a. The independent contractor must work exclusively for the real estate company.
   b. The independent contractor is compensated on a commission basis.
   c. The independent contractor is an employee of the real estate company.
   d. The contract may be terminated at any time by either party upon notice.

4. Which statement does *NOT* correctly describe the broker's responsibility for his or her own statements?
   a. A broker should not knowingly make a false representation.
   b. A broker should not make a statement of opinion without disclosing all facts known to him or her that may affect that statement.
   c. A broker may not disclose the racial characteristics of a neighborhood to a potential buyer.
   d. A broker may disclose the existence of a neighborhood group home for the handicapped to a potential buyer.

5. A broker is showing a house in which the previous owner committed suicide. The potential buyer asks whether the house has any stigma attached to it. The broker should
   a. reveal to the potential buyer that the owner committed suicide.
   b. Reveal to the potential buyer that the house is stigmatized, but that by law the broker is not allowed to reveal the nature of the stigma.
   c. Not disclose the owner's suicide to the potential buyer.
   d. Tell the potential buyer that the owner committed suicide, but it is not important because it had no effect on the physical condition of the house.

6. A salesperson is conducting an open house when a couple comes through and asks questions about the physical condition of the house. The salesperson is aware that the seller had a qualified third party provide a report on the physical condition of the house. The salesperson should *NOT*
   a. disclose any information that contradicts the written report.
   b. disclose information on the physical condition of the house if the written report is available.
   c. reveal the existence of the written report.
   d. discuss the physical condition except for the major problems.

7. According to Wisconsin Statutes Chapter 709, a completed real estate condition report must be given to a buyer no later than
   a. three days prior to the acceptance of the offer to purchase.
   b. two days after the acceptance of the offer to purchase.
   c. five days after the acceptance of the offer to purchase.
   d. ten days after the acceptance of the offer to purchase.

8. If a real estate condition report required by Wisconsin Statutes Chapter 709 discloses a serious defect that was *NOT* already known to a buyer prior to accepting an offer to purchase, the buyer has how many business days to rescind the offer?
   a. One business day
   b. Two business days
   c. Three business days
   d. Four business days

9. The Wisconsin Statutes Chapter 709 Seller Disclosure Law covers all but which type of property?
   a. An owner-occupied single-family home
   b. An eight-unit apartment building
   c. A duplex
   d. A four-unit apartment building

10. A mobile home is defined as real property if
   a. the land upon which it is located is not owned by a mobile home owner.
   b. it is not set upon a foundation.
   c. it is not connected to utilities.
   d. it is off its wheels and set upon some other support on land owned by the owner of the mobile home.

11. The new lead paint disclosure requirement on all residential real estate became effective on
   a. July 1, 1996.
   b. Sept. 6, 1996.
   c. Dec. 6, 1996.
   d. July 1, 1997.

12. The lead paint disclosure requirements cover residential real estate built before
   a. 1963.
   b. 1968.
   c. 1978.
   d. 1996.

13. Follow-up calls to previous customers or clients may be made within
   a. 6 months of the previous sale involving the agent.
   b. 12 months of the previous sale involving the agent.
   c. 18 months of the previous sale involving the agent.
   d. 24 months of the previous sale involving the agent.

14. How many Wisconsin "Do Not Call" lists are there?
   a. One
   b. Two
   Three
   Four

15. Which activity would *NOT* be allowed without the agent having established an agency relationship?
   a. An agent provides a buyer with information about the marketplace.
   b. An agent shows a property to a buyer.
   c. An agent takes the buyer on a tour of several neighborhoods.
   d. An agent is just beginning to negotiate with a buyer.

16. How many representation choices for clients are provided under Wisconsin law?
   a. One
   b. Two
   c. Three
   d. Four

17. Which statement correctly describes the impact of agency law on limited services brokers?
   a. Limited service brokerage is no longer legal.
   b. Limited service brokers must negotiate on behalf of their clients.
   c. The clients of limited service brokers are required to provide an express written waiver of negotiation duties.
   d. None of the above

18. Under Wisconsin agency law, brokers are responsible for
   a. the acts of their agents.
   b. only for brokerage services provided on behalf of the broker by the broker's licensed employees.
   c. none of their agents' actions.
   d. all of their agents' actions with the exception of supervising them.

19. Which statement defines negotiation in Wisconsin?
   a. The agent drafts an offer to purchase for the buyer.
   b. The agent presents his or her buyer's offer to a seller.
   c. The agent drafts a counter-offer for his or her buyer.
   d. All of the above

20. Agent A has a listing contract with a seller and agent B, who works for the same broker and has a buyer agency agreement with a buyer. Under agency law in Wisconsin
   a. agents A and B must enter into a written multiple representation agreement and maintain neutrality with regard to their clients.
   b. agent B is not allowed to negotiate on agent A's listing.
   c. agents A and B may negotiate on behalf of their clients if the clients of both parties have agreed to multiple representation with designated agency.
   d. None of the above

Listing Agreements

THE LISTING CONTRACT

The Wisconsin Statute of Frauds stipulates that in order for a listing to be valid it must: (1) be *in writing*; (2) state the *rate* or *exact amount of commission* to be earned by the broker; (3) specify a *definite termination date* or the period during which the agent or broker shall procure a buyer or seller for the agreement; (4) state the *price of the real estate* and the *terms of the sale*; (5) include a *description specifically identifying the property*; (6) name the *broker*; and (7) bear the *signature* of the person who is to pay the broker's commission. Under the Statute of Frauds, an oral listing agreement is *unenforceable*; Wisconsin courts have been reluctant to enforce any oral listing agreements but may require a broker to finish their performance with no duty on the part of the seller to pay.

Types of Listings

Wisconsin brokers may use open listing, exclusive-agency listing, and exclusive-right-to-sell listing agreements. However, the state-approved exclusive-right-to-sell listing form would have to be modified to accommodate the first two types. Real estate licensees are prohibited from using net listings (Wis. ADMCode RL24.10). The current WB-1 Residential Listing Contract—Exclusive Right to Sell was approved by the Wisconsin Department of Regulation and Licensing and required for use by licensees as of July 2008.

Changes in forms approved by the Department of Regulation and Licensing are being made as this book is being published. You can refer to the instructor resource site at *www.dearborn.com* to get an update on newly approved forms, as well as an explanation of the new forms.

In general, the exclusive-right-to-sell listing provides the greatest advantage for both broker and property owner. If brokers are assured of fair compensation, they can justify expending time and money on a property. When they control the sale, they can afford to advertise the property extensively and spend the necessary time on it. The owner or seller who gives an exclusive-right-to-sell listing has the right to demand the broker's preferred attention to the property. For this reason, brokers should not take such a listing unless they believe the property can be sold and intend to give it preferred attention.

Override Clauses

In Wisconsin, an override clause is included in a listing agreement in order to protect the broker's commission. The override clause provides that a broker is entitled to a commission if the property is sold or exchanged within 12 months after the listing expires to anyone with whom the seller, broker, or any of the broker's agents negotiated during the life of the contract and whose name or names the broker submitted in writing to the seller not later than three days after the expiration of the contract. A written offer to purchase submitted to the seller during the term of the listing also will constitute such notice. The override clause is effective for 12 months in all approved listing contracts.

Listing Considerations

While a real estate listing is the broker's employment contract, it is also a means of securing real estate to sell. Success depends to a great extent on the quantity and quality of the real estate that a broker has available for sale. Because a broker's public image is created partly by the real estate he or she handles, many factors should be considered before accepting employment and taking a listing.

Owners' reason for selling. Have the owners been transferred to another city? Have they outgrown their present home, or do they want a smaller home? Do they want a nicer home or a less expensive one? Are they selling the house as part of the property settlement in a divorce, or do they just dislike the neighbors? Perhaps they do not need to sell and are simply speculating on the market to make a profit. The owners' reasons for selling will determine how anxious they are to sell. In taking a listing, a broker also may identify a prospect who is willing to trade properties or purchase a different property. Information between the seller and the listing agent should remain confidential unless the seller authorizes the agent to disclose motives for selling.

Supply and demand. How much demand is there in a given market for a specific type of property? Compare a parcel of real estate with similar properties. If the supply is great and the demand is small, it may be necessary to compensate by offering the property at a reduced price or with an extra bonus in order to sell the property within a given time.

Potential. The broker also must consider the buyer appeal that one property has over another. How will the property look to prospective purchasers? Will prospective purchasers realize the property's full potential when they see it? Is it neat and clean? Does it look as nice as other properties in the neighborhood? Are there too many or too few furnishings? Will the property be accessible at reasonable times for the broker to show it to prospective purchasers? Remember the maxim that "a property well listed is half sold." The broker should seek only as many listings as he or she can handle, emphasizing the quality rather than the quantity of the inventory.

Termination of Listing

In Wisconsin, a listing contract may be terminated by: (1) mutual consent; (2) performance of the broker; (3) the expiration of the contract; (4) renunciation by the broker; (5) revocation by the principal; (6) the death, incapacity, or bankruptcy of either the principal or the broker; and (7) destruction of the property. A material breach by one party is usually required to allow the other party to rescind without liability for damages. A Cancellation and Mutual Release form (WB-46) does not generally relieve a broker from liability and should not be entered into by buyers or sellers if they have unresolved issues they may wish to sue over.

ADVERTISING

The Wisconsin Real Estate Board enforces a regulation concerning the advertising of real property by real estate licensees. Brokers and salespeople must always present a true picture of property being offered for sale. A broker may not advertise any service free of charge unless the service is available without any contingencies or strings attached. For example, a broker may offer free market analysis as an inducement to encourage listings. *Blind ads are prohibited* by Wisconsin law. These regulations and other rules relating to advertising are discussed more thoroughly in Chapter 10.

AN EXPLANATION OF THE RESIDENTIAL LISTING CONTRACT—EXCLUSIVE RIGHT-TO-SELL

Information contained in this chapter is provided to assist applicants as well as licensees to understand the WB-1 Residential Listing Contract which is four pages long. (See Figure 2.1.) This chapter includes both a sample problem and a line-by-line explanation of the listing contract. These explanations are primarily for your review and consideration. For advice in handling particular situations, you are strongly encouraged to obtain the services of an attorney.

Sample Listing

John James, a salesperson from Newhouse Realty, which is a member of the local REALTORS® multiple-listing service, secured a four-month, exclusive-right-to-sell listing on September 13, 2009, from George and Martha Carter. The listing was for their home at 1400 Regas Lane, Madison, Wisconsin. The legal description is Lot 2, Block 4, Fairmont Subdivision, NW 1/4 of Section 8, T9N, R7E, Dane County, Wisconsin. The Carters agreed to include the refrigerator, washer, dryer, carpeting, drapes, and drapery rods in the total selling price of $249,900. The Carters will give occupancy on the date of closing. James has agreed to hold at least one open house and to list the property with a multiple-listing service. The Carters have completed a sellers' condition report on the same day of the listing. The sellers have consented to designated agency as described in the listing contract, and the Carters have agreed to pay a commission of 6 percent. First Federal Bank of Madison holds a mortgage on the Carters' property with an unpaid balance of $176,650 as of September 1. The monthly payment, including interest, is $998.29. Interest is charged at the rate of 5 percent per annum and the final payment is to be made within 13 years. The bank had indicated that this mortgage may be assumed by a qualified buyer at the same rate of interest.

Line-by-Line Explanation of the WB-1 Residential Listing Contract

The new WB-1 Residential Listing Contract has an optional use date of January 1, 2008, and a mandatory use date of July 1, 2008. The residential listing is five pages long and is on letter-sized paper.

Line 1 makes clear that the listing is an exclusive-right-to-sell contract.

Lines 2–4 describe the property involved in the transaction. A street address is generally an adequate description if it identifies the property being sold. When the street address is not an adequate description, a complete legal description may be placed in the additional provisions section of the Residential Listing (lines 242–250) or in an addendum on lines 251–254.

Lines 5–14 identify the listing price as well as what the seller is including or not including in the list price. You, the licensee, must complete line 5 in the same manner that you prepare a personal check. Lines 6–9 indicate what property will be included in the list price. Line 6 refers to lines 199–210, which define fixtures and gives a list of non-exclusive fixtures to be considered as part of the list price, unless otherwise indicated on line 11. Lines 10–14 identify fixtures to be excluded by the seller as well as those that are rented and will continue to be owned by the lessor, such as a water softener or satellite dish component as indicated on lines 199–210.

Lines 15–22 provide the marketing agreement. On lines 17–18 you must indicate any steps you plan to use in selling the property. The licensee should add "as may be necessary" after the marketing plan in order to protect the commission in the event that the property sells before the licensee has actually performed the actual marketing activities indicated. Firms, however, often refer to a general marketing plan that has already been presented to the seller.

Lines 19–20 provide for the broker to advertise any special incentives offered by the seller, such as the seller being willing to sell on a land contract with a low down payment. Line 20 makes clear the seller's responsibility to cooperate with the broker's marketing efforts, such as cleaning the house prior to a showing. Lines 21–22 refer to lines 74–80 regarding the seller's duty to cooperate with the broker's marketing efforts. Lines 74–80 also reflect the seller's duty to notify the broker of any potential buyers known to the seller.

Line 22 makes clear to the seller that the broker may market other properties during the term of the listing. Lines 23–25 state that unless otherwise provided, the seller will give occupancy of the property to the buyer at the time of closing and ensure that the property is free of all debris.

Lines 26–33 state that the seller agrees that the broker will work and cooperate with other brokers in marketing the property, including buyer brokers and subagents, with the exception of any brokers or buyers identified on lines 31–32. Lines 28–30 define cooperation as providing access for showings and presenting offers. Lines 31–32 not only specify excluded buyers and brokers, but also excluded contract terms. Section RL24.13 (2) specifies that the listing broker shall permit all buyers and their agents access to the listed property for showings unless such access is contrary to the seller's written instructions. If the seller wishes to limit the agreement in some way, these limitations would be placed on lines 31–32. For

FIGURE 2.1

Sample Residential Listing Contract—Exclusive Right to Sell

Approved by Wisconsin Department of Regulation and Licensing
1-1-08 (Optional Use Date) 7-1-08 (Mandatory Use Date)

Wisconsin Legal Blank Co., Inc.
Milwaukee, Wisconsin

WB-1 RESIDENTIAL LISTING CONTRACT - EXCLUSIVE RIGHT TO SELL

page 1 of 5

SELLER GIVES BROKER THE EXCLUSIVE RIGHT TO SELL THE PROPERTY ON THE FOLLOWING TERMS:

■ **PROPERTY DESCRIPTION:** Street address is: 1400 Regas Lane ____________ in the City of Madison, County of Dane, Wisconsin. Insert additional description, if any, at lines 242-250 or attach as an addendum per lines 251-254.

■ **LIST PRICE:** Two Hundred Forty-Nine Thousand Nine Hundred and 00/100 Dollars ($ 249,900.00).

■ **INCLUDED IN LIST PRICE:** Seller is including in the list price the Property, all Fixtures not excluded on lines 11-14, and the following items: All carpeting, drapes, drapery rods, washer, dryer and refrigerator ____________.

■ **NOT INCLUDED IN LIST PRICE:** CAUTION: Identify Fixtures to be excluded by Seller or which are rented and will continue to be owned by the lessor. (See lines 199-210): ____________.

■ **MARKETING:** Seller authorizes and Broker agrees to use reasonable efforts to procure a buyer for the Property. Seller agrees that Broker may market Seller's personal property identified on lines 7-9 during the term of this Listing. Broker's marketing may include: ____________.

Broker may advertise the following special financing and incentives offered by Seller: ____________. Seller has a duty to cooperate with Broker's marketing efforts. See lines 74-80 regarding Broker's role as marketing agent and Seller's duty to notify Broker of any potential buyer known to Seller. Seller agrees that Broker may market other properties during the term of this Listing.

■ **OCCUPANCY:** Unless otherwise provided, Seller agrees to give buyer occupancy of the Property at time of closing and to have the Property in broom swept condition and free of all debris and personal property except for personal property belonging to current tenants, sold to buyer or left with buyer's consent.

■ **COOPERATION, ACCESS TO PROPERTY OR OFFER PRESENTATION:** The parties agree that Broker will work and cooperate with other brokers in marketing the Property, including brokers from other firms acting as subagents (agents from other companies engaged by Broker - See lines 138-141) and brokers representing buyers. Cooperation includes providing access to the Property for showing purposes and presenting offers and other proposals from these brokers to Seller. Note any brokers with whom Broker shall not cooperate, any brokers or buyers who shall not be allowed to attend showings, and the specific terms of offers which should not be submitted to Seller: ____________.

CAUTION: Limiting Broker's cooperation with other brokers may reduce the marketability of the Property.

■ **EXCLUSIONS:** All persons who may acquire an interest in the Property as a Protected Buyer under a prior listing contract are excluded from this Listing to the extent of the prior broker's legal rights, unless otherwise agreed to in writing. Within seven days of the date of this Listing, Seller agrees to deliver to Broker a written list of all such prospective buyers. The following other buyers are excluded from this Listing until ____________ [INSERT DATE]: ____________. These other buyers are no longer excluded from this Listing after the specified date unless, on or before the specified date, Seller has either accepted an offer from the buyer or sold the Property to the buyer.

■ **COMMISSION:** Broker's commission shall be 6%.

Seller shall pay Broker's commission, which shall be earned, if, during the term of this Listing:

1) Seller sells or accepts an offer which creates an enforceable contract for the sale of all or any part of the Property;
2) Seller grants an option to purchase all or any part of the Property which is subsequently exercised;
3) Seller exchanges or enters into a binding exchange agreement on all or any part of the Property;
4) A transaction occurs which causes an effective change in ownership or control of all or any part of the Property; or
5) A buyer is procured for the Property by Broker, by Seller, or by any other person, at no less than the price and on substantially the same terms set forth in this Listing and in the standard provisions of the current WB-11 RESIDENTIAL OFFER TO PURCHASE, even if Seller does not accept this buyer's offer. (See lines 215-218 regarding procurement.)

A percentage commission, if applicable, shall be calculated based on the purchase price if commission is earned under 1) or 2) above, or calculated based on the list price under 3), 4) or 5). A percentage commission shall be calculated on the fair market value of the Property exchanged under 3) if the exchange involves less than the entire Property or on the fair market value of the Property to which an effective change in ownership or control takes place, under 4) if the transaction involves less than the entire Property.

Once earned, Broker's commission is due and payable in full at the earlier of closing or the date set for closing, unless otherwise agreed in writing. Broker's commission shall be earned if, during the term of the Listing, one owner of the Property sells, conveys, exchanges or options an interest in all or any part of the Property to another owner, except by divorce judgment.

NOTE: A sale, option, exchange or procurement of a buyer for a portion of the Property does not terminate the Listing as to any remaining Property.

■ **COMPENSATION TO OTHERS:** Broker offers the following commission to cooperating brokers: ____________. (Exceptions if any): ____________.

FIGURE 2.1 (CONTINUED)

Sample Residential Listing Contract—Exclusive Right to Sell

Wisconsin Legal Blank Co., Inc.
Milwaukee, Wisconsin

page 2 of 5, WB-1

■ **EXTENSION OF LISTING:** The Listing term is extended for a period of one year as to any Protected Buyer. Upon receipt of a written request from Seller or a broker who has listed the Property, Broker agrees to promptly deliver to Seller a written list of those buyers known by Broker to whom the extension period applies. Should this Listing be terminated by Seller prior to the expiration of the term stated in this Listing, this Listing shall be extended for Protected Buyers, on the same terms, for one year after the Listing is terminated.

■ **TERMINATION OF LISTING:** Neither Seller nor Broker has the legal right to unilaterally terminate this Listing absent a material breach of contract by the other party. Seller understands that the parties to the Listing are Seller and the Broker (firm). Agents (salespersons) for Broker (firm) do not have the authority to enter into a mutual agreement to terminate the Listing, amend the commission amount or shorten the term of this Listing, without the written consent of the agent(s)' supervising broker. Seller and Broker agree that any termination of this Listing by either party before the date stated on line 259 shall be indicated to the other party in writing and shall not be effective until delivered to the other Party in accordance with lines 193-198. CAUTION: Early termination of this Listing may be a breach of contract, causing the terminating party to potentially be liable for damages.

■ **SELLER COOPERATION WITH MARKETING EFFORTS:** Seller agrees to cooperate with Broker in Broker's marketing efforts and to provide Broker with all records, documents and other material in Seller's possession or control which are required in connection with the sale. Seller authorizes Broker to do those acts reasonably necessary to effect a sale and Seller agrees to cooperate fully with these efforts which may include use of a multiple listing service, Internet advertising or a lockbox system on Property. Seller shall promptly notify Broker in writing of any potential buyers with whom Seller negotiates during the term of this Listing and shall promptly refer all persons making inquiries concerning the Property to Broker.

■ **LEASED PROPERTY:** If Property is currently leased and lease(s) will extend beyond closing, Seller shall assign Seller's rights under the lease(s) and transfer all security deposits and prepaid rents (subject to agreed upon prorations) thereunder to buyer at closing. Seller acknowledges that Seller remains liable under the lease(s) unless released by tenants. CAUTION: Seller should consider obtaining an indemnification agreement from buyer for liabilities under the lease(s) unless released by tenants.

■ **BROKER DISCLOSURE TO CLIENTS:**

UNDER WISCONSIN LAW, A BROKER OWES CERTAIN DUTIES TO ALL PARTIES TO A TRANSACTION:

(a) The duty to provide brokerage services to you fairly and honestly.
(b) The duty to exercise reasonable skill and care in providing brokerage services to you.
(c) The duty to provide you with accurate information about market conditions within a reasonable time if you request it, unless disclosure of the information is prohibited by law.
(d) The duty to disclose to you in writing certain material adverse facts about a property, unless disclosure of the information is prohibited by law. (See Lines 211-214)
(e) The duty to protect your confidentiality. Unless the law requires it, the broker will not disclose your confidential information or the confidential information of other parties. (See Lines 147-163)
(f) The duty to safeguard trust funds and other property the broker holds.
(g) The duty, when negotiating, to present contract proposals in an objective and unbiased manner and disclose the advantages and disadvantages of the proposals.

■ **BECAUSE YOU HAVE ENTERED INTO AN AGENCY AGREEMENT WITH A BROKER, YOU ARE THE BROKER'S CLIENT. A BROKER OWES ADDITIONAL DUTIES TO A CLIENT:**

(a) The broker will provide, at your request, information and advice on real estate matters that affect your transaction, unless you release the broker from this duty.
(b) The broker must provide you with all material facts affecting the transaction, not just adverse facts.
(c) The broker will fulfill the broker's obligations under the agency agreement and fulfill your lawful requests that are within the scope of the agency agreement.
(d) The broker will negotiate for you, unless you release the broker from this duty.
(e) The broker will not place the broker's interests ahead of your interests. The broker will not, unless required by law, give information or advice to other parties who are not the broker's clients, if giving the information or advice is contrary to your interests.
(f) If you become involved in a transaction in which another party is also the broker's client (a "multiple representation relationship"), different duties may apply.

■ **MULTIPLE REPRESENTATION RELATIONSHIPS AND DESIGNATED AGENCY:**

■ A multiple representation relationship exists if a broker has an agency agreement with more than one client who is a party in the same transaction. In a multiple representation relationship, if all of the broker's clients in the transaction consent, the broker may provide services to the clients through designated agency.

■ Designated agency means that different salespersons employed by the broker will negotiate on behalf of you and the other client or clients in the transaction, and the broker's duties will remain the same. Each salesperson will provide

FIGURE 2.1 (CONTINUED)

Sample Residential Listing Contract—Exclusive Right to Sell

Wisconsin Legal Blank Co., Inc.
Milwaukee, Wisconsin
page 3 of 5, WB-1

information, opinions, and advice to the client for whom the salesperson is negotiating, to assist the client in the negotiations. Each client will be able to receive information, opinions, and advice that will assist the client, even if the information, opinions, or advice gives the client advantages in the negotiations over the broker's other clients. A salesperson will not reveal any of your confidential information to another party unless required to do so by law.

■ If a designated agency relationship is not in effect you may authorize or reject a multiple representation relationship. If you authorize a multiple representation relationship the broker may provide brokerage services to more than one client in a transaction but neither the broker nor any of the broker's salespersons may assist any client with information, opinions, and advice which may favor the interests of one client over any other client. If you do not consent to a multiple representation relationship the broker will not be allowed to provide brokerage services to more than one client in the transaction.

INITIAL ONLY ONE OF THE THREE LINES BELOW:

GC & NC I consent to designated agency.

_______ I consent to multiple representation relationships, but I do not consent to designated agency.

_______ I reject multiple representation relationships.

NOTE: YOU MAY WITHDRAW YOUR CONSENT TO DESIGNATED AGENCY OR TO MULTIPLE REPRESENTATION RELATIONSHIPS BY WRITTEN NOTICE TO THE BROKER AT ANY TIME. YOUR BROKER IS REQUIRED TO DISCLOSE TO YOU IN YOUR AGENCY AGREEMENT THE COMMISSION OR FEES THAT YOU MAY OWE TO YOUR BROKER. IF YOU HAVE ANY QUESTIONS ABOUT THE COMMISSION OR FEES THAT YOU MAY OWE BASED UPON THE TYPE OF AGENCY RELATIONSHIP YOU SELECT WITH YOUR BROKER YOU SHOULD ASK YOUR BROKER BEFORE SIGNING THE AGENCY AGREEMENT.

■ **SUBAGENCY:** The broker may, with your authorization in the agency agreement, engage other brokers who assist your broker by providing brokerage services for your benefit. A subagent will not put the subagent's own interests ahead of your interests. A subagent will not, unless required by law, provide advice or opinions to other parties if doing so is contrary to your interests.

PLEASE REVIEW THIS INFORMATION CAREFULLY. A broker or salesperson can answer your questions about brokerage services, but if you need legal advice, tax advice, or a professional home inspection, contact an attorney, tax advisor, or home inspector. This disclosure is required by section 452.135 of the Wisconsin statutes and is for information only. It is a plain language summary of a broker's duties to you under section 452.133 (2) of the Wisconsin statutes.

■ **CONFIDENTIALITY NOTICE TO CLIENTS:** Broker will keep confidential any information given to Broker in confidence, or any information obtained by Broker that he or she knows a reasonable person would want to be kept confidential, unless the information must be disclosed by law or you authorize Broker to disclose particular information. Broker shall continue to keep the information confidential after Broker is no longer providing brokerage services to you.

The following information is required to be disclosed by law:

1) Material adverse facts, as defined in section 452.01 (5g) of the Wisconsin statutes (lines 211-214).
2) Any facts known by the Broker that contradict any information included in a written inspection report on the property or real estate that is the subject of the transaction.

To ensure that the Broker is aware of what specific information you consider confidential, you may list that information below (see lines 158-160). At a later time, you may also provide the Broker with other information you consider to be confidential.

CONFIDENTIAL INFORMATION: ____

____

____.

NON-CONFIDENTIAL INFORMATION (The following may be disclosed by Broker): ____

____

____.

■ **REAL ESTATE CONDITION REPORT:** Seller agrees to complete the real estate condition report provided by Broker to the best of Seller's knowledge. Seller agrees to amend the report should Seller learn of any defect(s) after completion of the report but before acceptance of a buyer's offer to purchase. Seller authorizes Broker to distribute the report to all interested parties and agents inquiring about the Property. Seller acknowledges that Broker has a duty to disclose all material adverse facts as required by law.

■ **SELLER REPRESENTATIONS REGARDING DEFECTS:** Seller represents to Broker that as of the date of this Listing, Seller has no notice or knowledge of any defects affecting the Property other than those noted on the real estate condition report.

WARNING: IF SELLER REPRESENTATIONS ARE INCORRECT OR INCOMPLETE, SELLER MAY BE LIABLE FOR DAMAGES AND COSTS.

■ **OPEN HOUSE AND SHOWING RESPONSIBILITIES:** Seller is aware that there is a potential risk of injury, damage and/or theft involving persons attending an "individual showing" or an "open house." Seller accepts responsibility for preparing the Property to minimize the likelihood of injury, damage and/or loss of personal property. Seller agrees to hold Broker harmless for any losses or liability resulting from personal injury, property damage, or theft occurring during "individual showings" or "open houses" other than those caused by Broker's negligence or intentional wrongdoing. Seller acknowledges that individual showings and open houses may be conducted by licensees other than Broker, that appraisers and inspectors may conduct appraisals and inspections without being accompanied by Broker or other licensees, and that buyers or licensees may be present at all inspections and testing and may photograph or videotape Property unless otherwise provided for in additional provisions at lines 242-250 or in an addendum per lines 251-254.

FIGURE 2.1 (CONTINUED)

Sample Residential Listing Contract—Exclusive Right to Sell

Wisconsin Legal Blank Co., Inc.
Milwaukee, Wisconsin

[page 4 of 5, WB-1]

■ **DEFINITIONS:**

ADVERSE FACT: An "adverse fact" means any of the following:

(a) A condition or occurrence that is generally recognized by a competent licensee as doing any of the following:

1) Significantly and adversely affecting the value of the Property;
2) significantly reducing the structural integrity of improvements to real estate; or
3) presenting a significant health risk to occupants of the Property.

(b) Information that indicates that a party to a transaction is not able to or does not intend to meet his or her obligations under a contract or agreement made concerning the transaction.

DEADLINES - DAYS: Deadlines expressed as a number of "days" from an event are calculated by excluding the day the event occurred and by counting subsequent calendar days.

DELIVERY: Delivery of documents or written notices related to this Listing may only be accomplished by:
1) giving the document or written notice personally to the party;
2) depositing the document or written notice postage or fees prepaid or charged to an account in the U.S. Mail or a commercial delivery system, addressed to the party, at the party's address (See lines 265, 271 and 277.);
3) electronically transmitting the document or written notice to the party's fax number (See lines 267, 273 and 279.); and,
4) as otherwise agreed in additional provisions on lines 242-250 or in an addendum to this Listing.

FIXTURES: A "fixture" is an item of property which is physically attached to or so closely associated with land or buildings so as to be treated as part of the real estate, including, without limitation, physically attached items not easily removable without damage to the premises, items specifically adapted to the premises, and items customarily treated as fixtures, including, but not limited to, all: garden bulbs; plants; shrubs and trees; screen and storm doors and windows; electric lighting fixtures; window shades; curtain and traverse rods; blinds and shutters; central heating and cooling units and attached equipment; water heaters and treatment systems; sump pumps; attached or fitted floor coverings; awnings; attached antennas, garage door openers and remote controls; installed security systems; central vacuum systems and accessories; in-ground sprinkler systems and component parts; built-in appliances; ceiling fans; fences; storage buildings on permanent foundations and docks/piers on permanent foundations.

CAUTION: Exclude any Fixtures to be retained by Seller or which are rented (e.g., water softener or other water conditioning systems, home entertainment and satellite dish components, L.P. tanks, etc.) on lines 11-14 and in the offer to purchase.

MATERIAL ADVERSE FACT: A "material adverse fact" means an adverse fact that a party indicates is of such significance, or that is generally recognized by a competent licensee as being of such significance to a reasonable party, that it affects or would affect the party's decision to enter into a contract or agreement concerning a transaction or affects or would affect the party's decision about the terms of such a contract or agreement.

PROCURE: A buyer is procured when, during the term of the Listing, an enforceable contract of sale is entered into between the Seller and the buyer or when a ready, willing and able buyer submits to the Seller or the Listing Broker a written offer at the price and on substantially the terms specified in this Listing. A buyer is ready, willing and able when the buyer submitting the written offer has the ability to complete the buyer's obligations under the written offer. (See lines 46-49)

PROPERTY: Unless otherwise stated, "Property", means the real estate described at lines 2-4.

PROTECTED BUYER: Means a buyer who personally, or through any person acting for such buyer: 1) delivers to Seller or Broker a written offer to purchase, exchange or option on the Property during the term of this Listing; 2) negotiates directly with Seller by discussing with Seller the potential terms upon which buyer might acquire an interest in the Property; or 3) attends an individual showing of the Property or discusses with Broker or cooperating brokers the potential terms upon which buyer might acquire an interest in the Property, but only if Broker delivers the buyer's name to Seller, in writing, no later than three days after the expiration of the Listing. The requirement in 3), to deliver the buyer's name to Seller in writing, may be fulfilled as follows: a) If the Listing is effective only as to certain individuals who are identified in the Listing, by the identification of the individuals in the Listing; or, b) if a buyer has requested that the buyer's identity remain confidential, by delivery of a written notice identifying the broker with whom the buyer negotiated and the date(s) of any showings or other negotiations.

■ **FAIR HOUSING: Seller and Broker agree that they will not discriminate against any prospective buyer on account of race, color, sex, sexual orientation as defined in Wisconsin Statutes, Section 111.32 (13m), disability, religion, national origin, marital status, lawful source of income, age, ancestry, familial status, or in any other unlawful manner.**

■ **EARNEST MONEY:** If Broker holds trust funds in connection with the transaction, they shall be retained by Broker in Broker's trust account. Broker may refuse to hold earnest money or other trust funds. Should Broker hold the earnest money, Seller authorizes Broker to disburse the earnest money as directed in a written earnest money disbursement agreement signed by or on behalf of all parties having an interest in the trust funds. If the transaction fails to close and the earnest money is disbursed to Seller, then upon disbursement to Seller the earnest money shall be paid first to reimburse Broker for cash advances made by Broker on behalf of Seller and one half of the balance, but not in excess of the agreed commission, shall be paid to Broker as Broker's full commission in connection with said purchase transaction and the balance shall belong to Seller. This payment to Broker shall not terminate this Listing.

FIGURE 2.1 (CONTINUED)

Sample Residential Listing Contract—Exclusive Right to Sell

Wisconsin Legal Blank Co., Inc.
Milwaukee, Wisconsin

■ **ADDITIONAL PROVISIONS:** Legal Description: Lot 2, Block 4, Fairmont Subdivision, NW 1/4 of Section 8, T9N, R7/E, Dane County, Wisconsin

■ **ADDENDA:** The attached addenda ______________________ is/are made part of this Listing.

■ **NOTICE ABOUT SEX OFFENDER REGISTRY:** You may obtain information about the sex offender registry and persons registered with the registry by contacting the Wisconsin Department of Corrections on the Internet at http://www.widocoffenders.org or by telephone at (608)240-5830.

■ **TERM OF THE CONTRACT:** From the 13th day of September, 2005, up to and including midnight of the 12th day of January, 2010.

■ **READING/RECEIPT: BY SIGNING BELOW, SELLER ACKNOWLEDGES RECEIPT OF A COPY OF THIS LISTING CONTRACT AND THAT HE/SHE HAS READ ALL FIVE PAGES AS WELL AS ANY ADDENDA AND ANY OTHER DOCUMENTS INCORPORATED INTO THE LISTING.**

(x)______________ George Carter September 13, 2009
Seller's Signature ▲ Print Name Here: ▲ Date ▲

1400 Regas Lane, Madison, WI ______________
Seller's Address ▲ Seller's Phone # ▲

______________ ______________
Seller's Fax # ▲ `Seller's E-Mail Address ▲

(x)______________ Martha Carter September 13, 2009
Seller's Signature ▲ Print Name Here: ▲ Date ▲

______________ ______________
Seller's Address ▲ Seller's Phone # ▲

______________ ______________
Seller's Fax # ▲ `Seller's E-Mail Address ▲

(x)______________ John James New House Realty September 13, 2009
Agent for Broker ▲ Print Name Here ▲ Broker/Firm Name ▲ Date ▲

______________ ______________
Broker/Firm Address ▲ Broker/Firm Phone # ▲

______________ ______________
Broker/Firm Fax # ▲ Broker/Firm E-Mail Address ▲

example, if the seller wanted to exclude a specific broker, the name of that person would be inserted on lines 31–32.

Lines 34–39 cover exclusions to the listing contract, used to list the names of those people with whom the seller has been dealing on their own whom the seller considers as potential purchasers to be excluded from the contract. Line 37 includes a date if the sellers' exceptions are to end before the listing expires. The seller's list must be provided within *seven days* of the listing date.

Lines 38–39 make clear that the seller must have accepted an offer to purchase from the excluded buyer, or sold (deeded) the property to the buyers by the stated deadline. If either event occurs by the stated deadline, the listing broker does not earn his or her commission.

Lines 40–60 cover the commission agreement. This section indicates that the commission earned by the broker can be based on either the purchase price or the list price. The commission is based on the purchase price if the property is conveyed as shown on lines 42 and 43. Line 40 states that the commission may be a percentage or dollar value or both if the broker and seller agree that the seller is willing to pay an administrative fee in addition to the commission on the purchase price or list price. If the property is conveyed as shown on lines 44–49, the commission will be based on the list price. Line 44 indicates that the broker's commission will be earned if the seller exchanges or sells an interest in all or any part of the property to another person during the term of the listing.

For example, if a rental property owner deeds his or her listed duplex directly to his or her cousin in exchange for another duplex during the term of the listing, the commission will be based on the list price. Another example would be someone quitclaiming his or her listed house to his or her daughter during the term of the listing; this would result in the commission being earned based on the list price.

An example of line 45 would be a situation in which a limited liability company (LLC) owns a listed property and one of the LLC members sells his or her ownership interest to a friend. The effect of this transaction would be the same as if the listed property owned by the LLC had been sold. The title to the property would remain the same; however, the person having voting control over the disposition of the property will have changed. This transaction will result in the listing broker earning his or her commission.

Lines 55–56 make clear that the broker's commission will be earned if, during the term of the listing, one owner of the property sells, exchanges, or options an interest in all or any part of the listed property to another owner, except by divorce judgment. For example, four sisters decide to buy out the other two sisters' ownership interest in the property. It is likely in this situation that the commissions earned will be proportioned to the value of the interest actually transferred. The broker will earn a commission even if the two sisters do not enter into an offer to buy, rather just quitclaim their interest to sisters who are buying their interests. In the case of divorce, a broker will earn a commission if the wife voluntarily sells her interest in the listed home to her husband. However, if the wife is required by the divorce judgment to convey her interest to her husband, the broker will not earn a commission.

Lines 57–58 indicate that a sale, option, exchange, or procurement of a buyer for a portion of the property does not terminate the listing as to any remaining property. Line 219 defines the property as the real estate described on line 204. Thus, lines 57–58 apply only to the real estate and not to any personal property included in the list price on lines 6–9.

Lines 59–60 require the listing broker to disclose what commission will be paid to other brokers who cooperate in the sale of the property. For example, if Broker A lists the property and Broker B sells it, Broker B would be the cooperating broker and receive part of the commission paid to the listing broker. Line 60 can be used to indicate any exceptions to the commission to be paid to cooperating brokers, such as a policy letter agreement the listing broker has that pays a lesser commission to certain cooperating brokers. It is likely that the listing broker will include wording such as "see Addendum A" on lines 59–60 rather than place detailed information on commission agreements with cooperating brokers on lines 59–60.

Lines 61–65 provide the broker with extended listing protection for protected buyers for a period of one year. The definition of "protected buyer" is found on lines 220–229 on page 4 of the listing. There are four ways in which a buyer may be covered for listing protection, including: (1) the buyer delivers a written offer to purchase during the term of the listing; (2) the buyer negotiates directly with the seller by discussing with the seller the potential terms upon which the buyer might acquire an interest in the property; (3) the buyer attends an individual showing of the property during the term of the listing; and (4) the buyer negotiates with the broker or cooperating brokers during the term of the listing.

It is important to emphasize that the term *negotiate* refers to the buyer discussing the potential terms upon which the buyer might acquire an interest in the property. The requirements in (3) and (4) will protect the buyers only if the listing broker delivers the buyer's names to the seller, in writing, no later than three days after the expiration of the listing. Lines 227–228 state that if a buyer has requested that his or her identity remain confidential, the requirement for that buyer to be protected may be carried out by delivery of a written notice identifying the broker with whom the buyer negotiated and the dates(s) of any showings or other negotiations. It is also important to note that lines 63–65 state that if either the seller or broker terminate the listing prior to the expiration date, the notice of termination must be in writing and is not effective until delivered to the other party in accordance with lines 197–202 on page 4 of the listing. The caution on lines 72–73 indicates that early termination of the listing may be a breach of contact, causing the terminating party to potentially be liable for damages.

You should be aware that the seller has the power, but not necessarily the right, to revoke a listing contract at any time. Early revocation might create a breach of contract providing the broker with the right to demand compensation for damages resulting form the early termination. The broker cannot, however, require the seller to remain a party to the listing contract. If the listing broker does not perform according to the terms of the listing contract, then the seller will have the power as well as the right to terminate the listing contract.

If the listing is terminated prior to the expiration date stated in the listing, the broker will have a listing for protected buyers for one year after the listing is terminated. The broker will have three days from the date of termination to deliver a list of any protected buyers for whom notice has not already been given.

Lines 66–73 deal with termination of the listing. Lines 66–67 state that neither the seller nor the broker has the legal right to unilaterally terminate the listing unless a material breach of contract has been made by the other party. You should be aware that the seller has the power, but not necessarily the right, to revoke a listing contract at any time. Early revocation might create a breach of contract providing the broker with the right to demand compensation for damages resulting from the early termination. The broker cannot, however, require the seller to remain a party to the listing contract. If the listing broker does not perform according to the terms of the listing contract, then the seller will have the power as well as the right to terminate the listing contract. Lines 68–70 state that salespersons for the broker have no authority to sign amendments to the listing contract that shorten the term of the listing or cancel the listing. Lines 70–72 state that the parties agree that any termination of the listing by either the seller or the broker prior to the expiration date stated in the listing must be in writing and will not be effective until delivered to the other party in accordance with lines 193–198 on page 4 of the listing.

Lines 72–73 make clear that early termination of the listing by either party may be a breach of contract, resulting in possible liability for damages for the terminating party.

Lines 74–80 identify the responsibilities of the seller in cooperating with the broker's marketing efforts. For example, the seller is responsible for promptly notifying the broker in writing of any potential buyers with whom the seller negotiates during the term of the listing. The seller is also responsible for promptly referring all persons making inquiries concerning the property to the broker.

Lines 81–85 cover a property that has been leased. For example, lines 81–82 state that if current leases on the property extend beyond the closing, the seller will assign all rights under the leases, as well as transfer all security deposits and prepaid rents to the buyer at closing.

Lines 86–98 identify the broker disclosures that must be provided to all parties under Wisconsin law. More specifically, these lines state certain duties that the broker owes to all parties (both customers and clients) in a transaction, such as the duty to provide brokerage services that are fair and honest. It is important to emphasize that among the other duties is the duty to protect the confidentiality of all parties in a transaction. If the broker has an agency agreement with a buyer or seller, that party becomes a client of the agent. If a buyer works with an agent without an agency agreement, that buyer is a customer of the agent. Thus, the parties in a transaction may include clients and or customers.

Lines 99–111 present the broker's disclosure responsibilities with regard to clients that are comparable with those owed all parties. The primary difference between the type of information that a broker can provide to a client rather than a customer is that a broker can provide information to a client which favors the client as opposed to a customer. For example, a broker may favor a client who is a buyer by stating that a property is overpriced, which could not be revealed to a customer who is a buyer.

Lines 184–190 define an adverse fact and lines 211–214 define a material adverse fact.

Lines 112–127 provide an explanation of multiple representation relationships and designated agency.

Under designated agency, as stated in lines 116–127, the different salespersons for the broker will negotiate on behalf of their clients and other clients in the transaction and the broker's duties will remain the same to each of the clients. Each salesperson will provide information and advice to the client for whom the salesperson is negotiating to assist the client in the negotiations, even if the information or advice gives the client advantages over the broker's other clients.

Lines 128–131 are used to indicate which type of agency relationship the client is choosing; the client will indicate his or her choice by initialing one of the choices on lines 129–131.

Lines 132–137 state that the client may withdraw consent to the designated agency or multiple representation relationship by written notice at any time. In addition, the broker is required to disclose in the agency agreement any commission or fees the client may owe to the broker.

Lines 138–141 indicate that a subagent will not place his or her own interests ahead of the client.

Lines 142–146 make clear to the client that licensees are not home inspectors, tax advisors, or attorneys and that if the client needs this type of advice, he or she should contact a person with the required expertise.

Lines 147–157 describe the confidentiality owed to the client by the broker with the exception of information required to be disclosed by law on lines 151–157.

Lines 155–163 provide the client with the opportunity to state information that is confidential (lines 158–160), as well as information that is not confidential (lines 161–163).

An example of information that might be placed on lines 158–160 would be that the sellers are getting a divorce. An example of non-confidential information on lines 161–163 would be that the property is in foreclosure.

Lines 164–168 ask the seller to complete the Real Estate Condition Report (RECR) to the best of the seller's knowledge.

You should be aware that there is nothing in the listing that requires the seller to complete the RECR.

Lines 169–173 deal with seller representations regarding defects other than those showing on the RECR. Lines 172–173 make clear that if the seller representations are incorrect or incomplete, the seller may be liable for damages and costs.

Lines 174–182 address the responsibilities of the seller in regard to open house and showing responsibilities. On lines 175–176, the seller accepts responsibility for preparing the property to minimize the likelihood of injury, damage or loss of property during an open house or showing. This section also states that the seller agrees to hold the broker harmless for any losses or liability resulting from personal injury, damage, and so on, occurring during the open house or showing other than those caused by the broker's negligence or intentional wrongdoing. This section also states that individual showings and open houses may be conducted by licensees other than the broker and that appraisers and inspectors may conduct appraisals and inspections without being accompanied by the broker or other licensees, and that buyers or licensees may be present at all inspections and testing and may photograph or videotape the property unless otherwise provided for in additional provisions at lines 242–250 or in an addendum per lines 251–254.

Page 4 (lines 183–241) of the listing contract defines selected terms, some of which were discussed above.

Lines 191–192 indicate that when a deadline is expressed as a number of days from an event such as acceptance of the offer, the date of the acceptance is excluded and subsequent calendar days are counted. This procedure is based upon the language in the offer to purchase.

Lines 193–198 describe the alternative methods for delivery of documents or written notices related to the listing. The alternative methods of delivery include: (1) personal delivery; (2) U.S. Mail or commercial delivery; and (3) fax transmission. A fourth alternative identified on line 198 refers to "as otherwise agreed," which may be used for e-mail delivery and e-commerce. **The Wisconsin Department of Regulation and Licensing has stated that it is permissible for brokers to authorize e-mail in additional provisions on lines 242–250 or in an addendum to the listing contract.**

Lines 199–210 define a fixture as well as specific items that are considered to be fixtures.

Lines 211–214 define a material adverse fact.

Lines 215–218 define the term "procure" and require that procurement of a buyer is based on an enforceable contract of sale.

Line 219 states that unless otherwise indicated, "property" refers to the real estate described in lines 2–4.

Lines 220–229 define a protected buyer.

Lines 230–233 identify the protected classes in Wisconsin. Protected classes are groups of people against whom one may not discriminate. Under the federal fair housing law, the owner of up to four units of rental housing who is living on the premises may discriminate against protected classes with the exception of race. However, in Wisconsin, one may not discriminate in either the sale or rental of an owner-occupied home.

Lines 234–241 state that if the broker holds trust funds in connection with the transaction, they shall be retained in the broker's trust account. It is important to emphasize that the broker may refuse to hold earnest money or other trust funds. Lines 236–237 authorize the broker to disburse the earnest money as directed in a written earnest money disbursement agreement signed by or on behalf of all parties having an interest in the trust funds. Lines 237–241 deal with how earnest money will be shared between the seller and the broker if the transaction fails to close.

Lines 242–250 are used to identify anything the seller does not want disclosed. For example, if the seller does not want a For Sale sign on the property, that stipulation would be included in this section. If there is an assumable mortgage, the specifics could also be stated in this section. A legal description or the conveyance of the property by something other than a warranty deed could also be placed in this section or in separate addenda.

Lines 251–254 provide space for any addenda used to add further terms and conditions to the listing contract, thus incorporating them into the legal document. The addenda may or may not require preparation by an attorney.

Lines 255–257 provide notice about the Sex Offender Registry. The language on these lines provides the notice required to be given to sellers under state law, thus providing the broker with immunity relating to the disclosure of information on sex offenders.

Lines 259–260 refer to the term of the contract. The statute of frauds covering listing contracts (S.240.10 Wis. Stats.) requires that the listing have a definite duration in order to be enforceable. There is, however, no state law regarding the length of the listing; it is negotiable between the seller and the broker.

Lines 260–280 provide for the signatures of all of the parties to the contract as well as the date on which the listing contract is being drafted. This date is generally the same as the date on which the listing is to begin (lines 263, 269 and 275). However, the date the seller signs the contract may differ from lines 258 and 259 (term of contract). For example, the seller might need a week to get the house ready for marketing. The sellers sign on lines 263 and 269. Someone other than the seller or owner, such as a personal representative, could sign. The key point is that whoever signs the listing contract agrees to pay the commission.

AN EXPLANATION OF THE WB-4 RESIDENTIAL CONDOMINIUM LISTING CONTRACT—EXCLUSIVE RIGHT-TO-SELL

The Residential Condominium Listing Contract is similar to the Residential Listing Contract.

Students should be familiar with the following basic condominium law concepts found in Chapter 703 of the Wisconsin Statutes:

Highlights of WB-4: Residential Condominium Listing Contract

- The condominium form of ownership includes an individual interest in a unit, such as an apartment, and an interest in undivided common elements, such as land, parking areas, or elevators.
- The recording of a document called a *declaration* creates a condominium.
- A *condominium plat* refers to a survey of the land and improvements as well as the floor plans of the buildings in the project.
- The property developer or owner who creates the condominium is called the *declarant*.
- The part of the condominium intended for independent use is referred to as the *unit*. The unit can take the form of an apartment, house, or a lot as well as a patio, parking space in a garage, or a storage area. Close attention should be paid to how the unit is defined in the condominium declaration and plat.
- Everything in the condominium that is not a unit is referred to as a *common element*. Examples of common elements include the land, elevators, and meeting rooms.
- Common elements reserved for the exclusive use of a unit owner are referred to as *limited common elements*. Examples include a patio or a parking space.

WB-4 includes language related to the limited common elements assigned to the unit as well as the parking and parking fee.

Line 24 of WB-4 deals with whether or not the condominium association has a right of first refusal on the unit.

Lines 100–111 of WB-4 identify condominium disclosure materials to be provided to the buyer according to S. 703.33 no later than 15 days prior to closing.

The seller cooperation section of WB-4 states that the seller is to provide the broker with various records, documents, and materials related to the condominium.

A complete line-by-line explanation follows:

Line-by-Line Explanation of the WB-4 Residential Condominium Listing Contract

Line 1 makes clear that the listing is an exclusive-right-to-sell contract. (See Figure 2.2.)

Lines 2–7 describe the property involved in the transaction. The street address and the condominium unit description are generally included on these lines.

Lines 8–10 cover the terms of the listing.

Lines 12–19 state that the seller will include his or her interest in any common surplus and reserves of the condominium and all fixtures in or on the unit as of the date of the listing.

Lines 20–21 identify any common elements assigned to the unit such as an assigned parking space.

FIGURE 2.2

Sample Residential Condominium Listing Contract—Exclusive Right to Sell

Approved by the Wisconsin Department of Regulation and Licensing
4-1-00 (Optional Use Date)
9-1-00 (Mandatory Use Date)

Wisconsin Legal Blank Co., Inc.
Milwaukee, Wisconsin 53208

WB-4 RESIDENTIAL CONDOMINIUM LISTING CONTRACT-EXCLUSIVE RIGHT TO SELL

SELLER GIVES BROKER THE EXCLUSIVE RIGHT TO SELL THE PROPERTY ON THE TERMS SET FORTH IN THIS LISTING.

■ ***PROPERTYDESCRIPTION:*** The street address of the Unit is: _____________ _____________ in the _____________ of _____________, County of _____________, Wisconsin, particularly described as Unit: _____________ (Building _____________) of _____________ Condominium; Seller's undivided interest in the common elements appurtenant to the Unit, together with and subject to the rights, interests, obligations and limitations as set forth in the declaration and condominium plat (and all amendments to them) creating the Condominium, which altogether constitute the Property.

■ ***TERMS OF LISTING:*** *LIST PRICE:* _____________ _____________ Dollars ($ _____________).

TERMS: Cash or equivalent at closing or _____________.

OCCUPANCY DATE: _____________ *OCCUPANCY CHARGE* (if Seller occupies after closing): $ _____________ per day or part thereof.

PROPERTY INCLUDED IN LIST PRICE: Seller agrees to include in the list price and to transfer free and clear of encumbrances Seller's interest in any common surplus and reserves of the Condominium allocated to the Unit; and all fixtures as defined at lines 180 to 188 and as may be in or on the Unit as of the date of this Listing, unless excluded at lines 18 to 19. ***CAUTION: Exclude fixtures not owned by Seller such as rented water softeners. The terms of the Offer to Purchase will determine what property is included or excluded.***

ADDITIONAL ITEMS INCLUDED IN THE LIST PRICE: _____________ _____________

ITEMS NOT INCLUDED IN THE LIST PRICE: _____________ _____________

LIMITED COMMON ELEMENTS: The limited common elements assigned to the Unit include: _____________ _____________. See condominium declaration for complete list.

■ ***PARKING:*** The parking for the Unit is: _____________. The parking fee is: $ _____________.

■ ***ASSOCIATION FEE:*** The association fee for this Unit is $ _____________ per _____________.

■ ***RIGHT OF FIRST REFUSAL:*** The condominium association (does) (does not) [STRIKE ONE] have a right of first refusal on the Unit.

■ ***CONDITION OF TITLE:*** Upon payment of the purchase price, Seller shall convey the Property by warranty deed (or other conveyance as provided herein) free and clear of all liens and encumbrances, except: municipal and zoning ordinances and agreements entered under them, recorded easements for the distribution of utility, municipal and association services, recorded building and use restrictions and covenants, general taxes levied in the year of closing, Wisconsin Condominium Ownership Act, condominium declaration and plat and association articles of incorporation, bylaws and rules and amendments to the above, and _____________ _____________ (provided none of the foregoing prohibit present use of the Property).

■ ***TITLE EVIDENCE:*** Seller shall provide evidence of the condition of Seller's title in the form agreed to in the offer to purchase.

■ ***SELLER REPRESENTATIONS REGARDING PROPERTY CONDITIONS:*** Seller represents to Broker that as of the date of this Listing, Seller has no notice or knowledge of any conditions affecting the Property or transaction (as defined at lines 156 - 179) other than those identified in the attached real estate condition report dated _____________ (see lines 112 - 120 regarding real estate condition reports) and _____________.

WARNING: IF SELLER REPRESENTATIONS ARE INCORRECT, SELLER MAY BE LIABLE FOR DAMAGES AND COSTS.

■ ***MARKETING:*** Broker agrees to use reasonable efforts to procure a purchaser for the Property, including, but not limited to, the following: _____________ _____________.

Seller agrees that Broker may market other properties during the term of this Listing. SEE LINES 90 - 99 AND 264 - 269 REGARDING SELLER'S DUTY TO NOTIFY BROKER OF ANY POTENTIAL PURCHASER OF WHICH SELLER HAS KNOWLEDGE, SELLER'S DUTY TO COOPERATE WITH BROKER'S MARKETING EFFORTS AND PROVISIONS REGARDING BROKER'S ROLE AS MARKETING AGENT.

■ ***OTHER BROKERS:*** The Parties agree that Broker will work and cooperate with other brokers in marketing the Property, including brokers from other firms acting as subagents (agents of Seller retained by Broker) and brokers representing buyers, except: _____________ _____________.

CAUTION: LIMITING BROKER'S COOPERATION WITH OTHER BROKERS MAY REDUCE THE MARKETABILITY OF THE PROPERTY.

■ ***TERM OF THE CONTRACT:*** FROM THE _____________ DAY OF _____________, _____________, UP TO AND INCLUDING MIDNIGHT OF THE _____________ DAY OF _____________, _____________.

■ ***EXCLUSIONS:*** All persons whose purchase, exchange or exercise of grant of option would earn a prior listing broker a commission under a prior listing contract are excluded from this Listing to the extent of the prior broker's legal rights, unless otherwise agreed to in writing. Within one week of this Listing, Seller agrees to deliver to Broker a list of all persons whose procurement as purchaser would earn another broker a commission under a prior listing contract. ***CAUTION: Contact previous listing broker if the identity of potential protected buyers from previous listings is uncertain.*** The following other buyers are excluded from this Listing until _____________ [INSERT DATE]: _____________. These other buyers are no longer excluded from this Listing after the specified date unless, on or before the specified date, Seller has either accepted an offer from the buyer or sold the Property to the buyer.

■ ***COMMISSION:*** Broker's commission shall be _____________% or _____________

FIGURE 2.2 (CONTINUED)

Sample Residential Condominium Listing Contract—Exclusive Right to Sell

whichever is greater. The percentage commission, if applicable, shall be calculated based on the purchase price if commission is earned under 1) or 2) below, or calculated based on the list price under 3) (if an exchange of the entire Property), 4) or 5). If less than the entire Property is exchanged, the percentage commission shall be calculated on the fair market value of the Property exchanged. Seller shall pay Broker's commission, which shall be earned if, during the term of this Listing:

1) Seller sells or accepts an offer which creates an enforceable contract for the sale of all or any part of the Property;

2) Seller grants an option to purchase all or any part of the Property which is subsequently exercised;

3) Seller exchanges or enters into a binding exchange agreement on all or any part of the Property;

4) A transaction occurs which causes an effective change in ownership or control of all or any part of the Property; or

5) A purchaser is procured for the Property by the Broker, by Seller, or by any other person, at the price and on substantially the same terms set forth in this Listing and the standard provisions of the current WB-14 CONDOMINIUM OFFER TO PURCHASE, even if Seller does not accept this purchaser's offer. See lines 193 - 196 regarding procurement.

Once earned, Broker's commission is due and payable in full at the earlier of closing or the date set for closing, unless otherwise agreed in writing.

Broker's commission also shall be earned if, during the term of the Listing, one owner of the Property sells, exchanges or options an interest in all or any part of the Property to another owner, except by divorce judgment.

■ ***EXTENSION OF LISTING:*** This Listing may be extended by agreement of the Parties. The Listing term is extended for a period of one year as to any buyer who personally or through any person acting for such buyer either negotiated to acquire an interest in the Property or submitted a written offer to purchase, exchange or option during the term of this Listing (protected buyer). If the extension is based on negotiation, the extension shall only be effective if the buyer's name is delivered to Seller, in writing, no later than three days after the expiration of the Listing, unless Seller was directly involved in discussions of the potential terms upon which buyer might acquire an interest in the Property. The requirement of this Listing to deliver the buyer's name in order to make the extension of the Listing term effective also may be fulfilled as follows: 1) If the Listing is effective only as to certain individuals who are identified in the Listing (One Party Listing), the identification of the individuals in the Listing shall fulfill the delivery of the buyer's name requirement and 2) if buyer has requested that buyer's identity remain confidential, delivery of a notice identifying the broker with whom the buyer negotiated and the date(s) of any showings or other negotiations shall fulfill the delivery of the buyer's name requirement. "Negotiated" for the purpose of this paragraph means to discuss the potential terms upon which buyer might acquire an interest in the Property or to attend an individual showing of the Property. "Submitted" for the purposes of this paragraph means that a written offer has been delivered to Seller or Broker. Upon receipt of a written request from Seller or a broker who has listed the Property, Broker agrees to promptly deliver to Seller a written list of those buyers known by Broker to whom the extension period applies. Should this Listing be terminated by Seller prior to the expiration of the term stated in this Listing, Broker shall have a Listing for one year after the Listing is terminated for "protected" buyers.

■ ***TERMINATION OF LISTING:*** Neither Seller nor Broker have the legal right to unilaterally terminate this listing absent a material breach of contract by the other Party. Seller understands that the Parties to the listing are Seller and the Broker (firm). Agents (salespersons) for Broker (firm) do not have the authority to enter into a mutual agreement to terminate the Listing, amend the commission amount or shorten the term of this Listing, without the written consent of the agent's supervising broker.

■ ***SELLER COOPERATION WITH MARKETING EFFORTS:*** Seller agrees to cooperate with Broker in Broker's marketing efforts and to provide Broker with all records, documents and other material in Seller's possession or control which are required in connection with the sale including, but not limited to, copies of the condominium association's financial statements for the last two years, the minutes of the last unit owner's meetings, the minutes of condominium board meetings during the 12 months prior to acceptance, copies of the association's certificate of insurance, a statement from the association indicating the balance of reserve accounts controlled by the association, a statement from the association of the amount of any unpaid assessments on the unit (per Wis. Stat. §703.16(5)) and the declaration and bylaws of the master association, if any. Seller authorizes Broker to do those acts reasonably necessary to effect a sale and Seller agrees to cooperate fully with these efforts which may include obtaining condominium disclosure materials at Seller's expense (see Wis. Stat. §703.20(2)), use of a multiple listing service, the Internet or a key lockbox system on Property. Seller shall promptly notify Broker in writing of any potential purchasers with whom Seller negotiates during the term of this Listing and shall promptly refer all persons making inquiries concerning the Property to Broker.

■ ***CONDOMINIUM DISCLOSURE MATERIALS:*** Seller agrees to provide buyer with complete, current and accurate copies of the condominium disclosure materials required by Wisconsin Stat. §703.33. The condominium disclosure materials are required to be delivered to buyer no later than 15 days prior to closing. The condominium disclosure materials include copies of the condominium declaration, bylaws, rules and regulations, together with an index of contents, articles of incorporation, management contracts, current year's association budget (including reasonable details concerning monthly assessment charges and charges for rental of facilities), latest annual association operating statements, leases to which unit owners will be a party, description of any contemplated expansion of condominium, the unit floor plan with information necessary to show location of common elements and other facilities available to unit owners, and any amendments to any of these (except as limited for small residential condominiums per Wis Stat. §703.365). If the condominium was an occupied structure prior to the recording of the condominium declaration, it is a "conversion condominium" and the "condominium disclosure materials" also include: 1) a statement based on an engineer's or architect's report describing the present condition of structural, mechanical and electrical installations; 2) a statement of the useful life of the items covered in 1), unless a statement that no representations are being made is provided, and 3) a list of notices of code or other municipal violations, including an estimate of the costs of curing the violations.

■ ***REAL ESTATE CONDITION REPORT:*** Seller agrees to complete the real estate condition report provided by Broker to the best of Seller's ability. Seller acknowledges that failure to deliver a complete and accurate report to Buyer within ten days after acceptance of an offer to purchase may provide Buyer with rights to rescind that offer to purchase under Wis. Statute Chapter 709. Wis. Stat. §709.03 provides that when the Property

FIGURE 2.2 (CONTINUED)

Sample Residential Condominium Listing Contract—Exclusive Right to Sell

Wisconsin Legal Blank Co., Inc.
Page 3 of 5, WB-4

is a condominium unit, the property to which the real estate condition report applies is the condominium unit, the common elements of the condominium and any limited common elements that may be used only by the owner of the condominium unit being transferred. Wis. Stat. §709.035 requires Sellers to deliver an amended report to buyer should Seller learn of any defects after completion of the report but before acceptance of the buyer's offer to purchase. Seller agrees to promptly amend the report to include any defects (as defined in the report) which Seller learns of after completion of the report. Seller authorizes Broker to distribute the report to all interested parties and their agents and to disclose all adverse material facts as required by law.

■ ***ATTORNEY FEES:*** SHOULD LITIGATION ARISE BETWEEN THE PARTIES IN CONNECTION WITH THIS LISTING, THE PREVAILING PARTY SHALL HAVE THE RIGHT TO RECOVER REASONABLE ATTORNEY FEES.

■ ***FAIR HOUSING:*** SELLER AND BROKER AGREE THAT THEYWILL NOTDISCRIMINATE AGAINSTANY PROSPECTIVE PURCHASER ON ACCOUNT OF RACE, COLOR, SEX, SEXUAL ORIENTATION AS DEFINED IN WISCONSIN STATUTES, SECTION 111.32 (13M), DISABILITY, RELIGION, NATIONALORIGIN, MARITALSTATUS, LAWFULSOURCE OF INCOME, AGE, ANCESTRY, FAMILIALSTATUS, OR IN ANY OTHER UNLAWFUL MANNER.

■ ***EARNEST MONEY:*** If Broker holds trust funds in connection with the transaction, they shall be retained by Broker in Broker's trust account. Broker may refuse to hold earnest money or other trust funds. Should Broker hold the earnest money, Seller authorizes Broker to disburse the earnest money pursuant to the terms of the offer to purchase, option or exchange agreement used in the transaction. If the transaction fails to close and the earnest money is disbursed to Seller, then upon disbursement to Seller the earnest money shall be paid first to reimburse Broker for cash advances made by Broker on behalf of Seller and one half of the balance, but not in excess of the agreed commission, shall be paid to Broker as Broker's full commission in connection with said purchase transaction and the balance shall belong to Seller. This payment to Broker shall not terminate this Listing.

■ ***OPEN HOUSE AND SHOWING RESPONSIBILITIES:***
Seller is aware that there is a potential risk of injury, damage and or theft involving persons attending an "individual showing" or an "open house". Seller accepts responsibility for preparing the Property to minimize the likelihood of injury, damage and/or loss of personal property. Seller agrees to hold Broker harmless for any losses or liability resulting from personal injury, property damage, or theft occurring during "individual showings" or "open houses" other than those caused by Broker's negligence or intentional wrongdoing. **Seller acknowledges that individual showings may be conducted by licensees other than Broker, that appraisers and inspectors may conduct appraisals and inspections without being accompanied by Broker or other licensees and that buyers may photograph or videotape Property unless otherwise provided for at lines 254 - 262 or in an addendum per line 263.**

■ ***LEASED PROPERTY:*** If Property is currently leased and lease(s) will extend beyond closing, Seller shall assign Seller's rights under the lease(s) and transfer all security deposits and prepaid rents (subject to agreed upon prorations) thereunder to Buyer at closing. Seller acknowledges that Seller remains liable under the lease(s) unless released by tenants. ***CAUTION: Seller should consider obtaining an indemnification agreement from buyer for liabilities under the lease(s) unless released by tenants.***

■ ***DEFINITIONS:***
ADVERSE FACT: An "Adverse fact" means any of the following:
(a) A condition or occurrence that is generally recognized by a competent licensee as doing any of the following: 1) Significantly and adversely affecting the value of the Property; 2) Significantly reducing the structural integrity of improvements to real estate; 3) Presenting a significant health risk to occupants of the Property.
(b) Information that indicates that a party to a transaction is not able to or does not intend to meet his or her obligations under a contract or agreement made concerning the transaction.

MATERIAL ADVERSE FACT: A "material adverse fact" means an adverse fact that a party indicates is of such significance, or that is generally recognized by a competent licensee as being of such significance to a reasonable party, that it affects or would affect the party's decision to enter into a contract or agreement concerning a transaction or affects or would affect the party's decision about the terms of such a contract or agreement.

CONDITIONS AFFECTING THE PROPERTY OR TRANSACTION:
A "condition affecting the Property or transaction" is defined as follows:
(a) planned or commenced public improvements by government authorities or the homeowner's or condominium association which may result in special assessments or otherwise materially affect the Property or the present use of the Property;
(b) completed or pending reassessment of the Property for property tax purposes;
(c) government agency, court, homeowner's or condominium association order requiring repair, alteration or correction of any existing condition;
(d) construction or remodeling on Property for which required state or local permits had not been obtained;
(e) any land division involving the subject Property, for which required state or local approvals had not been obtained;
(f) violation of applicable state or local smoke detector laws; ***NOTE: State law requires operating smoke detectors on all levels of all residential properties.***
(g) any portion of the Condominium being in a 100 year floodplain, a wetland or a shoreland zoning area under local, state or federal laws;
(h) a structure on the Property is designated as a historic building or that any part of Property is in a historic district;
(i) structural inadequacies which if not repaired will significantly shorten the expected normal life of the Condominium;
(j) mechanical systems inadequate for the present use of the Condominium;
(k) insect or animal infestation of the Condominium;
(l) conditions constituting a significant health or safety hazard for occupants of Property; ***NOTE: Specific federal lead paint disclosure requirments must be complied with in the sale of most residential properties built before 1978.***
(m) underground or aboveground storage tanks on the Condominium for storage of flammable or combustible liquids including but not limited to

FIGURE 2.2 (CONTINUED)

Sample Residential Condominium Listing Contract—Exclusive Right to Sell

gasoline and heating oil which are currently or which were previously located on the Condominium; ***NOTE: Wis. Adm. Code, Chapter COMM 10 contains registration and operation rules for such underground and aboveground storage tanks.***

(n) material violations of environmental laws or other laws or agreements regulating the use of the Condominium;

(o) high voltage electric (100 KV or greater) or steel natural gas transmission lines located on but not directly serving the Condominium;

(p) other conditions or occurrences which would significantly reduce the value of the Property to a reasonable person with knowledge of the nature and scope of the condition or occurrence.

FIXTURES: A "fixture" is an item of property which is physically attached to or so closely associated with land or buildings so as to be treated as part of the real estate, including, without limitation, physically attached items not easily removable without damage to the premises, items specifically adapted to the premises, and items customarily treated as fixtures including but not limited to all: garden bulbs; plants; shrubs and trees; screen and storm doors and windows; electric lighting fixtures; window shades; curtain and traverse rods; blinds and shutters; central heating and cooling units and attached equipment; water heaters and softeners; sump pumps; attached or fitted floor coverings; awnings; attached antennas, satellite dishes and component parts; garage door openers and remote controls; installed security systems; central vacuum systems and accessories; in-ground sprinkler systems and component parts; built-in appliances; ceiling fans; fences; storage buildings on permanent foundations and docks/piers on permanent foundations. See lines 12 - 19. ***CAUTION: Address rented fixtures, if any (e.g., water softener, L.P. tanks, etc.).***

DELIVERY: Unless otherwise stated, delivery of documents or written notices related to this Listing may be accomplished by: 1) giving the document or written notice personally to the Party; 2) by depositing the document or written notice postage or fees prepaid or charged to an account in the U.S. Mail or a commercial delivery system, addressed to the Party, at the Party's address (See lines 275, 279); 3) by electronically transmitting the document or written notice to the Party's fax number (See lines 275, 279).

PROCURE: A purchaser is procured when a valid and binding contract of sale is entered into between the Seller and the purchaser or when a ready, willing and able purchaser submits a written offer at the price and on substantially the terms specified in this Listing. A purchaser is ready, willing and able when the purchaser submitting the written offer has the ability to complete the purchaser's obligations under the written offer. See lines 65 - 67.

■ ***AGENCY DISCLOSURE PROVISIONS:***

■ AGENCY DISCLOSURE AND CONSENT TO MULTIPLE REPRESENTATION: Wisconsin Statute § 452.135(2) requires Broker to disclose that Seller is Broker's client. Broker's duties to Seller can be found at lines 218 - 226. Broker's duties to all parties can be found at lines 202 - 217. The confidentiality rights of all parties can be found at lines 238 - 245. See lines 245 - 249 for information regarding identification of confidential and non-confidential information at lines 250 - 253. If a multiple representation relationship is consented to and does occur, both parties will be Broker's clients.

■ DUTIES OWED TO ALL PARTIES: Wisconsin Statute § 452.133(1) states that in providing brokerage services to a party to a transaction (including both clients and customers), a broker shall do all of the following:

(a) Provide brokerage services to all parties to the transaction honestly, fairly and in good faith.

(b) Diligently exercise reasonable skill and care in providing brokerage services to all parties.

(c) Disclose to each party all material adverse facts that the broker knows and that the party does not know or cannot discover through reasonably vigilant observation, unless the disclosure of a material adverse fact is prohibited by law.

(d) Keep confidential any information given to the broker in confidence, or any information obtained by the broker that he or she knows a reasonable party would want to be kept confidential, unless the information must be disclosed under par. (c) or Wis. Stat. § 452.23 (information contradicting third party inspection or investigation reports) or is otherwise required by law to be disclosed or the party whose intrests may be adversely affected by the disclosure specifically authorizes the disclosure of particular confidential information. A broker shall continue to keep the information confidential after the transaction is complete and after the broker is no longer providing brokerage services to the party.

(e) Provide accurate information about market conditions that affect a transaction, to any party who requests the information, within a reasonable time of the party's request, unless disclosure of the information is prohibited by law.

(f) Account for all property of the parties coming into the possession of a broker within a reasonable time of receipt.

(g) When negotiating on behalf of a party, present contract proposals in an objective and unbiased manner and disclose the advantages and disadvantages of the proposals.

■ DUTIES OWED TO CLIENTS ONLY: Wisconsin Statute § 452.133(2) states that in addition to his or her duties under lines 202 - 217, a broker providing brokerage services to his or her client shall do all of the following:

(a) Loyally represent the client's interests by placing the client's interests ahead of the interests of any other party, unless loyalty to a client violates the broker's duties under lines 202 - 217 or Wis. Stat. § 452.137(2) (duties to all clients in multiple representation situations).

(b) Disclose to the client all information known by the broker that is material to the transaction and that is not known by the client or discoverable by the client through reasonably vigilant observation, except for confidential information (see lines 208 - 212) and other information, the disclosure of which is prohibited by law.

(c) Fulfill any obligation required by the agency agreement, and any order of the client that is within the scope of the agency agreement, that are not inconsistent with another duty that the broker has under this chapter or any other law.

■ MULTIPLE REPRESENTATION (DUAL AGENCY): Wisconsin Statute § 452.137 states that Broker may represent both parties in the same transaction only with the written consent of both Parties. A multiple representation relationship would exist if Broker was the buyer's agent for a buyer seeking to acquire an interest in the Property. In a multiple representation relationship, Broker will provide the marketing and other services agreed upon in this Listing. Broker will continue to provide information and advice to both parties, but is not allowed to place the interests of either party ahead of the other in negotiations. During negotiations, Broker will prepare approved forms to accomplish the intent of the party making the

FIGURE 2.2 (CONTINUED)

Sample Residential Condominium Listing Contract—Exclusive Right to Sell

Wisconsin Legal Blank Co., Inc.
Page 5 of 5, WB-4

proposal. Broker will present the proposal in an objective and unbiased manner, disclosing the proposal's advantages and disadvantages. Broker shall not disclose confidential information of either party unless required by law. ***(NOTE: Wisconsin Administrative Code section RL 24.07 requires disclosure of adverse material facts to all interested parties).*** If Seller consents to the multiple representation relationship, Seller is indicating that Seller understands Broker's duties to all parties to a transaction (see lines 202 - 217) and Broker's duties to a client (see lines 218 - 226) and that if a multiple representation relationship arises, Broker will owe the same duties to buyer that Broker owes to Seller (See lines 218 - 226).
SELLER (DOES)(DOES NOT) STRIKE ONE **CONSENT TO A MULTIPLE REPRESENTATION RELATIONSHIP (DUALAGENCY).**

■ CONFIDENTIALITY NOTICE:
A BROKER IS REQUIRED TO MAINTAIN THE CONFIDENTIALITYOF ALLINFORMATION GIVEN TO THE BROKER IN CONFIDENCE AND OF ALL INFORMATION OBTAINED BYTHE BROKER THAT HE OR SHE KNOWS A REASONABLE PARTY WOULD WANT TO BE KEPT CONFIDENTIAL, UNLESS THE INFORMATION IS REQUIRED TO BE DISCLOSED BY LAW. THE FOLLOWING INFORMATION IS REQUIRED TO BE DISCLOSED BY LAW:
1) MATERIALADVERSE FACTS AS DEFINED IN § 452.01(5g) OF THE WISCONSIN STATUTES. (See lines 147 to 155)
2) ANY FACTS KNOWN BY THE BROKER THAT CONTRADICT ANY INFORMATION INCLUDED IN A WRITTEN INSPECTION REPORT ON THE PROPERTYOR REALESTATE THAT IS THE SUBJECTOF THE TRANSACTION. TO ENSURE THAT THE BROKER IS AWARE OF WHAT SPECIFIC INFORMATION YOU CONSIDER CONFIDENTIAL, YOU MAY LISTTHAT INFORMATION AT LINE 250 - 251. AT A LATER TIME, YOU ALSO MAY PROVIDE THE BROKER WITH OTHER WRITTEN NOTIFICATION OF WHAT INFORMATION YOU CONSIDER TO BE CONFIDENTIAL. YOU MAY IDENTIFY INFORMATION WHICH MIGHT OTHERWISE BE CONSIDERED CONFIDENTIAL (SUCH AS SELLER'S MOTIVATION TO SELL) AS NON-CONFIDENTIAL AT LINES 252 - 253.

■ CONFIDENTIAL INFORMATION: ______________________________
____

■ NON-CONFIDENTIAL INFORMATION: ______________________________
____

■ ***ADDITIONAL PROVISIONS:*** ______________________________
____
____
____
____
____
____
____
____

■ **ADDENDA:** The attached ______________________________ is/are made part of this Listing.

CAUTION: IF SIGNED, THIS LISTING CAN CREATE A LEGALLY ENFORCEABLE CONTRACT. BROKERS MAY PROVIDE A GENERAL EXPLANATION OF THE PROVISIONS OF THIS LISTING OR OTHER REAL ESTATE CONTRACTS, BUT ARE PROHIBITED BY LAW FROM GIVING ADVICE OR OPINIONS CONCERNING YOUR LEGAL RIGHTS UNDER THIS LISTING OR ANY OTHER REAL ESTATE CONTRACT. AN ATTORNEY SHOULD BE CONSULTED IF LEGAL ADVICE IS NEEDED. SELLER SHOULD CONSULT OTHER EXPERTS AS APPROPRIATE, FOR EXAMPLE, APPRAISERS, TAX ADVISORS, OR HOME INSPECTORS IF SERVICES BEYOND BROKER'S MARKETING SERVICES ARE REQUIRED.

Dated this ______________ day of ______________________________, ______________

(x)______________________________ ______________________________ ______________
Seller's Signature ▲ Print Name Here: ▶ Social Security No. or FEIN (Optional) ▲ Date ▲

(x)______________________________ ______________________________ ______________
Seller's Signature ▲ Print Name Here: ▶ Social Security No. or FEIN (Optional) ▲ Date ▲

______________________________ ______________ ______________
Seller's Address ▲ Phone # ▲ Fax # ▲

(x)______________________________ ______________________________
Agent for Broker ▲ (Print Name) ▶ Broker/Firm Name ▲

______________________________ ______________ ______________
Broker/Firm Address ▲ Phone # ▲ Fax # ▲

Line 22 identifies whether parking rights are included with the unit. It also indicates whether parking rights are included with the unit or whether they are to be purchased separately or rented in addition to the monthly condominium assessments.

Line 23 indicates the amount of the association fee as well as the payment schedule.

Line 24 indicates whether the condominium association has a right of first refusal on the unit. The existence of a right of first refusal should be disclosed in writing by the listing agent to a potential buyer because it has a potential to be a material adverse fact. It creates uncertainty over whether the seller will be able to sell the unit to a third party because it gives a person the first opportunity to purchase a property. You should be aware that the person holding a right-of-first refusal doesn't have a right to purchase until the owner offers to sell the property or receives an offer to purchase from a third party that the owner is willing to accept.

Lines 25–30 state that upon payment of the purchase price the seller will convey title to the buyer free and clear of all liens and encumbrances other than those items identified on lines 26–29.

Line 31 indicates that the seller will provide title insurance as evidence of title.

Lines 32–36 indicate information provided to the broker by the seller as identified in the attached Real Estate Condition Report. If there is no condition report, the seller should return a signed copy with a counter-offer or accepted offer or by itself within ten days of an accepted offer. Licensees must always disclose adverse material facts not disclosed in the condition report.

Lines 37–42 reflect the marketing agreement.

Lines 38 and 39 indicate any steps you plan to use in selling the property.

Lines 41 and 42 state the seller's responsibility to cooperate with regard to notification of potential buyers as well as broker attempts to market the property.

Lines 43–46 provide that the broker will cooperate with other brokers including subagents and brokers representing the buyer. If the seller wishes to limit the agreement in some way, these limitations would be placed on lines 44 and 45.

Lines 47 and 48 cover the terms of the contract.

Lines 49–55 are used to list the names of those people with whom the seller has been negotiating on his or her own and whom the seller considers as potential buyers and wants to be excluded from the contract. This section is similar to the section discussed above in the Residential Listing Contract.

Lines 56–70 cover the commission agreement as discussed above in the Residential Listing Contract.

Lines 71–85 provide for extended listing protection for the brokers discussed above in the residential listing contract.

Lines 86–89 state that neither the seller nor the broker have the legal right to unilaterally terminate the listing unless a material breach of contract has been made by the other party.

Lines 90–99 identify the responsibilities of the seller in cooperating with the broker marketing efforts. This section also states that the seller is to provide the broker with all records, documents, and other material in the seller's possession or control which are required in connection with the sale as indicated on lines 92–95.

Lines 100–111 state that the seller agrees to provide the buyer with a copy of the condominium disclosure materials no later than 15 days prior to closing. Materials to be provided include copies of the condominium declarations and bylaws as well as other materials stated on lines 102–111.

Lines 121–122 state that if there is any litigation in connection with the listing, the prevailing party has the right to recover reasonable attorney fees. Only recently have brokers been given the right to collect attorney fees in successful litigation.

Lines 123–126 identify the protected classes in Wisconsin according to the Wisconsin fair housing laws.

Lines 127–133 relate to earnest money. This section is similar to the Residential Listing Contract discussed above.

Lines 134–141 also include language that is similar to the Residential Listing Contract section above.

Lines 142–145 cover a property that has been leased.

Lines 147–155 define an adverse fact and a material adverse fact.

Lines 156–179 identify conditions affecting the property transaction.

Lines 180–188 cover *fixtures*, while *delivery* is defined on lines 189–192.

Lines 193–196 define the term *procure*.

Lines 197–217 identify duties owed to all parties while lines 218 and 226 identify duties owed to clients only. Multiple representation (dual agency) is covered on lines 227–237 while lines 238–253 provide notice of confidentiality.

Lines 254–262 are used to identify any negatives such as anything the seller does not want. For example, if the seller does not want a For Sale sign on the property, it would be included in this section. The fact that a right of first refusal exists would also be placed in this section.

Line 263 covers any attached addendum.

Line 270 is used to indicate the date on which the listing contract is being drafted. The sellers or persons agreeing to pay the commission must sign on lines 271 and 273.

THE WB-36 BUYER AGENCY/TENANT REPRESENTATION AGREEMENT

The new WB-36 Buyer Agency/Tenant Representation Agreement has an optional use date of January 1, 2008, and a mandatory use date of July 1, 2008. You should be aware of the following five points with regard to buyer agency in general and the WB-36 Buyer Agency/Tenant Representation Agreement in particular.

1. The WB-36 agreement authorizes the broker to act as agent of the buyer; the buyer is a client of the broker.
2. The WB-36 explains that exclusive right to act as buyer agent means that the buyer may *not* enter into another buyer agency agreement with another agent. The buyer may still work with an attorney to assist with negotiations or get business strategies from other professionals or friends.
3. The WB-36 indicates the type of performance required for the broker to earn a success fee.
4. A licensee may provide brokerage services to any party up to the point of negotiation of terms of a contract. After negotiation has started, the licensee must have an agency contract with at least one of the parties to the transaction. *Negotiate* means to provide assistance to a party within the scope of the knowledge, skills, and training required in developing a proposal or agreement relating to a transaction, including doing *any* of the following:
   a. Acting as an intermediary by facilitating or participating in communications between parties. Providing advice or opinions on matters that are material to a transaction in which a person is engaged or intends to engage to show a party real estate does not, in and of itself, constitute acting as an intermediary by facilitating or participating in communications between parties.
   b. Completing approved forms or other writings to document the party's proposal consistent with the party's intent.
   c. Presenting to a party the proposals of other parties to the transaction and giving the party a general explanation of the provisions of the proposal.
5. The WB-36 makes clear that the buyer broker earns a "success fee" if the buyer acquires the described property or enters into an enforceable contract to acquire such a property during the term of the agreement, regardless of whether the buyer's agent located the property or negotiated the contract.

Line-by-Line Explanation of the WB-36 Buyer Agency/Tenant Representation Agreement

Lines 1–5 deal with the buyer giving the broker the exclusive right to represent the buyer as a buyer's agent. Thus, no other party can serve as a buyer's agent for the buyer with regard to any properties not excluded from the WB-36 agreement.

However, the exclusive right does not prevent the buyer from personally contacting sellers or seller agents concerning properties in which the buyer may be interested. Lines 3–5 make it clear, however, that the buyer may not enter into a buyer

FIGURE 2.3

Sample Buyer Agency/Tenant Representation Agreement

Approved by Wisconsin Department of Regulation and Licensing
1-1-08 (Optional Use Date) 7-1-08 (Mandatory Use Date)

Wisconsin Legal Blank Co., Inc.
Milwaukee, Wisconsin

Page 1 of 5, WB-36

WB-36 BUYER AGENCY/TENANT REPRESENTATION AGREEMENT

■ **BROKER THE SOLE AUTHORITY TO ACT FOR BUYER AS A BUYER'S AGENT:** Buyer (see lines 154-155) gives Broker the exclusive right to act as Buyer's agent to locate an interest in property and to negotiate the procurement of an interest in property, except as excluded under lines 11-20. Except for excluded properties described in lines 11-20, Buyer agrees that during the term of this Agreement, Buyer will not enter into any other agreements to retain any other buyer's agent.

NOTE: IF BUYER WORKS WITH OWNER OR AGENTS OF OWNER IN LOCATING AND/OR NEGOTIATING AN INTEREST IN PROPERTY, BUYER MAY BE RESPONSIBLE FOR BROKER'S FULL COMPENSATION IF BUYER'S CONTACTS WITH OWNER OR OWNER'S AGENT RESULT IN NO COMPENSATION BEING RECEIVED BY BROKER FROM OWNER OR OWNER'S AGENT.

■ **PURCHASE PRICE RANGE:** ____________________

■ **EXCLUDED PROPERTIES:** The following properties are excluded from this Agreement until __________ [INSERT DATE]

Note: Identify any specific excluded properties or limitations on the scope of this Agreement including geographic limitations, or limitations on property type included under this Agreement ____________________

■ **COMPENSATION:** Broker's compensation shall be: [Check "SUCCESS FEE", "OTHER COMPENSATION", OR BOTH, as applicable] ☐ *SUCCESS FEE:* _______ % of the purchase price or ____________________ whichever is greater. ☐ *OTHER COMPENSATION:* ____________________

[INSERT THE AMOUNT AND TYPE OF OTHER FEE, E.G. RETAINER FEE, OR HOURLY FEE]

If this Agreement calls for a success fee, it is agreed that Broker has earned the success fee if, during the term of this Agreement (or any extension of it), Buyer or any person acting on behalf of Buyer acquires an interest in property or enters into an enforceable written contract between owner and Buyer to acquire an interest in property, at any terms and price acceptable to owner and Buyer. Broker's compensation remains due and payable if an enforceable written contract entered into by Buyer per lines 26-29 fails to close. Once earned, Broker's compensation is due and payable at the earlier of closing or the date set for closing, unless otherwise agreed in writing.

Broker (may) (may not) [STRIKE ONE] accept compensation from owner or owner's agent. (Broker may accept compensation from owner or owner's agent if neither is struck.) Broker's compensation from Buyer will be reduced by any amounts received from owner or owner's agent.

■ **BROKER'S DUTIES:** In consideration for Buyer's agreements, Broker agrees to use professional knowledge and skills, and reasonable efforts, to: 1) locate an interest in property, unless Broker is being retained solely to negotiate the procurement of an interest in a specific property, and 2) negotiate the procurement of an interest in property, as required, by giving advice to Buyer within the scope of Broker's license, facilitating or participating in the discussions of the terms of a potential contract, completing appropriate contractual forms, presenting either party's contractual proposal with an explanation of the proposal's advantages and disadvantages and other efforts including but not limited to the following: ____________________, unless Broker is retained solely to locate an interest in property.

■ **EARNEST MONEY:** If Broker holds trust funds in connection with the transaction, they shall be retained by Broker in Broker's trust account. Broker may refuse to hold earnest money or other trust funds. Should Broker hold the earnest money, Buyer authorizes Broker to disburse the earnest money as directed in a written earnest money disbursement agreement signed by all parties having an interest in the trust funds. If the transaction fails to close and the earnest money is disbursed to Buyer, then upon disbursement to Buyer the earnest money shall be paid first to reimburse Broker for cash advances made by Broker on behalf of Buyer.

■ **NON DISCRIMINATION:** Buyer and Broker agree that they will not discriminate based on race, color, sex, sexual orientation as defined in Wisconsin Statutes §111.32(13m), disability, religion, national origin, marital status, lawful source of income, age, ancestry, familial status or in any other unlawful manner.

FIGURE 2.3 (CONTINUED)

Sample Buyer Agency/Tenant Representation Agreement

Wisconsin Legal Blank Co., Inc.
Milwaukee, Wis.

■ **BROKER DISCLOSURE TO CLIENTS:**

UNDER WISCONSIN LAW, A BROKER OWES CERTAIN DUTIES TO ALL PARTIES TO A TRANSACTION:

(a) The duty to provide brokerage services to you fairly and honestly.

(b) The duty to exercise reasonable skill and care in providing brokerage services to you.

(c) The duty to provide you with accurate information about market conditions within a reasonable time if you request it, unless disclosure of the information is prohibited by law.

(d) The duty to disclose to you in writing certain material adverse facts about a property, unless disclosure of the information is prohibited by law. (See lines 170-173)

(e) The duty to protect your confidentiality. Unless the law requires it, the broker will not disclose your confidential information or the confidential information of other parties. (See lines 109-122)

(f) The duty to safeguard trust funds and other property the broker holds.

(g) The duty, when negotiating, to present contract proposals in an objective and unbiased manner and disclose the advantages and disadvantages of the proposals.

BECAUSE YOU HAVE ENTERED INTO AN AGENCY AGREEMENT WITH A BROKER, YOU ARE THE BROKER'S CLIENT. A BROKER OWES ADDITIONAL DUTIES TO A CLIENT:

(a) The broker will provide, at your request, information and advice on real estate matters that affect your transaction, unless you release the broker from this duty.

(b) The broker must provide you with all material facts affecting the transaction, not just adverse facts.

(c) The broker will fulfill the broker's obligations under the agency agreement and fulfill your lawful requests that are within the scope of the agency agreement.

(d) The broker will negotiate for you, unless you release the broker from this duty.

(e) The broker will not place the broker's interests ahead of your interests. The broker will not, unless required by law, give information or advice to other parties who are not the broker's clients, if giving the information or advice is contrary to your interests.

(f) If you become involved in a transaction in which another party is also the broker's client (a "multiple representation relationship"), different duties may apply.

■ **MULTIPLE REPRESENTATION RELATIONSHIPS AND DESIGNATED AGENCY:**

A multiple representation relationship exists if a broker has an agency agreement with more than one client who is a party in the same transaction. In a multiple representation relationship, if all of the broker's clients in the transaction consent, the broker may provide services to the clients through designated agency.

Designated agency means that different salespersons employed by the broker will negotiate on behalf of you and the other client or clients in the transaction and the broker's duties will remain the same. Each salesperson will provide information, opinions, and advice to the client for whom the salesperson is negotiating, to assist the client in the negotiations. Each client will be able to receive information, opinions, and advice that will assist the client, even if the information, opinions, or advice gives the client advantages in the negotiations over the broker's other clients. A salesperson will not reveal any of your confidential information to another party unless required to do so by law.

If a designated agency relationship is not in effect you may authorize or reject a multiple representation relationship. If you authorize a multiple representation relationship the broker may provide brokerage services to more than one client in a transaction but neither the broker nor any of the broker's salespersons may assist any client with information, opinions, and advice which may favor the interests of one client over any other client. If you do not consent to a multiple representation relationship the broker will not be allowed to provide brokerage services to more than one client in the transaction.

FIGURE 2.3 (CONTINUED)

Sample Buyer Agency/Tenant Representation Agreement

Wisconsin Legal Blank Co., Inc.
Milwaukee, Wis.

page 3 of 5, WB-36

INITIAL ONLY ONE OF THE THREE LINES BELOW:

_______I consent to designated agency.

_______I consent to multiple representation relationships, but I do not consent to designated agency.

_______I reject multiple representation relationships.

NOTE: You may withdraw your consent to designated agency or to multiple representation relationships by written notice to the broker at any time. Your broker is required to disclose to you in your agency agreement the commission or fees that you may owe to your broker. If you have any questions about the commission or fees that you may owe based upon the type of agency relationship you select with your broker you should ask your broker before signing the agency agreement.

■ **SUBAGENCY:** The broker may, with your authorization in the agency agreement, engage other brokers who assist your broker by providing brokerage services for your benefit. A subagent will not put the subagent's own interests ahead of your interests. A subagent will not, unless required by law, provide advice or opinions to other parties if doing so is contrary to your interests. **PLEASE REVIEW THIS INFORMATION CAREFULLY. A broker or salesperson can answer your questions about brokerage services, but if you need legal advice, tax advice, or a professional home inspection, contact an attorney, tax advisor, or home inspector. This disclosure is required by section 452.135 of the Wisconsin statutes and is for information only. It is a plain language summary of a broker's duties to you under section 452.133 (2) of the Wisconsin statutes.**

■ **CONFIDENTIALITY NOTICE TO CLIENTS:** Broker will keep confidential any information given to Broker in confidence, or any information obtained by Broker that he or she knows a reasonable person would want to be kept confidential, unless the information must be disclosed by law or you authorize Broker to disclose particular information. Broker shall continue to keep the information confidential after Broker is no longer providing brokerage services to you.

THE FOLLOWING INFORMATION IS REQUIRED TO BE DISCLOSED BY LAW:

1. Material adverse facts, as defined in section 452.01 (5g) of the Wisconsin statutes (See lines 170-173).
2. Any facts known by the broker that contradict any information included in a written inspection report on the property or real estate that is the subject of the transaction. To ensure that the broker is aware of what specific information you consider confidential, you may list that information below (See lines 119-120). At a later time, you may also provide the broker with other information you consider to be confidential.

CONFIDENTIAL INFORMATION: ____

____

NON-CONFIDENTIAL INFORMATION (The following may be disclosed by Broker):______________________

____

■ **WAIVER OF CONFIDENTIALITY:** Buyer may wish to authorize Broker to disclose information which might otherwise be considered confidential. An example of this type of information might be financial qualification information which may be disclosed to strengthen Buyer's offer to purchase/lease proposal in the eyes of prospective sellers/landlords. Broker's authorization to disclose may be indicated at lines 121-122. Unless otherwise provided at lines 119-120, Broker has permission to disclose Buyer's identity to owner, owner's agents and other third parties without prior consent from Buyer. Buyer acknowledges that pursuant to Wisconsin Statute section 706.03(1)(b)(1m) a conveyance, such as an offer to purchase, is not binding if it is signed by a representative properly authorized by Buyer (e.g., with a power of attorney) until such time as Buyer is identified in the conveyance.

■ **NON-EXCLUSIVE RELATIONSHIP:** Buyer acknowledges and agrees that Broker may act for other buyers in connection with the location of properties and may negotiate on behalf of such buyers with the owner or owner's agent. In the event that Broker undertakes to represent and act for other buyers, Broker shall not disclose to Buyer, or any other buyer, any confidential information of any buyer, unless required by law.

■ **COOPERATION:** Buyer agrees to cooperate with Broker and to provide Broker accurate copies of all relevant records, documents and other materials in Buyer's possession or control which are required in connection with the purchase, option, exchange or lease of property. Buyer agrees to be reasonably available for showings of properties. Buyer authorizes Broker to do those acts reasonably necessary to fulfill Broker's responsibilities under this Agreement including retaining subagents. Buyer shall promptly notify Broker in writing of the description of any property Buyer locates. Buyer shall also notify Broker of the identity of all persons making inquiries concerning Buyer's objectives stated in this Agreement.

FIGURE 2.3 (CONTINUED)

Sample Buyer Agency/Tenant Representation Agreement

Wisconsin Legal Blank Co., Inc.
Milwaukee, Wis.

[page 4 of 5, WB-36]

■ **PROPERTY DIMENSIONS:** Buyer acknowledges that property dimensions, total square footage and total acreage information provided to Buyer may be approximate due to rounding and may vary due to different formulas which can be used to calculate these figures. Unless otherwise indicated, property dimension figures have not been verified by survey. **CAUTION: Buyer should verify any property dimension or total square footage/acreage calculation which is material to Buyer.**

■ **DEFINITIONS:**

ADVERSE FACT: An "adverse fact" means any of the following:

(a) A condition or occurrence that is generally recognized by a competent licensee as doing any of the following:
  1) Significantly and adversely affecting the value of the property;
  2) Significantly reducing the structural integrity of improvements to real estate; or
  3) Presenting a significant health risk to occupants of the property.

(b) Information that indicates that a party to a transaction is not able to or does not intend to meet his or her obligations under a contract or agreement made concerning the transaction.

BUYER: "Buyer", as used in this Agreement, is the party executing this Agreement and seeking to acquire an interest in real estate or a business opportunity by purchase, lease, option, exchange or any other manner.

DEADLINES-DAYS: Deadlines expressed as a number of "days" from an event, such as acceptance, are calculated by excluding the day the event occurred and by counting subsequent calendar days.

DELIVERY: Delivery of documents or written notices related to this Agreement may only be accomplished by:
  1) giving the document or written notice personally to the party;
  2) depositing the document or written notice postage or fees prepaid or charged to an account in the U.S. Mail or a commercial delivery system, addressed to the party, at the party's address (See lines 220, 226 and 232);
  3) electronically transmitting the document or written notice to the party's fax number (See lines 222, 228 and 234); and
  4) as otherwise agreed in additional provisions on lines 182-190 or in an addendum to this Agreement.

INTEREST IN PROPERTY: The "interest in property" to be obtained by Buyer includes a purchase, leasehold, option, exchange agreement or any other procured interest in real property unless restricted at lines 11-20, in additional provisions (lines 182-190) or elsewhere in this Agreement.

LOCATE AN INTEREST IN PROPERTY: "Locate an interest in property" shall mean, as used in this Agreement, to identify, evaluate according to the standards set by Buyer, and determine the availability of the interest sought by Buyer in a property.

MATERIAL ADVERSE FACT: A "material adverse fact" means an adverse fact that a party indicates is of such significance, or that is generally recognized by a competent licensee as being of such significance to a reasonable party, that it affects or would affect the party's decision to enter into a contract or agreement concerning a transaction or affects or would affect the party's decision about the terms of such a contract or agreement.

NEGOTIATE THE PROCUREMENT OF AN INTEREST IN PROPERTY: "Negotiate the procurement of an interest in property" shall mean, as used in this Agreement, to contact the owner of the property or the owner's agent to ascertain the terms and conditions upon which the interest may be obtained and to otherwise assist Buyer in reaching an agreement to procure the interest sought by Buyer in the property as may be specified in this Agreement.

PERSON ACTING ON BEHALF OF BUYER: In this Agreement "Person acting on behalf of Buyer" shall mean any person joined in interest with Buyer, or otherwise acting on behalf of Buyer, including but not limited to Buyer's immediate family, agents, servants, employees, as well as any and all corporations, partnerships, limited liability companies or other entities controlled by, affiliated with or owned by Buyer in whole or in part.

FIGURE 2.3 (CONTINUED)

Sample Buyer Agency/Tenant Representation Agreement

Wisconsin Legal Blank Co., Inc.
page 5 of 5, WB-36

■ **ADDITIONAL PROVISIONS:** ____________________

■ **ADDENDA:** The attached addenda ____________________ is/are made a part of this Agreement.

■ **TERM OF THE AGREEMENT:** From the __________ day of __________, ______, up to and including midnight of the __________ day of __________, ______. Notwithstanding lines 193-194, Broker and Buyer agree that this Agreement shall/shall not [STRIKE ONE] end [if neither struck, this Agreement shall end] when Buyer procures an interest in property.

■ **TERMINATION OF AGREEMENT:** Neither Buyer nor Broker has the legal right to unilaterally terminate this Agreement absent a material breach of contract by the other party. Buyer understands that the parties to this Agreement are Buyer and the Broker (firm). Agents (salespersons) for Broker (firm) do not have the authority to terminate this Agreement, amend the compensation terms or shorten the term of this Agreement, without the written consent of the agent(s)' supervising broker. Buyer and Broker agree that any termination of this Agreement by either party before the date stated on line 194 shall be indicated to the other party in writing and shall not be effective until delivered to the other party in accordance with lines 158-163. CAUTION: Early termination of this Agreement may be a breach of contract, causing the terminating party to potentially be liable for damages.

■ **EXTENSION OF AGREEMENT TERM:** The Agreement term is extended for a period of one year as to any property which during the term of this Agreement was: 1) located or negotiated for by Broker, Broker's agent, Buyer or any person acting on behalf of Buyer, or 2) which was the subject of a written offer to purchase submitted by Buyer or any person acting on behalf of Buyer. If this extension is based on Broker's or Broker's agent's location or negotiation, this extension shall only be effective if a written description of the property is delivered to Buyer no later than three days after expiration of this Agreement.

■ **NOTICE ABOUT SEX OFFENDER REGISTRY:** You may obtain information about the sex offender registry and persons registered with that registry by contacting the Wisconsin Department of Corrections on the Internet at http://www.widocoffenders.org or by telephone at (608)240-5830.

■ **READING/RECEIPT: BY SIGNING BELOW, BUYER ACKNOWLEDGES RECEIPT OF A COPY OF THIS AGREEMENT AND THAT HE/SHE HAS READ ALL FIVE PAGES AS WELL AS ANY ADDENDA AND ANY OTHER DOCUMENTS INCORPORATED INTO THIS AGREEMENT.**

Dated this __________ day of __________, ______

(x)__________ Buyer's Signature ▲ | Print Name Here: ▲ | Date ▲

Buyer's Address ▲ | Buyer's Phone # ▲

Buyer's Fax # ▲ | `Buyer's E-Mail Address ▲

(x)__________ Buyer's Signature ▲ | Print Name Here: ▲ | Date ▲

Buyer's Address ▲ | Buyer's Phone # ▲

Buyer's Fax # ▲ | `Buyer's E-Mail Address ▲

(x)__________ Agent for Broker ▲ | Print Name Here ▲ | Broker/Firm Name ▲ | Date ▲

Broker/Firm Address ▲ | Broker/Firm Phone # ▲

Broker/Firm Fax # ▲ | Broker/Firm E-Mail Address ▲

agency agreement with another broker regarding properties already included in his or her current buyer agency agreement.

Lines 154–155 on page 4 of the WB-36 agreement define the "buyer." The term *buyer* includes buyers as well as optionees, investors in business, tenants, and exchangers.

Line 3 refers to an "interest in property," which is defined on lines 164–166. An *interest in property* is used to include a purchase, option, exchange, leasehold, or any other procured interest, unless restricted in lines 11–20, in additional provisions, or elsewhere in the WB-36.

Line 2 refers to the phrase "locate an interest in property," which is defined on lines 167–169 to mean identifying and evaluating based on the buyer's standards, and determining the availability of the interest that the buyer is seeking. The broker would generally utilize the multiple listing service as a primary source for locating an interest in property.

Lines 2–3 refer to negotiating the procurement of an interest in property, except as excluded under lines 11–20. Lines 174–177 define the above statement meaning that the broker will contact owner's agents or property owners to determine the terms and conditions under which the interest may be obtained. Negotiation is also defined as assisting the buyer to reach an agreement to procure the interest sought by the buyer.

Lines 1–3 identify the different types of duties that the broker might be asked to perform for the buyer. For example, the buyer might ask the broker to only locate a property and not be involved in the procurement of the buyer's interest.

Lines 1–5 make clear that the broker's authorization to act for the buyer does not apply to any properties listed on lines 11–20.

Lines 6–9 make clear to the buyer that the buyer is responsible for paying the fee for the buyer broker if the buyer works with the owner's agents or the owner to acquire his or her interest in property that results in no compensation being received by the broker from the owner's agent or the owner. For example, if the buyer negotiates directly with a FSBO (for sale by owner), buys the property, and the owner refuses to pay a commission, the language in this section makes clear that the buyer will be responsible for paying a success fee to the buyer broker.

Line 10 states the range of the purchase price that is required to have an enforceable contract. The buyer broker should make the range sufficiently wide so as not to exclude properties in which the buyer might be interested.

Lines 11–20 list excluded properties. The language on these lines makes clear that the buyer's broker will not earn a fee if the buyer acquires an interest in a property identified in this section.

Line 11 identifies property excluded until a certain date. For example, if the buyer has made an offer on another property with another broker under a previous buyer agency agreement, the end of the protection period would be the date indicated in this section. The extension of this agreement term is described in lines 205–210.

Lines 11–20 provide space for identifying any specific properties or limitation, such as location or property type. For example, the buyer might state that she is not interested in any properties that are located more than 40 miles from Madison or that she does not want for sale by owner (FSBO) property included in this contract. This agency agreement includes all property listed or unlisted, unless otherwise stated on lines 13–20.

Lines 21–34 state that if the contract calls for a success fee, that fee is earned if the buyer acquires a property *not excluded* on lines 13–20 or enters into an enforceable contract to acquire such property during the term of the contract, regardless of whether the buyer's agent located the property or negotiated the contract.

You should also be aware of lines 29–30, which state that the broker's compensation is due and payable, even if the transaction fails to close.

Line 32 indicates whether the broker may accept compensation from the owner or the owner's agent.

Lines 35–42 emphasize that the buyer's broker must provide minimum service to the buyer, such as providing a reasonable effort to locate a property in order to be entitled to compensation. For example, a buyer's agent might indicate on line 41 that he will conduct a property search on the multiple listing service as may be necessary to locate a property.

Lines 43–48 state that all earnest money and other trust funds shall be held in the broker's trust account. This section also authorizes the broker to disburse earnest money according to a written earnest money disbursement agreement signed by all parties having an interest in the trust funds.

Lines 49–51 prohibit discrimination, which is discussed in the state statute and the listing contract.

Lines 52–122 concern agency disclosure and consent to multiple representation similar to the agency disclosure material discussed in the WB-1 Residential Listing Contract on lines 86–163.

Lines 131–134 state the non-exclusive nature of the relationship in that the buyer agrees that the broker can act for and negotiate on behalf of other buyers. Lines 133–134 stress that the broker will not disclose any confidential information, unless required by law.

Lines 135–140 indicate that the buyer agrees to cooperate with the broker. For example, the buyer agrees to be reasonably available for showings and promptly notify the broker in writing of any property located by the buyer.

Lines 141–145 caution the buyer that the property dimensions may vary due to different formulas that may be used to calculate dimensions, square footage, or acreage. It makes clear that the buyer should verify any dimensions that are material to the buyer.

Lines 146–181 include various definitions.

Lines 154–155 define *buyer*, which was discussed in the explanation of lines 1–5.

Lines 156–157 explain deadlines, which were discussed in lines 191–192 of the residential listing contract.

Lines 158–163 describe the alternative methods for delivery of documents or written notices discussed on lines 193–198 of the residential listing contract.

Lines 164–166 define an interest in property, which was discussed in lines 3–5.

Locating an interest in property (lines 167–169) was also discussed in lines 3–5.

Negotiating the procurement of an interest in property (lines 174–177) was also discussed in lines 3–5.

Lines 178–181 define *person acting for buyer* to include parties such as the buyer's immediate family or a limited liability company controlled by the buyer.

Lines 182–190 provide space for additional provisions discussed in lines 242–250 of the residential listing contract. For example, the buyer may wish to make the contract contingent upon getting a job at XYZ Company.

The addenda (lines 191–192) were discussed in lines 251–254 of the residential listing contract.

Lines 193–196 cover the term of the agreement discussed in lines 258–259 of the residential listing contract. Lines 195–196 would apply to a situation in which a buyer purchases more than one property during the term of the agreement.

Termination of agreement on lines 197–204 is similar to the termination of listing language discussed on lines 66–73 of the residential listing contract. Lines 201–203 explain that termination of the contract by either party before the date stated on line 194 shall be indicated to the other party in writing and shall not be effective until delivered to the other party in accordance with lines 158–163.

Lines 205–210 cover the extension of agreement term, which is similar to the extension of listing section discussed on lines 61–65 of the residential listing section. It is important to emphasize that while the listing language provides automatic exclusion of protected properties from a previous listing contract, that is not the case with the WB-36 agreement. The contract does not automatically exclude properties protected under a previous buyer agency agreement. If a broker is entering into a contract with a buyer who had a previous buyer agency agreement with another broker, the second buyer agent will have to ask the buyer about any negotiations that occurred during the previous contract and whether a list of protected properties was submitted by the previous buyer broker within three days after the previous buyer agency agreement expired. Any such properties would be placed on lines 13–20 of the excluded properties section of the contract.

Lines 211–213 covering notice about sex offender registry are identical to lines 255–257 of the residential listing contract.

Lines 217–235 provide for the signatures of all of the parties to the contract, as well as the date on which the buyer agency agreement is being drafted. You should be aware that any address or fax number placed in this section constitutes authorization for purposes of delivery. (Placement of an e-mail address in this section, however, does not constitute authorization for delivery purposes.)

QUESTIONS

1. Which type of listing agreement *BEST* assures the seller that the broker will give the property preferred attention and that the broker will receive fair compensation?
   a. Open
   b. Net
   c. Exclusive agency
   d. Exclusive-right-to-sell

2. According to the Wisconsin Statute of Frauds, a listing agreement
   a. must be in writing to be enforceable.
   b. must not be made for a period of longer than 60 days.
   c. need not state the price of the real estate.
   d. need not state the rate of the commission.

Use the information in the Residential Listing Contract on pages 34–38 to answer questions 3 through 8.

3. According to the listing contract, which is *TRUE*?
   a. The override is good for five months.
   b. The sellers prohibit prospective buyers from assuming the mortgage.
   c. The refrigerator is included in the sale.
   d. The broker will receive a 7 percent commission on the sale of the house.

4. Which statement is *TRUE* regarding the sellers?
   a. They will list an asking price of $240,000.
   b. They will promise to include the carpeting and drapes as part of the sales price.
   c. They will not include the washer in the sales price.
   d. They will not consent to designated agency.

5. The listing contract does *NOT*
   a. require the broker to hold at least one open house.
   b. expire after midnight on January 12, 2009.
   c. provide for the broker to use MLS.
   d. list any prospective buyers as excluded from the agency agreements.

6. Information on the override clause is found in which lines of the listing contract?
   a. 2–14
   b. 169–171
   c. 34–39
   d. 61–65

7. A broker is preparing a listing contract for the seller of a home. The broker is explaining how the property will be marketed. This information would be inserted in which lines of a listing contract?
   a. 5–14
   b. 164–167
   c. 15–22
   d. 174–182

8. The listing contract is approved by the
   a. Wisconsin Department of Regulation and Licensing.
   b. Wisconsin Department of Industry, Labor and Human Relations.
   c. Wisconsin Real Estate Board.
   d. Wisconsin Department of Development.

9. If a listed property is exchanged, the commission will be based on
   a. the list price.
   b. the sales price.
   c. the average of the list price and the sales price.
   d. either the list price or the sale price, whichever is preferred by the seller.

10. If a seller terminates a listing with a broker prior to the expiration of the term stated in the listing, the listing shall be extended for protected buyers, on the same terms for
    a. six months after the listing is terminated.
    b. one year after the listing is terminated.
    c. two years after the listing is terminated.
    d. three years after the listing is terminated.

11. Which is *NOT* a protected class under Wisconsin Fair Housing Law?
   a. Sex
   b. Sexual orientation
   c. Marital status
   d. Arrest or conviction record

12. Alice entered into an exclusive-right-to-sell listing contract with Broker Clyde. If Alice sells her property during the term of the listing without Clyde's services, she owes Clyde
   a. the marketing expenses related to Alice's listing.
   b. the full commission.
   c. nothing.
   d. a partial commission.

13. If the person signing a listing contract is promising to convey by a personal representative deed, on which lines should that information be inserted?
   a. 5–7
   b. 34–38
   c. 59–60
   d. 242–250

14. The type of title evidence primarily used in Wisconsin is
   a. title insurance.
   b. abstract opinion.
   c. certificate of title.
   d. the Torrens system.

15. Kelly listed her house, filled out a real estate condition report for the broker, and discovered the next day that the roof was leaking. Kelly is required to
   a. say nothing.
   b. amend the condition report upon discovering the problem.
   c. amend the condition report when the offer to purchase is submitted.
   d. amend the condition report within ten days after the offer to purchase has been accepted.

16. You are in the process of filling out a listing contract for a seller when he informs you that he will *NOT* allow a particular broker to market his home. You should place the broker on which lines?
   a. 15–22
   b. 26–28
   c. 30–32
   d. 34–39

17. The term of a listing contract may be for
   a. one day.
   b. four months.
   c. one year.
   d. All of the above

18. Which would *NOT* be required for a listing contract to be valid?
   a. It must be in writing.
   b. It must be acknowledged.
   c. It must contain a definite termination date.
   d. It must name the broker.

19. Adam listed his house with Broker Laura and stated that he had been negotiating with Selma, his coworker. Adam indicated that he did *NOT* want to pay a commission to Laura if Selma bought his home. Selma's name would appear on which line in the listing contract?
   a. 17–18
   b. 31–32
   c. 37–38
   d. 60

20. Pat listed Quincy's four-unit property for four months. Two weeks after listing his other property with Pat, Quincy deeded his four-unit to a limited liability company (LLC) controlled by Quincy and his spouse. Pat's commission will be based on
   a. the list price.
   b. the selling price.
   c. the average of the list and the selling price.
   d. negotiation with the seller at closing.

21. Kristin listed a motel owned by a limited liability company (LLC). One of the LLC's members sold his ownership interest in the LLC to his brother. Kristin will earn a commission based on

   a. the list price.
   b. the selling price.
   c. the average of the list and the selling price.
   d. negotiation with the seller at closing.

22. Baker listed a property for a couple in the process of getting a divorce. During the term of the listing, the husband was required by divorce judgment to convey his interest to his wife. Baker will earn a commission based on the

   a. list price.
   b. selling price.
   c. the average of the list and selling price.
   d. negotiation with the seller at closing.

23. Extended listing protection for buyers with whom the broker negotiated is available if the broker submits a list of names to the seller no later than

   a. one day after the expiration of the listing.
   b. two days after the expiration of the listing.
   c. three days after the expiration of the listing.
   d. four days after the expiration of the listing.

24. The salesperson for the broker has the authority to

   a. draft a listing contract.
   b. amend the listing contract.
   c. cancel the listing.
   d. All of the above

25. You are preparing the listing contract for Seller Diane when Diane states that she does *NOT* want the property marketed on the Internet. This information should be placed on

   a. lines 10–14.
   b. lines 31–32.
   c. lines 37–38.
   d. lines 242–250.

26. Which is *NOT* a protected class in Wisconsin?

   a. Race
   b. Marital status
   c. Political beliefs
   d. Sexual orientation

27. If the seller does *NOT* want his property videotaped, the broker should indicate this information on

   a. lines 10–14.
   b. lines 17–18.
   c. lines 31–32.
   d. lines 242–250.

28. Which statement does *NOT* correctly describe the process of terminating a listing?

   a. A salesperson for a broker may amend the commission amount with the written consent of his supervising broker.
   b. Termination of the listing prior to its expiration by either the seller or broker must be in writing and will not be effective until properly delivered.
   c. Early termination of the listing may be a breach of contract.
   d. A salesperson for a broker may shorten the term of a listing without the written consent of her supervising broker.

29. The Buyer Agency/Tenant Representation Agreement is approved by the

   a. Wisconsin Department of Workforce Development.
   b. Wisconsin Real Estate Board.
   c. Wisconsin Department of Agriculture, Trade and Consumer Protection.
   d. Wisconsin Department of Regulation and Licensing.

30. You have provided a list of properties to your buyer's client that you have negotiated on behalf of your buyer client. The term of the WB-36 agreement will be extended on the listed properties for

   a. three months.
   b. six months.
   c. one year.
   d. two years.

31. Broker A entered into a Buyer/Tenant Agreement with Broker B and successfully negotiated for the purchase of C's home, which was listed with Broker D. Which correctly describes the relationship of the parties in this transaction?
   a. A is serving as dual agent for B and C.
   b. B is A's client and C is A's customer.
   c. D is B's client and C's customer.
   d. D is serving as subagent for B.

32. The WB-36 agreement creates a(n)
   a. exclusive-agency relationship between the broker and the buyer.
   b. exclusive-agent-to-negotiate relationship between the broker and the buyer.
   c. open buyer agency relationship between the broker and the buyer.
   d. net agency relationship between the broker and the buyer.

33. Which statement correctly describes the language in the Residential Condominium Listing Contract?
   a. A complete legal description is required.
   b. The seller's interest in any common surplus of the condominium is not included in the purchase price.
   c. The broker may obtain the disclosure material at the seller's expense.
   d. All assessments are to be paid through the day prior to the closing.

34. The residential Condominium Listing Contract requires the seller to provide the buyer with a copy of condominium disclosure materials, including
   a. the declaration.
   b. the bylaws.
   c. the annual operating budget.
   d. All of the above

35. The broker protection clause on the Residential Condominium Listing Contract is good for
   a. 30 days.
   b. 3 months.
   c. 6 months.
   d. 1 year.

36. The seller agrees to provide the broker with copies of the condominium association's financial statements for the
   a. last year.
   b. last two years.
   c. last three years.
   d. last four years.

37. Condominium disclosure materials are required to be delivered to the buyer no later than
   a. 3 days prior to closing.
   b. 5 days prior to closing.
   c. 10 days prior to closing.
   d. 15 days prior to closing.

38. Delivery of written notices may be accomplished by
   a. personal delivery.
   b. commercial delivery.
   c. electronic transmission.
   d. All of the above

39. Which statement does *NOT* correctly describe the WB-36 agency agreement?
   a. The buyer gives the broker the exclusive right to work as her only buyer's agent during the term of the agreement.
   b. The WB-36 does not create an exclusive right to locate and negotiate agency relationship.
   c. The buyer is not prohibited from personally contacting the seller's agents about properties in which she might be interested.
   d. The buyer may employ another buyer agent during the term of her previous WB-36 with regard to the properties subject to her previous WB-36.

40. Which party would be considered a buyer under the terms of the WB-36 agreement?
   a. Tenants
   b. Business investors
   c. An exchange
   d. All of the above

41. Which would be defined as an interest in property under the terms of the WB-36 agreement?

a. A purchase
b. An option
c. An exchange
d. All of the above

42. A buyer broker submits an offer to purchase on behalf of his client that is rejected by the seller. The broker will be protected under the extension of agreement term for a period of

a. four months.
b. eight months.
c. one year.
d. two years.

43. According to the WB-36, who would be considered to be a person acting for the buyer?

a. The buyer's wife
b. The buyer's son
c. The buyer's employee
d. All of the above

44. According to the WB-36, documents or written notices may be delivered by

a. personal delivery.
b. electronic transmission to the party's fax number.
c. depositing fees prepaid to a commercial delivery system, addressed to the party at the party's address.
d. All of the above

45. Which duty would the buyer broker *NOT* owe to all parties to a transaction?

a. The duty to provide brokerage services fairly and honestly
b. The duty to protect your confidentiality
c. The duty to disclose to you in writing certain material adverse facts about a property, unless disclosure of the information is prohibited by law
d. The duty to provide you with all material facts affecting the transaction, not just adverse facts

46. A buyer client tells his buyer broker that he does *NOT* want any property that is located more than 40 miles from Wausau. This type of information would be placed in which line(s) on a buyer agency agreement?

a. Line 10
b. Lines 12–20
c. Line 24
d. Line 41

Interests in Real Estate

ESTATES IN LAND

Wisconsin recognizes freeholds in fee simple, fee determinable, fee subject to a condition subsequent, and life estates.

Legal Life Estates

Homestead. (See S. 706.01 and S. 766.605 Wis. Stats.) Every resident of Wisconsin is entitled to claim a homestead exemption from a court sale of property to pay unsecured debts. Homestead includes both single and married homeowners. Generally, a homeowner must claim such an exemption to be entitled to it. A homeowner who is being sued by an unsecured creditor may notify the officer making the levy that he or she is claiming a homestead exemption. Exemptions do not have to be filed before a claim is lodged. The officer involved in a levy is usually a local sheriff who officially seizes the property of a judgment debtor and holds it until the claim is settled. Failure to make this claim for a specific property at the time of levy may result in a waiver of the right to selection of homestead.

In Wisconsin, a homestead is specifically defined for both urban and rural dwellings. An *urban homestead* consists of the home and the lot on which it is located (including any rented space, as in the case of a duplex) and any space within the building used for commercial purposes. A *rural homestead* includes the house in which a homeowner dwells and the surrounding land necessary for the use of the dwelling as a home, but not less than one-quarter acre and not more than 40 acres.

The amount of the homestead exemption is $40,000. Homestead does not exempt payment of mortgages, laborers' and construction liens, purchase-money liens, or taxes. These kinds of debts must be satisfied from the sale proceeds before the homeowner receives the exempt portion. For example, a homeowner owes $10,000 to a judgment creditor. Sale of the homestead brings $55,000. Because the homeowner owes $5,000 on the mortgage, this amount is paid before the homestead exemption of $40,000 is applied. From the $50,000 left from the proceeds of the sale after payment of the mortgage, the first $40,000 goes to the homeowner and the remaining $10,000 is applied to the homeowner's debts. If one spouse dies, the homestead rights in any property he or she owned at the time of death go to the surviving spouse.

Dower and Curtesy

Dower and curtesy do not exist as common-law rights in Wisconsin. Prior to 1986, however, the rights of the surviving spouse, whether widow or widower, were protected by statutory dower rights. The statutes pertaining to dower prior to 1986 gave the surviving spouse rights to one-third of any property that the decedent owned at death. Under those laws, the surviving spouse was entitled to a fee-simple interest in the real estate on the death of the spouse.

Prior to 1986 in Wisconsin, the surviving spouse was able to renounce dower in order to elect a share in the estate under the laws of descent and distribution. Election was the right to take one-third of the estate minus the value of any property given outright to the spouse in a will. The right to elect could be barred by the written consent of both parties before or after marriage. It also could be barred if the spouse received at least one-half of certain specific properties.

The Wisconsin Marital Property Act, discussed in greater detail in Chapter 4, presumes that all property of spouses is marital property unless otherwise classified. The dower right to an elective share is abolished because the spouse acquires a one-half interest in all marital property. More specifically, each spouse has a present undivided one-half interest in each item of marital property. If one spouse dies, that spouse dies owning a one-half interest and the surviving spouse owns the other half. The deceased spouse's one-half interest will be probated as that spouse's estate.

EASEMENTS

An easement is a right acquired by one person to use the land owned by another person for a specific purpose. The state purchases conservation easements from private landowners, including scenic easements, hunting rights, and the right not to have the land drained or not to have game cover cut. Public easements usually are acquired by a state in order to preserve the land for the enjoyment of the public and to prevent private development. Public easements usually are preserved for their aesthetic value, for their historical interest, or for the preservation of wildlife. Public and private easements are becoming increasingly important encumbrances on land. Licensees are required to know of existing easements so that prospective buyers can be informed.

Easement by Prescription

In Wisconsin, a person may acquire an easement by prescription in the land of another provided that he or she has had continuous and uninterrupted use of the easement property for a period of 20 years. Such use also must be open, so that the owner easily knows of it, and hostile, that is, without the owner's permission.

WATER RIGHTS

The water laws of Wisconsin are based on the public trust doctrine contained in the state constitution. This doctrine maintains that all navigable waters are held in trust by the state for the public. A stream is navigable if it has a bed and banks and a person can float the stream in a canoe or other small craft at some time of the year, even if only during spring floods. The beds of natural lakes also are owned by the state and held in trust for the public. Owners of adjoining upland have title to the land above the ordinary high watermark and a qualified right in the exposed lakebed in front of their property. The owner of land adjoining rivers and streams owns the streambed to the center, but the rights to use the stream are subject to regulation.

Some activities require permits from local municipalities, county zoning administrators, the U.S. Army Corps of Engineers, or similar sources. In Wisconsin, the principles that relate to regulating the use of water are: (1) the riparian right doctrine of reasonable use, which provides that all riparians have the right to use the water adjacent to their land, and (2) the doctrine of prior appropriation, which is used for allocating water among private users when water supplies are short.

In response to a relative shortage of water and a Wisconsin Supreme Court decision, the right of prior appropriation has been emphasized recently in the state. The court decision held that prior beneficial users of water, in effect, have a property right and that they may refuse consent to a future irrigator if they are beneficially using the water that would be diverted. Under prior appropriation, the rights of an existing user take precedence over the rights of a person applying for use. Prior-appropriation rights have been upheld for many reasons, including the recognition by the courts that substantial investment usually is required for many uses of water, especially irrigation. Under the pure system of prior appropriation used in many of the western states, all users of water must obtain an appropriation permit for the use of a specific quantity of water. Because the oldest permit in force has the superior rights, if the water supply diminishes, the most recent permittees must cease their use in favor of the more senior users.

Wisconsin does not use a pure prior-appropriation system, but under Wisconsin's system, consent is required from an existing user before a new permit can be issued. The relative rights of existing permittees are looked into only when complaints are received. After a hearing, a junior user might be required to modify his or her use of water to protect the rights of a senior user. In all cases, however, the public right to use water prevails over private rights. The Wisconsin Department of Natural Resources (DNR) regulates water use in the state. The department determines the amount of surplus water available and the time water diversions must cease. The DNR may revoke most permits if the diversion of waters is found to be harmful to a lake or stream or to other riparians.

QUESTIONS

1. Faced with a court sale of the family home to satisfy debts, a homeowner may claim a homestead exemption against
   a. real estate taxes.
   b. a mortgage loan.
   c. general creditors.
   d. a construction lien.
2. The homestead exemption from claims of unsecured creditors granted by Wisconsin law to a homeowner is
   a. $40,000 of equity.
   b. $25,000 of equity.
   c. $10,000 of equity.
   d. 5 percent of the property's market value.
3. In Wisconsin, a person may claim an easement by prescription to the land of another if he or she
   a. lived secretly on the land for 20 years.
   b. lived on the land openly for 14 years.
   c. had continuous, open, and hostile use of the land for 20 years.
   d. lived on the land openly for 10 years.
4. Which of the following statements does *NOT* correctly describe the water laws of Wisconsin?
   a. Wisconsin water laws are based on the public trust doctrine.
   b. All navigable waters are held in trust by the state for the public.
   c. Wisconsin uses a pure prior-appropriation system.
   d. The public right to use water always prevails over private rights.
5. Which of the following statements does *NOT* correctly describe the impact of the Wisconsin Marital Property Act on the rights of the spouse?
   a. All property of the spouses is presumed to be marital property unless otherwise classified.
   b. The dower right to an elective share is abolished.
   c. Each spouse acquires a one-third interest in all marital property.
   d. Each spouse has a present undivided one-half interest in each item of marital property.
6. The amount of land for a rural homestead in Wisconsin is defined as not less than one-quarter acre and not more than how many acres?
   a. 10
   b. 20
   c. 40
   d. 160

How Ownership Is Held

FORMS OF OWNERSHIP

Wisconsin recognizes the three forms of ownership: *ownership in severalty*, *co-ownership (joint tenancy* and *tenancy in common*), and *marital property*. The Wisconsin Marital Property Act creates new forms of ownership that are similar to community property.

Co-Ownership

Under the Wisconsin Marital Property Act, all property of married persons is presumed to be marital property unless another classification, such as individual property, is established. Tenancy by the entirety has been abolished in Wisconsin. A conveyance to two persons who are not married automatically creates a tenancy in common, unless the deed expressly states the intention to create a joint tenancy.

Partition. Any joint tenant, tenant in common, or spouse under the Marital Property Act may file a *suit for partition*. If the land involved cannot be partitioned or divided fairly among the co-owners, the court may order the property sold and the proceeds distributed to the former co-owners.

The Wisconsin Marital Property Act (Chapter 766 Wis. Stats.)

The Wisconsin Marital Property Act became effective January 1, 1986. Wisconsin is the first state in the country to adopt a version of the Uniform Marital Property Act written by a group of legal scholars. The law creates a different property law system for married people. The system is based on the assumption that property acquired during a marriage belongs equally to both partners. The law recognizes the family as an economic unit and the equal value of the contribution made by each spouse to the family, whether the contribution is money or services or both.

The act shifts Wisconsin from a common-law property system to a community property system. Under the common-law property system, each spouse owns the property he or she earns, inherits, or is given. Under the community property system, the wife and husband are considered as one economic unit and share equally in most assets and debts during the marriage.

Under the Marital Property Act, all property acquired by spouses during a marriage and after January 1, 1986, is classified as either marital property or individual property. All property of spouses is marital property except as otherwise classified by the act, and all property is presumed to be marital property. Each spouse has a present undivided one-half interest in each item of marital property.

The presumption of marital property means that a person wishing to maintain individual ownership of an asset is responsible for proving its individual classification. Unless it can be proved otherwise, the asset is classified as marital property. With the exception of its income, property brought to the marriage at its beginning by one spouse, or property later inherited by or given to that spouse alone, or a personal injury recovery to that spouse alone, is classified as individual property. Should a spouse do something to substantially increase the value of the other spouse's individual property during a marriage, a percentage of ownership could be awarded to the nonowning spouse.

The new law applies only to property acquired by spouses after January 1, 1986. Property already owned by married persons prior to the act's effective date is not classified. If individual property is mixed with marital property, it will become marital property unless the individual property can be traced. Property acquired during the marriage before the determination date is deferred marital property if still owned by the spouse at the date of death, if the property would have been marital property if acquired after the determination date. The Marital Property Act affects spouses whenever the determination date applies. The determination date is the date on which the new marital property law becomes effective for spouses. The Marital Property Act applies to spouses when the *last* of the following three occurs:

1. January 1, 1986
2. The date on which a Wisconsin couple is married
3. The date on which spouses establish a marital residence in Wisconsin

Deferred marital property will be treated in probate as marital property. The Marital Property Act also permits all spouses to title property as survivorship marital property. This new form of title is similar to joint tenancy in that the property goes to the surviving spouse without probate when one spouse dies.

Moreover, if spouses acquire property after January 1, 1986, and title the property in joint tenancy, the property becomes survivorship marital property. If the spouses take title to the property as tenants in common, the property becomes marital property. If the spouses purchase real estate after January 1, 1986, and use it as their personal home, the real estate will be presumed to be survivorship marital property unless the deed or document of transfer indicates a contrary intent.

Condominiums (Chapter 703)

Wisconsin law permits ownership of condominium units. Legally, they are called *unit ownerships*. The unit owner's interest is like any other fee simple because it may be sold, and upon the owner's death, the interest passes to heirs unless disposed of by a will.

The Condominium Statute, Chapter 703 of the Wisconsin Statutes, also known as the Condominium Ownership Act, became effective August 1, 1978. Included among the provisions of Chapter 703 are various consumer-protection requirements regarding disclosures, conversions, sweetheart contracts, and declarant control. For example, Section 703.33 requires that the *declarant of a residential condominium provide a prospectus to interested purchasers* of units. These disclosure materials must be *delivered not later than 15 days prior to the closing* and must contain copies of the condominium documents, contracts, leases, and budgets, all in a prescribed format. The act further specifies in Section 703.33(2) that conspicuous disclosure statements must be printed on the cover of the materials.

Recent changes in the Condominium Statute include the following:

1. **Executive Summary**
   The executive summary is like an index, summarizing what the most important buyers want or need to know from the condominium disclosures (declarations, bylaws, etc.).

   It is created, or filled out, by the Condominium Association or declarant (developer) and is produced with the other condominium documents. Agents do not fill out the executive summary.

   The agent may let condominium sellers know about the regulations, but it is the declarant or association who will have to fill out the executive summary.
2. **Statutory Reserve Account** (SRA)
   A Statutory Reserve Account is a reserve account for repair or replacement of common elements. All condominium associations have to choose whether to have an SRA or not.
3. **Annual Budget**
   All condominium associations must establish and distribute an annual budget.
4. **Disclosure Documents/Revisions**
   The new law continues to require that the condominium documents be produced at least 15 days before closing. Like the previous law, delivery of complete documents leaves the buyer with the same five business day time period to rescind.

   However, unlike previous law, a new step is built in to shorten the time for the buyer's rescissions and to deal with situations where the documents are not complete.

   If the documents are not complete, the buyer has the same five business days to rescind, or the buyer may *request* that the missing documents be produced. That request (in writing) triggers a new five business day time period.

   If the seller does produce complete documents within that time, or supplies the missing documents, the buyer then has five days to rescind.

   However, if the seller does not supply the missing documents within those five business days, the buyer then has five business days to decide whether to rescind or not.

If the buyer does not rescind, the buyer loses that right. In other words, the buyer has to recognize that the documents are complete or incomplete and do something about it.

5. **Small Condominium Definition**

The term "small condominium" under Wisconsin law is revised to 12 units or less, and includes residential or nonresidential condominiums.

You should be aware that an executive summary may not be required as part of the disclosure materials for a "small condominium" of no more than 12 units.

Small condominium declarants or associations may elect to use abbreviated disclosure materials that would not include an executive summary.

Condominium conversion is another area in which consumer-protection requirements are addressed in the current condominium law, although the *provisions on conversion apply only to residential properties*. Section 703.08 provides that the property may not be converted without prior written notice to existing tenants. Following the delivery of the notice, the tenants have an exclusive 60-day option to purchase a unit. Furthermore, the tenants must be given 120 days' advance written notice of the proposed conversion. Thus, existing tenants are allowed a period of time to relocate and acquire new accommodations if they elect not to purchase a unit in the converted condominium pursuant to the notice. The tenants may not be required to vacate the property during the 120-day notice period except for violation of the lease or nonpayment of rent.

Section 703.35 grants the unit owners the right to terminate sweetheart contracts and leases entered into by the declarant on behalf of the association. *Sweetheart contracts* are contracts with affiliates of the declarant or contracts that are advantageous or remunerative for the declarant rather than in the best interests of the association. Section 703.35 states that any contract with the declarant or affiliates of the declarant, any contract or lease that is not bona fide or reasonable, and other specified contracts and leases entered into before the association officers are elected by unit owners *may be terminated* by the association at any time without penalty on 90 *days' notice*.

The consumer orientation of the current condominium law also is apparent in the manner in which declarant control is treated. The declarant is permitted only limited control of an association subject to restrictions. For example, Section 703.15(2)(c) states that a declarant may not control an association for more than 3 years (10 years in the case of an expandable condominium) or 30 days after the sale of 75 percent of the common-element interest. In addition, Section 703.15(2)(d) specifies that the unit owners (other than declarant) are entitled to elect directors to the Board of the Association as sales of units progress (25 percent of the directors prior to the sale of 25 percent of the common-element interest and one-third of the directors prior to the sale of 50 percent of the common-element interest).

Partnerships

Both the Uniform Partnership Act and the Uniform Limited Partnership Act have been adopted to regulate partnerships in Wisconsin.

Land Trusts

Land trusts are permitted in Wisconsin provided that the terms of the trust agreement and the powers of the trustee are stated clearly and specifically.

Time-Shares

Chapter 707 of the Wisconsin Statutes states that a disclosure statement must be given to the purchaser of a time-share prior to transferring the title. The purchaser has five business days after the disclosure information has been delivered to cancel the contract in writing without penalty.

Prior to the sale of any time-shares in a project, the developer must establish an escrow account and designate an escrow agent for the purpose of protecting the deposits of purchasers. The escrow agent must be independent of the developer. In addition, the developer, as well as any affiliate of the developer or any officer, director, subsidiary, or employee of the developer, may not serve as escrow agent. The statute identifies the responsibilities of the escrow agent, including that the agent retain for five years all affidavits requesting the release of the escrowed deposit received by the developer or the buyer in the case of cancellation. Until the deposit can be released from escrow, an amount equal to 50 percent of the deposit must be deposited in an escrow account under an escrow agreement.

Limited Liability Companies and Limited Liability Partnerships

Limited liability companies (LLCs) and limited liability partnerships (LLPs) have recently been authorized by the Wisconsin Statutes and provide some benefits as ownership vehicles. They are used primarily for commercial properties.

Ownership of Land by Nonresident Aliens or Foreign-Based Corporations

Chapter 710 of the Wisconsin Statutes states that nonresident aliens or foreign-based corporations in Wisconsin cannot hold or purchase more than 640 acres of land in Wisconsin. The statute does identify exceptions, such as a foreign-based corporation involved in an exploration mining lease, or inherited property, or property acquired through foreclosure for a debt owed and not paid. However, the mining corporation cannot use the land for a different activity while or before the land is converted or developed for the permitted activity. Interests exceeding 640 acres, acquired by persons covered by the statute, are generally to be divested within four years after acquiring the interest unless the interest is classified as an exception. Interests in land in excess of 640 acres acquired or held in violation of the statute are forfeited to the state. Any person required by this statute to file a report with the state who fails to do so will forfeit not less than $500 nor more than $5,000.

QUESTIONS

1. A deed grants title to a parcel of real estate to Jane and Lisa. They will acquire title to the parcel as
   a. owners in severalty.
   b. tenants in common.
   c. owners in trust.
   d. joint tenants.

2. A conveyance to two persons who are husband and wife automatically creates a(n)
   a. tenancy in common.
   b. marital property.
   c. tenancy by the entirety.
   d. ownership in severalty.

3. Wisconsin law permits ownership of condominiums that are legally described as
   a. time-shares.
   b. unit ownerships.
   c. cooperatives.
   d. planned unit developments.

4. Under the Wisconsin Marital Property Act, all property acquired by spouses during a marriage and after January 1, 1986, is classified as what type of property?
   a. Individual
   b. Marital
   c. Separate
   d. Community

5. Which of the following types of property would *NOT* be a classification of property under the Wisconsin Marital Property Act?
   a. Marital
   b. Separate
   c. Deferred marital
   d. Mixed

6. Harry and Rita were married in Illinois on December 1, 2003, moved to Wisconsin, and established a marital residence on February 1, 2004. The date on which the Wisconsin Marital Property Act becomes effective for Harry and Rita is
   a. December 1, 2003.
   b. January 1, 2004.
   c. February 1, 2004.
   d. March 1, 2004.

7. According to Wisconsin law, the declarant of a residential condominium must provide a prospectus to interested purchasers of units *NOT* later than how many days prior to closing?
   a. 3
   b. 5
   c. 15
   d. 30

8. The purchaser of a time-share in Wisconsin has the right to cancel the contract, in writing, without penalty after the disclosure information has been delivered. The right to cancel exists for
   a. one business day.
   b. three business days.
   c. five business days.
   d. ten business days.

9. Nonresident aliens in Wisconsin may own no more than
   a. 100 acres of land in Wisconsin.
   b. 240 acres of land in Wisconsin.
   c. 640 acres of land in Wisconsin.
   d. 1,200 acres of land in Wisconsin.

10. Any person required by Chapter 710 of the Wisconsin Statutes to file a report with the state who fails to do so will forfeit
    a. not less than $100, but no more than $1,200.
    b. not less than $200, but no more than $2,000.
    c. not less than $500, but no more than $5,000.
    d. not less than $1,000, but no more than $10,000.

11. The executive summary should *NOT* be prepared by the
    a. agent.
    b. declarant.
    c. association.
    d. developer.

12. An executive summary may *NOT* be required as part of the disclosure materials for a "small condominium" of no more than
    a. 4 units.
    b. 6 units.
    c. 8 units.
    d. 12 units.

13. Which statement does *NOT* correctly describe the condominium buyer's rescission rights?
    a. If the buyer receives all of the condominium disclosure documents required by law, the buyer will have five business days to rescind the offer in writing, without stating any reason and without liability.
    b. If the buyer receives incomplete condominium documents, the buyer will have five business days to request that the seller deliver the missing documents.
    c. If the buyer neither rescinds nor requests missing documents within five business days, then the delivered materials will be deemed satisfactory and the buyer will have no further right to rescind based upon those materials.
    d. The condominium buyer continues to have a limitless right of rescission.

14. Under the new Wisconsin condominium law, which entity should adopt an annual budget and distribute it to all of the owners?
    a. Any condominium with at least one residential unit
    b. Any condominium with at least four residential units
    c. Any condominium with at least eight residential units
    d. All of the above

Legal Descriptions

LEGAL DESCRIPTIONS

In Wisconsin, land may be identified by *rectangular survey* or by the *subdivision lot and block* as stipulated in a recorded plat. Both of these methods are acceptable as legal descriptions. Description by *metes and bounds* also may be used in connection with either the rectangular survey or the lot-and-block method. Land may also be described by reference to a certified survey map. *A legal description of the property must be included in deeds, land contracts, mortgages, or other instruments to be recorded in the register of deeds office. A street address alone is not an acceptable legal description* because it does not by itself accurately describe the boundaries of the property. An example of an acceptable legal description in Wisconsin is:

> *Lot 2, Block 4, Fairmont Subdivision, NW 1/4 of Section 8, Township 9 North, Range 7 East, Dane County, Wisconsin.*

Rectangular Survey

Rectangular survey descriptions are determined from the Fourth Principal Meridian and baseline. The *Fourth Principal Meridian* is a north-south line that runs about 50 miles west of Madison, while the *baseline* is the southern boundary of the state. The map in Figure 5.1 illustrates the numbering of townships in Wisconsin and shows the baseline and meridian.

Plats

Any property owner who intends to subdivide one piece of property into five or more parcels of one and one-half acres or less within five years and offer them for sale is required by Wisconsin law to file a plat of subdivision in the public record of the county in which the property is located. Once land has been subdivided, it must be described, in all future conveyances, by reference to the recorded plat or certified survey map. An example of a plat as it may appear on the licensing exam is shown in Figure 5.2.

FIGURE 5.1

Wisconsin Township Maps

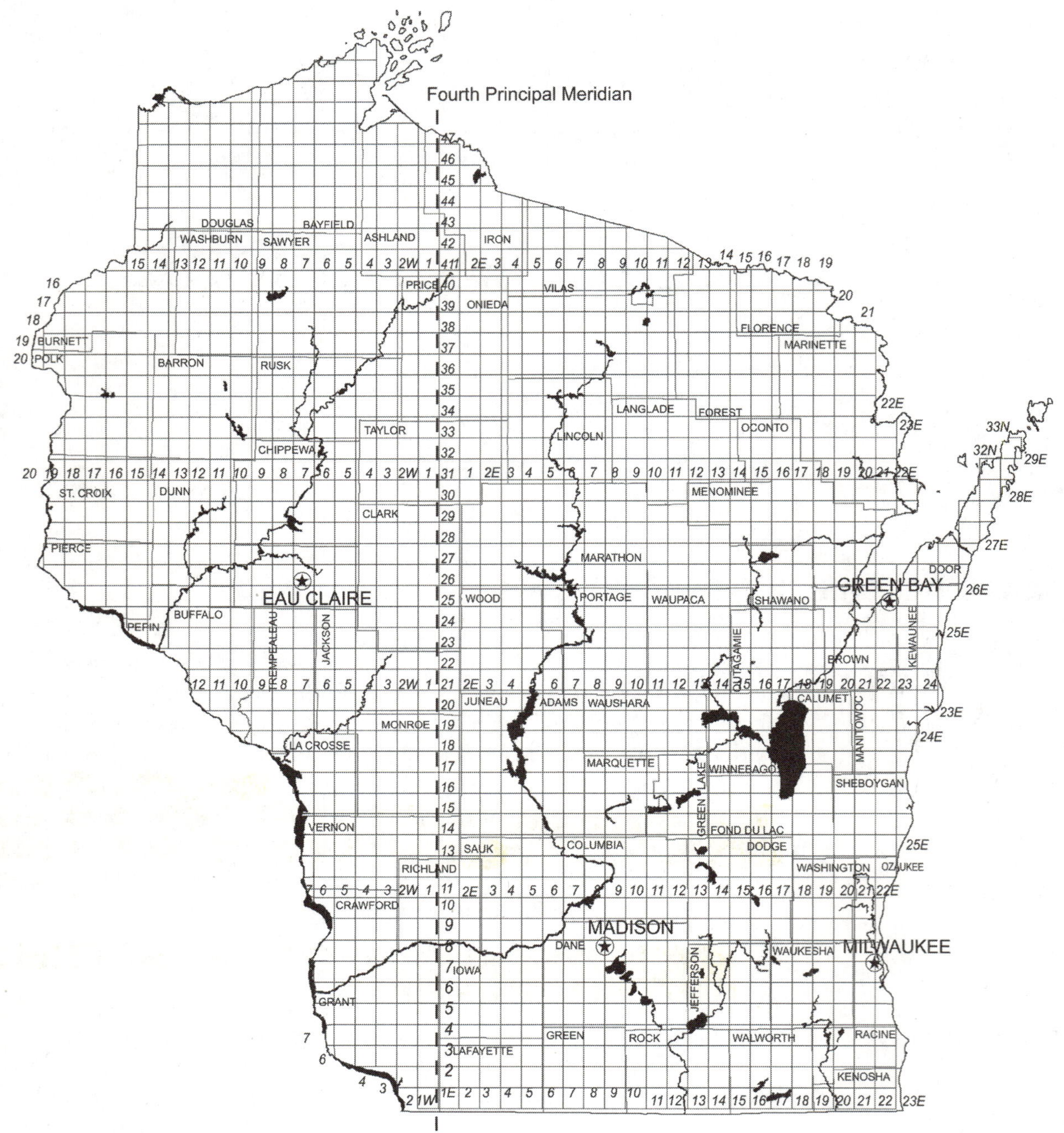

Certified survey maps are used to create subdivisions of four or fewer lots. A typical description of a lot in a certified survey map follows:

> *Lot 1 of Certified Survey Map 2040 which is recorded in Volume 23 of Certified Survey Maps, page 25, #2345678, in the City of Madison, Dane County, Wis.*

FIGURE 5.2

Plat of Grassland Acres Estates Subdivision Map

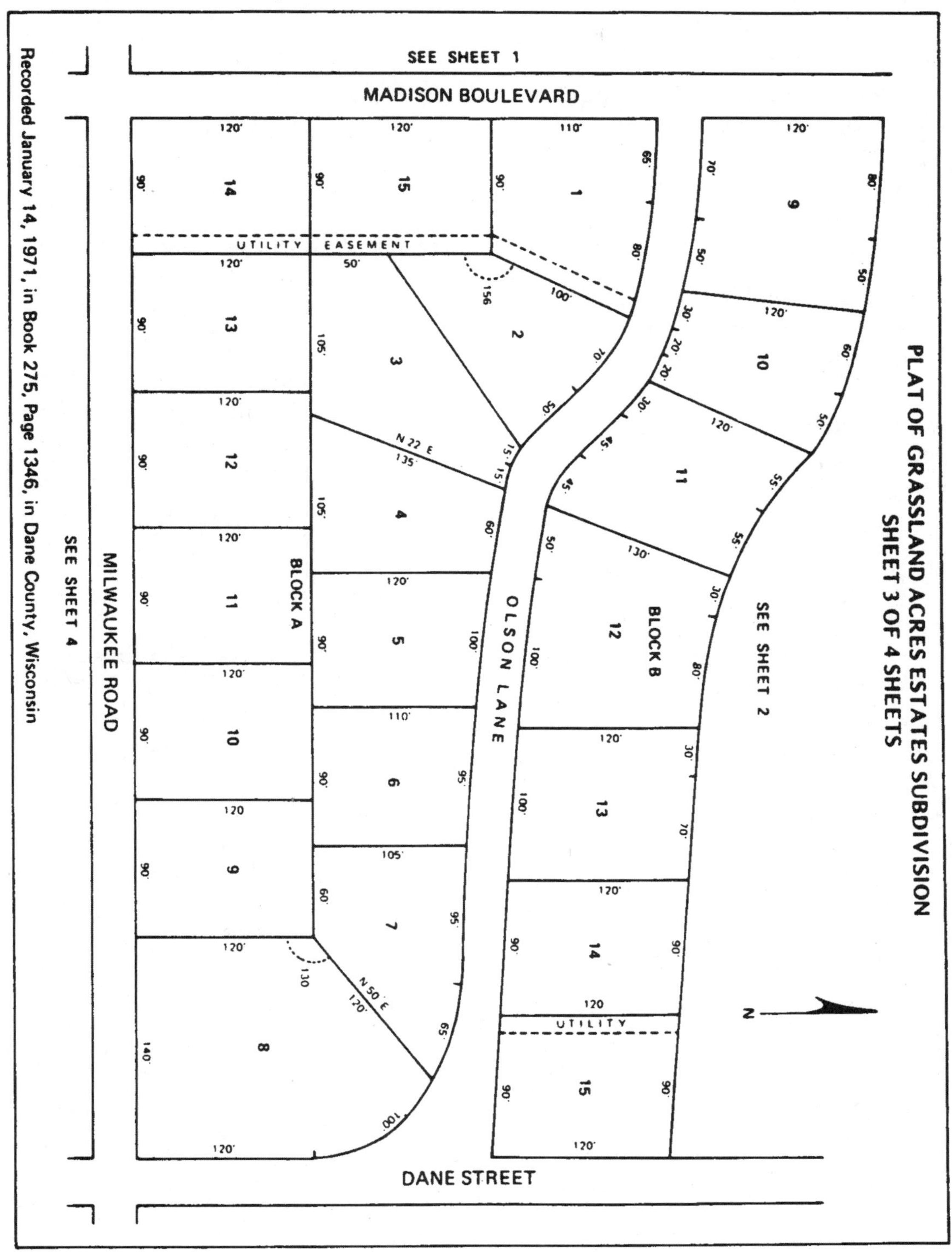

QUESTIONS

1. Which of the following does *NOT* constitute a proper legal description of a parcel of real estate in Wisconsin?
   a. Identification by subdivision lot and block
   b. Identification according to the rectangular-survey system
   c. Identification by metes and bounds in connection with the rectangular survey
   d. Property's street address
2. A property owner must file a plat of subdivision for record if he or she plans to divide a parcel of real estate and offer it for sale as:
   a. four or more separate parcels, each two acres or less within four years
   b. five or more separate parcels, each one and one-half acres or less within five years
   c. six or more separate parcels, each one and one-half acres or less within five years
   d. three or more separate parcels, each one acre or less within four years
3. A Wisconsin property located in Township 2 North, Range 4 East, is in what county?
   a. Green
   b. Lafayette
   c. Grant
   d. Iowa

Use the information given on the plat of Grassland Acres Estates in Figure 5.2 to answer Question 4 and Question 5.

4. Which of the following statements is true?
   a. Lot 9, Block A is larger than Lot 12 in the same block.
   b. The plat for the lots on the southerly side of Milwaukee Road between Madison Boulevard and Dane Street is found on Sheet 3 of 4 Sheets.
   c. Lot 9, Block A is the same size as Lot 12 in the same block.
   d. Lot 14, Block A is larger than Lot 15 in the same block.
5. Which of the following lots has the most frontage on Olson Lane?
   a. Lot 10, Block B
   b. Lot 11, Block B
   c. Lot 1, Block A
   d. Lot 2, Block A

Use the information given on the Wisconsin Townships Map in Figure 5.1 to answer Question 6 and Question 7.

6. Which of the following statements is true of the Wisconsin baseline?
   a. It runs about 50 miles west of Madison.
   b. It is the northern boundary of the state.
   c. It runs about 20 miles south of Madison.
   d. It is the southern boundary of the state.
7. Certified survey maps are used to create subdivisions of:
   a. 4 or fewer lots.
   b. 5 or fewer lots.
   c. 50 or fewer lots.
   d. 100 or fewer lots.

Real Estate Taxes and Other Liens

REAL ESTATE TAX

Exemptions

In Wisconsin, as in other states, exemptions from real estate taxes are permitted for educational, religious, benevolent, and charitable institutions. There are also numerous other exemptions specified in the law. *In most cases, if the use, occupancy, and ownership changes in a way that would make it exempt, the owner must submit to the assessor by March 1 a prescribed form describing how the property qualifies for exemption.* Exemptions are not given to members of the armed forces, but extended payment privileges usually are permitted.

Levy and Assessment

The annual real estate tax is *levied as of January 1 for that calendar year, and taxes become a lien from that date*. Generally, taxes are levied on the basis of a property assessment made by the assessor for each municipality. However, taxes also may be levied on a countywide basis under a county-assessor system. This system may be established for any county if 60 percent of the members of the county board approve and pass a resolution or ordinance adopting such a system. Each municipality has an assessor who is in charge of the tax roll and assessments. Certified appraisers may work under the assessor and help establish the value of property in the municipality for placement on the tax roll.

The assessed valuation, as determined by the assessor, may be at a percentage of the market value. The specific percentage of the assessor's market determination can vary from one municipality to another. If a real property assessment has changed from the previous year, the property owner should receive a notice of changed assessment in March or April of the year the tax as determined by the assessor may be a percentage of market value. Notice may be mailed at a later date, however. Objections to the assessed valuation may be made to the *board of review* of a municipality up to the date of the board's fifth meeting of the year. One tax bill is sent to each condominium owner, and one tax bill is sent to each building unit within a time-share property, which entry shall consist of the cumulative real property value of all time-share interest in the unit.

Lottery Tax and Gaming Credit

A Lottery and Gaming Credit is available to owners of residential properties who used their property as their primary residence and properly claimed their lottery and gaming credit. Property owners must have used their home as their primary residence on January 1 of the year in which property taxes are levied. The *primary residence* is defined as the home where an individual lives more than six months of the year. Only one primary residence may be claimed.

Qualified property owners are required to file an application with the county treasurer or City of Milwaukee treasurer to receive the lottery and gaming credit. The credit is determined in November of each year and depends on the amount of revenues from the lottery, pari-mutual ontrack betting, and bingo during the year. The credit amount on the tax bill is based on the owner's school tax rate and the maximum credit value.

As mentioned, to claim the lottery and gaming credit, property owners must file an application they receive from the county treasurer or City of Milwaukee treasurer. The application will be valid for the five-year certification cycle. Property owners must notify the county treasurer or City of Milwaukee treasurer within 30 days if the property no longer is the primary residence of the owner.

If the owners sell their home, the lottery and gaming credit stays with the property and will be deducted from the net tax payable on the next property bill. When a property is sold, the lottery and gaming credit is "sold" with it. Ideally, the amount of the credit should be considered when prorating the property taxes between buyer and seller.

For more information about the lottery and gaming credit, check the Web site for the Wisconsin Department of Revenue:

WEB LINK

http://www.dor.state.wi.us.

Tax Rate

The property tax is stated as so many mills for each $1 of assessed valuation. A *mill* is one-tenth of a cent ($.001), and there are 1,000 mills in one dollar ($1). For example, a levy of 54.4 mills can be computed as 54.4 mills divided by 1,000, which is a tax of $.0544, or 5.44 cents per dollar. An easy way to convert mills to dollars is to move the decimal three places to the left.

Tax Payment

Real estate taxes in Wisconsin are paid in arrears. The taxpayer may pay the tax for the calendar year in *one payment on or before January 31 of the year following the property tax assessment.* Various installment payment options are offered throughout the state by various municipalities.

Tax Delinquency

A monthly interest charge of 1 percent on the unpaid balance (computed from January 1) is added to each tax installment that is not paid by the January 31 due date. The county board or city council also may impose an additional penalty of one-half percent per month on any delinquent real estate taxes or special assessments. Property owners may redeem their property from delinquent taxes by paying all past-due taxes, penalties, interest, and costs. This redemption must be made within the time periods prescribed in Section 74 of the Wisconsin Statues. If an installment payment is even one day late, the government is entitled to charge the one and one-half percent penalty and interest for that entire month, plus for each month backwards through January of that year.

Tax Sale

When property taxes are *past due for three years*, the county may give notice in the local newspapers and hold a *tax sale*. The county issues a deed to the property to itself, and when the property is later sold to a new owner, the county issues a deed to the new owner. No tax deed may be issued without notice to the property owner.

Municipalities can sue for delinquent real estate taxes in lieu of foreclosure, thereby avoiding the acquisition of unreliable and burdensome real estate. Senior citizens with low incomes can apply for the Property Tax Deferral Loan Program offered by the Wisconsin Housing and Economic Development Authority (WHEDA). WHEDA will pay the county taxes and take a lien against the home. Information can be obtained by calling 800-334-6873, or on the Web at:

WEB LINK

http://www.wheda.com.

OTHER LIENS

Special Assessments

In Wisconsin, the municipality sets up a time schedule and bills the taxpayer for an annual prorated portion of the total unpaid assessment. For example, a $1,000 charge for curbs and gutters prorated over five years would be added to the annual tax bill at a rate of $200 per year. The length of the repayment period is determined by each municipality. Interest is usually charged by the municipality and added to each required installment.

Construction Lien Claims (Mechanics' Liens)

In Wisconsin, mechanics' liens are referred to as *construction liens* and may be obtained by those who furnish labor, materials, or professional services in the improvement of an owner's land or buildings. Construction liens in Wisconsin take priority from the date of visible commencement of the work on an improvement or from the beginning of substantial excavation for foundation footing or base in any new construction.

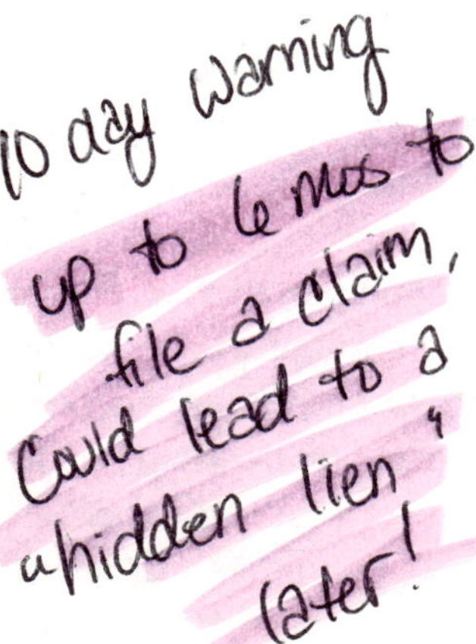

Lien notice. A *prime contractor*—that is, one who deals directly with an owner—must, within *ten days* after labor has begun or materials have been furnished, give the owner written notice that any person who furnishes labor or materials has lien rights in the event that payment is not made. If payment is not made, the contractor must give the owner a warning notice within five months after completing the work that a lien is pending. The contractor also must file a lien claim with the clerk of the circuit court within six months after completing the work but no sooner than 30 days after the warning notice has been given.

A *subcontractor or material supplier* must (except on large projects) give the owner notice within 60 *days* after first furnishing the labor or materials and must comply with the warning notice and filing requirements that apply to the prime contractor.

To collect on a properly perfected construction lien claim, a claimant may commence foreclosure proceedings. Such proceedings must be commenced within two years of the date the lien claim was filed.

Judgments

Money judgments become a lien on all real property that the judgment debtor owns or acquires, for a period of ten years from the date the judgment is docketed with the clerk of courts. It is only a lien on real estate owned by the debtor in the county in which the judgment is docketed. A transcript (copy certified by the court) of a judgment may be docketed in other counties.

Up to $40,000 of equity in a homestead is exempt from execution for money judgments. Judgment creditors can be required by homestead owners to release an exempt homestead from the lien of the judgment without being paid anything.

Assessors

An assessor is a public official who appraises property for tax purposes. The Wisconsin Department of Revenue certifies assessors and assessment personnel in the state.

Assessor Certification in Wisconsin

An assessor certification program for Wisconsin was authorized in 1975. Its objective is to upgrade the quality of the individual assessor. The program requires training, which is available from the Wisconsin Department of Revenue, the Wisconsin Technical College districts, and other private sources. As of January 1977, all local assessors in Wisconsin must be certified by representatives of the Wisconsin Department of Revenue prior to assuming office as local assessors. *The goal of the program is to establish, by means of a testing* procedure, minimum standards of knowledge for local assessors and *other assessment personnel* (excluding clerical support personnel) and, thus, to improve the equity of assessments made at the local level. The certification program does not guarantee that assessors will be proficient in their work, but it does ensure, through written examination, that they have sufficient preparation and knowledge to perform the complex functions associated with property assessment in accordance with Wisconsin law. The law does not affect the selection of assessors. The program merely requires that the candidates for assessment offices obtain the proper certification prior to assuming office.

Each municipality in Wisconsin is rated for a specific level of certification for the statutory assessor, depending on the complexity of the property-assessment function. *New assessors, whether elected or appointed, must obtain the level of certification appropriate for their municipalities prior to being eligible to assume office.* If a person is elected to the office of assessor on or after January 1, 1977, and is not certified at the appropriate level for that municipality, the office is declared vacant and the proper authority must appoint an appropriately certified person to assume the office of assessor. The certification rules also apply to new property-assessment personnel, other than the statutory assessor, who are appointed on or after January 1, 1977. The level of required certification for assessment personnel is determined by their duties. Each certification level has a description of the duties authorized within that level. To legally perform any or all of the duties described at a particular level of certification, a person must be certified at that level.

Assessor Certification Examination

Certification may be attained by successfully completing the examination required by the Wisconsin Department of Revenue for that particular level of certification. All certifications expire five years after the date of issue. Individuals may be recertified by successfully completing the current certification examination or by meeting the established continuing-education requirements and attending at least four of the five annual assessor schools held during the five years preceding their certification expiration dates.

On January 1, 1981, a temporary certification status was initiated. A temporarily certified individual is authorized to perform, in accordance with the Wisconsin Property Assessment Manual and under the direct supervision of the certified assessor, the duties defined for the lowest assessment-technician level of assessor certification. Applications for temporary certification must be in writing on the prescribed form. Approval is based on the conditions that the applicant has not been temporarily certified before and has a job commitment in the assessment field. Temporary certification becomes effective with the mailing of the approval letter. Temporary certification is valid until the results of the next assessor certification exam are issued or 100 days have expired since the temporary certification became effective, whichever occurs first. An applicant is restricted to challenging only one examination per exam cycle. A $20 examination fee is required for each examination.

The assessor certification program offers five levels of certification, three of which are for assessors and two of which are for other assessment personnel. Certification levels from lowest to highest are: assessment technician, property appraiser, assessor 1, assessor 2, and assessor 3. With the exception of the assessor 3 level, which is unique, each level of certification is progressively more demanding and encompasses the duties of the lower levels. A person certified as an assessor 2 thus automatically is certified and eligible to perform the duties of an assessor 1, a property appraiser, or an assessment technician. The assessor 3 level is primarily for administrative property-assessment positions, so certification at that level authorizes an individual to perform only the duties prescribed at that level.

Examinations for each of the five certification levels are independent of each other and are not progressive in nature. In other words, a person does not need to complete a certification examination at one level before taking the examination for the next higher level. The exams are offered quarterly. Assessor certification and continuing education information is available at *www.revenue.wi.gov* under "Training."

QUESTIONS

1. Real estate taxes in Wisconsin are usually
   a. paid to the assessor of each municipality.
   b. prepaid on January 31 of the tax year.
   c. prepaid on May 1 of the tax year.
   d. paid in arrears on or before January 31 of the year following the levy.
2. A property owner may redeem his or her property from delinquent taxes by paying all past-due taxes plus
   a. a penalty of 2 percent per month.
   b. a penalty of 3 percent per month.
   c. a penalty of 5 percent per month.
   d. penalties and interest within the time periods prescribed in Section 74 of the Wisconsin Statutes.
3. For Wisconsin, a construction-lien claim made by a prime contractor must be filed
   a. with the treasurer of the municipality.
   b. with the building inspector of the municipality.
   c. within two months after completing the work.
   d. within six months after completing the work and at least 30 days after the warning notice.
4. The market value of a residence is established at $53,400. If the municipality assesses at 60 percent of the market value, what is the assessed value of the property?
   a. $8,900
   b. $21,360
   c. $32,040
   d. $37,380
5. The assessed value of a home is $48,650. If the tax rate is $.0184 per $1 of assessed value, what is the amount of property tax due on the property?
   a. $264.40
   b. $447.58
   c. $895.16
   d. $943.81
6. To take an assessor certification test, an applicant must
   a. be a licensed real estate broker.
   b. pay a $20 examination fee.
   c. be 18 years of age.
   d. be an experienced appraiser.
7. An assessor elected or appointed in Wisconsin after January 1977 must
   a. be certified at the assessor 3 level.
   b. be certified at the assessor 1 level.
   c. be certified at the appropriate level for his or her municipality before being eligible to assume office.
   d. apply to take a certification exam after being elected.
8. The annual real estate tax in Wisconsin is levied as of what date for each calendar year?
   a. December 31
   b. January 1
   c. January 31
   d. February 28
9. You are filing an objection to the assessed valuation on your home. To whom of the following do you object?
   a. The mayor's office
   b. The Register of Deeds
   c. The Wisconsin Department of Revenue
   d. The Board of Review
10. The maximum charge for delinquent real estate in Wisconsin is how much interest per month?
    a. 7½ percent
    b. 1 percent
    c. 1½ percent
    d. 2 percent

11. One of your tenants recently moved out of his apartment prior to the expiration of his lease. The court has issued a judgment against the tenant, and it has been docketed. The judgment will remain a lien against the tenant for how many years?

a. one year
b. five years
c. three years
d. ten years

12. Money judgments become a lien on all real property that the judgment debtor owns or acquires for a period of

a. one year from the date the judgment is docketed with the clerk of courts.
b. three years from the date the judgment is docketed with the clerk of courts.
c. five years from the date the judgment is docketed with the clerk of courts.
d. ten years from the date the judgment is docketed with the clerk of courts.

Real Estate Contracts

The contract for the sale of real estate, known in Wisconsin as an *offer to purchase*, is the most important document in a real estate sales transaction. It fixes the rights and duties of the parties to the transaction and controls all the subsequent proceedings, including the consummation of the transaction (the closing).

LICENSEE'S AUTHORITY TO PREPARE DOCUMENTS

A Wisconsin licensee is prohibited from giving advice or opinions regarding the legal rights or obligations of parties to a transaction, the legal effect of contracts or conveyances, or the state of title to real estate. Any licensee or registrant who violates these rules is in violation of the Wisconsin Statutes and may be disciplined by the Real Estate Board.

Contract Forms

Under RL16.03 only a broker can use certain forms prepared and approved by the state bar and Uniform Commercial Code forms. A salesperson or broker can use out-of-state forms if some are for the sale of out-of-state real estate and are filled out in Wisconsin and legally used in the other state. Real estate forms prepared by government agencies and property management agreements may also be used by both brokers and salespersons in Wisconsin. The approved forms may be prepared and used subject to the following five conditions:

1. Approved forms may be used only when a licensee is acting as an agent or a party in a real estate or business opportunity transaction. A broker must now use approved listing contracts, except as otherwise provided in RL16.04.
2. Salespeople may use any WB form prepared by the Department of Regulation and Licensing.

3. A nonapproved form may be used when the department has no approved form for a given kind of real estate or business opportunity transaction.
4. A nonapproved form may be used for a property management agreement between a broker and a landlord—prepared by the broker entering into the agreement, the broker's attorney, or the landlord—that contains provisions relating to leasing, managing, marketing, and the overall management of the landlord's property.
5. RL16.06 covers specifics relating to the use of addenda to real estate contracts. For example, a licensee may use a preprepared addendum that supplants or alters the printed provisions of an approved form only if the addendum is drafted by an attorney who is identified on the addendum.

Licensees who use outdated forms violate Chapters 452.14(3)(m) and RL16 of the Wisconsin Statutes. Some of these forms appear on all salesperson and broker license examinations.

ESSENTIALS OF A VALID CONTRACT

Statute of Frauds

The Wisconsin Statute of Frauds requires that all documents conveying interest in real estate, including transactions by which an interest or estate in land is created, transferred, mortgaged, assigned, or otherwise affected, are in writing and are signed by the parties. Leases for one year or less are not subject to the statute of frauds. The Statute of Frauds on agency contracts (Chapter 240.10) and the Statute of Frauds on conveyances (Chapter 706) are covered on the salesperson's exam.

Competent Parties

In Wisconsin, the legal age for entering into a contract is 18 years old. *A contract entered into with a minor is voidable at the option of the minor* because the minor can renounce, or void, the contract at any time during the minority period and for a reasonable time thereafter. After reaching legal age, the former minor can ratify, or confirm in writing and be bound by, any such contract that previously has not been voided. However, the laws are constructed to protect young persons from adults who might take advantage of them. Persons entering into a contract with a minor do so at their own risk.

Offer and Acceptance

After an offer to purchase is accepted by the seller and delivered to the buyer, it becomes a binding contract on both buyer and seller. If the meaning of a contract is questioned by either the buyer or the seller, or its wording is vague, the courts usually will rule against the party who drafted it. Licensees, therefore, must be careful when drafting the offer to purchase.

Equitable Title

In Wisconsin, after a contract is accepted, *the doctrine of equitable conversion* takes effect. Under this doctrine, *the buyer becomes the owner, subject to his or her liability to pay the rest of the purchase price.* The seller has only a claim for the rest of the purchase price and holds legal title to the property only as security to ensure that the price is paid. In other words, the seller is still in possession but holds the property subject to a legal obligation to take care of it for the buyer. The buyer, then, holds *equitable title* to the real estate and even has the right to sell to a third party prior to closing, under certain circumstances, and to demand that the deed be made out to the third party buyer.

TERMS OF THE CONTRACT

The offer to purchase should contain the following elements: *the nature of the estate to be conveyed, whether it is fee simple or some other estate*; the *form of the deed to be used*; the *total consideration*; the *method of payment*; an *accurate description of the property*; and the *date and place for the closing*. When a contract provides that "time is of the essence," its terms must be carried out exactly by the date specified unless an extension is mutually agreed on by the parties.

If a *counter-offer* is made, it should be made on the department-approved counter-offer forms (WB-44 or WB-46). WB-44 is a simple counter-offer form that limits a seller to negotiations with just one buyer. WB-46 is a multiple counter-proposal form that allows a seller to negotiate with more than one buyer. WB-46 is a non-binding proposal that may be made to more than one buyer. The seller may accept what is considered to be the most favorable response to the multiple counter-proposal.

If a later change must be made that is mutually agreeable to the parties, Form WB-40 (Amendment to Offer to Purchase) should be used. If one party is giving notice that the other party does not need to approve, the WB-41 (Notice Relating to Offer to Purchase) should be used.

Encumbrances and Other Conditions

Sellers should be careful to include in the sale only what they own. All restrictions, limitations, or encumbrances on the property or its use should be stated fully and the contract should specify that the property is being sold subject to them. If applicable, *the offer to purchase also should state any contingencies or conditions* that must be met before the contract can be performed. For example, if the purchaser must borrow money in order to make the purchase, the details of the mortgage loan he or she expects to obtain should be included, along with a statement that the contract is to be performed subject to the purchaser obtaining such a loan. The more details included in describing contingencies, the less confusion there will be as to whether they have been met. Provisions also should be made for the division of any rents, insurance premiums, taxes, water charges, or interest on existing mortgages. Title insurance cannot be assumed or transferred in Wisconsin.

Personal Property

Any personal property to be included in the sale, such as air-conditioning units, carpets, drapes, refrigerators, or ranges, *also should be specified in the sales contract*. This will minimize the possibility of a conflict between the buyer and seller regarding what constitutes fixtures and what constitutes personal property. The broker or salesperson should bring to both parties' attention any property that might be in question. The disposition of annual crops in the sale of farmland is included in the personal property classification and must be specified in the offer to purchase. The final arbiter of what is included in the sale is the offer to purchase. Personal property listed in an MLS sheet or some other document drafted before the offer may not legally have to be included. Changes to the items listed in the offer should be accomplished through a counteroffer or an amendment.

Signatures

The offer to purchase must be signed by the parties. When selling property owned by a married person, it is important to *obtain the signatures of both spouses* in order to release any *homestead rights* the owner's spouse may have in the property, and all deadlines do not begin to run until the last signature is obtained. When financing is necessary for the buyers, the lender will want both spouses to sign the accepted offer to show the willingness of both spouses to sign the mortgage and the note.

The Marital Property Act raises the question of what role real estate licensees play in clarifying with married sellers how their property was owned or controlled by one or the other or both of them and, with married buyers, how they will want to own and take title to the property. Under the law, title does not determine who has ownership rights to property. However, title generally does determine management and control rights of the property. In much the same way that title determined management rights under the common-law property system, the marital property law generally looks at who "holds" (has title to) the property and at the classification of the property. *Management* and *control* are broadly defined under the law as "the right to buy, sell, use, transfer, exchange, abandon, lease, consume, expend, assign, create a security interest in, mortgage, encumber, dispose of, institute or defend a civil action regarding, or otherwise deal with property as if it were property of an unmarried person."

The law provides that a spouse acting alone may manage and control

- the spouse's individual property;
- marital property, unless otherwise provided, held in the spouse's name alone or not held in the name of either spouse;
- marital property held in the names of both spouses in the alternative (e.g., John or Mary);
- all marital property, subject to exceptions, for the purpose of obtaining an extension of certain kinds of credit for an obligation in the interest of the marriage or family;
- a policy of insurance, if the spouse is designated as the owner on the records of the issuer of the policy;
- any right of an employee under a deferred employment benefit plan (e.g., pension plan) that accrues as a result of the spouse's employment; and
- any legal claim for relief of the spouse.

Only by *acting together* may spouses manage and control marital property held in the names of both spouses (e.g., "John and Mary") unless the property is held in the alternative.

The right to manage and control marital property transferred to a trust is determined by the terms of the trust.

The classifications of property are more complex than before the Marital Property Act went into effect, and licensees will have to avoid giving legal advice, especially concerning how buyers will hold property.

The real estate board has taken the position in the past that interspousal disputes concerning the disposition of their property may require disclosure to buyers who could be inconvenienced and adversely affected by the situation. This position is not changed by the Marital Property Act.

AN EXPLANATION OF THE RESIDENTIAL OFFER TO PURCHASE

Information contained in this chapter is provided to assist applicants as well as licensees to understand the WB-11 Residential Offer to Purchase form. This chapter includes both a sample (see Figure 7.1) and a line-by-line explanation of the Residential Offer to Purchase.

Sample Offer to Purchase

On November 15, 2009, salesperson James obtained an offer from Jay and Linda Jones to purchase the Carter property at 1400 Regas Lane, Madison, Wisconsin. The legal description is Lot 2, Block 4, of the Fairmont Subdivision, NW 1/4 of Chapter 8, T9N, R7E, Dane County, Wisconsin. The Joneses have written an offer for $248,000. The offer was made on the basis of the buyers' assumption of the balance of the existing mortgage and the balance of the selling price being paid in cash at closing. Possession was desired as of the date of closing, which was to be no later than December 15, 2009. The Joneses received a copy of the sellers' condition report prior to signing the offer to purchase. The sellers' condition report was dated September 13, 2009. Buyers would like the washer and dryer. The Joneses paid earnest money of $2,000 with another $2,000 to be paid on acceptance of the offer. The offer was accepted by the Carters on November 15, 2009.

An Overview of the WB-11 Residential Offer to Purchase

The WB-11 Residential Offer to Purchase is five pages long and includes optional contingency provisions presented on page three and five of the contract.

The licensee must indicate on line 1 who he or she is representing, the buyer or seller. The licensee, of course, will have already given an agency disclosure to the client or customer for whom the offer is being drafted. For example, it is possible that the agent has become a dual agent.

See the discussion in Chapter 2 of lines 2–5 in the listing contract. Fill in the buyer's name(s) on line 2 making sure that the name(s) are complete.

You must complete lines 6 and 7—purchase price—in the same manner that you prepare a personal check, as also is done in the listing contract.

Lines 8–10 refer to earnest money. There is no law in Wisconsin regarding the amount of earnest money to be paid when preparing an offer to purchase. However, when the buyer pays earnest money, it constitutes a show of good faith and might serve as liquidated damages to the seller if the buyer defaults. You should also be aware that in Wisconsin earnest money is not required for an offer to purchase to be enforceable because the numerous mutual promises involved with an offer to purchase constitute consideration in Wisconsin.

Lines 248–250 state that the earnest money will be held in the listing broker's trust account. If the property is not listed, the buyer's agent will hold the earnest money in his trust account. If there are no brokers involved in the transaction, the seller will hold the earnest money. Line 10 is self-explanatory.

FIGURE 7.1

Residential Offer to Purchase

Approved by Wisconsin Department of Regulation and Licensing
4-1-99 (Optional Use Date)
11-1-99 (Mandatory Use Date)

WB-11 RESIDENTIAL OFFER TO PURCHASE

Wisconsin Legal Blank Co., Inc.
Milwaukee, Wis.

Page 1 of 5

BROKER DRAFTING THIS OFFER ON Nov. 15, 2009 **[DATE] IS (AGENT OF SELLER) (AGENT OF BUYER) (DUAL AGENT)** [STRIKE TWO]

GENERAL PROVISIONS The Buyer, Jay and Linda Jones, offers to purchase the Property known as [Street Address] 1400 Regas Lane ______ in the City of Madison, County of Dane Wisconsin (Insert additional description, if any, at lines 180 - 186, 317 - 320 or attach as an addendum per line 316), on the following terms:

■ PURCHASE PRICE: Two Hundred Forty Eight Thousand and 00/100-- Dollars ($ 248,000.00).

■ EARNEST MONEY of $ 2,000.00 accompanies this Offer and earnest money of $ 2,000.00 will be paid within ______ days of acceptance.

■ THE BALANCE OF PURCHASE PRICE will be paid in cash or equivalent at closing unless otherwise provided below.

■ ADDITIONAL ITEMS INCLUDED IN PURCHASE PRICE: Seller shall include in the purchase price and transfer, free and clear of encumbrances, all fixtures, as defined at lines 124 - 132 and as may be on the Property on the date of this Offer, unless excluded at lines 15 - 16, and the following additional items: washer and dryer

■ ITEMS NOT INCLUDED IN THE PURCHASE PRICE: ______

ACCEPTANCE Acceptance occurs when all Buyers and Sellers have signed an identical copy of the Offer, including signatures on separate but identical copies of the Offer. ***CAUTION: Deadlines in the Offer are commonly calculated from acceptance. Consider whether short term deadlines running from acceptance provide adequate time for both binding acceptance and performance.***

BINDING ACCEPTANCE This Offer is binding upon both Parties only if a copy of the accepted Offer is delivered to Buyer on or before November 15, 2009. ***CAUTION: This Offer may be withdrawn prior to delivery of the accepted Offer.***

DELIVERY OF DOCUMENTS AND WRITTEN NOTICES Unless otherwise stated in this Offer, delivery of documents and written notices to a Party shall be effective only when accomplished by one of the methods specified at lines 24 - 33.

(1) By depositing the document or written notice postage or fees prepaid in the U.S. Mail or fees prepaid or charged to an account with a commercial delivery service, addressed either to the Party, or to the Party's recipient for delivery designated at lines 27 or 29 (if any) for delivery to the Party's delivery address at lines 28 or 30.

Seller's recipient for delivery (optional): ______

Seller's delivery address: ______

Buyer's recipient for delivery (optional): ______

Buyer's delivery address: ______

(2) By giving the document or written notice personally to the Party, or the Party's recipient for delivery if an individual is designated at lines 27or 29.

(3) By fax transmission of the document or written notice to the following telephone number:

Buyer: (______)______ Seller: (______)______

OCCUPANCY Occupancy of the entire Property shall be given to Buyer at time of closing unless otherwise provided in this Offer (lines 293 through 297). At time of Buyer's occupancy, Property shall be free of all debris and personal property except for personal property belonging to current tenants, or that sold to Buyer or left with Buyer's consent. Occupancy shall be given subject to tenant's rights, if any.

LEASED PROPERTY If Property is currently leased and lease(s) extend beyond closing, Seller shall assign Seller's rights under said lease(s) and transfer all security deposits and prepaid rents thereunder to Buyer at closing. The terms of the (written) (oral) [STRIKE ONE] lease(s), if any, are ______.

RENTAL WEATHERIZATION This transaction (is) (is not) [STRIKE ONE] exempt from State of Wisconsin Rental Weatherization Standards (Wis. Admin. Code Comm 67). If not exempt, (Buyer) (Seller) [STRIKE ONE] will be responsible for compliance, including all costs. If Seller is responsible for compliance, Seller shall provide a Certificate of Compliance at closing.

PLACE OF CLOSING This transaction is to be closed at the place designated by Buyer's mortgagee or To be determined ______ no later than December 15, 2009 unless another date or place is agreed to in writing.

CLOSING PRORATIONS The following items shall be prorated at closing: real estate taxes, rents, water and sewer use charges, garbage pick-up and other private and municipal charges, property owner's association assessments, fuel and ______. Any income, taxes or expenses shall accrue to Seller, and be prorated, through the day prior to closing. Net general real estate taxes shall be prorated based on (the net general real estate taxes for the current year, if known, otherwise on the net general real estate taxes for the preceding year) (______). [STRIKE AND COMPLETE AS APPLICABLE]

CAUTION: If proration on the basis of net general real estate taxes is not acceptable (for example, completed/pending reassessment, changing mill rate, lottery credits), insert estimated annual tax or other formula for proration.

PROPERTY CONDITION PROVISIONS

■ PROPERTY CONDITION REPRESENTATIONS: Seller represents to Buyer that as of the date of acceptance Seller has no notice or knowledge of conditions affecting the Property or transaction (see below) other than those identified in Seller's Real Estate Condition Report dated ______, which was received by Buyer prior to Buyer signing this Offer and which is made a part of this Offer by reference [COMPLETE DATE OR STRIKE AS APPLICABLE] and ______ [INSERT CONDITIONS NOT ALREADY INCLUDED IN THE CONDITION REPORT].

FIGURE 7.1 (CONTINUED)

Residential Offer to Purchase

■ A "condition affecting the Property or transaction" is defined as follows: [page 2 of 5, WB-11]

(a) planned or commenced public improvements which may result in special assessments or otherwise materially affect the Property or the present use of the Property;
(b) completed or pending reassessment of the Property for property tax purposes;
(c) government agency or court order requiring repair, alteration or correction of any existing condition;
(d) construction or remodeling on Property for which required state or local permits had not been obtained;
(e) any land division involving the subject Property, for which required state or local approvals had not been obtained;
(f) violation of applicable state or local smoke detector laws; ***NOTE: State law requires operating smoke detectors on all levels of all residential properties.***
(g) any portion of the Property being in a 100 year floodplain, a wetland or a shoreland zoning area under local, state or federal laws;
(h) that a structure on the Property is designated as an historic building or that any part of Property is in an historic district;
(i) structural inadequacies which if not repaired will significantly shorten the expected normal life of the Property;
(j) mechanical systems inadequate for the present use of the Property;
(k) insect or animal infestation of the Property;
(l) conditions constituting a significant health or safety hazard for occupants of Property; ***Note: Specific federal lead paint disclosure requirements must be complied with in the sale of most residential properties built before 1978.***
(m) underground or aboveground storage tanks on the Property for storage of flammable or combustible liquids including but not limited to gasoline and heating oil which are currently or which were previously located on the Property; ***NOTE: Wis. Adm. Code, Chapter Comm 10 contains registration and operation rules for such underground and aboveground storage tanks.***
(n) material violations of environmental laws or other laws or agreements regulating the use of the Property;
(o) high voltage electric (100 KV or greater) or steel natural gas transmission lines located on but not directly serving the Property;
(p) other conditions or occurrences which would significantly reduce the value of the Property to a reasonable person with knowledge of the nature and scope of the condition or occurrence.

■ REAL ESTATE CONDITION REPORT: Wisconsin law requires owners of property which includes 1-4 dwelling units to provide buyers with a Real Estate Condition Report. Excluded from this requirement are sales of property that has never been inhabited, sales exempt from the real estate transfer fee, and sales by certain court-appointed fiduciaries, (for example, personal representatives who have never occupied the Property). The form of the Report is found in Wis. Stat. § 709.03. The law provides: "709.02 Disclosure . . . the owner of the property shall furnish, not later than 10 days after acceptance of the contract of sale . . . , to the prospective buyer of the property a completed copy of the report . . . A prospective buyer who does not receive a report within the 10 days may, within 2 business days after the end of that 10 day period, rescind the contract of sale . . . by delivering a written notice of rescission to the owner or the owner's agent." Buyer may also have certain rescission rights if a Real Estate Condition Report disclosing defects is furnished before expiration of the 10 days, but after the Offer is submitted to Seller. Buyer should review the report form or consult with an attorney for additional information regarding these rescission rights.

■ PROPERTY DIMENSIONS AND SURVEYS: Buyer acknowledges that any land, building or room dimensions, or total acreage or building square footage figures, provided to Buyer by Seller or by a broker, may be approximate because of rounding or other reasons, unless verified by survey or other means. Buyer also acknowledges that there are various formulas used to calculate total square footage of buildings and that total square footage figures will vary dependent upon the formula used. ***CAUTION: Buyer should verify total square footage formula, total square footage/acreage figures, land, building or room dimensions, if material.***

■ INSPECTIONS: Seller agrees to allow Buyer's inspectors reasonable access to the Property upon reasonable notice if the inspections are reasonably necessary to satisfy the contingencies in this Offer. Buyer agrees to promptly provide copies of all such inspection reports to Seller, and to listing broker if Property is listed. Furthermore, Buyer agrees to promptly restore the Property to its original condition after Buyer's inspections are completed, unless otherwise agreed with Seller. An "inspection" is defined as an observation of the Property which does not include testing of the Property, other than testing for leaking carbon monoxide, or testing for leaking LP gas or natural gas used as a fuel source, which are hereby authorized.

■ TESTING: Except as otherwise provided, Seller's authorization for inspections does not authorize Buyer to conduct testing of the Property. A "test" is defined as the taking of samples of materials such as soils, water, air or building materials from the Property and the laboratory or other analysis of these materials. If Buyer requires testing, testing contingencies must be specifically provided for at lines 180 - 186, 317 - 320 or in an addendum per line 316. Note: Any contingency authorizing such tests should specify the areas of the Property to be tested, the purpose of the test, (e.g., to determine if environmental contamination is present), any limitations on Buyer's testing and any other material terms of the contingency (e.g., Buyer's obligation to return the Property to its original condition). Seller acknowledges that certain inspections or tests may detect environmental pollution which may be required to be reported to the Wisconsin Department of Natural Resources.

■ PRE-CLOSING INSPECTION: At a reasonable time, pre-approved by Seller or Seller's agent, within 3 days before closing, Buyer shall have the right to inspect the Property to determine that there has been no significant change in the condition of the Property, except for ordinary wear and tear and changes approved by Buyer, and that any defects Seller has elected to cure have been repaired in a good and workmanlike manner.

■ PROPERTY DAMAGE BETWEEN ACCEPTANCE AND CLOSING: Seller shall maintain the Property until the earlier of closing or occupancy of Buyer in materially the same condition as of the date of acceptance of this Offer, except for ordinary wear and tear. If, prior to closing, the Property is damaged in an amount of not more than five per cent (5%) of the selling price, Seller shall be obligated to repair the Property and restore it to the same condition that it was on the day of this Offer. If the damage shall exceed such sum, Seller shall promptly notify Buyer in writing of the damage and this Offer may be canceled at option of Buyer. Should Buyer elect to carry out this Offer despite such damage, Buyer shall be entitled to the insurance proceeds relating to the damage to the Property, plus a credit towards the purchase price equal to the amount of Seller's deductible on such policy. However, if this sale is financed by a land contract or a mortgage to Seller, the insurance proceeds shall be held in trust for the sole purpose of restoring the Property.

FIXTURES A "Fixture" is defined as an item of property which is physically attached to or so closely associated with land or improvements so as to be treated as part of the real estate, including, without limitation, physically attached items not easily removable without damage to the Property, items specifically adapted to the Property, and items customarily treated as fixtures, including, but not limited to, all: garden bulbs; plants; shrubs and trees; screen and storm doors and windows; electric lighting fixtures; window shades; curtain and traverse rods; blinds and shutters; central heating and cooling units and attached equipment; water heaters and softeners; sump pumps; attached or fitted floor coverings; awnings; attached antennas, satellite dishes and component parts; garage door openers and remote controls; installed security systems; central vacuum systems and accessories; in-ground sprinkler systems and component parts; built-in appliances; ceiling fans; fences; storage buildings on permanent foundations and docks/piers on permanent foundations. ***NOTE: The terms of the Offer will determine what items are included/excluded. Address rented fixtures (e.g., water softeners), if any.***

FIGURE 7.1 (CONTINUED)

Residential Offer to Purchase

Wisconsin Legal Blank Co., Inc.

PROPERTY ADDRESS: 1400 Regas Lane, Madison, WI ______ [page 3 of 5, WB-11]

TIME IS OF THE ESSENCE "Time is of the Essence" as to: (1) earnest money payment(s); (2) binding acceptance; (3) occupancy; (4) date of closing; (5) contingency deadlines STRIKE AS APPLICABLE and all other dates and deadlines in this Offer except: ______ ______. If "Time is of the Essence" applies to a date or deadline, failure to perform by the exact date or deadline is a breach of contract. If "Time is of the Essence" does not apply to a date or deadline, then performance within a reasonable time of the date or deadline is allowed before a breach occurs.

DATES AND DEADLINES Deadlines expressed as a number of "days" from an event, such as acceptance, are calculated by excluding the day the event occurred and by counting subsequent calendar days. The deadline expires at midnight on the last day. Deadlines expressed as a specific number of "business days" exclude Saturdays, Sundays, any legal public holiday under Wisconsin or Federal law, and other day designated by the President such that the postal service does not receive registered mail or make regular deliveries on that day. Deadlines expressed as a specific number of "hours" from the occurrence of an event, such as receipt of a notice, are calculated from the exact time of the event, and by counting 24 hours per calendar day. Deadlines expressed as a specific day of the calendar year or as the day of a specific event, such as closing, expire at midnight of that day.

THE FINANCING CONTINGENCY PROVISIONS AT LINES 149 - 163 ARE A PART OF THIS OFFER IF LINE 149 IS MARKED, SUCH AS WITH AN "X". THEY ARE NOT PART OF THIS OFFER IF LINE 149 IS MARKED N/A OR IS NOT MARKED.

☐ **FINANCING CONTINGENCY:** This Offer is contingent upon Buyer being able to obtain a ______ INSERT LOAN PROGRAM OR SOURCE first mortgage loan commitment as described below, within ______ days of acceptance of this Offer. The financing selected shall be in an amount of not less than $______ for a term of not less than ______ years, amortized over not less than ______ years. Initial monthly payments of principal and interest shall not exceed $______. Monthly payments may also include 1/12th of the estimated net annual real estate taxes, hazard insurance premiums, and private mortgage insurance premiums. The mortgage may not include a prepayment premium. Buyer agrees to pay a loan fee not to exceed ______% of the loan. (Loan fee refers to discount points and/or loan origination fee, but DOES NOT include Buyer's other closing costs.) If the purchase price under this Offer is modified, the financed amount, unless otherwise provided, shall be adjusted to the same percentage of the purchase price as in this contingency and the monthly payments shall be adjusted as necessary to maintain the term and amortization stated above. **CHECK AND COMPLETE APPLICABLE FINANCING PROVISION AT LINE 159 OR 160.**

☐ **FIXED RATE FINANCING:** The annual rate of interest shall not exceed ______%.

☐ **ADJUSTABLE RATE FINANCING:** The initial annual interest rate shall not exceed ______%. The initial interest rate shall be fixed for ______ months, at which time the interest rate may be increased not more than ______% per year. The maximum interest rate during the mortgage term shall not exceed ______%. Monthly payments of principal and interest may be adjusted to reflect interest changes.

LOAN COMMITMENT: Buyer agrees to pay all customary financing costs (including closing fees), to apply for financing promptly, and to provide evidence of application promptly upon request by Seller. If Buyer qualifies for the financing described in this Offer or other financing acceptable to Buyer, Buyer agrees to deliver to Seller a copy of the written loan commitment no later than the deadline for loan commitment at line 150. **Buyer's delivery of a copy of any written loan commitment to Seller (even if subject to conditions) shall satisfy the Buyer's financing contingency unless accompanied by a notice of unacceptability. *CAUTION: BUYER, BUYER'S LENDER AND AGENTS OF BUYER OR SELLER SHOULD NOT DELIVER A LOAN COMMITMENT TO SELLER WITHOUT BUYER'S PRIOR APPROVAL OR UNLESS ACCOMPANIED BY A NOTICE OF UNACCEPTABILITY.***

SELLER TERMINATION RIGHTS: If Buyer does not make timely delivery of said commitment, Seller may terminate this Offer if Seller delivers a written notice of termination to Buyer prior to Seller's actual receipt of a copy of Buyer's written loan commitment.

FINANCING UNAVAILABILITY: If financing is not available on the terms stated in this Offer (and Buyer has not already delivered an acceptable loan commitment for other financing to Seller), Buyer shall promptly deliver written notice to Seller of same including copies of lender(s)' rejection letter(s) or other evidence of unavailability. Unless a specific loan source is named in this Offer, Seller shall then have 10 days to give Buyer written notice of Seller's decision to finance this transaction on the same terms set forth in this Offer, and this Offer shall remain in full force and effect, with the time for closing extended accordingly. If Seller's notice is not timely given, this Offer shall be null and void. Buyer authorizes Seller to obtain any credit information reasonably appropriate to determine Buyer's credit worthiness for Seller financing.

ADDITIONAL PROVISIONS/CONTINGENCIES Buyer will assume seller's mortgage

TITLE EVIDENCE

■ CONVEYANCE OF TITLE: **Upon payment of the purchase price, Seller shall convey the Property by warranty deed (or other conveyance as provided herein)** free and clear of all liens and encumbrances, except: municipal and zoning ordinances and agreements entered under them, recorded easements for the distribution of utility and municipal services, recorded building and use restrictions and covenants, general taxes levied in the year of closing and latest known mill rate latest known assessed value ______ (provided none of the foregoing prohibit present use of the Property), which constitutes merchantable title for purposes of this transaction. Seller further agrees to complete and execute the documents necessary to record the conveyance. ***WARNING: Municipal and zoning ordinances, recorded building and use restrictions, covenants and easements may prohibit certain improvements or uses and therefore should be reviewed, particularly if Buyer contemplates making improvements to Property or a use other than the current use.***

■ FORM OF TITLE EVIDENCE: Seller shall give evidence of title in the form of an owner's policy of title insurance in the amount of the purchase price on a current ALTA form issued by an insurer licensed to write title insurance in Wisconsin. ***CAUTION: IF TITLE EVIDENCE WILL BE GIVEN BY ABSTRACT, STRIKE TITLE INSURANCE PROVISIONS AND INSERT ABSTRACT PROVISIONS.***

FIGURE 7.1 (CONTINUED)

Residential Offer to Purchase

[page 4 of 5, WB-11]

■ PROVISION OF MERCHANTABLE TITLE: Seller shall pay all costs of providing title evidence. For purposes of closing, title evidence shall be acceptable if the commitment for the required title insurance is delivered to Buyer's attorney or Buyer not less than 3 business days before closing, showing title to the Property as of a date no more than 15 days before delivery of such title evidence to be merchantable, subject only to liens which will be paid out of the proceeds of closing and standard title insurance requirements and exceptions, as appropriate. ***CAUTION: BUYER SHOULD CONSIDER UPDATING THE EFFECTIVE DATE OF THE TITLE COMMITMENT PRIOR TO CLOSING OR A "GAP ENDORSEMENT" WHICH WOULD INSURE OVER LIENS FILED BETWEEN THE EFFECTIVE DATE OF THE COMMITMENT AND THE DATE THE DEED IS RECORDED.***

■ TITLE ACCEPTABLE FOR CLOSING: If title is not acceptable for closing, Buyer shall notify Seller in writing of objections to title by the time set for closing. In such event, Seller shall have a reasonable time, but not exceeding 15 days, to remove the objections, and the time for closing shall be extended as necessary for this purpose. In the event that Seller is unable to remove said objections, Buyer shall have 5 days from receipt of notice thereof, to deliver written notice waiving the objections, and the time for closing shall be extended accordingly. If Buyer does not waive the objections, this Offer shall be null and void. Providing title evidence acceptable for closing does not extinguish Seller's obligations to give merchantable title to Buyer.

■ SPECIAL ASSESSMENTS: Special assessments, if any, for work actually commenced or levied prior to date of this Offer shall be paid by Seller no later than closing. All other special assessments shall be paid by Buyer. ***CAUTION: Consider a special agreement if area assessments, property owner's association assessments or other expenses are contemplated.*** "Other expenses" are one-time charges or ongoing use fees for public improvements (other than those resulting in special assessments) relating to curb, gutter, street, sidewalk, sanitary and stormwater and storm sewer (including all sewer mains and hook-up and interceptor charges), parks, street lighting and street trees, and impact fees for other public facilities, as defined in Wis. Stat. §66.55(1)(c) & (f).

DELIVERY/RECEIPT Unless otherwise stated in this Offer, any signed document transmitted by facsimile machine (fax) shall be treated in all manner and respects as an original document and the signature of any Party upon a document transmitted by fax shall be considered an original signature. Personal delivery to, or actual receipt by, any named Buyer or Seller constitutes personal delivery to, or actual receipt by Buyer or Seller Once received, a notice cannot be withdrawn by the Party delivering the notice without the consent of the Party receiving the notice. A Party may not unilaterally reinstate a contingency after a notice of a contingency waiver has been received by the other Party. **The delivery/receipt provisions in this Offer may be modified when appropriate (e.g., when mail delivery is not desirable (see lines 24 - 30) or when a party will not be personally available to receive a notice (see line 286)).** Buyer and Seller authorize the agents of Buyer and Seller to distribute copies of the Offer to Buyer's lender, appraisers, title insurance companies and any other settlement service providers for the transaction as defined by the Real Estate Settlement Procedures Act (RESPA).

DEFAULT Seller and Buyer each have the legal duty to use good faith and due diligence in completing the terms and conditions of this Offer. A material failure to perform any obligation under this Offer is a default which may subject the defaulting party to liability for damages or other legal remedies.

If Buyer defaults, Seller may:

(1) sue for specific performance and request the earnest money as partial payment of the purchase price; or

(2) terminate the Offer and have the option to: (a) request the earnest money as liquidated damages; or (b) direct Broker to return the earnest money and have the option to sue for actual damages.

If Seller defaults, Buyer may:

(1) sue for specific performance; or

(2) terminate the Offer and request the return of the earnest money, sue for actual damages, or both.

In addition, the Parties may seek any other remedies available in law or equity.

The Parties understand that the availability of any judicial remedy will depend upon the circumstances of the situation and the discretion of the courts. If either Party defaults, the Parties may renegotiate the Offer or seek nonjudicial dispute resolution instead of the remedies outlined above. By agreeing to binding arbitration, the Parties may lose the right to litigate in a court of law those disputes covered by the arbitration agreement.

NOTE: IF ACCEPTED, THIS OFFER CAN CREATE A LEGALLY ENFORCEABLE CONTRACT. BOTH PARTIES SHOULD READ THIS DOCUMENT CAREFULLY. BROKERS MAY PROVIDE A GENERAL EXPLANATION OF THE PROVISIONS OF THE OFFER BUT ARE PROHIBITED BY LAW FROM GIVING ADVICE OR OPINIONS CONCERNING YOUR LEGAL RIGHTS UNDER THIS OFFER OR HOW TITLE SHOULD BE TAKEN AT CLOSING. AN ATTORNEY SHOULD BE CONSULTED IF LEGAL ADVICE IS NEEDED.

EARNEST MONEY

■ HELD BY: Unless otherwise agreed, earnest money shall be paid to and held in the trust account of the listing broker (buyer's agent if Property is not listed or Seller's account if no broker is involved), until applied to purchase price or otherwise disbursed as provided in the Offer. ***CAUTION: Should persons other than a broker hold earnest money, an escrow agreement should be drafted by the Parties or an attorney. If someone other than Buyer makes payment of earnest money, consider a special disbursement agreement.***

■ DISBURSEMENT: If negotiations do not result in an accepted offer, the earnest money shall be promptly disbursed (after clearance from payor's depository institution if earnest money is paid by check) to the person(s) who paid the earnest money. At closing, earnest money shall be disbursed according to the closing statement. If this Offer does not close, the earnest money shall be disbursed according to a written disbursement agreement signed by all Parties to this Offer (Note: Wis. Adm. Code s. RL 18.09(1)(b) provides that an offer to purchase is not a written disbursement agreement pursuant to which the broker may disburse). If said disbursement agreement has not been delivered to broker within 60 days after the date set for closing, broker may disburse the earnest money: (1) as directed by an attorney who has reviewed the transaction and does not represent Buyer or Seller; (2) into a court hearing a lawsuit involving the earnest money and all Parties to this Offer; (3) as directed by court order; or (4) any other disbursement required or allowed by law. Broker may retain legal services to direct disbursement per (1) or to file an interpleader action per (2) and broker may deduct from the earnest money any costs and reasonable attorneys fees, not to exceed $250, prior to disbursement.

■ LEGAL RIGHTS/ACTION: Broker's disbursement of earnest money does not determine the legal rights of the Parties in relation to this Offer. Buyer's or Seller's legal right to earnest money cannot be determined by broker. At least 30 days prior to disbursement per (1) or (4) above, broker shall send Buyer and Seller notice of the disbursement by certified mail. If Buyer or Seller disagree with broker's proposed disbursement, a lawsuit may be filed to obtain a court order regarding disbursement. Small Claims Court has jurisdiction over all earnest money disputes arising out of the sale of residential property with 1-4 dwelling units and certain other earnest money disputes. Buyer and Seller should consider consulting attorneys regarding their legal rights under this Offer in case of a dispute. Both Parties agree to hold the broker harmless from any liability for good faith disbursement of earnest money in accordance with this Offer or applicable Department of Regulation and Licensing regulations concerning earnest money. See Wis. Adm. Code Ch. RL 18.

ENTIRE CONTRACT This Offer, including any amendments to it, contains the entire agreement of the Buyer and Seller regarding the transaction. All prior negotiations and discussions have been merged into this Offer. This agreement binds and inures to the benefit of the Parties to this Offer and their successors in interest.

FIGURE 7.1 (CONTINUED)

Residential Offer to Purchase

Wisconsin Legal Blank Co., Inc.

PROPERTY ADDRESS: 1400 Regas Lane, Madison, WI ____ [page 5 of 5, WB-11]

OPTIONAL PROVISIONS: THE PROVISIONS ON LINES 278 THROUGH 316 ARE A PART OF THIS OFFER IF MARKED, SUCH AS WITH AN "X". THEY ARE NOT PART OF THIS OFFER IF MARKED N/A OR ARE LEFT BLANK (EXCEPT AS PROVIDED AT LINES 280 - 281).

☐ **SALE OF BUYER'S PROPERTY CONTINGENCY:** This Offer is contingent upon the sale and closing of Buyer's property located at ____, no later than ____. Seller may keep Seller's Property on the market for sale and accept secondary offers. **If this contingency is made a part of this Offer, lines 282 - 286 are also a part of this offer unless marked N/A at line 282 or otherwise deleted.**

☐ **CONTINUED MARKETING:** If Seller accepts a bona fide secondary offer, Seller may give written notice to Buyer of acceptance. If Buyer does not deliver to Seller a written waiver of sale of Buyer's property contingency and ____ **[INSERT OTHER REQUIREMENTS, IF ANY (e.g., PAYMENT OF ADDITIONAL EARNEST MONEY, WAIVER OF ALL CONTINGENCIES, OR PROVIDING EVIDENCE OF SALE OR BRIDGE LOAN, etc.)]** within ____ hours of Buyer's actual receipt of said notice, this Offer shall be null and void.

☐ **SECONDARY OFFER:** This Offer is secondary to a prior accepted offer. This Offer shall become primary upon delivery of written notice to Buyer that this Offer is primary. Unless otherwise provided, Seller is not obligated to give Buyer notice prior to any deadline, nor is any particular secondary buyer given the right to be made primary ahead of other secondary buyers. Buyer may declare this Offer null and void by delivering written notice of withdrawal to Seller prior to delivery of Seller's notice that this Offer is primary. Buyer may not deliver notice of withdrawal earlier than ____ days after acceptance of this Offer. All other Offer deadlines which are run from acceptance shall run from the time this Offer becomes primary.

☐ **PRE/POST CLOSING OCCUPANCY:** Occupancy of ____ shall be given to Buyer on ____ at ____ am/pm. (Seller)(Buyer) [STRIKE ONE] shall pay an occupancy charge of $____ per day or partial day of pre/post-closing occupancy. Payment shall be due at the beginning of the occupancy period. Any unearned post closing occupancy fee (shall)(shall not) [STRIKE ONE] be refunded based on actual occupancy. ***CAUTION: Consider a special agreement regarding occupancy escrow, insurance, utilities, maintenance, keys, etc.***

☐ **INSPECTION CONTINGENCY:** This Offer is contingent upon a Wisconsin registered home inspector performing a home inspection of the Property, and an inspection, by a qualified independent inspector, of ____ which discloses no defects as defined below. This contingency shall be deemed satisfied unless Buyer, within ____ days of acceptance, delivers to Seller, and to listing broker if Property is listed, a copy of the inspector's written inspection report(s) and a written notice listing the defect(s) identified in the inspection report(s) to which Buyer objects. ***CAUTION: A proposed amendment will not satisfy this notice requirement.*** Buyer shall order the inspection and be responsible for all costs of inspection, including any inspections required by lender or as follow-up inspections to the home inspection. **Note: This contingency only authorizes inspections, not testing. (See lines 97 - 110.)**

■ RIGHT TO CURE: Seller (shall) (shall not) [STRIKE ONE] have a right to cure the defects. (Seller shall have a right to cure if no choice is indicated.) If Seller has right to cure, Seller may satisfy this contingency by: (1) delivering a written notice within 10 days of receipt of Buyer's notice of Seller's election to cure defects, (2) curing the defects in a good and workmanlike manner and (3) delivering to Buyer a written report detailing the work done no later than 3 days prior to closing. This Offer shall be null and void if Buyer makes timely delivery of the above notice and report and: (1) Seller does not have a right to cure or (2) Seller has a right to cure but: a) Seller delivers notice that Seller will not cure or b) Seller does not timely deliver the notice of election to cure.

■ "DEFECT" DEFINED: For the purposes of this contingency, a defect is defined as a structural, mechanical or other condition that would have a significant adverse effect on the value of the Property; that would significantly impair the health or safety of future occupants of the Property; or that if not repaired, removed or replaced would significantly shorten or have a significant adverse effect on the expected normal life of the Property. Defects do not include structural, mechanical or other conditions the nature and extent of which Buyer had actual knowledge or written notice before signing this Offer.

☐ **ADDENDA:** The attached ____ is/are made part of this Offer.

ADDITIONAL PROVISIONS/CONTINGENCIES Legal description: Lot 2, Block 4, Fairmont Subdivision, NW 1/4 of Section 8, T9N, R7E, Dane County, Wisconsin

This Offer was drafted on 11/15/05 [date] by [Licensee and firm] John James, New House Realty.

(x) ____ 11/15/09
Buyer's Signature ▲ Print Name Here: ▶ Jay Jones — Social Security No. or FEIN ▲ (Optional) — Date ▲

(x) ____ 11/15/09
Buyer's Signature ▲ Print Name Here: ▶ Linda Jones — Social Security No. or FEIN ▲ (Optional) — Date ▲

EARNEST MONEY RECEIPT Broker acknowledges receipt of earnest money as per line 8 of the above Offer. **(See lines 247 - 271.)**

____ Broker (By) ____

SELLER ACCEPTS THIS OFFER. THE WARRANTIES, REPRESENTATIONS AND COVENANTS MADE IN THIS OFFER SURVIVE CLOSING AND THE CONVEYANCE OF THE PROPERTY. SELLER AGREES TO CONVEY THE PROPERTY ON THE TERMS AND CONDITIONS AS SET FORTH HEREIN AND ACKNOWLEDGES RECEIPT OF A COPY OF THIS OFFER.

(x) ____ 11/15/09
Seller's Signature ▲ Print Name Here: ▶ George Carter — Social Security No. or FEIN ▲ (Optional) — Date ▲

(x) ____ 11/15/09
Seller's Signature ▲ Print Name Here: ▶ Martha Carter — Social Security No. or FEIN ▲ (Optional) — Date ▲

This Offer was presented to Seller by John James on November 15, 2005, at ____ a.m./p.m.

THIS OFFER IS REJECTED ____ ____ THIS OFFER IS COUNTERED [See attached counter] ____ ____
Seller Initials ▲ Date ▲ — Seller Initials ▲ Date ▲

Lines 11–16 are almost identical to lines 9–16 of the listing contract and were discussed under the listing contract. Lines 132–133 of the offer to purchase state that the terms of the offer will determine what the seller is willing to have included in an acceptable offer to purchase.

Lines 17–21 distinguish between acceptance and binding acceptance. Acceptance occurs when all buyers and sellers have signed an identical copy of the offer to purchase, including signatures on separate but identical copies of the offer. Binding acceptance occurs when a copy of the accepted offer is delivered to the buyer on or before the acceptance date. Line 21 also makes clear that an offer may be withdrawn prior to delivery of the accepted offer.

Lines 22–33 describe the alternative methods for delivery of the accepted offer to the buyer as well as delivery of other documents and written notices. The alternative methods for delivery include: (1) U.S. mail or commercial delivery, (2) personal delivery, and (3) fax transmission—but absent an amendment, fax transmission delivery is allowed only if a fax number is listed in the offer.

If a document or written notice is being mailed to a recipient, the document or written notice may be addressed to either the party or the party's designated recipient for delivery. Thus the party may choose the licensee with whom he or she is working, or any other person, as the recipient of his or her written notices or commercially delivered or mailed documents. The delivery address on line 28 is for receiving written notices or documents that are commercially delivered or mailed; the address is not relevant for fax or personal deliveries.

It is important to emphasize that a written notice or document that is commercially delivered or mailed must be addressed to either the party or the person designated as recipient for delivery at the party's designated address for delivery. If the documents are mailed to an address other than the one shown on line 28 or line 30, it will not constitute notice.

You should also be aware that personal delivery occurs when the person designated as recipient has actually been given the written notice or document. Finally, faxed written notices or documents are considered delivered when they are actually transmitted to the fax number designated by the party. If the notice or document is faxed to a number other than the one indicated in the offer, the delivery is ineffective and does not constitute notice.

Lines 34–36 include a provision for occupancy and related property including leased property and tenant's rights. It is important to note that lines 34–35 state that occupancy of the entire property will be given at closing unless indicated otherwise on lines 293–297. Lines 35–36 also state that occupancy is subject to tenant's rights, if any.

Lines 37–38 state that if the property is currently leased and the leases extend beyond the closing, the seller will assign his or her rights under the leases and transfer all prepaid rents and security deposits to the buyer at closing. If the property is rented, you should request a copy of the leases and state the terms of the lease if known. Information on leases could go on line 39 or lines 180–186 or in an addendum.

Lines 40–42 relate to the Rental Weatherization Standards administered by the Wisconsin Department of Commerce. If the property is not exempt from the standards, the buyer and seller must determine who is to be responsible for the weatherization requirements. Line 42 makes clear that if the seller is responsible for compliance, the seller must provide a Certificate of Compliance at closing; the certificate is good indefinitely. Note: residential property of one to four units that will be occupied by the buyer for at least one year after transfer is exempt from the weatherization program, as discussed in Chapter 8 of this book.

Lines 43–44 indicate where the transaction will be closed unless another place or date is agreed to in writing.

Lines 45–52 of the offer state that prorations are to be made as of the day prior to closing, which is consistent with the Internal Revenue Code's requirement that sellers prorate as of the date prior to closing. Lines 51–52 state that real estate tax proration may have to be based on an amount other than net general taxes for the current or previous year. Reassessed properties are an example of the type of potential problem recognized on lines 51–52.

Lines 54–58 were discussed on lines 23–27 of the listing contract. Lines 59–81 were discussed on lines 133–156 of the listing contract.

Lines 82–91 were discussed on lines 103–109 of the listing contract.

Lines 92–96 state that there are various formulas used to calculate square footage, total acreage, and so on, and they caution the buyer to verify total square footage, acreage, or building dimensions if they are material to the buyer's decision to purchase.

Lines 97–102 state that the seller agrees to allow the buyer's inspectors reasonable access to the property upon reasonable notice if reasonably necessary to satisfy the contingencies in the offer. The buyer agrees to provide copies of inspection reports to the seller, and listing broker if the property is listed.

Lines 100–102 define an *inspection* as an observation of the property that does not include testing of the property other than authorized testing such as for leaking carbon monoxide, leaking LP gas, or natural gas used for fuel.

Lines 103–110 state that the buyer is not authorized to conduct tests other than those types of tests authorized on lines 100–102. Lines 104–105 define a test. If a buyer requires testing, appropriate contingencies must be placed on lines 180–186, 317–320, or in an addendum per line 316. Testing contingencies should specify areas of the property to be tested as well as the purpose and any limitations on the buyer's testing. The seller acknowledges that certain tests may detect environmental pollution that may be referred to the Wisconsin Department of Natural Resources.

Lines 111–114 give the buyer the right to have a final inspection within three days before closing. This section also states that if the buyer finds damage beyond ordinary wear and tear during this inspection, the seller will be responsible for all repairs.

Lines 115–123 state that the seller will maintain the property until the earlier of closing or occupancy of the buyer. For example, a buyer who takes possession prior to closing cannot argue that the seller is responsible for damage that occurred due to the buyer's negligence. This section also states that the seller is to repair any damage not exceeding 5 percent of the selling price that occurs between acceptance and closing. This section also gives the buyer the option to cancel the contract if the damage amount is over 5 percent of the selling price.

Lines 124–133 define a fixture and include items that will be classified as fixtures. Lines 132–133 state that the terms of the offer will determine what items are either included in or excluded from the transaction.

Line 134 calls for the property address to be sure that pages 1 and 2 are connected to pages 3 and 4 of the offer to purchase.

Lines 135–139 state that "time is of the essence" for all dates and deadlines unless indicated otherwise on line 137. Lines 137–139 state that if time is of the essence does not apply to a date or deadline, the performance within a reasonable time of the date or deadline is allowed. If performance does not occur within a reasonable time, a breach will occur.

Lines 140–141 indicate that when a deadline is expressed as a number of "days" from an event such as acceptance of the offer, the date of the acceptance is excluded and subsequent calendar days are counted. For example, if the financing contingency deadline is "within 30 days of acceptance," the date of acceptance is excluded. You should be aware that deadlines expire at midnight of the last day.

Deadlines expressed as a specific number of "business days" exclude Saturdays, Sundays, and any legal public holiday under Wisconsin or federal law, or other holidays designated by the president such that the postal service does not receive registered mail or make regular deliveries on that day.

Deadlines expressed as a specific number of hours after the occurrence of an event are calculated from the exact time of the event and by counting 24 hours per calendar day. For example, if the deadline is within 48 hours of the buyer's actual receipt of notice and the notice is personally delivered to the buyer at 6:30 P.M. on Friday, the deadline would be 6:30 P.M. on Sunday.

The financing contingency is worded so as to comply with any loan program. However, programs that require specific additional provisions, such as FHA or VA requirements, will need to be supplemented with an addendum or other attachment. Lines 149–151 make clear that the contingency is based on the buyer obtaining a loan commitment rather than a loan. The financing contingency begins with basic terms, such as the deadline and loan amount, and concludes with the maximum loan fee the buyer will pay.

Lines 159–163 are used to indicate whether the financing is based on a fixed rate or on an adjustable rate of interest.

Lines 164–168 deal with responsibilities of the buyer with regard to obtaining a loan commitment. For example, line 164 states that the buyer agrees to apply for financing promptly and to provide evidence of application promptly upon request of the seller. Lines 173–179 refer to financing unavailability. If the buyer is unable to obtain financing from any lender, the buyer must promptly deliver written notice to the seller of the rejection with evidence such as a rejection letter from the lender. The seller then has ten days to provide the required loan unless a specific loan source was named in the financing contingency.

Licensees may use lines 180–186 to state a legal description if needed or contingencies not included in the offer such as an attorney's review of the offer for the buyer.

Lines 187–196 are similar to lines 17–21 of the listing contract, discussed earlier in Chapter 2.

Lines 197–212 make clear that the seller is responsible for all costs of providing evidence of title. The remainder of this section identifies the various deadlines that must be met by the parties to the transaction. For example, if title is not acceptable for closing, the buyer must notify the seller in writing of objections to title by the time set for closing.

Lines 204–206 suggest the use of a "gap endorsement." The gap insurance may be requested in the additional provisions section or in an addendum. The gap insurance can be paid by either the buyer or the seller.

Lines 213–218 state that the seller will pay special assessments actually commenced or levied prior to the date of the offer. The buyer is to pay all other special assessments.

Lines 219–227 state that any signed document transmitted by fax is to be treated as an original document, and any signatures on that document are to be considered original signatures. Once binding acceptance occurs, the party delivering the notice cannot withdraw the notice unless the party receiving the notice consents to the withdrawal.

Licensees cannot give legal advice, but if a licensee asks about his or her rights in the event of a default, licensees can refer to the language on lines 228–246 and suggest that the buyers and sellers seek legal advice if they have legal questions.

Lines 247–271 indicate that unless otherwise agreed, earnest money is to be paid to and held in the listing broker's trust account. If the property is not listed, the buyer's agent is to hold the earnest money. If there is no broker involved, the seller is to hold the earnest money. If the offer is not accepted and money has been paid by a check deposited in the listing broker's trust account, the earnest money will be transferred to the person who paid the earnest money upon the earnest money checks clearing the trust account of the listing broker. If the offer does not close, a written disbursement agreement signed by all parties will serve as the basis for the disbursement of the earnest money.

Line 263 makes clear that the buyer's or seller's legal right to the earnest money cannot be determined by the broker.

Lines 272–274 clearly state that the offer reflects the entire agreement of the parties to the transaction. Lines 273–274 stress that the agreement is binding on the parties' heirs as well as their estate.

Lines 278–292 state that if the sale of Buyer's Property Contingency is included in the offer, the Continued Marketing language is also automatically included unless indicated otherwise.

Lines 287–292 state that unless otherwise provided, the seller is not obligated to give the buyer notice before any deadline. Line 289 also makes clear that a secondary buyer has no rights over other secondary buyers regardless of the timing of the secondary offers.

Line 297 encourages licensees to consider a special agreement regarding occupancy escrow, and so on, when this contingency has been made part of the offer.

Lines 298–315 state that a home inspector should be requested in Wisconsin. The section also provides for a second inspection for some part of the property identified on lines 299–300. For example, a plumber could be asked to inspect the septic system.

Lines 306–310 make clear that if the buyer gives the seller a list of defects, the seller has substantial control over the transaction (lines 309–310). A notice of defects is provided on a WB-41 *Notice Relating to Offer to Purchase* shown in Figure 7.5. A copy of the inspection report must accompany the notice and they must be delivered by the deadline to both the seller and the listing broker. Line 303 states that a proposed amendment will not satisfy this notice requirement.

If the buyer does not give the seller a notice of defects prior to the deadline and the seller refuses to accept the proposed amendment, the buyer will have to purchase the property in its present condition.

Lines 304–305 make clear that the buyer must order the inspection and is responsible for the cost of that inspection, including any inspections required by the lender or as follow-up inspections to the home inspections. Line 305 states that this contingency only authorizes inspections, not testing. Thus if the buyer would like a separate inspection of the roof, this language would be placed on line 300. Lines 306–307 indicate that the seller has a right to cure the defects unless the offer indicates otherwise.

Finally, licensees should be aware that defects do not include structural, mechanical, or other conditions that the buyer had actual knowledge of or written notice of prior to signing the offer.

Line 316 provides for the licensee to include other documents such as a lead-based paint disclosure form as part of the offer to purchase.

Lines 317–320 may be used for contingencies not provided in the offer, such as review by the buyer's attorney to the satisfaction of the buyer.

Line 321 provides for the date on which the offer was drafted and by whom and on which form. Signatures of the buyer include Social Security numbers since Form 1099 may have to be sent to the Internal Revenue Service. Lines 326–327 provide an earnest money receipt if earnest money is collected by the broker.

If the sellers accept the offer, they will sign on lines 331–334 and include their Social Security numbers.

Line 335 requires the date and time at which the offer was presented, reflecting RL24 which requires offers to be presented promptly. If the sellers reject or counter the offer, they will place their initials and date on line 336.

WB-14 RESIDENTIAL CONDOMINIUM OFFER TO PURCHASE

Highlights of the Residential Condominium Offer to Purchase include the following:

Highlights of WB-14: Residential Condominium Offer to Purchase

- The sale of the unit includes the limited common elements assigned to the unit which is covered in the condominium declaration.
- Immediately after the closing, the buyer and the seller must notify the condominium of the transfer.
- Chapter 703 of the Wisconsin Statutes, which is very important to know, is reflected in lines 81–94.
- Also important are lines 279–284, which cover inspections and make clear that inspections are inspections of the unit and limited common elements assigned to the unit.
- Unique to this form is the condominium association's right of first refusal.

Line-by-Line Explanation of WB-14 Residential Condominium Offer to Purchase

Line 1 (see Figure 7.2) is similar to line 1 in the Residential Offer to Purchase form which was discussed above.

Lines 2–8 cover the general provision of the offer including the identification of the property. This section includes both the street address and the condominium unit description (letter, number, etc.).

Lines 6–8 cover the rights, interests, obligations, and limitations stated in the condominium declaration and plat.

Lines 9–13 are similar to lines 6–10 of the Residential Offer to Purchase.

Lines 14–19 state that the seller's interest in any common surplus and reserves as well as fixtures will be included in the purchase price. This section also states that the seller's interests are to be transferred free and clear of encumbrances; this requirement is not explicitly stated in the Residential Offer to Purchase.

Line 20 makes clear that the sale of the unit includes the limited common elements assigned to the unit that is covered in the condominium declaration. An example would include assigned parking stalls or storage units.

FIGURE 7.2

Sample Residential Condominium Offer to Purchase

Approved by the Wisconsin Department of Regulation and Licensing
4-1-00 (Optional Use Date)
9-1-00 (Mandatory Use Date)

Wisconsin Legal Blank Co., Inc.
Milwaukee, Wisconsin 53208

WB-14 RESIDENTIAL CONDOMINIUM OFFER TO PURCHASE

Page 1 of 6, WB-14

BROKER DRAFTING THIS OFFER ON ____________ [DATE] IS (AGENT OF SELLER) (AGENT OF BUYER) (DUAL AGENT) [STRIKE TWO]

GENERAL PROVISIONS The Buyer, ____________________, offers to purchase the Property known as [Street Address] ____________________ in the ____________________ of ____________________, County of ____________________, Wisconsin, particularly described as Unit: __________ (Building __________) of ____________________ Condominium; Seller's undivided interest in the common elements appurtenant to the Unit, together with and subject to the rights, interests, obligations and limitations as set forth in the declaration and condominium plat (and all amendments to them) creating the Condominium, which altogether constitute the Property, on the following terms:

■ PURCHASE PRICE: ____________________ Dollars ($ ____________________).

■ EARNEST MONEY of $ ____________ accompanies this Offer and earnest money of $____________ will be paid within ________ days of acceptance.

■ THE BALANCE OF PURCHASE PRICE will be paid in cash or equivalent at closing unless otherwise provided below.

■ ADDITIONAL ITEMS INCLUDED IN PURCHASE PRICE: Seller shall include in the purchase price and transfer free and clear of encumbrances Seller's interest in: any common surplus and reserves of the condominium allocated to the Unit; and all fixtures, as defined at lines 242 to 251and as may be in or on the Unit on the date of this Offer, unless excluded at lines 18-19, and the following additional items: ____________________.

■ ITEMS NOT INCLUDED IN THE PURCHASE PRICE: ____________________.

■ LIMITED COMMON ELEMENTS: Note, the limited common elements are those assigned in the condominium declaration.

■ PARKING: The parking for the Unit is: ____________________. The parking fee is:$____________.

■ ASSOCIATION FEE: The association fee for the Unit is $____________ per ____________.

BINDING ACCEPTANCE This Offer is binding upon both Parties only if a copy of the accepted Offer is delivered to Buyer on or before ____________. ***CAUTION: This Offer may be withdrawn prior to delivery of the accepted Offer.***

DELIVERY OF DOCUMENTS AND WRITTEN NOTICES Unless otherwise stated in this Offer, delivery of documents and written notices to a Party shall be effective only when accomplished by one of the methods specified at lines 27 - 36.

(1) By depositing the document or written notice postage or fees prepaid in the U.S. Mail or fees prepaid or charged to an account with a commercial delivery service, addressed either to the Party, or to the Party's recipient for delivery designated at lines 30 or 32 (if any), for delivery to the Party's delivery address at lines 31 or 33.

Seller's recipient for delivery (optional): ____________________

Seller's delivery address: ____________________

Buyer's recipient for delivery (optional): ____________________

Buyer's delivery address: ____________________

(2) By giving the document or written notice personally to the Party or the Party's recipient for delivery if an individual is designated at lines 30 or 32.

(3) By fax transmission of the document or written notice to the following telephone number:

Buyer: (________) ____________________ Seller: (________) ____________________

LEASED PROPERTY If Property is currently leased and lease(s) extends beyond closing, Seller shall assign Seller's rights under said lease(s) and transfer all security deposits and prepaid rents thereunder to Buyer at closing. The terms of the (written)(oral) [STRIKE ONE] lease(s), if any, are ____________________.

CAUTION: The Association may have the right to review and approve the terms of any lease of the unit.

PLACE OF CLOSING This transaction is to be closed at the place designated by Buyer's mortgagee or ____________________ no later than ____________________, __________ unless another date or place is agreed to in writing. Immediately after closing Buyer and Seller shall notify the condominium association of the transfer.

CLOSING PRORATIONS The following items shall be prorated at closing: real estate taxes, rents, water and sewer use charges, garbage pick-up and other private and municipal charges, property owner's or condominium association fees and assessments, fuel and ____________. Any income, taxes or expenses shall accrue to Seller and be prorated through the day prior to closing. Net general real estate taxes shall be prorated based on (the net general real estate taxes for the current year, if known, otherwise on the net general real estate taxes for the preceding year) (____________________).

[STRIKE AND COMPLETE AS APPLICABLE] ***CAUTION: If proration on the basis of net general real estate taxes is not acceptable (for example, completed/pending reassessment, changing mill rate, lottery credits), insert estimated annual tax or other formula for proration.***

PROPERTY CONDITION PROVISIONS

■ PROPERTY CONDITION REPRESENTATIONS: Seller represents to Buyer that as of the date of acceptance Seller has no notice or knowledge of conditions affecting the Property or transaction other than those identified in Seller's Real Estate Condition Report dated ____________, which was received by Buyer prior to Buyer signing this Offer and which is made a part of this Offer by reference [COMPLETE DATE OR STRIKE AS APPLICABLE] and ____________________ [INSERT CONDITIONS NOT ALREADY INCLUDED IN THE CONDITION REPORT].

FIGURE 7.2 (CONTINUED)

Sample Residential Condominium Offer to Purchase

■ A "condition affecting the Property or transaction" is defined as follows:

(a) planned or commenced public improvements by government authorities or the homeowner's or condominium association which may result in special assessments or otherwise materially affect the Property or the present use of the Property;

(b) completed or pending reassessment of the Property for property tax purposes;

(c) government agency, court, homeowner's or condominium association order requiring repair, alteration or correction of any existing condition related to the Property;

(d) construction or remodeling on Property for which required state or local permits had not been obtained;

(e) any land division involving the subject Property, for which required state or local approvals had not been obtained;

(f) violation of applicable state or local smoke detector laws; ***NOTE:State law requires operating smoke detectors on all levels of all residential properties.***

(g) any portion of the Condominium being in a 100 year floodplain, a wetland or a shoreland zoning area under local, state or federal laws;

(h) that a structure on the Property is designated as a historic building or that any part of Property is in a historic district;

(i) structural inadequacies which if not repaired will significantly shorten the expected normal life of the Condominium;

(j) mechanical systems inadequate for the present use of the Condominium;

(k) insect or animal infestation of the Condominium;

(l) conditions constituting a significant health or safety hazard for occupants of Property; ***Note: Specific federal lead paint disclosure requirements must be complied with in the sale of most residential properties built before 1978.***

(m)underground or aboveground storage tanks on the Condominium for storage of flammable or combustible liquids including but not limited to gasoline and heating oil which are currently or which were previously located on the Condominium; ***NOTE: Wis. Adm. Code, Chapter COMM 10 contains registration and operation rules for such underground and aboveground storage tanks.***

(n) material violations of environmental laws or other laws or agreements regulating the use of the Condominium;

(o) high voltage electric (100 KV or greater) or steel natural gas transmission lines located on but not directly serving the Condominium;

(p) other conditions or occurrences which would significantly reduce the value of the Property to a reasonable person with knowledge of the nature and scope of the condition or occurrence.

■ CONDOMINIUM DISCLOSURES: Seller agrees to provide Buyer with complete, current and accurate copies of the condominium disclosure materials required by Wisconsin Statute §703.33. The condominium disclosure materials are required to be delivered to Buyer no later than 15 days prior to closing. The condominium disclosure materials include copies of the condominium declaration, bylaws, rules and regulations, together with an index of contents, articles of incorporation, management contracts, current year's association budget (including reasonable details concerning monthly assessment charges and charges for rental of facilities), latest annual association operating statements, leases to which unit owners will be a party, description of any contemplated expansion of condominium, the unit floor plan with information necessary to show location of common elements and other facilities available to unit owners, and any amendments to any of these (except as limited for small residential condominiums per Wis Stat.§703.365). If the condominium was an occupied structure prior to the recording of the condominium declaration, it is a "conversion condominium" and the "condominium disclosure materials" also include: 1) a statement based on an engineer's or architect's report describing the present condition of structural, mechanical and electrical installations; 2) a statement of the useful life of the items covered in 1), unless a statement that no representations are being made is provided, and 3) a list of notices of code or other municipal violations, including an estimate of the costs of curing the violations. These materials are available at cost from the condominium association. As provided in Wisconsin Statutes §703.33(4), Buyer may, within five business days after receipt of these documents, including any material modification thereto, rescind this Offer by written notice mailed or delivered to Seller, the date of mailing or actual delivery being the effective date of notice.

■ ADDITIONAL CONDOMINIUM ISSUES: In addition to review of the disclosure materials required to be provided by Wisconsin Statute §703.33, Buyer may wish to consider reviewing other condominium materials as may be available, such as: copies of the condominium association's financial statements for previous years, the minutes of previous unit owner's meetings, the minutes of condominium board meetings during the months prior to acceptance, copies of the association's certificate of insurance, a statement from the association indicating the balance of reserve accounts controlled by the association, a statement from the association of the amount of any unpaid assessments on the unit (per Wis. Stats. §703.16(5)) and the declaration and bylaws of the master association, if any. Contingencies for review and approval of those additional materials which may be available may be provided for in additional contingencies per lines 157-163, or in an addendum per line 347. Because not all of these materials may exist or be available from the condominium association, Seller may wish to verify availability prior to acceptance if the Offer is contingent upon Seller providing these materials to Buyer.

■ REAL ESTATE CONDITION REPORT: Wisconsin law requires owners of property which includes 1-4 dwelling units to provide buyers with a Real Estate Condition Report. Wisconsin Statutes §709.03 provides that when the Property is a condominium unit, the property to which the real estate condition report applies is the condominium unit, the common elements of the condominium and any limited common elements that may be used only by the owner of the condominium unit being transferred. Excluded from this requirement are sales of property that has never been inhabited, sales exempt from the real estate transfer fee, and sales by certain court-appointed fiduciaries, (for example, personal representatives who have never occupied the Property). The form of the Report is found in Wisconsin Statutes §709.03. The law provides: "709.02 Disclosure . . . the owner of the property shall furnish, not later than 10 days after acceptance of the contract of sale . . . , to the prospective buyer of the property a completed copy of the report . . . A prospective buyer who does not receive a report within the ten days may, within two business days after the end of that 10 day period, rescind the contract of sale . . . by delivering a written notice of rescission to the owner or the owner's agent." Buyer may also have certain rescission rights if a Real Estate Condition Report disclosing defects is furnished before expiration of the 10 days, but after the Offer is submitted to Seller. Buyer should review the report form or consult with an attorney for additional information regarding these rescission rights.

■ PROPERTY DIMENSIONS AND SURVEYS: Buyer and Seller acknowledge that any land, unit or room dimensions, or total acreage or unit square footage figures, provided to Buyer or Seller, may be approximate because of rounding or other reasons, unless verified by survey or other means. Buyer and Seller also acknowledge that there are various formulas used to calculate total square footage of units and that total square footage figures will vary dependent upon the formula used. ***CAUTION: Buyer should verify total square footage formula, total square footage/acreage figures, land, unit or room dimensions, if material.***

ACCEPTANCE Acceptance occurs when all Buyers and Sellers have signed an identical copy of the Offer, including signatures on separate but identical copies of the Offer. ***CAUTION: Deadlines in the Offer are commonly calculated from acceptance. Consider whether short term deadlines running from acceptance provide adequate time for both binding acceptance and performance.***

FIGURE 7.2 (CONTINUED)

Sample Residential Condominium Offer to Purchase

Wisconsin Legal Blank Co., Inc.

PROPERTYADDRESS: ____ [page 3 of 6, WB-14]

THE FINANCING CONTINGENCY PROVISIONS AT LINES 127 - 156 ARE A PART OF THIS OFFER IF LINE 127 IS MARKED, SUCH AS WITH AN "X". THEYARE NOT PART OF THIS OFFER IF LINE 127 IS MARKED N/A OR IS NOT MARKED.

☐ **FINANCING CONTINGENCY:** This Offer is contingent upon Buyer being able to obtain a ____________________ [INSERT LOAN PROGRAM OR SOURCE] first mortgage loan commitment as described below, within _____ days of acceptance of this Offer. The financing selected shall be in an amount of not less than $ ____________________ for a term of not less than _______ years, amortized over not less than _______ years. Initial monthly payments of principal and interest shall not exceed $________________. Monthly payments may also include 1/12th of the estimated net annual real estate taxes, hazard insurance premiums, and private mortgage insurance premiums. The mortgage may not include a prepayment premium. Buyer agrees to pay a loan fee not to exceed ______ % of the loan. (Loan fee refers to discount points and/or loan origination fee, but DOES NOT include Buyer's other closing costs.) If the purchase price under this Offer is modified, the financed amount, unless otherwise provided, shall be adjusted to the same percentage of the purchase price as in this contingency and the monthly payments shall be adjusted as necessary to maintain the term and amortization stated above. **CHECK AND COMPLETE APPLICABLE FINANCING PROVISION AT LINE 137 OR 138.**

☐ **FIXED RATE FINANCING** The annual rate of interest shall not exceed _______________ %.

☐ **ADJUSTABLE RATE FINANCING** The initial annual interest rate shall not exceed _____________ %. The initial interest rate shall be fixed for ________ months, at which time the interest rate may be increased not more than _____________ % per year. The maximum interest rate during the mortgage term shall not exceed __________________ %. Monthly payments of principal and interest may be adjusted to reflect interest changes.

LOAN COMMITMENT: Buyer agrees to pay all customary financing costs (including closing fees), to apply for financing promptly, and to provide evidence of application promptly upon request of Seller. If Buyer qualifies for the financing described in this contingency or other financing acceptable to Buyer, Buyer agrees to deliver to Seller, or Seller's agent, a copy of the written loan commitment no later than the deadline for loan commitment at line 128. **Buyer's delivery of a copy of any written loan commitment to Seller shall satisfy the Buyer's financing contingency unless accompanied by a notice of unacceptability.** ***CAUTION: NEITHER BUYER, LENDER OR AGENTS OF BUYER OR SELLER SHOULD DELIVER A LOAN COMMITMENT TO SELLER WITHOUT BUYER'S PRIOR APPROVAL OR UNLESS ACCOMPANIED BY A NOTICE OF UNACCEPTABILITY.***

SELLER TERMINATION RIGHTS: If Buyer does not make timely delivery of the loan commitment, Seller may terminate this Offer provided that Seller delivers a written notice of termination to Buyer prior to Seller's actual receipt of a copy of Buyer's written loan commitment.

FINANCING UNAVAILABILITY: If financing is not available on the terms stated in this Offer (and Buyer has not already delivered an acceptable loan commitment for other financing to Seller), Buyer shall promptly deliver written notice to Seller of same including copies of lender(s)' rejection letter(s) or other evidence of unavailability. Unless a specific loan source is named in this Offer, Seller shall then have 10 days to give Buyer written notice of Seller's decision to finance this transaction on the same terms set forth in this Offer, and this Offer shall remain in full force and effect, with the time for closing extended accordingly. If Seller's notice is not timely given, this Offer shall be null and void. Buyer authorizes Seller to obtain any credit information reasonably appropriate to determine Buyer's credit worthiness for Seller financing.

ADDITIONAL PROVISIONS/CONTINGENCIES ____

____

____

____

____

____

____

TIME IS OF THE ESSENCE "Time is of the Essence" as to: (1) earnest money payment(s); (2) binding acceptance; (3) occupancy; (4) date of closing; (5) contingency deadlines; (6) delivery of condominium disclosure materials (see lines 81 to 94) [STRIKE AS APPLICABLE] and all other dates and deadlines in this Offer except: ____. If "Time is of the Essence" applies to a date or deadline, failure to perform by the exact date or deadline is a breach of contract. If "Time is of the Essence" does not apply to a date or deadline, then performance within a reasonable time of the date or deadline is allowed before a breach occurs.

RENTAL WEATHERIZATION This transaction (is) (is not) [STRIKE ONE] exempt from State of Wisconsin Rental Weatherization Standards (COMM 67, Wisconsin Administrative Code). If not exempt, (Buyer) (Seller) [STRIKE ONE] will be responsible for compliance, including all costs. If Seller is responsible for compliance, Seller shall provide a Certificate of Compliance at closing.

TITLE EVIDENCE

■ CONVEYANCE OF TITLE: Upon payment of the purchase price, Seller shall convey the Property by warranty deed (or other conveyance as provided herein) free and clear of all liens and encumbrances, except: municipal and zoning ordinances and agreements entered under them, recorded easements for the distribution of utility, municipal and association service, easements for performance of association duties, recorded building and use restrictions and covenants, general taxes levied in the year of closing, Wisconsin Condominium Act, condominium declaration and plat and association articles of incorporation, bylaws and rules and amendments to the above and ____________________ ____ (provided none of the foregoing prohibit present use of the Property), which constitutes merchantable title for purposes of this transaction. Seller further agrees to complete and execute the documents necessary to record the conveyance. ***WARNING: Municipal and zoning ordinances, recorded building and use restrictions, covenants and easements may prohibit certain improvements or uses and therefore should be reviewed, particularly if Buyer contemplates making improvements to Property or a use other than the current use.***

FIGURE 7.2 (CONTINUED)

Sample Residential Condominium Offer to Purchase

■ PROVISION OF MERCHANTABLE TITLE: Seller shall pay all costs of providing title evidence. For purposes of closing, title evidence shall be acceptable if the commitment for the required title insurance is delivered to Buyer's attorney or Buyer not less than 3 business days before closing, showing title to the Property as of a date no more than 15 days before delivery of such title evidence to be merchantable, subject only to liens which will be paid out of the proceeds of closing and standard title insurance requirements and exceptions, as appropriate. ***CAUTION: BUYER SHOULD CONSIDER UPDATING THE EFFECTIVE DATE OF THE TITLE COMMITMENT PRIOR TO CLOSING OR A "GAP ENDORSEMENT" WHICH WOULD INSURE OVER LIENS FILED BETWEEN THE EFFECTIVE DATE OF THE COMMITMENT AND THE DATE THE DEED IS RECORDED.***

■ FORM OF TITLE EVIDENCE: Seller shall give evidence of title in the form of an owner's policy of title insurance in the amount of the purchase price on a current ALTA form (including the ALTA Condominium 4 Endorsement or equivalent) issued by an insurer licensed to write title insurance in Wisconsin. ***CAUTION: IF TITLE EVIDENCE WILL BE GIVEN BY ABSTRACT, STRIKE TITLE INSURANCE PROVISIONS AND INSERT ABSTRACT PROVISIONS.***

■ TITLE ACCEPTABLE FOR CLOSING: If title is not acceptable for closing, Buyer shall notify Seller in writing of objections to title by the time set for closing. In such event, Seller shall have a reasonable time, but not exceeding 15 days, to remove the objections, and the time for closing shall be extended as necessary for this purpose. In the event that Seller is unable to remove the objections, Buyer shall have 5 days from receipt of notice thereof, to deliver written notice waiving the objections, and the time for closing shall be extended accordingly. If Buyer does not waive the objections, this Offer shall be null and void. Providing title evidence acceptable for closing does not extinguish Seller's obligations to give merchantable title to Buyer.

■ SPECIAL ASSESSMENTS: Special assessments, if any, including those by the homeowner's or condominium association, for work actually commenced or levied prior to date of this Offer shall be paid by Seller no later than closing. All other special assessments shall be paid by Buyer. ***CAUTION: Consider a special agreement if area assessments, property owner's or condominium owner's association assessments or other expenses are contemplated.*** "Other expenses" are one-time charges or ongoing use fees for public improvements (other than those resulting in special assessments) relating to curb, gutter, street, sidewalk, sanitary and stormwater and storm sewer (including all sewer mains and hook-up and interceptor charges), parks, street lighting and street trees, and impact fees for other public facilities, as defined in Wis. Stats. §66.55(1)(c) & (f).

OCCUPANCY Occupancy of the entire Property shall be given to Buyer at time of closing unless otherwise provided in this Offer (lines 324 - 327 or in an addendum per line 347). At time of Buyer's occupancy, the Unit and any limited common elements assigned exclusively to the Unit shall be free of all debris and personal property, except for personal property belonging to current tenants or personal property sold to Buyer or left with Buyer's consent. Occupancy shall be given subject to tenant's rights, if any.

DATES AND DEADLINES Deadlines expressed as a number of "days" from an event, such as acceptance, are calculated by excluding the day the event occurred and by counting subsequent calendar days. The deadline expires at midnight on the last day. Deadlines expressed as a specific number of "business days" exclude Saturdays, Sundays and any legal public holiday under Wisconsin or Federal law, or other day designated by the President such that the postal service does not receive registered mail or make regular deliveries on that day. Deadlines expressed as a specific number of "hours" from the occurrence of an event, such as receipt of a notice, are calculated from the exact time of the event, and by counting 24 hours per calendar day. Deadlines expressed as a specific day of the calendar year or as the day of a specific event, such as closing, expire at midnight of that day.

DELIVERY/RECEIPT Unless otherwise stated in this Offer, any signed document transmitted by facsimile machine (fax) shall be treated in all manner and respects as an original document and the signature of any Party upon a document transmitted by fax shall be considered an original signature. Personal delivery to, or actual receipt by, any named Buyer or Seller constitutes personal delivery to, or actual receipt by Buyer or Seller. Once received, a notice cannot be withdrawn by the Party delivering the notice without the consent of the Party receiving the notice. A Party may not unilaterally reinstate a contingency after a notice of a contingency waiver has been received by the other Party. **The delivery/receipt provisions in this Offer may be modified when appropriate (e.g., when mail delivery is not desirable (see lines 27 - 33) or when a party will not be personally available to receive a notice (see line 317)).** Buyer and Seller authorize the agents of Buyer and Seller to distribute copies of the Offer to Buyer's lender, appraisers, title insurance companies and any other settlement service providers for the transaction as defined by the Real Estate Settlement Procedures Act (RESPA).

ENTIRE CONTRACT This Offer, including any amendments to it, contains the entire agreement of the Buyer and Seller regarding the transaction. All prior negotiations and discussions have been merged into this Offer. This agreement binds and inures to the benefit of the Parties to this Offer and their successors in interest.

DEFAULT ***IF ACCEPTED, THIS OFFER CAN CREATE A LEGALLY ENFORCEABLE CONTRACT. BOTH PARTIES SHOULD READ THIS DOCUMENT CAREFULLY. BROKERS MAY PROVIDE A GENERAL EXPLANATION OF THE PROVISIONS OF THE OFFER BUT ARE PROHIBITED BY LAW FROM GIVING ADVICE OR OPINIONS CONCERNING YOUR LEGAL RIGHTS UNDER THIS OFFER OR HOW TITLE SHOULD BE TAKEN AT CLOSING. AN ATTORNEY SHOULD BE CONSULTED IF LEGAL ADVICE IS NEEDED.*** Seller and Buyer each have the legal duty to use good faith and due diligence in completing the terms and conditions of this Offer. A material failure to perform any obligation under this Offer is a default which may subject the defaulting party to liability for damages or other legal remedies.

If Buyer defaults, Seller may:

(1) sue for specific performance and request the earnest money as partial payment of the purchase price; or

(2) terminate the Offer and have the option to: (a) request the earnest money as liquidated damages; or (b) direct Broker to return the earnest money and have the option to sue for actual damages.

If Seller defaults, Buyer may:

(1) sue for specific performance; or

(2) terminate the Offer and request the return of the earnest money, sue for actual damages, or both.

In addition, the Parties may seek any other remedies available in law or equity.

The Parties understand that the availability of any judicial remedy will depend upon the circumstances of the situation and the discretion of the courts. If either Party defaults, the Parties may renegotiate the Offer or seek nonjudicial dispute resolution instead of the remedies outlined above. By agreeing to binding arbitration, the Parties may lose the right to litigate in a court of law those disputes covered by the arbitration agreement.

FIGURE 7.2 (CONTINUED)

Sample Residential Condominium Offer to Purchase

FIXTURES

A "Fixture" is defined as an item of property, which may or may not be a common element of the Condominium, which is physically attached to or so closely associated with land or improvements so as to be treated as part of the real estate, including, without limitation, physically attached items not easily removable without damage to the Property, items specifically adapted to the Property, and items customarily treated as fixtures including, but not limited to, all: garden bulbs; plants; shrubs and trees; screen and storm doors and windows; electric lighting fixtures; window shades; curtain and traverse rods; blinds and shutters; central heating and cooling units and attached equipment; water heaters and softeners; sump pumps; attached or fitted floor coverings; awnings; attached antennas, satellite dishes and component parts; garage door openers and remote controls; installed security systems; central vacuum systems and accessories; in-ground sprinkler systems and component parts; built-in appliances; ceiling fans; fences; storage buildings on permanent foundations and docks/piers on permanent foundations. ***NOTE: The terms of the Offer will determine what items are included/excluded. Address rented fixtures (e.g., water softeners), if any.***

EARNEST MONEY

■ HELD BY: Unless otherwise agreed, earnest money shall be paid to and held in the trust account of the listing broker (buyer's agent if Property is not listed or Seller's account if no broker is involved), until applied to purchase price or otherwise disbursed as provided in the Offer. ***CAUTION: Should persons other than a broker hold earnest money, an escrow agreement should be drafted by the Parties or an attorney. If some - one other than Buyer makes payment of earnest money, consider a special disbursement agreement.***

■ DISBURSEMENT: If negotiations do not result in an accepted offer, the earnest money shall be promptly disbursed (after clearance from payor's depository institution if earnest money is paid by check) to the person(s) who paid the earnest money. At closing, earnest money shall be disbursed according to the closing statement. If this Offer does not close, the earnest money shall be disbursed according to a written disbursement agreement signed by all Parties to this Offer (Note: Wis. Adm. Code s. RL 18.09(1)(b) provides that an offer to purchase is not a written disbursement agreement pursuant to which the broker may disburse). If the disbursement agreement has not been delivered to broker within 60 days after the date set for closing, broker may disburse the earnest money: (1) as directed by an attorney who has reviewed the transaction and does not represent Buyer or Seller; (2) into a court hearing a lawsuit involving the earnest money and all Parties to this Offer; (3) as directed by court order; or (4) any other disbursement required or allowed by law. Broker may retain legal services to direct disbursement per (1) or to file an interpleader action per (2) and broker may deduct from the earnest money any costs and reasonable attorneys fees, not to exceed $250, prior to disbursement.

■ LEGAL RIGHTS/ACTION: Broker's disbursement of earnest money does not determine the legal rights of the Parties in relation to this Offer. Buyer's or Seller's legal right to earnest money cannot be determined by broker. At least 30 days prior to disbursement per (1) or (4) above, broker shall send Buyer and Seller notice of the disbursement by certified mail. If Buyer or Seller disagree with broker's proposed disbursement, a lawsuit may be filed to obtain a court order regarding disbursement. Small Claims Court has jurisdiction over all earnest money disputes arising out of the sale of residential property with 1-4 dwelling units and certain other earnest money disputes. The Buyer and Seller should consider consulting attorneys regarding their legal rights under this Offer in case of a dispute. Both Parties agree to hold the broker harmless from any liability for good faith disbursement of earnest money in accordance with this Offer or applicable Department of Regulation and Licensing regulations concerning earnest money. See Wis. Adm. Code Ch. RL 18.

NOTE: WISCONSIN LICENSE LAW PROHIBITS A BROKER FROM GIVING ADVICE OR OPINIONS CONCERNING THE LEGAL RIGHTS OR OBLIGATIONS OF PARTIES TO A TRANSACTION OR THE LEGAL EFFECT OF A SPECIFIC CONTRACT OR CONVEYANCE. AN ATTORNEY SHOULD BE CONSULTED IF LEGAL ADVICE IS REQUIRED.

ADDITIONAL PROPERTY CONDITION PROVISIONS

■ INSPECTIONS: Seller agrees to allow Buyer's inspectors reasonable access to the Unit and limited common elements assigned to the Unit, upon reasonable notice, if the inspections are reasonably necessary to satisfy the contingencies in this Offer. Buyer agrees to promptly provide copies of all such inspection reports to Seller, and to listing broker if Property is listed. Furthermore, Buyer agrees to promptly restore the Unit to it's original condition after Buyer's inspections are completed, unless otherwise agreed with Seller. An "inspection" is defined as an observation of the Unit which does not include testing of the Property other than testing for leaking carbon monoxide, or testing for leaking LP gas or natural gas used as a fuel source, which are hereby authorized.

■ TESTING: Except as otherwise provided, Seller's authorization for inspections does not authorize Buyer to conduct testing of the Property. A "test" is defined as the taking of samples of materials such as soils, water, air or building materials from the Property and the laboratory or other analysis of these materials. If Buyer requires testing, testing contingencies must be specifically provided for at lines 157 - 163 or in an addendum per line 347. Note: Any contingency authorizing such tests should specify the areas of the Property to be tested, the purpose of the test, (e.g. to determine if environmental contamination is present), any limitations on Buyer's testing and any other material terms of the contingency (e.g. Buyer's obligation to return the Property to its original condition). Seller acknowledges that certain inspections or tests may detect environmental pollution which may be required to be reported to the Wisconsin Department of Natural Resources.

■ PRE-CLOSING INSPECTION: At a reasonable time, pre-approved by Seller or Seller's agent, within 3 days before closing, Buyer shall have the right to inspect the Unit to determine that there has been no significant change in the condition of the Unit and the limited common elements assigned to the Unit, except for ordinary wear and tear and changes approved by Buyer, and that any defects Seller has elected to cure have been repaired in a good and workmanlike manner.

■ PROPERTY DAMAGE BETWEEN ACCEPTANCE AND CLOSING: Seller shall maintain the Unit and the limited common elements assigned to the Unit until the earlier of closing or occupancy of Buyer in materially the same condition as of the date of acceptance of this Offer, except for ordinary wear and tear. If, prior to the earlier of closing or occupancy of Buyer, the Unit is damaged in an amount of not more than five per cent (5%) of the selling price, Seller shall be obligated to repair the Unit and restore it to the same condition that it was on the day of this Offer. If the damage shall exceed such sum, Seller shall promptly notify Buyer in writing of the damage and this Offer may be canceled at option of Buyer. Should Buyer elect to carry out this Offer despite such damage, Buyer shall be entitled to the insurance proceeds relating to the damage to the Unit, plus a credit towards the purchase price equal to the amount of Seller's deductible on such policy. However, if this sale is financed by a land contract or a mortgage to Seller, the insurance proceeds shall be held in trust for the sole purpose of restoring the Unit.

FIGURE 7.2 (CONTINUED)

Sample Residential Condominium Offer to Purchase

PROPERTY ADDRESS: ______________________________ [page 6 of 6, WB-14]

OPTIONAL PROVISIONS: THE PROVISIONS ON LINES 307 THROUGH 347 ARE A PART OF THIS OFFER IF MARKED, SUCH AS WITH AN "X". THEY ARE NOT PART OF THIS OFFER IF MARKED N/A OR ARE LEFT BLANK (EXCEPT AS PROVIDED AT LINES 311 - 312).

☐ **ASSOCIATION APPROVAL OF SALE OF UNIT CONTINGENCY:** This Offer is contingent upon Seller delivering to Buyer a waiver of the association's right of first refusal within _______ days of acceptance. Seller shall promptly submit the Offer and waiver request to the association.

☐ **SALE OF BUYER'S PROPERTY CONTINGENCY:** This Offer is contingent upon the sale and closing of Buyer's property located at ______________________________, no later than ______________. Seller may keep Seller's Property on the market for sale and accept secondary offers. **If this contingency is made a part of this Offer, lines 313 - 317 are also a part of this offer unless marked N/A at line 313 or otherwise deleted.**

☐ **CONTINUED MARKETING:** If Seller accepts a bona fide secondary offer, Seller may give written notice to the Buyer of acceptance. If Buyer does not deliver to Seller a written waiver of sale of Buyer's property contingency and ______________________________ **[INSERT OTHER REQUIREMENTS, IF ANY (e.g., PAYMENT OF ADDITIONAL EARNEST MONEY, WAIVER OF ALL CONTINGENCIES, OR PROVIDING EVIDENCE OF SALE OR BRIDGE LOAN, etc.)]** within ___________ hours of Buyer's actual receipt of the notice, this Offer shall be null and void.

☐ **SECONDARY OFFER:** This Offer is secondary to a prior accepted offer. This Offer shall become primary upon delivery of written notice to Buyer that this Offer is primary. Unless otherwise provided, Seller is not obligated to give Buyer notice prior to any deadline, nor is any particular secondary Buyer given the right to be made primary ahead of other secondary buyers. Buyer may declare this Offer null and void by delivering written notice of withdrawal to Seller prior to delivery of Seller's notice that this Offer is primary. Buyer may not deliver notice of withdrawal earlier than _______ days after acceptance of this Offer. All other Offer deadlines which are run from acceptance shall run from the time this Offer becomes primary.

☐ **PRE/POST CLOSING OCCUPANCY:** Occupancy of ______________________________ shall be given to Buyer on __________________ at _____ am/pm. At closing (Seller)(Buyer) [STRIKE ONE] shall pay an occupancy charge of $__________ per day or partial day of pre/post-closing occupancy. Any unearned post closing occupancy fee (shall) (shall not) [STRIKE ONE] be refunded based on actual occupancy. ***CAUTION: Consider a special agreement regarding occupancy escrow, insurance, utilities, maintenance, keys, etc.***

☐ **INSPECTION CONTINGENCY:** This Offer is contingent upon a Wisconsin registered home inspector performing a home inspection of the Unit and the limited common elements assigned to the Unit, and an inspection, by a qualified independent inspector, of: ______________________________ which discloses no defects as defined below. This contingency shall be deemed satisfied unless Buyer, within _____ days of acceptance, delivers to Seller, and to listing broker if the Unit is listed, a copy of the inspector's written inspection report(s) and a written notice listing the defect(s) identified in the inspection report(s) to which Buyer objects. ***CAUTION: A proposed amendment will not satisfy this notice requirement.*** Buyer shall order the inspection and be responsible for all costs of inspection, including any inspections required by lender or as follow-up inspections to the home inspection. **Note: This contingency only authorizes inspections, not testing, see lines 279 - 291.**

■ RIGHT TO CURE: Seller (shall) (shall not) [STRIKE ONE] have a right to cure the defects. (Seller shall have a right to cure if no choice is indicated.) If Seller has right to cure, Seller may satisfy this contingency by: (1) delivering a written notice of Seller's election to cure defects within 10 days of receipt of Buyer's notice, (2) curing the defects in a good and workmanlike manner and (3) delivering to Buyer a written report detailing the work done no later than 3 days prior to closing. This Offer shall be null and void if Buyer makes timely delivery of the above notice and report and: (1) Seller does not have a right to cure or (2) Seller has a right to cure but: a) Seller delivers notice that Seller will not cure or b) Seller does not timely deliver the notice of election to cure.

■ "DEFECT" DEFINED: For the purposes of this contingency, a defect is defined as a structural, mechanical or other condition that would have a significant adverse effect on the value of the Property; that would significantly impair the health or safety of future occupants of the Unit; or that if not repaired, removed or replaced would significantly shorten or have a significant adverse effect on the expected normal life of the Unit. Defects do not include structural, mechanical or other conditions the nature and extent of which Buyer had actual knowledge or written notice before signing this Offer.

☐ **ADDENDA:** The attached ______________________________ is/are made part of this Offer.

This Offer was drafted on _________ [date] by [Licensee and firm] ______________________________.

(x)______________________________ ____________________ ____________
Buyer's Signature ▲ Print Name Here: ▶ Social Security No. or FEIN (optional)▲ Date ▲

(x)______________________________ ____________________ ____________
Buyer's Signature ▲ Print Name Here: ▶ Social Security No. or FEIN (optional)▲ Date ▲

EARNEST MONEY RECEIPT Broker acknowledges receipt of earnest money as per line 11 of the above Offer. (See lines 252 - 277)

______________________________ Broker (By) ______________________________

SELLER ACCEPTS THIS OFFER. THE WARRANTIES, REPRESENTATIONS AND COVENANTS MADE IN THIS OFFER SURVIVE CLOSING AND THE CONVEYANCE OF THE PROPERTY. SELLER AGREES TO CONVEY THE PROPERTY ON THE TERMS AND CONDITIONS AS SET FORTH HEREIN AND ACKNOWLEDGES RECEIPT OF A COPY OF THIS OFFER.

(x)______________________________ ____________________ ____________
Seller's Signature ▲ Print Name Here: ▶ Social Security No. or FEIN (optional)▲ Date ▲

(x)______________________________ ____________________ ____________
Seller's Signature ▲ Print Name Here: ▶ Social Security No. or FEIN (optional)▲ Date ▲

This Offer was presented to Seller by ______________________________ on _______________, _______, at _____ a.m./p.m.

THIS OFFER IS REJECTED ___________ ___________ THIS OFFER IS COUNTERED [See attached counter] ___________ ___________
Seller Initials ▲ Date▲ Seller Initials ▲ Date▲

Line 21 indicates whether parking rights are included with the unit and, if so, the description of the parking space as well as the fee is relevant.

Line 22 states the amount of the assessment on the unit that is generally payable on a monthly basis.

Lines 23–36 have language that is similar to the Residential Offer to Purchase as discussed.

Lines 41–80 have language which is similar to the Residential Offer to Purchase as discussed.

Lines 81–94 indicate the condominium disclosures required by Wisconsin Statute 703.33. It is important to note that the buyer may, "within five business days after receipt of these documents, including any material modification thereto, rescind the offer by written notice mailed or delivered to the seller the date of mailing or actual receipt being the effective date of notice." You should be aware that the buyer does not have to indicate a reason for the rescission.

Lines 95–103 (Additional Condominium Issues) state that the buyer may wish to consider reviewing other condominium materials as may be available, such as copies of the condominium association's financial statements for previous years. Contingencies for review and approval of these additional materials may be placed on lines 157–163 in an addendum as indicated on line 347.

Lines 104–115 cover the Real Estate Condition Report. You should be aware that Wisconsin Statute 709.03 provides that when the property is a condominium unit, the property to which the real estate condition report applies is the condominium unit, the common elements of the condominium, and any limited common elements that may be used only by the owner of the condominium unit being transferred (line 105–107).

Lines 116–120 on property dimensions and surveys are similar to the Residential Offer to Purchase.

Lines 121–196 are also similar to the Residential Offer to Purchase discussed above.

Lines 197–202 on special assessments are not found in the Residential Offer to Purchase.

Lines 199–200 urge the buyer to consider a special agreement if area assessments or other expenses are contemplated.

Lines 199–200 state that if, for example, the minutes of the condominium owners association indicate that the roof will be replaced, the seller and buyer should enter into a special agreement regarding the cost of the anticipated roof assessment.

Lines 203–206 also differ from the Residential Offer to Purchase. They indicate that when the buyer takes occupancy, the unit and any limited common elements assigned exclusively to the unit shall be free of all debris and personal property, except for personal property belonging to current tenants or personal property sold to the buyer or left with the buyer's consent.

Lines 207–241: Dates and deadlines covering delivery, receipt and default are similar to the Residential Offer to Purchase.

Lines 242–251: The fixtures section refers to common elements; the rest of the language is similar to the offer to purchase.

Lines 252–277: Earnest money is similar to the Residential Offer to Purchase.

Lines 279–284 on inspections is similar to the Residential Offer to Purchase except for providing reasonable access to the unit and limited common elements assigned to the unit.

Lines 285–303 are also similar to the residential offer. Line 293 refers to the unit and limited common elements assigned to the unit.

Lines 304–364 also are similar to the Residential Offer to Purchase with the exception of lines 307–308 that provide a contingency for an association approval of the sale of the unit.

WB-13 VACANT LAND OFFER TO PURCHASE

The Vacant Land Offer to Purchase form is similar to the Residential Offer to Purchase form but differs in that there is no residential or commercial structure, etc., involved.

The Vacant Land Offer to Purchase concentrates on the adaptability of land as a residential or commercial development, etc.

Line-by-Line Explanation of WB-13 Vacant Land Offer to Purchase

Lines 1–18 (see Figure 7.3) are similar to the language in lines 1–14 in the Residential Offer to Purchase as discussed above.

Line 19 states how the land is zoned.

The provisions on lines 20–88 are basically the same as the provisions in the Residential Offer to Purchase.

Lines 89–97 vary significantly from the Residential Offer to Purchase. These lines cover issues related to property development; they warn a buyer considering the purchase or development of a property to ensure the development or new use is feasible. The buyer is made aware of issues such as zoning, restrictions, easements, environmental audits, and subsoil tests. The buyer is informed of optional contingencies as well as the opportunity to add contingencies.

Lines 98–103 cover inspections; this section, of course, differs from the general structural inspections contingency in the residential and condominium offers to purchase. The seller agrees to allow the buyers' inspectors reasonable access to

FIGURE 7.3

Sample Vacant Land Offer to Purchase

Approved by Wisconsin Department of Regulation and Licensing
7-1-99 (Optional Use Date)
1-1-00 (Mandatory Use Date)

Wisconsin Legal Blank Co., Inc.
Milwaukee, Wis.

WB-13 VACANT LAND OFFER TO PURCHASE

Page 1 of 5

BROKER DRAFTING THIS OFFER ON __________ [DATE] IS (AGENT OF SELLER) (AGENT OF BUYER) (DUAL AGENT) STRIKE TWO

GENERAL PROVISIONS The Buyer ____________________, offers to purchase the Property known as [Street Address] ____________________ __________ in the __________ of ____________________, County of _______________, Wisconsin, (Insert additional description, if any, at lines 179 - 187 or attach as an addendum, line 188), on the following terms:

■ PURCHASE PRICE: ____ Dollars ($_______________).

■ EARNEST MONEY of $_______________ accompanies this Offer and earnest money of $_______________ will be paid within ______ days of acceptance.

■ THE BALANCE OF PURCHASE PRICE will be paid in cash or equivalent at closing unless otherwise provided below.

■ ADDITIONAL ITEMS INCLUDED IN PURCHASE PRICE: Seller shall include in the purchase price and transfer, free and clear of encumbrances, all fixtures, as defined at lines 15 - 18 and as may be on the Property on the date of this Offer, unless excluded at line 14, and the following additional items: ____________________

■ ITEMS NOT INCLUDED IN THE PURCHASE PRICE: ____________________

A "Fixture" is defined as an item of property which is physically attached to or so closely associated with land so as to be treated as part of the real estate, including, without limitation, physically attached items not easily removable without damage to the Property, items specifically adapted to the Property, and items customarily treated as fixtures including but not limited to all: perennial crops; garden bulbs; plants; shrubs and trees. CAUTION: Annual crops are not included in the purchase price unless otherwise agreed at line 13.

■ ZONING: Seller represents that the Property is zoned ____________________.

ACCEPTANCE Acceptance occurs when all Buyers and Sellers have signed an identical copy of the Offer, including signatures on separate but identical copies of the Offer. ***CAUTION: Deadlines in the Offer are commonly calculated from acceptance. Consider whether short term deadlines running from acceptance provide adequate time for both binding acceptance and performance.***

BINDING ACCEPTANCE This Offer is binding upon both Parties only if a copy of the accepted Offer is delivered to Buyer on or before ____________________. ***CAUTION: This Offer may be withdrawn prior to delivery of the accepted Offer.***

DELIVERY OF DOCUMENTS AND WRITTEN NOTICES Unless otherwise stated in this Offer, delivery of documents and written notices to a Party shall be effective only when accomplished by one of the methods specified at lines 27 - 36.

(1) By depositing the document or written notice postage or fees prepaid in the U.S. Mail or fees prepaid or charged to an account with a commercial delivery service, addressed either to the Party, or to the Party's recipient for delivery designated at lines 30 or 32 (if any), for delivery to the Party's delivery address at lines 31 or 33.

Seller's recipient for delivery (optional): ____________________

Seller's delivery address: ____________________

Buyer's recipient for delivery (optional): ____________________

Buyer's delivery address: ____________________

(2) By giving the document or written notice personally to the Party or the Party's recipient for delivery if an individual is designated at lines 30 or 32.

(3) By fax transmission of the document or written notice to the following telephone number:

Buyer: (______)_______________ Seller: (______)_______________

OCCUPANCY Occupancy of the entire Property shall be given to Buyer at time of closing unless otherwise provided in this Offer (lines 179 - 187 or in an addendum per line 188). Occupancy shall be given subject to tenant's rights, if any. **Caution: Consider an agreement which addresses responsibility for clearing the Property of personal property and debris, if applicable.**

LEASED PROPERTY If Property is currently leased and lease(s) extend beyond closing, Seller shall assign Seller's rights under said lease(s) and transfer all security deposits and prepaid rents thereunder to Buyer at closing. The terms of the (written) (oral) STRIKE ONE lease(s), if any, are ____________________.

PLACE OF CLOSING This transaction is to be closed at the place designated by Buyer's mortgagee or _______________ _______________ no later than _______________, __________ unless another date or place is agreed to in writing.

CLOSING PRORATIONS The following items shall be prorated at closing: real estate taxes, rents, private and municipal charges, property owner's association assessments, fuel and ____________________ _______________. Any income, taxes or expenses shall accrue to Seller, and be prorated, through the day prior to closing. Net general real estate taxes shall be prorated based on (the net general real estate taxes for the current year, if known, otherwise on the net general real estate taxes for the preceding year) (____________________ ____________________). STRIKE AND COMPLETE AS APPLICABLE

CAUTION: If proration on the basis of net general real estate taxes is not acceptable (for example, completed/pending reassessment, changing mill rate, lottery credits), insert estimated annual tax or other formula for proration.

PROPERTY CONDITION PROVISIONS

■ PROPERTY CONDITION REPRESENTATIONS: Seller represents to Buyer that as of the date of acceptance Seller has no notice or knowledge of conditions affecting the Property or transaction (see below) other than those identified in Seller's Real Estate Condition Report dated _______________, which was received by Buyer prior to Buyer signing this Offer and which is made a part of this Offer by reference COMPLETE DATE OR STRIKE AS APPLICABLE and ____________________ ____________________ INSERT CONDITIONS NOT ALREADY INCLUDED IN THE CONDITION REPORT.

FIGURE 7.3 (CONTINUED)

Sample Vacant Land Offer to Purchase

A "condition affecting the Property or transaction" is defined as follows: [page 2 of 5, WB-13]

(a) planned or commenced public improvements which may result in special assessments or otherwise materially affect the Property or the present use of the Property;
(b) completed or pending reassessment of the Property for property tax purposes;
(c) government agency or court order requiring repair, alteration or correction of any existing condition;
(d) any land division involving the subject Property, for which required state or local approvals had not been obtained;
(e) any portion of the Property being in a 100 year floodplain, a wetland or a shoreland zoning area under local, state or federal laws;
(f) conditions constituting a significant health or safety hazard for occupants of Property;
(g) underground or aboveground storage tanks on the Property for storage of flammable or combustible liquids including but not limited to gasoline and heating oil which are currently or which were previously located on the Property; ***NOTE: Wis. Adm. Code, Chapter Comm 10 contains registration and operation rules for such underground and aboveground storage tanks.***
(h) material violations of environmental laws or other laws or agreements regulating the use of the Property;
(i) high voltage electric (100 KV or greater) or steel natural gas transmission lines located on but not directly serving the Property;
(j) any portion of the Property being subject to, or in violation of, a Farmland Preservation Agreement under a County Farmland Preservation Plan or enrolled in, or in violation of, a Forest Crop, Woodland Tax, Managed Forest, Conservation Reserve or comparable program;
(k) boundary disputes or material violation of fence laws (Wis. Stats. Chapter 90) which require the erection and maintenance of legal fences between adjoining properties where one or both of the properties is used and occupied for farming or grazing purposes;
(l) wells on the Property required to be abandoned under state regulations (Wis. Adm. Code NR 112.26) but which are not abandoned;
(m) cisterns or septic tanks on the Property which are currently not servicing the Property;
(n) subsoil conditions which would significantly increase the cost of the development proposed at lines 271-272, if any, including, but not limited to, subsurface foundations, organic and non-organic fill, dumpsites or containers on Property which contained or currently contain toxic or hazardous materials, high groundwater, soil conditions (e.g. low load bearing capacity) or excessive rocks or rock formations on the Property;
(o) a lack of legal vehicular access to the Property from public roads;
(p) prior reimbursement for corrective action costs under the Agricultural Chemical Cleanup Program; (Wis. Stats. §94.73.)
(q) other conditions or occurrences which would significantly increase the cost of the development proposed at lines 271 to 272 or reduce the value of the Property to a reasonable person with knowledge of the nature and scope of the condition or occurrence.

■ PROPERTY DIMENSIONS AND SURVEYS: Buyer acknowledges that any land dimensions, total square footage/acreage figures, or allocation of acreage information, provided to Buyer by Seller or by a broker, may be approximate because of rounding or other reasons, unless verified by survey or other means. ***CAUTION: Buyer should verify land dimensions, total square footage/acreage figures or allocation of acreage if material to Buyer's decision to purchase.***

■ ISSUES RELATED TO PROPERTY DEVELOPMENT: WARNING: If Buyer contemplates developing Property or a use other than the current use, there are a variety of issues which should be addressed to ensure the development or new use is feasible. Municipal and zoning ordinances, recorded building and use restrictions, covenants and easements may prohibit certain improvements or uses and therefore should be reviewed. Building permits, zoning variances, Architectural Control Committee approvals, estimates for utility hook-up expenses, special assessments, charges for installation of roads or utilities, environmental audits, subsoil tests, or other development related fees may need to be obtained or verified in order to determine the feasibility of development of, or a particular use for, a property. Optional contingencies which allow Buyer to investigate certain of these issues can be found at lines 271 - 314 and Buyer may add contingencies as needed in addenda (see line 188). Buyer should review any plans for development or use changes to determine what issues should be addressed in these contingencies.

■ INSPECTIONS: Seller agrees to allow Buyer's inspectors reasonable access to the Property upon reasonable notice if the inspections are reasonably necessary to satisfy the contingencies in this Offer. Buyer agrees to promptly provide copies of all such inspection reports to Seller, and to listing broker if Property is listed. Furthermore, Buyer agrees to promptly restore the Property to its original condition after Buyer's inspections are completed, unless otherwise agreed in this Offer. An "inspection" is defined as an observation of the Property which does not include testing of the Property, other than testing for leaking LP gas or natural gas used as a fuel source, which are hereby authorized.

■ TESTING: Except as otherwise provided, Seller's authorization for inspections does not authorize Buyer to conduct testing of the Property. A "test" is defined as the taking of samples of materials such as soils, water, air or building materials from the Property and the laboratory or other analysis of these materials. If Buyer requires testing, testing contingencies must be specifically provided for at lines 179-187 or in an addendum per line 188. Note: Any contingency authorizing testing should specify the areas of the Property to be tested, the purpose of the test, (e.g., to determine if environmental contamination is present), any limitations on Buyer's testing and any other material terms of the contingency (e.g., Buyer's obligation to return the Property to its original condition). Seller acknowledges that certain inspections or tests may detect environmental pollution which may be required to be reported to the Wisconsin Department of Natural Resources.

■ PRE-CLOSING INSPECTION: At a reasonable time, pre-approved by Seller or Seller's agent, within 3 days before closing, Buyer shall have the right to inspect the Property to determine that there has been no significant change in the condition of the Property, except for changes approved by Buyer.

■ PROPERTY DAMAGE BETWEEN ACCEPTANCE AND CLOSING: Seller shall maintain the Property until the earlier of closing or occupancy of Buyer in materially the same condition as of the date of acceptance of this Offer, except for ordinary wear and tear. If, prior to closing, the Property is damaged in an amount of not more than five per cent (5%) of the selling price, Seller shall be obligated to repair the Property and restore it to the same condition that it was on the day of this Offer. If the damage shall exceed such sum, Seller shall promptly notify Buyer in writing of the damage and this Offer may be canceled at option of Buyer. Should Buyer elect to carry out this Offer despite such damage, Buyer shall be entitled to the insurance proceeds relating to the damage to the Property, plus a credit towards the purchase price equal to the amount of Seller's deductible on such policy. However, if this sale is financed by a land contract or a mortgage to Seller, the insurance proceeds shall be held in trust for the sole purpose of restoring the Property.

FENCES Wisconsin Statutes section 90.03 requires the owners of adjoining properties to keep and maintain legal fences in equal shares where one or both of the properties is used and occupied for farming or grazing purposes. ***CAUTION: Consider an agreement addressing responsibility for fences if Property or adjoining land is used and occupied for farming or grazing purposes.***

DELIVERY/RECEIPT Unless otherwise stated in this Offer, any signed document transmitted by facsimile machine (fax) shall be treated in all manner and respects as an original document and the signature of any Party upon a document transmitted by fax shall be considered an original signature. Personal delivery to, or actual receipt by, any named Buyer or Seller constitutes personal delivery to, or actual receipt by Buyer or Seller. Once received, a notice cannot be withdrawn by the Party delivering the notice without the consent of the Party receiving the notice. A Party may not unilaterally reinstate a contingency after a notice of a contingency waiver has been received by the other Party. **The delivery provisions in this Offer may be modified when appropriate (e.g., when mail delivery is not desirable (see lines 25-36).** Buyer and Seller authorize the agents of Buyer and Seller to distribute copies of the Offer to Buyer's lender, appraisers, title insurance companies and any other settlement service providers for the transaction as defined by the Real Estate Settlement Procedures Act (RESPA).

FIGURE 7.3 (CONTINUED)

Sample Vacant Land Offer to Purchase

Wisconsin Legal Blank Co., Inc.

PROPERTY ADDRESS: ______________________________ [page 3 of 5, WB-13]

TIME IS OF THE ESSENCE "Time is of the Essence" as to: (1) earnest money payment(s); (2) binding acceptance; (3) occupancy; (4) date of closing; (5) contingency deadlines [STRIKE AS APPLICABLE] and all other dates and deadlines in this Offer except: ______________________________. If "Time is of the Essence" applies to a date or deadline, failure to perform by the exact date or deadline is a breach of contract. If "Time is of the Essence" does not apply to a date or deadline, then performance within a reasonable time of the date or deadline is allowed before a breach occurs.

DATES AND DEADLINES Deadlines expressed as a number of "days" from an event, such as acceptance, are calculated by excluding the day the event occurred and by counting subsequent calendar days. The deadline expires at midnight on the last day. Deadlines expressed as a specific number of "business days" exclude Saturdays, Sundays, any legal public holiday under Wisconsin or Federal law, and other day designated by the President such that the postal service does not receive registered mail or make regular deliveries on that day. Deadlines expressed as a specific number of "hours" from the occurrence of an event, such as receipt of a notice, are calculated from the exact time of the event, and by counting 24 hours per calendar day. Deadlines expressed as a specific day of the calendar year or as the day of a specific event, such as closing, expire at midnight of that day.

THE FINANCING CONTINGENCY PROVISIONS AT LINES 148 - 162 ARE A PART OF THIS OFFER IF LINE 148 IS MARKED, SUCH AS WITH AN "X". THEY ARE NOT PART OF THIS OFFER IF LINE 148 IS MARKED N/A OR IS NOT MARKED.

☐ **FINANCING CONTINGENCY:** This Offer is contingent upon Buyer being able to obtain a ______________________________ [INSERT LOAN PROGRAM OR SOURCE] first mortgage loan commitment as described below, within _______ days of acceptance of this Offer. The financing selected shall be in an amount of not less than $________________ for a term of not less than ________ years, amortized over not less than ________ years. Initial monthly payments of principal and interest shall not exceed $________________. Monthly payments may also include 1/12th of the estimated net annual real estate taxes, hazard insurance premiums, and private mortgage insurance premiums. The mortgage may not include a prepayment premium. Buyer agrees to pay a loan fee not to exceed ____________% of the loan. (Loan fee refers to discount points and/or loan origination fee, but DOES NOT include Buyer's other closing costs.) If the purchase price under this Offer is modified, the finance amount, unless otherwise provided, shall be adjusted to the same percentage of the purchase price as in this contingency and the monthly payments shall be adjusted as necessary to maintain the term and amortization stated above. **CHECK AND COMPLETE APPLICABLE FINANCING PROVISION AT LINE 158 OR 159.**

☐ **FIXED RATE FINANCING:** The annual rate of interest shall not exceed ________________%.

☐ **ADJUSTABLE RATE FINANCING:** The initial annual interest rate shall not exceed __________%. The initial interest rate shall be fixed for _________ months, at which time the interest rate may be increased not more than _________% per year. The maximum interest rate during the mortgage term shall not exceed ________%. Monthly payments of principal and interest may be adjusted to reflect interest changes.

LOAN COMMITMENT: Buyer agrees to pay all customary financing costs (including closing fees), to apply for financing promptly, and to provide evidence of application promptly upon request by Seller. If Buyer qualifies for the financing described in this Offer or other financing acceptable to Buyer, Buyer agrees to deliver to Seller a copy of the written loan commitment no later than the deadline for loan commitment at line 149. **Buyer's delivery of a copy of any written loan commitment to Seller (even if subject to conditions) shall satisfy the Buyer's financing contingency unless accompanied by a notice of unacceptability.** ***CAUTION: BUYER, BUYER'S LENDER AND AGENTS OF BUYER OR SELLER SHOULD NOT DELIVER A LOAN COMMITMENT TO SELLER WITHOUT BUYER'S PRIOR APPROVAL OR UNLESS ACCOMPANIED BY A NOTICE OF UNACCEPTABILITY.***

SELLER TERMINATION RIGHTS: If Buyer does not make timely delivery of said commitment, Seller may terminate this Offer if Seller delivers a written notice of termination to Buyer prior to Seller's actual receipt of a copy of Buyer's written loan commitment.

FINANCING UNAVAILABILITY: If financing is not available on the terms stated in this Offer (and Buyer has not already delivered an acceptable loan commitment for other financing to Seller), Buyer shall promptly deliver written notice of same including copies of lender(s)' rejection letter(s) or other evidence of unavailability. Unless a specific loan source is named in this Offer, Seller shall then have 10 days to give Buyer written notice of Seller's decision to finance this transaction on the same terms set forth in this Offer and this Offer shall remain in full force and effect, with the time for closing extended accordingly. If Seller's notice is not timely given, this Offer shall be null and void. Buyer authorizes Seller to obtain any credit information reasonably appropriate to determine Buyer's credit worthiness for Seller financing.

ADDITIONAL PROVISIONS/CONTINGENCIES ______________________________

☐ **ADDENDA:** The attached ______________________________ is/are made part of this Offer.

TITLE EVIDENCE

■ CONVEYANCE OF TITLE: **Upon payment of the purchase price, Seller shall convey the Property by warranty deed (or other conveyance as provided herein)** free and clear of all liens and encumbrances, except: municipal and zoning ordinances and agreements entered under them, recorded easements for the distribution of utility and municipal services, recorded building and use restrictions and covenants, general taxes levied in the year of closing and ______________________________ (provided none of the foregoing prohibit present use of the Property), which constitutes merchantable title for purposes of this transaction. Seller further agrees to complete and execute the documents necessary to record the conveyance.

FIGURE 7.3 (CONTINUED)

Sample Vacant Land Offer to Purchase

[page 4 of 5, WB-13]

■ FORM OF TITLE EVIDENCE: Seller shall provide evidence of title in the form of an owner's policy of title insurance in the amount of the purchase price on a current ALTA form issued by an insurer licensed to write title insurance in Wisconsin. ***CAUTION: IF TITLE EVIDENCE WILL BE GIVEN BY ABSTRACT, STRIKE TITLE INSURANCE PROVISIONS AND INSERT ABSTRACT PROVISIONS.***

■ PROVISION OF MERCHANTABLE TITLE: Seller shall pay all costs of providing title evidence. For purposes of closing, title evidence shall be acceptable if the commitment for the required title insurance is delivered to Buyer's attorney or Buyer not less than 3 business days before closing, showing title to the Property as of a date no more than 15 days before delivery of such title evidence to be merchantable, subject only to liens which will be paid out of the proceeds of closing and standard title insurance requirements and exceptions, as appropriate. ***CAUTION: BUYER SHOULD CONSIDER UPDATING THE EFFECTIVE DATE OF THE TITLE COMMITMENT PRIOR TO CLOSING OR A "GAP ENDORSEMENT" WHICH WOULD INSURE OVER LIENS FILED BETWEEN THE EFFECTIVE DATE OF THE COMMITMENT AND THE DATE THE DEED IS RECORDED.***

■ TITLE ACCEPTABLE FOR CLOSING: If title is not acceptable for closing, Buyer shall notify Seller in writing of objections to title by the time set for closing. In such event, Seller shall have a reasonable time, but not exceeding 15 days, to remove the objections, and the time for closing shall be extended as necessary for this purpose. In the event that Seller is unable to remove said objections, Buyer shall have 5 days from receipt of notice thereof, to deliver written notice waiving the objections, and the time for closing shall be extended accordingly. If Buyer does not waive the objections, this Offer shall be null and void. Providing title evidence acceptable for closing does not extinguish Seller's obligations to give merchantable title to Buyer.

■ SPECIAL ASSESSMENTS: Special assessments, if any, for work actually commenced or levied prior to date of this Offer shall be paid by Seller no later than closing. All other special assessments shall be paid by Buyer. ***CAUTION: Consider a special agreement if area assessments, property owner's association assessments or other expenses are contemplated.*** "Other expenses" are one-time charges or ongoing use fees for public improvements (other than those resulting in special assessments) relating to curb, gutter, street, sidewalk, sanitary and stormwater and storm sewer (including all sewer mains and hook-up and interceptor charges), parks, street lighting and street trees, and impact fees for other public facilities, as defined in Wis. Stat. §66.55(1)(c) & (f).

ENTIRE CONTRACT This Offer, including any amendments to it, contains the entire agreement of the Buyer and Seller regarding the transaction. All prior negotiations and discussions have been merged into this Offer. This agreement binds and inures to the benefit of the Parties to this Offer and their successors in interest.

DEFAULT

Seller and Buyer each have the legal duty to use good faith and due diligence in completing the terms and conditions of this Offer. A material failure to perform any obligation under this Offer is a default which may subject the defaulting party to liability for damages or other legal remedies.

If Buyer defaults, Seller may:

(1) sue for specific performance and request the earnest money as partial payment of the purchase price; or

(2) terminate the Offer and have the option to: (a) request the earnest money as liquidated damages; or (b) direct Broker to return the earnest money and have the option to sue for actual damages.

If Seller defaults, Buyer may:

(1) sue for specific performance; or

(2) terminate the Offer and request the return of the earnest money, sue for actual damages, or both.

In addition, the Parties may seek any other remedies available in law or equity.

The Parties understand that the availability of any judicial remedy will depend upon the circumstances of the situation and the discretion of the courts. If either Party defaults, the Parties may renegotiate the Offer or seek nonjudicial dispute resolution instead of the remedies outlined above. By agreeing to binding arbitration, the Parties may lose the right to litigate in a court of law those disputes covered by the arbitration agreement.

NOTE: IF ACCEPTED, THIS OFFER CAN CREATE A LEGALLY ENFORCEABLE CONTRACT. BOTH PARTIES SHOULD READ THIS DOCUMENT CAREFULLY. BROKERS MAY PROVIDE A GENERAL EXPLANATION OF THE PROVISIONS OF THE OFFER BUT ARE PROHIBITED BY LAW FROM GIVING ADVICE OR OPINIONS CONCERNING YOUR LEGAL RIGHTS UNDER THIS OFFER OR HOW TITLE SHOULD BE TAKEN AT CLOSING. AN ATTORNEY SHOULD BE CONSULTED IF LEGAL ADVICE IS NEEDED.

EARNEST MONEY

■ HELD BY: Unless otherwise agreed, earnest money shall be paid to and held in the trust account of the listing broker (buyer's agent if Property is not listed or seller if no broker is involved), until applied to purchase price or otherwise disbursed as provided in the Offer. ***CAUTION: Should persons other than a broker hold earnest money, an escrow agreement should be drafted by the Parties or an attorney. If someone other than Buyer makes payment of earnest money, consider a special disbursement agreement.***

■ DISBURSEMENT: If negotiations do not result in an accepted offer, the earnest money shall be promptly disbursed (after clearance from payor's depository institution if earnest money is paid by check) to the person(s) who paid the earnest money. At closing, earnest money shall be disbursed according to the closing statement. If this Offer does not close, the earnest money shall be disbursed according to a written disbursement agreement signed by all Parties to this Offer (Note: Wis. Adm. Code § RL 18.09(1)(b) provides that an offer to purchase is not a written disbursement agreement pursuant to which the broker may disburse). If said disbursement agreement has not been delivered to broker within 60 days after the date set for closing, broker may disburse the earnest money: (1) as directed by an attorney who has reviewed the transaction and does not represent Buyer or Seller; (2) into a court hearing a lawsuit involving the earnest money and all Parties to this Offer; (3) as directed by court order; or (4) any other disbursement required or allowed by law. Broker may retain legal services to direct disbursement per (1) or to file an interpleader action per (2) and broker may deduct from the earnest money any costs and reasonable attorneys fees, not to exceed $250, prior to disbursement.

■ LEGAL RIGHTS/ACTION: Broker's disbursement of earnest money does not determine the legal rights of the Parties in relation to this Offer. Buyer's or Seller's legal right to earnest money cannot be determined by broker. At least 30 days prior to disbursement per (1) or (4) above, broker shall send Buyer and Seller notice of the disbursement by certified mail. If Buyer or Seller disagree with broker's proposed disbursement, a lawsuit may be filed to obtain a court order regarding disbursement. Small Claims Court has jurisdiction over all earnest money disputes arising out of the sale of residential property with 1-4 dwelling units and certain other earnest money disputes. Buyer and Seller should consider consulting attorneys regarding their legal rights under this Offer in case of a dispute. Both Parties agree to hold the broker harmless from any liability for good faith disbursement of earnest money in accordance with this Offer or applicable Department of Regulation and Licensing regulations concerning earnest money. See Wis. Adm. Code Ch. RL 18. **NOTE: WISCONSIN LICENSE LAW PROHIBITS A BROKER FROM GIVING ADVICE OR OPINIONS CONCERNING THE LEGAL RIGHTS OR OBLIGATIONS OF PARTIES TO A TRANSACTION OR THE LEGAL EFFECT OF A SPECIFIC CONTRACT OR CONVEYANCE. AN ATTORNEY SHOULD BE CONSULTED IF LEGAL ADVICE IS REQUIRED.**

FIGURE 7.3 (CONTINUED)

Sample Vacant Land Offer to Purchase

Wisconsin Legal Blank Co., Inc.

PROPERTY ADDRESS: ______________________________ [page 5 of 5, WB-13]

OPTIONAL PROVISIONS: THE PARAGRAPHS AT LINES 271 - 314 WHICH ARE PRECEDED BY A BOX ARE A PART OF THIS OFFER IF MARKED, SUCH AS WITH AN "X". THEY ARE NOT PART OF THIS OFFER IF MARKED N/A OR ARE LEFT BLANK.

☐ **PROPOSED USE CONTINGENCY:** Buyer is purchasing the property for the purpose of: ______________________________. This Offer is contingent upon Buyer obtaining the following:

☐ Written evidence at (Buyer's) (Seller's) [STRIKE ONE] expense from a qualified soils expert that the Property is free of any subsoil condition which would make the proposed development impossible or significantly increase the costs of such development.

☐ Written evidence at (Buyer's) (Seller's) [STRIKE ONE] expense from a certified soils tester or other qualified expert that indicates that the Property's soils at locations selected by Buyer and all other conditions which must be approved to obtain a permit for an acceptable private septic system for: ______________________________ [insert proposed use of Property; e.g., three bedroom single family home] meet applicable codes in effect as of the date of this offer. An acceptable system includes all systems approved for use by the State for the type of property identified at line 277. An acceptable system does not include a holding tank, privy, composting toilet or chemical toilet or other systems (e.g. mound system) excluded in additional provisions or an addendum per lines 179 - 188.

☐ Copies at (Buyer's) (Seller's) [STRIKE ONE] expense of all public and private easements, covenants and restrictions affecting the Property and a written determination by a qualified independent third party that none of these prohibit or significantly delay or increase the costs of the proposed use or development identified at lines 271 to 272.

☐ Permits, approvals and licenses, as appropriate, or the final discretionary action by the granting authority prior to the issuance of such permits, approvals and licenses at (Buyer's) (Seller's) [STRIKE ONE] expense for the following items related to the proposed development ______________________________.

☐ Written evidence at (Buyer's) (Seller's) [STRIKE ONE] expense that the following utility connections are located as follows (e.g., on the Property, at the lot line across the street, etc.): electricity ____________; gas ____________; sewer ____________; water ____________; telephone ____________; other ____________.

This proposed use contingency shall be deemed satisfied unless Buyer within ____________ days of acceptance delivers written notice to Seller specifying those items of this contingency which cannot be satisfied and written evidence substantiating why each specific item included in Buyer's notice cannot be satisfied.

☐ **MAP OF THE PROPERTY:** This offer is contingent upon (Buyer obtaining)(Seller providing) [STRIKE ONE] a map of the Property prepared by a registered land surveyor, within ____ days after acceptance, at (Buyer's) (Seller's) [STRIKE ONE] expense. The map shall identify the legal description of the Property, the Property's boundaries and dimensions, visible encroachments upon the Property, the location of improvements, if any, and: ______________________________. [STRIKE AND COMPLETE AS APPLICABLE] Additional map features which may be added include, but are not limited to: specifying how current the map must be; staking of all corners of the Property; identifying dedicated and apparent streets, lot dimensions, total acreage or square footage, easements or rights-of-way. ***CAUTION: Consider the cost and the need for map features before selecting them.*** The map shall show no significant encroachment(s) or any information materially inconsistent with any prior representations to Buyer. This contingency shall be deemed satisfied unless Buyer, within five days or the earlier of: 1) Buyer's receipt of the map, or 2) the deadline for delivery of said map, delivers to Seller, and to listing broker if Property is listed, a copy of the map and a written notice which identifies the significant encroachment or the information materially inconsistent with prior representations.

☐ **INSPECTION CONTINGENCY:** This offer is contingent upon a qualified independent inspector(s) conducting an inspection(s), at Buyer expense, of the Property and ______________________________ which discloses no defects as defined below. This contingency shall be deemed satisfied unless Buyer within ________ days after acceptance delivers to Seller, and to listing broker if Property is listed, a copy of the inspector's written inspection report and a written notice listing the defects identified in the report to which Buyer objects. This Offer shall be null and void upon timely delivery of the above notice and report. ***CAUTION: A proposed amendment will not satisfy this notice requirement.*** Buyer shall order the inspection and be responsible for all costs of inspection, including any inspections required by lender or follow-up to inspection. Note: This contingency only authorizes inspections, not testing, see lines 98 to 110. For the purposes of this contingency a defect is defined as any condition of the Property which constitutes a significant threat to the health or safety of persons who occupy or use the Property or gives evidence of any material use, storage or disposal of hazardous or toxic substances on the Property. Defects do not include conditions the nature and extent of which Buyer had actual knowledge or written notice before signing this Offer.

This Offer was drafted on ____________ [date] by [Licensee and firm] ______________________________.

(x)______________________________ ____________________ ____________
Buyer's Signature ▲ Print Name Here: ▶ Social Security No. or FEIN ▲ Date ▲

(x)______________________________ ____________________ ____________
Buyer's Signature ▲ Print Name Here: ▶ Social Security No. or FEIN ▲ Date ▲

EARNEST MONEY RECEIPT Broker acknowledges receipt of earnest money as per line 8 of the above Offer. **(See lines 242 - 267.)**

______________________________ Broker (By) ______________________________

SELLER ACCEPTS THIS OFFER. THE WARRANTIES, REPRESENTATIONS AND COVENANTS MADE IN THIS OFFER SURVIVE CLOSING AND THE CONVEYANCE OF THE PROPERTY. SELLER AGREES TO CONVEY THE PROPERTY ON THE TERMS AND CONDITIONS AS SET FORTH HEREIN AND ACKNOWLEDGES RECEIPT OF A COPY OF THIS OFFER.

(x)______________________________ ____________________ ____________
Seller's Signature ▲ Print Name Here: ▶ Social Security No. or FEIN ▲ Date ▲

(x)______________________________ ____________________ ____________
Seller's Signature ▲ Print Name Here: ▶ Social Security No. or FEIN ▲ Date ▲

This Offer was presented to Seller by ____________________ on ____________, ________, at ______ a.m./p.m.

THIS OFFER IS REJECTED ____________ ____________ THIS OFFER IS COUNTERED [See attached counter] ____________ ____________
Seller Initials ▲ Date ▲ Seller Initials ▲ Date ▲

the property upon reasonable notice if the inspections are reasonably necessary to satisfy the contingencies in the offer.

Lines 104–110 deal with testing.

Lines 107–109 make clear that any contingency authorizing testing should specify the areas of the property to be tested and the purpose of that test.

Lines 111–113 address the preclosing inspection and property damage between acceptance and closing.

Lines 114–121 are similar to lines 115–123 of the Residential Offer to Purchase.

Lines 122–124 cover fences and state that the parties should consider an agreement addressing responsibility for fences if the property or adjoining land is used and occupied for farming or grazing purposes.

Lines 125–132 on delivery/receipt, lines 134–138 on time is of the essence, and lines 139–145 on dates and deadlines are basically similar to lines addressing those topics on the Residential Offer to Purchase discussed above.

Lines 146–162 on the financing provisions and lines 163–178 on the loan commitment are also very similar to the Residential Offer to Purchase language.

The additional provisions/contingency section in lines 179–187 is also similar to that section in the Residential Offer to Purchase.

Line 188, Addenda, plays the same role as it does in the Residential Offer to Purchase.

Lines 189–267 are similar to the Residential Offer to Purchase language.

Lines 269–314 deal with contingencies that are different from those addressed in the Residential Offer to Purchase. The proposed use contingency (lines 271–292) covers issues such as subsoil conditions, copies of easements and restrictions, and approval for issuance of permits. Lines 293–303 state that the offer is contingent upon the preparation of a map meeting specified requirements.

The inspection contingency in lines 304–314 is also generally comparable to the language in the Residential Offer to Purchase.

Lines 315–331, remainder of the Vacant Land Offer to Purchase, are similar to the Residential Offer to Purchase.

EXPLANATION OF WB-40 AMENDMENT TO OFFER TO PURCHASE

The WB-40 (see Figure 7.4) is used if both parties must agree to modify the terms of the offer. For example, lines 1–33 provide for changing the closing date or occupancy date. Lines 34–42 deal with the date of binding acceptances and the

FIGURE 7.4

Sample Amendment to Offer to Purchase

Approved by the Wisconsin Department of Regulation and Licensing
7-1-99 (Optional Use Date) 1-1-00 (Mandatory Use Date)

Wisconsin Legal Blank Co., Inc.
Milwaukee, Wis.

WB-40 AMENDMENT TO OFFER TO PURCHASE

Caution: Use A WB-40 Amendment If Both Parties Will Be Agreeing To Modify The Terms Of The Offer. Use A WB-41 Notice If A Party Is Giving A Notice Which Does Not Require The Other Party's Agreement.

Buyer and Seller agree to amend the Offer dated ______________, ______, and accepted ______________, ______, for the purchase and sale of real estate at ____ as follows:

( ) Closing date is changed from ______________ to ______________.

( ) Purchase price is changed from $______________ to $______________.

( ) Occupancy date is changed from ______________ to ______________.

( ) Occupancy charge is changed from $______________ to $______________.

( ) Other: ____

ALL OTHER TERMS OF THE OFFER TO PURCHASE AND ANY PRIOR AMENDMENTS REMAIN THE SAME.

This Amendment is binding upon Seller and Buyer only if a copy of the accepted Amendment is delivered to the Party offering the Amendment on or before ______________________ (Time is of the essence). Delivery of the accepted Amendment may be made in any manner specified in the Offer to Purchase, unless otherwise provided in this Amendment. ***NOTE: The Party offering this Amendment may withdraw the offered Amendment prior to acceptance and delivery as provided at lines 34 to 37.***

This Amendment was drafted by ______________________ on ______________.
Licensee and Firm ▲ Date ▲

This Amendment was presented by ______________________ on ______________.
Licensee and Firm ▲ Date ▲

______________________ ______________________
Buyer's Signature ▲ Date ▲ Buyer's Signature ▲ Date ▲

______________________ ______________________
Seller's Signature ▲ Date ▲ Seller's Signature ▲ Date ▲

NOTE: ATTACH THIS AMENDMENT TO THE OFFER TO PURCHASE.

form of acceptable delivery as indicated in the offer to purchase, unless indicated otherwise in the amendment.

Both parties must sign on lines 43–46 in order for the offer to be amended.

EXPLANATION OF WB-41 NOTICE RELATING TO OFFER TO PURCHASE

The WB-41 (see Figure 7.5) is used if one party is giving notice that the other party does not need to approve.

Lines 1–34 would be used, for example, for the buyer to remove the financing contingency or to give notice to the seller of defects discovered by the buyers' third-party inspector.

The party giving notice signs on line 43.

EXPLANATION OF WB-44 COUNTER-OFFER

Lines 1–5 (see Figure 7.6) are used to place the date that appears on the offer as well as the buyer and the address of the property.

Lines 1–3 make clear that the prior offer is being rejected. This emphasizes the point that a counter-offer is a new offer being made in response to the prior offer which was unacceptable. You should also be aware that once a buyer has received a counter-offer from a seller, the seller may not withdraw the counter-offer and accept the original offer even if the time period for acceptance in the original offer has not expired.

You should also be sure to number each counter-offer at the top of the counter-offer sequentially and indicate by whom the counter-offer was made in order to maintain the proper sequence of counter-offers.

Lines 6–32 allow for any changes that you are making from the original offer, such as the purchase price or closing date. It is important to note that the formal contract is the original offer plus only the last counter-offer. Each counter-offer should restate any changes from the original. If you are changing a part of a contingency, it is better to restate the entire contingency so as to make clear what changes have occurred. Line 32 notes that any warranties and representations made in the counter-offer survive the closing.

Lines 33–43 allow for signatures and addresses as well as the deadline for acceptance of the counter-offer.

Lines 35–36 state that delivery may be made in any manner specified in the offer, unless otherwise stated in the counter-offer.

FIGURE 7.5

Sample Notice Relating to Offer to Purchase

Approved by the Wisconsin Department of Regulation and Licensing
7-1-99 (Optional Use Date) 1-1-00 (Mandatory Use Date)

Wisconsin Legal Blank Co., Inc.
Milwaukee, Wis.

WB-41 NOTICE RELATING TO OFFER TO PURCHASE

Caution: Use A WB-41 Notice If A Party Is Giving A Notice Which Does Not Require The Other Party's Agreement. Use A WB-40 Amendment If Both Parties Will Be Agreeing to Modify The Terms Of The Offer.

This Notice by (Seller)(Buyer) STRIKE ONE relates to the Offer to Purchase dated ______________, ________, and accepted ______________, ________, for the purchase and sale of real estate at ____.

(1) The following are no longer contingencies or conditions to the Offer to Purchase (Note: Attach supporting documents, if required): ____

(2) Notice is given that: ____

This Notice was drafted by ______________________________ on ______________.
Licensee and Firm ▲ Date ▲

This Notice was delivered by ______________________________ on ______________,
Date ▲

at ________ a.m./p.m. STRIKE ONE using the following method of delivery: ☐ mail, ☐ fax, ☐ personal delivery,
☐ other ______________________________ CHECK AS APPLICABLE.

This Notice was presented by ______________________________ on ______________, at ________
Licensee and Firm ▲ Date ▲ a.m./p.m. ▲

(x) ______________________________ ________ (x) ______________________________ ________
Signature of Party Giving Notice ▲ Date ▲ Signature of Party Giving Notice ▲ Date ▲

NOTE: ATTACH THIS NOTICE TO THE OFFER TO PURCHASE.

FIGURE 7.6

Sample Counter-Offer

Approved by Wisconsin Department of Regulation and Licensing
7-1-99 (Optional Use Date) 1-1-00 (Mandatory Use Date)

Wisconsin Legal Blank Co., Inc.
Milwaukee, Wis.

WB-44 COUNTER-OFFER

Counter-Offer No. _________ by (Buyer/Seller) STRIKE ONE

The Offer to Purchase dated ____________________ and signed by Buyer, ______________________________, for purchase of real estate at ____ is rejected and the following counter-offer is hereby made. **All terms and conditions remain the same as stated in the Offer to Purchase except the following: [CAUTION: This Counter-Offer does not include the terms or conditions in any other Counter-Offer unless incorporated by reference.]**

ANY WARRANTIES AND REPRESENTATIONS MADE IN THIS COUNTER-OFFER SURVIVE THE CLOSING OF THIS TRANSACTION. This Counter-Offer is binding upon Seller and Buyer only if a copy of the accepted Counter-Offer is delivered to the Party making the Counter-Offer on or before ____ (Time is of the essence). Delivery of the accepted Counter-Offer may be made in any manner specified in the Offer to Purchase, unless otherwise provided in this Counter-Offer. ***NOTE: The Party makng this Counter-Offer may withdraw the Counter-Offer prior to acceptance and delivery as provided at lines 33 to 36.***

This Counter-Offer was drafted by ____ on ______________.
Licensee and Firm ▲ Date ▲

Signature of Party Making Counter-Offer ▲ Date ▲ Signature of Party Making Counter-Offer ▲ Date ▲

Signature of Party Accepting Counter-Offer ▲ Date ▲ Signature of Party Accepting Counter-Offer ▲ Date ▲

This Counter-Offer was presented by ____ on ______________.
Licensee and Firm ▲ Date ▲

This Counter-Offer is **(rejected) (countered)** STRIKE ONE (Party's Initials) ______________ (Party's Initials) ______________

Note: Provisions from a previous Counter-Offer may be included by reproduction of the entire provision or incorporation be reference. Provisions incorporated by reference may be indicated in the subsequent Counter-Offer by specifying the number of the provision or the lines containing the provision. In transactions involving more than one Counter-Offer, the Counter-Offer referred to should be clearly specified. **NOTE: Number this Counter-Offer sequentially, e.g. Counter-Offer No. 1 by Seller, Counter-Offer No. 2 by Buyer, etc.**

ATTACH THIS COUNTER-OFFER TO THE OFFER TO PURCHASE-INSERT SOCIAL SECURITY NUMBERS OR FEIN ON OFFER.

You should have your buyer or seller sign on line 42 when an offer is accepted. The parties place their initials on line 46 if they are either rejecting or countering the counter-offer.

EXPLANATION OF WB-46 MULTIPLE COUNTER-PROPOSAL

Lines 1–4 (see Figure 7.7) provide an overview of the form and make clear that more than one buyer is receiving multiple counter-proposals.

Line 2 indicates that the seller is not obligated to issue the same multiple counter-proposal to all buyers.

Lines 2–4 state that once the buyer signs the seller's nonbinding proposal, it becomes an offer to the seller. The multiple counter-proposal becomes a binding contract only when it is signed and delivered by the seller as stated on line 45.

Lines 5–31 provide for any changes the seller is making from the original offer, such as the purchase price. It presents the terms of the seller's nonbinding proposal to the buyer.

Lines 24–25 identify an expiration date for the seller's multiple counter-proposal.

Lines 26–31 indicate the date and time of the seller's signature, the seller's Social Security number and the name of the licensee who drafted the counter-proposal on behalf of the seller.

Lines 33–42 state the procedure by which the buyer accepts the nonbinding proposal found on lines 5–22.

You should be aware of lines 35–36 which state that if the sellers' multiple's counter-proposal is not accepted by the buyer in its entirety, the buyer should not use the multiple counter-proposal for a counter-offer. The buyer is to submit a counter-offer (WB-44) or a new offer to purchase.

Lines 43–53 refer to confirmation by the seller. If the seller accepts the multiple counter-proposal that the buyer accepted above, the seller signs on line 48 to indicate acceptance.

HANDLING EARNEST MONEY DEPOSITS

The subject of commingling funds and the broker's responsibility for the funds of others is described in detail in Chapter 10 of this text as part of the rules and regulations enforced by the Real Estate Board. Whenever a real estate broker has monies belonging to another person, the broker must maintain a separate account in an authorized financial institution for monies belonging to and held for other persons, such as earnest money deposits.

FIGURE 7.7

Sample Multiple Counter-Proposal

Approved by Wisconsin Department of Regulation and Licensing
7-1-99 (Optional Use Date)
1-1-00 (Mandatory Use Date)

Wisconsin Legal Blank Co., Inc.
Milwaukee, Wis.

WB-46 MULTIPLE COUNTER-PROPOSAL

A Multiple Counter-Proposal is being made by Seller to one or more other prospective buyers. The terms of this Multiple Counter-Proposal may differ from the terms of multiple counter-proposals being submitted to other prospective buyers. This Multiple Counter-Proposal is not binding on Seller or Buyer until Seller's binding acceptance per lines 44-46. Seller or Buyer may withdraw their Multiple Counter-Proposal or accepted multiple counter-proposal, at any time prior to binding acceptance per lines 44-46.

The Offer to Purchase dated ____________________ and signed by Buyer, ____________________ for purchase of real estate at ____ is rejected and the following Multiple Counter-Proposal is made. **All terms and conditions remain the same as stated in the Offer to Purchase except the following: [CAUTION: This Multiple Counter-Proposal does not include the terms or conditions in any other counter-offer or multiple counter-proposal unless incorporated by reference.]**

____

Any warranties, covenants and representations made in this Multiple Counter-Proposal survive the closing of this transaction.
This Multiple Counter-Proposal by Seller will expire and be null and void unless a copy of the approved Multiple Counter-Proposal (see lines 33-35) is delivered to Seller in any manner authorized in the Offer to Purchase on or before ______________, ________ (Time is of the essence).
This Multiple Counter-Offer was drafted on ____________ by ________________________________.
Date ▲ Licensee and Firm ▲

(x)______________________ ______________________ ____________
Seller's Signature ▲Print Name Here: ▶ Social Security No. or FEIN ▲ Date ▲

(x)______________________ ______________________ ____________
Seller's Signature ▲Print Name Here: ▶ Social Security No. or FEIN ▲ Date ▲

APPROVAL BY BUYER

This Multiple Counter-Proposal by Seller is approved by Buyer. Approval of this Multiple Counter-Proposal is not binding on Buyer or Seller until binding acceptance of this approved Multiple Counter-Proposal by Seller (per lines 44-46) on or before ______________, ________ (Time is of the essence). **NOTE: If the above Multiple Counter-Proposal by Seller is not approved by Buyer in its entirety, do not use this form for a counter-offer by Buyer. Instead, submit a Counter-Offer (WB-44) or a new offer to purchase.**

(x)______________________ ______________________
Buyer's Signature ▲ Date ▲ Buyer's Signature ▲ Date ▲
This Multiple Counter-Proposal is **(rejected)(countered)** STRIKE ONE (Buyer's Initials) ______________
This Multiple Counter-Proposal was presented to Buyer by ________________________________
Licensee and Firm ▲
______________________ on ____________, at ____________
Date ▲ a.m./p.m. ▲

ACCEPTANCE BY SELLER

By signing below, Seller accepts Buyer's approved Multiple Counter-Proposal. The terms of this Multiple Counter-Proposal shall be binding on Seller and Buyer if Seller delivers a copy of the accepted Multiple Counter-Proposal to Buyer in any manner authorized in the Offer to Purchase on or before the deadline stated at line 34. **NOTE: Seller should not sign below if there is an existing accepted offer unless this Multiple Counter-Proposal provides for a secondary offer.**

(x)______________________ ______________________
Seller's Signature ▲ Date ▲ Seller's Signature ▲ Date ▲
The accepted Multiple Counter-Proposal was presented to Seller by ________________________________
Licensee and Firm ▲
______________________ on ____________, at ____________
Date ▲ a.m./p.m. ▲

ATTACH THIS MULTIPLE COUNTER-PROPOSAL TO THE OFFER TO PURCHASE - INSERT SOCIAL SECURITY NUMBERS OR FEIN ON OFFER.

RISK OF LOSS

In Wisconsin, the seller bears any risk of loss that may occur before title passes, as provided in the Uniform Vendor and Purchaser Risk Act, adopted in 1941.

STATUTE OF LIMITATIONS

The time during which parties to a contract may bring legal suit to enforce their rights is limited to six years in Wisconsin. Parties who do not take steps to enforce their legal rights within this time may lose them.

LAND OR INSTALLMENT CONTRACTS

Land contracts, or installment contracts, are frequently used in Wisconsin. The Wisconsin laws covering the use of land contracts are discussed in Chapter 11 of this book.

ESCROW CLOSINGS

Escrow closings are seldom used in Wisconsin. Escrow sometimes is used at the time of closing if the seller has failed to do something that he or she had agreed to do. Part of the purchase price may be withheld if, for example, the seller has failed to repair a window that has rotted out or has not fixed a broken stair as promised. The part of the purchase price retained is entrusted to an escrow agent. The escrow agent is a third person, usually an attorney or an officer of the lending institution. An agreement generally is signed providing that if the work is done on time and to the satisfaction of the buyer, the seller will receive the withheld money.

Escrows now are being used more widely in connection with construction loans in Wisconsin. Agreements of this kind are regulated by the title insurance companies where such escrows are arranged. There are no state regulations for escrows.

QUESTIONS

1. In Wisconsin, licensees may use forms prepared or approved by the Wisconsin
   a. Real Estate Board.
   b. Real Estate License Law.
   c. Department of Natural Resources.
   d. Department of Regulation and Licensing.
2. In Wisconsin, a salesperson may *NOT* prepare a(n)
   a. listing contract.
   b. residential lease.
   c. land contract.
   d. offer to purchase.
3. When a contract depends on its terms being carried out exactly by the date specified, the contract usually contains a(n)
   a. time is of the essence clause.
   b. statute of limitations.
   c. extension clause.
   d. equitable title form.
4. Personal property that is to be included in the sale of real estate should be
   a. specified in the sales contract.
   b. sold separately and listed in a separate contract.
   c. conveyed by a warranty deed.
   d. conveyed by a quitclaim deed.
5. Which of the following statements does *NOT* correctly describe the Marital Property Act?
   a. Title determines ownership rights to property.
   b. Title determines management rights of a property.
   c. Title determines control rights of a property.
   d. Title does not determine ownership rights to a property.

Use the information contained in the Residential Offer to Purchase form that appears in Figure 7.1 to answer Question 6 through Question 11.

6. Which statement is *TRUE* regarding the property?
   a. It is being purchased by George and Martha Carter.
   b. Legally, it is described as Lot 2, Block 4, Fairmont Subdivision, NW 1/4 of Section 8, T9N, R7E, Dane County, Wisconsin.
   c. It is being sold by Jay and Linda Jones.
   d. It is being purchased for a sales price of $248,000.
7. Information on an inspection contingency would be placed on which of the following lines on the offer to purchase?
   a. 53–58
   b. 298–305
   c. 180–186
   d. 317–320
8. According to the offer to purchase, the seller must provide evidence of title to the buyer at the seller's expense at least how long before closing?
   a. 30 days
   b. 3 business days
   c. 15 days
   d. 15 business days
9. The offer to purchase allows the seller to provide which of the following types of evidence of title to the buyer prior to closing?
   a. Certificate of registration
   b. Certificate of title
   c. Title insurance
   d. Torrens System
10. The buyers are *NOT* assuming the
    a. sellers' mortgage.
    b. sellers' owners' title insurance policy.
    c. sellers' real estate taxes.
    d. All of the above are being assumed by the buyers.

11. The transaction will be closed
    a. on or before September 13, 2009.
    b. on or before November 15, 2009.
    c. on or before December 15, 2009.
    d. at the offices of the First Federal Bank of Madison.

12. Broker Saidel listed North's property that was sold by broker Frank, the cooperative broker to Eagan, the buyer. Eagan's earnest money will be held by
    a. broker Eagan.
    b. broker North.
    c. broker Frank.
    d. broker Saidel.

13. Broker Krupp has been asked by Buyer Charles to place the legal description in the offer to purchase which Broker Krupp is preparing. Broker Krupp should place the legal description on which line(s)?
    a. 3–4
    b. 317–320
    c. 28
    d. 275

14. Seller Yost and Buyer Vern are arguing about which items were included in their transaction. The terms of their agreement will be determined by the
    a. listing contract.
    b. offer to purchase.
    c. oral agreements between Brokers Yost and Vern.
    d. MLS data sheet.

15. Binding acceptance occurs when the
    a. buyer signs the offer to purchase.
    b. buyer signs the offer to purchase and it is conveyed to the seller.
    c. seller signs the offer to purchase.
    d. seller signs the offer to purchase and it is delivered to the buyer.

16. Which of the following would *NOT* be an acceptable method for delivering an accepted offer to the buyer?
    a. Telephone
    b. Personal delivery
    c. U.S. mail
    d. fax transmission

17. Broker W has just completed an offer to purchase for Buyer T. Buyer T has indicated that any documents or written notices should be delivered to either Buyer T or Broker W's office. Which of the following would constitute appropriate delivery of documents to either Buyer T or Broker W?
    a. The document is addressed and mailed to Buyer T at his office.
    b. The document is addressed and mailed to Broker W at his home.
    c. The document is addressed and mailed to Buyer T at Broker W's office.
    d. The document is addressed and mailed to Buyer T at his home.

18. Home Inspector D is doing an inspection of Seller Q's house for Buyer K. The offer to purchase would authorize Home Inspector D to perform which of the following tests on Seller Q's house?
    a. A radon test
    b. A test of leaking carbon monoxide
    c. A test for asbestos
    d. A test to determine the quality of the water

19. Buyer Upton is requesting that the soil and water be tested on the house for which she has just signed an offer to purchase. Testing contingencies for soil and water would *NOT* be placed
    a. on lines 57–58.
    b. on lines 180–186.
    c. on lines 317–320.
    d. in addendum.

20. According to the offer to purchase, the preclosing inspection is to be conducted within
    a. 3 days before closing.
    b. 5 days before closing.
    c. 7 days before closing.
    d. 10 days before closing.

21. Buyer Aron and Seller Bork have mutually agreed to change the closing date of the accepted offer on Bork's house. Which one of the following forms should be used by the broker to change the closing date for the transaction?
    a. WB-40
    b. WB-41
    c. WB-44
    d. WB-46

22. Buyer Parks is notifying Seller Quinn that the financing contingency on the accepted offer has been satisfied. Which one of the following forms should be used by the broker to notify Quinn that the financing contingency has been satisfied?

a. WB-40
b. WB-41
c. WB-44
d. WB-46

23. Seller Victor is countering Buyer Uribe's offer. Which one of the following forms should be used by the broker to present the counter-offer?

a. WB-40
b. WB-41
c. WB-44
d. WB-46

24. Seller Tankel has received offers to purchase his home from four different buyers. Tankel would like to continue negotiating with all four of the buyers. Which one of the following forms should be used by the seller to counter the four buyers?

a. WB-40
b. WB-44
c. WB-41
d. WB-46

25. The amount of earnest money in the Residential Condominium Offer to Purchase would appear on lines

a. 9 and 10
b. 11 and 12.
c. 157–163.
d. 177 and 178.

26. Items not included in the purchase price in the Residential Condominium Offer to Purchase are covered on

a. lines 9 and 10.
b. lines 14–17.
c. lines 18 and 19.
d. lines 157–163.

27. The basis for proration of real estate tax in the Residential Condominium Offer to Purchase is covered on line(s)

a. 18 and 19.
b. 22.
c. 46–48.
d. 157–163.

28. According to the Residential Condominium Offer to Purchase, condominium disclosure materials are to be delivered to the buyer no later than

a. 3 days prior to closing.
b. 5 days prior to closing.
c. 10 days prior to closing.
d. 15 days prior to closing.

29. Wisconsin law requires that the seller of a condominium provide a Real Estate Condition Report to the buyer no later than

a. 3 days after acceptance of the contract of sale.
b. 5 days after acceptance of the contract of sale.
c. 10 days after acceptance of the contract of sale.
d. 30 days after acceptance of the contract of sale.

30. The Residential Condominium Offer to Purchase defines defects on lines:

a. 307–311
b. 328–335
c. 336–341
d. 342–346

31. A licensee is filling out a Vacant Land Offer to Purchase for a buyer when the buyer states that she would like the annual crops included in the purchase price. This request would appear on line

a. 13.
b. 19.
c. 42.
d. 57.

32. The Vacant Land Offer to Purchase includes a warning regarding issues related to property development. This is found on line(s)

a. 13.
b. 19.
c. 57–58.
d. 89–97.

33. The Vacant Land Offer to Purchase includes a contingency calling for written evidence regarding the location of utility connections that is found on lines

a. 273–274.
b. 275–280.
c. 284–286.
d. 287–289.

34. A buyer of vacant land has received a map before the deadline indicated in the Vacant Land Offer to Purchase. The buyer will have how many days to determine whether the map shows any significant encroachments or changes in information?

a. 3
b. 5
c. 10
d. 15

35. Which of the following does *NOT* correctly describe the language in the inspection contingency in the Vacant Land Offer to Purchase?

a. The contingency calls for an inspection by a qualified independent inspector.
b. The seller has a right to cure.
c. The contingency authorizes only inspections.
d. The seller has no right to cure.

Transfer of Title

SUCCESSION

The Wisconsin Law of Intestate Succession provides that real estate located in Wisconsin owned by a person who has died intestate (i.e., without leaving a valid will) is to be distributed in four possible ways:

1. The spouse receives the entire estate unless there are children of the decedent, who are not the children of the spouse.
2. If there are such children, the surviving spouse receives one-half of the estate and the remaining one-half of the estate is shared equally by all of the children of the decedent spouse. Classification under the Marital Property Act does not matter because the surviving spouse gets only one-half of the marital property that he or she already owned plus one-half of all of the deceased spouse's other property.
3. If there is neither a surviving spouse nor surviving children, the law lists parents, brothers and sisters, nieces and nephews, grandparents, then other kin as the order in which they are to inherit property.
4. The state school fund receives the property of those who die without heirs.

WILLS

A surviving spouse cannot be excluded totally by a will unless he or she agrees to such exclusion in a written marital agreement. By law, surviving spouses may elect to take up to a one-half interest in property owned by the decedent prior to

1986, which would have been marital property if it had been acquired after 1985. Moreover, a court may award a surviving spouse as much of the estate as necessary for that spouse's support.

If there are assets to be transferred, jointly owned property, survivorship marital property, or individually owned life insurance may substitute for a will. Jointly owned property and survivorship marital property automatically are transferred to the survivor(s); insurance policies can direct that proceeds be paid directly to a beneficiary. One must remember, however, that a will has various important functions, such as naming a guardian for minor children and saving taxes. One may need alternate heirs in case both joint owners, such as both spouses, die together.

Spouses may sign a marital agreement that provides that on the death of either spouse, any or either or both spouses' property will pass without probate to a designated person, trust, or other entity. Such a marital agreement, if properly drafted, can be a total will substitute.

INVOLUNTARY TRANSFER

Adverse Possession

In Wisconsin, legal title may be acquired by adverse possession after *continuous possession of the land for either 10 years or 20 years*, depending on the circumstances. If a *claim of title* is based on a written instrument such as a deed that later proves faulty, the occupant may claim ownership by *adverse possession* after possessing the land for ten years under color of title law. The payment of taxes and possession may also kick in the ten-year adverse possession law. Possession is established if the land is (1) improved, (2) usually cultivated, (3) enclosed, (4) used to supply fuel or fencing timber, or (5) set aside for the ordinary use of the possessor.

In some cases, land that has been improved but is a part of a plot that customarily is not cleared or enclosed also may be claimed. *This might happen when the legal description on a conveyance is incorrect or a surveyor's error causes incorrect boundary lines*. If such errors are discovered after a person has lived on the land for the ten-year prescriptive period, the occupant of the land may claim ownership by adverse possession and will not have to change the boundary lines or move any improvements.

If a claim of adverse possession is *not based on a written instrument*, the prescriptive period is *20 years* and only the premises actually occupied can be claimed. Actual occupancy in this circumstance is established if the land has been improved, cultivated, or enclosed.

Court action. Court action to defeat a claim by adverse possession must begin within one year after interrupting use by the one who is possessing the property and within the prescribed 10-year or 20-year possession period. Any claim by adverse possession, with or without an instrument, must be open, *continuous, notorious, and hostile*.

VOLUNTARY ALIENATION

Deeds

Any deed for the transfer of property in Wisconsin *is valid if it is signed by the grantor, identifies the parties and interest conveyed, and is delivered.* The names of all signers must be printed or typed under all signatures. A deed usually is turned over to the grantee at the closing of a real estate transaction. *Title is passed irrevocably when the deed is delivered to the grantee in return for the money.* The deed should be recorded by the grantee as soon as possible after it has been executed. Deeds are recorded at the office of the register of deeds in the county in which the described land is located. An unrecorded deed is still valid between the grantor and grantee. The recording fee usually is paid by the buyer.

Acknowledgment

Any instrument that is to be recorded must be acknowledged or authenticated by a notary public. In Wisconsin, a notary public is appointed for the state-at-large and may act anywhere in the state. Other officials, including clerks of the court of records, court commissioners, county clerks, and deputy clerks, also may acknowledge instruments. An instrument to be recorded also may be authenticated by an attorney.

Real Estate Transfer Fee

Wisconsin does not require a documentary stamp tax, but the state does impose a real estate transfer fee on most conveyances of real estate. The fee is $0.30 per $100 of the value of the property or fraction thereof.

For example, if the value of the property sold is $30,000, the fee is $90. If the value is $30,050, the sales price is rounded up to the next $100, so the $30,050 becomes $30,100 multiplied by 0.003, so the fee is $90.30. The tax applies to the full sales price of the property regardless of any liens or encumbrances that may stand against the property.

In addition, as of August 1, 1992, the transfer fee must be paid by the seller (grantor) at the time a land contract is recorded even though the deed will be recorded later. For example, the transfer tax would be $149.70 on a property sold for $49,900 even though there might be a $30,000 mortgage assumed by the buyer.

The transfer fee must be paid by the seller (grantor) to the register of deeds at the time the deed is recorded. A Wisconsin Real Estate Transfer Return form must be submitted at the time the fee is paid and must show the value of the property. Payment of a transfer fee is not required for: (1) conveyances between husband and wife or parent and child for nominal or no consideration; (2) correcting deeds; (3) liquidation deeds; and (4) conveyances of real estate with a value of $100 or less. Sections 77.22 and 77.27 of the Wisconsin Statutes cover taxation and the transfer fee and are included on the salesperson's exam.

For example, Section 77.27 states that any person who intentionally falsifies value on a transfer fee return required to be filed may be fined not more than $1,000 or imprisoned in the county jail not more than one year or both.

Rental Weatherization Requirements

Most residential rental properties in Wisconsin must meet minimum energy-conservation standards at the time of ownership transfer. Private state-centered inspectors are to be hired by owners to check properties for compliance with the standards. In order to enforce these standards, the statutes prohibit a county register of deeds from recording any transfer of a property that includes a rental dwelling unit unless: (1) an inspector has certified the property; (2) the buyer has filed a stipulation to bring the dwelling unit up to code within a year; (3) the property transfer is shown to be excluded from the code; or (4) the buyer has filed a statement that the building will be demolished within two years.

The code applies to a building only when its ownership is to be transferred. According to the code, *transfer* means a transfer of ownership by deed, land contract, or judgment. In the case of a land contract, transfer occurs when the contract is entered into, not when the deed is transferred. Ownership conveyance also includes transfer of a controlling stock or controlling partnership interest and interest in a lease in excess of one year that was contracted after January 1, 1985.

Excluded from coverage by the code are seven transfers that are

1. for security purposes;
2. between agent and principal or trustee and beneficiary without consideration;
3. part of a divorce settlement;
4. for no or nominal consideration between husband and wife or parent and children;
5. part of the probate process;
6. involuntary, including foreclosures, bankruptcies and delinquent taxes, or assessments; or
7. to declare a building a condominium.

Only residential rental properties are covered by the code. However, a number of these are excluded, including:

- seasonal dwelling units not rented any time between November 1 and March 31 each year;
- buildings with four or fewer units, if the buyer will live in one of the units;
- one-family or two-family dwellings constructed after December 1, 1978;
- buildings with more than two dwelling units constructed after April 15, 1976;
- mobile homes and manufactured homes;
- bed and breakfast establishments;
- condominium buildings of three or more dwelling units;
- hotels and motels used primarily for transient residency; and
- health care facilities.

Unless a property or transfer is shown to be excluded from the code, a Department of Commerce transfer authorization must accompany the documents of transfer for rental property when the register of deeds is asked to record them. There are three types of transfer authorizations:

1. Certificate of compliance: If a property meets the weatherization standards of the code, it may receive a certificate of compliance that will cover any transfers for the life of the building. A certificate can be issued only by an inspector certified by the Department of Commerce. Inspectors are paid by building owners at an agreed upon fee, subject to a state-set maximum.

2. Stipulation: The purchaser of a rental property can accept the responsibility for bringing the building into compliance by signing a stipulation, which requires that a certificate of compliance be obtained within one year after transfer. The stipulation form is obtained from the Department of Commerce, a Department of Commerce agent, or an authorized municipality. The stipulation is submitted for authorization with a fee to the Department of Commerce, a Department of Commerce agent, or an authorized municipality. A list of agents is available from the Department of Commerce.
3. Waiver: If demolition of a structure is planned within two years of transfer, an owner can apply for a waiver that will allow transfer of the property without meeting the weatherization standards. The waiver form is obtained and submitted in the same manner as the stipulation form described previously.

Before recording the documents of a transfer, proof of an exclusion will be required by the register of deeds to certify that the property being transferred is excluded from the code.

The Rental Unit Energy Efficiency Code also provides penalties for inspectors or owners attempting to evade the requirements of the code. Any inspector falsifying a certificate will have his or her certification revoked by the department and may be required to forfeit not more than $500 per dwelling unit in the rental unit for which the certificate is issued. Any person who offers documents evidencing transfer of ownership for recondition and who, with intent to evade the requirements of the code, falsely states that the property involved does not include a rental unit, may be required to forfeit not more than $500 per dwelling unit in the rental unit being transferred. COMM 67.03 and 67.08 on weatherization are covered on the salesperson's exam. For more information, consult the following Web site:

WEB LINK

http://www.commerce.state.wi.us/SB/SB-RentalWeatherizationProgram.html.

QUESTIONS

1. John James died intestate, leaving a wife and daughter. Under the law of intestate succession, Mrs. James should receive the
   a. first $50,000 plus one-third of the remaining estate.
   b. first $25,000 plus one-half of the remaining estate.
   c. entire estate.
   d. first $25,000 plus one-third of the remaining estate.

2. Which of the following statements does *NOT* apply to a deed filed in Wisconsin?
   a. The deed must be signed by the grantor and delivered.
   b. The deed should be recorded.
   c. The buyer (grantee) must sign the deed.
   d. The deed must identify the parties involved.

3. Eleanor Roche owned property in joint tenancy with Carmen Renato. Carmen died intestate, leaving only her husband, Raul. The property goes to
   a. Raul, by right of survivorship.
   b. Raul, the husband, as surviving spouse under the law of intestate succession.
   c. Eleanor, because she is now a tenant in common.
   d. Eleanor, by right of survivorship as joint tenant.

4. For 25 years, Nora Shelley has lived on a parcel of land in the northern woods of Wisconsin without title to the land. She has had a garden farm on the land and has built a cabin. Nora can claim the land that she has used as her own by
   a. advertising in the local newspaper that she has a claim on the land.
   b. placing a sign on the land indicating that she has a claim on the land.
   c. informing the owners that she has a claim on the land.
   d. filing a claim of ownership by adverse possession.

5. A house in Wisconsin is sold for $145,050. The buyer has a mortgage for $116,040. How much must the seller pay as a real estate transfer fee when the deed is recorded?
   a. $435
   b. $348
   c. $435.60
   d. $435.30

6. The Rental Weatherization Code is administered by the
   a. Department of Natural Resources.
   b. Real Estate Board.
   c. Department of Commerce.
   d. Department of Regulation and Licensing.

7. Unless a property or transfer is shown to be excluded from the code, a Department of Commerce transfer authorization must accompany the documents of transfer for rental property when the register of deeds is asked to record them. Which would *NOT* be an acceptable type of transfer authorization?
   a. Waiver
   b. Certificate of occupancy
   c. Stipulation
   d. Certificate of compliance

8. If a property meets the weatherization standards of the code, it may receive a certificate of compliance, which will cover any transfer of the property for
   a. one year.
   b. two years.
   c. three years.
   d. the life of the building.

9. Which type of residential rental property would be covered by the Rental Weatherization Code?
   a. A mobile home
   b. A single-family home built in 1975
   c. A motel used primarily for transient residency
   d. An owner-occupied, four-unit apartment building

10. Which of the following parties is responsible for paying the real estate transfer fee?

a. Broker
b. Grantee
c. Grantor
d. Lendor

11. Any person who intentionally falsifies value on a transfer fee return may be

a. fined not more than $500.
b. imprisoned not more than six months.
c. fined not more than $1,000.
d. imprisoned not more than three months.

Title Records

RECORDING DOCUMENTS

Any document affecting real estate that is signed and acknowledged may be recorded. The documents must disclose who drafted it, must conform to the layout requirements of the statutes, and must contain, in some counties, the tax parcel number of the property being conveyed.

A purchaser is charged with constructive notice of the contents of all recorded documents that are in the chain of title to the property he or she is purchasing. This means that they are treated as though they actually know about each recorded document even though they may not.

Wisconsin is a "Race Notice" state. That is, in the event the owner conveys a property to two different buyers, the one who records his or her deed first, provided that he or she has no actual knowledge of the other competing interest, becomes the owner.

Foreign Language Documents

An instrument must be *written in English* in order to be recorded in Wisconsin. To record a foreign language instrument, a *translated duplicate of the instrument* must be attached to the original along with a written authentication of the instrument.

Title Evidence

In most real estate sales transactions that take place in Wisconsin, *the seller is required to furnish evidence of his or her good title to the property that is being sold.* In Wisconsin, *the title abstract is acceptable evidence of title*. This history of recorded documents affecting the title to a parcel of real estate must be examined and evaluated by a real estate attorney, who then prepares his or her opinion of the title or ownership rights.

Title Insurance

Title insurance is used extensively in Wisconsin because lenders who sell their loans in the secondary market require it.

Title insurance generally protects the insured (buyer) against the effects of undiscovered and undisclosed title defects. Some examples are forged conveyances, improperly delivered deeds, and deeds given by sellers who are incompetent. Matters that are not covered are set forth in Schedule B of both the commitment and the policy. Forms have been standardized by the American Land Title Association (ALTA). The loan policy insures the priority of the lien of a mortgage. When a loan policy is issued at the same time as an owner's policy, the charge for the lender's policy is generally under $100. An owner's policy insures only the current owner. This means that each time the property is sold, a new policy, insuring the interest of the new buyer, must be purchased.

Torrens System

The Torrens system of registering title to real estate has not been adopted in Wisconsin.

Business Opportunity Sales

Every business, no matter how small, must have a place of operation. Whether it is a small, direct-mail sales enterprise operated from the owner's home or a large manufacturing concern with numerous factories and sales offices, the operation of a business involves the use of real estate. Consequently, when a business is sold, the title or lease to real estate used in the business usually is included in the sale. For this reason, *a person who sells or negotiates the sale of businesses for others for a fee is required to be licensed as a real estate broker or must be a licensed salesperson who is employed by a broker*; salespeople may use business offers.

When the sale includes chattel (that is, trade fixtures and other items of personal property) as well as an interest in the real estate, personal property may be listed in the offer to purchase or an additional agreement must be executed by the seller. At the closing of a business sales transaction, a separate bill of sale should be executed by the seller for all chattel, stock, materials, and other items of personal property that are included in the sale. Personal property should not be listed in the deed.

A license to act as a real estate broker or salesperson does not entitle the licensee to negotiate the sale of an incorporated business where the transfer is to be made by transfer of any controlling common stock; such a transaction requires the license of a security dealer.

Uniform Commercial Code

The Uniform Commercial Code was adopted in Wisconsin in 1965. The sections of the code that are most applicable to the real estate business concern bulk transfers and security agreements.

In most businesses, supplies, goods, and services constantly are being purchased on credit and paid for periodically as the suppliers submit their bills. *The regulations relating to bulk transfers are designed to protect the creditors of a business from the fraud that may be perpetrated by a business owner who sells the business, including equipment and stock, and then disappears without paying the creditors*. In such a case, the creditors cannot follow the conveyed goods and demand payment from the new owner unless it can be proved that the new owner had actual knowledge of the fraud.

To prevent such a fraud from occurring in the sale of a business, the purchaser should require the seller to execute a *bulk sales affidavit—a sworn statement listing any liens or unpaid bills that might become liens* against the stock, fixtures, or furniture included in the sale. A list of creditors should be included, specifying the amount due to each creditor. In addition, the purchaser must notify each creditor of the pending sale by registered mail at least ten days before the sale takes place. The purchaser of a business who fails to obtain a bulk sales affidavit from the seller or fails to give creditors due notice can be held responsible for unpaid invoices, even though he or she paid the seller in good faith for the full value of the items involved.

The Bulk Transfer law, Chapter 406 of the Wisconsin Statutes, is covered on the salesperson's exam.

Lis Pendens

Wisconsin law requires that notice be recorded when filing a suit that may result in a lien or title claim against any property. This notice, called *lis pendens*, gives constructive notice of the action against the property to any person who has or will acquire an interest in the property. Such notice may create a *cloud on the title*, which will prevent conveyance of the property until the suit is settled.

QUESTIONS

1. To be placed in the public record, documents must be
   a. filed under the grantee's name.
   b. filed under the grantor's name.
   c. acknowledged or authenticated.
   d. filed in the tract index.
2. Which of the following statements is true of unrecorded deeds?
   a. They are valid between parties to a transaction.
   b. They are not valid between parties to a transaction.
   c. They protect the rights of subsequent purchasers and lenders.
   d. They protect the grantee against the claims of subsequent purchasers and lenders.
3. In Wisconsin, deeds may be recorded
   a. under the Torrens system of title registration.
   b. in the office of the local zoning administrator.
   c. in the assessor's office.
   d. in the register of deeds office of the county in which the property is located.
4. Which of the following describes foreign language documents in Wisconsin?
   a. May be recorded if they are acknowledged
   b. Must have an English translation attached to the original in order to be recorded
   c. May be recorded as they appear
   d. May be recorded as they appear if they are authenticated
5. Which of the following statements is true of a title abstract and attorney's opinion?
   a. It is acceptable evidence of title in Wisconsin.
   b. It commonly is used in many parts of Wisconsin.
   c. It proves that the holder has title to the property.
   d. It protects the purchaser and lender against undetected title defects.
6. Which of the following statements does *NOT* correctly describe the Uniform Commercial Code?
   a. The code does not cover bulk transfers.
   b. The code has been adopted in Wisconsin.
   c. The code covers security agreements.
   d. The code affects requirements for the sale of a business property, among other things.
7. The purchaser of a business must notify each creditor of the pending sale at *LEAST*
   a. 3 days before the sale takes place.
   b. 5 days before the sale takes place.
   c. 10 days before the sale takes place.
   d. 30 days before the sale takes place.

10 CHAPTER

Real Estate License Laws

WISCONSIN REAL ESTATE LAW

The real estate business in Wisconsin is regulated by the laws contained in Chapter 440 and Chapter 452 of the Wisconsin Statutes and by rules adopted by the Department of Regulation and Licensing and enforced by the Wisconsin Real Estate Board. These rules elaborate on the basic law and provide additional guidelines for Wisconsin real estate licensees. The laws became effective in 1919, the same year the Wisconsin Real Estate Examining Board was established. In 1982, the Real Estate Examining Board became the Real Estate Board.

The department is totally responsible for the creation and administration of the licensing examinations, which essentially reflect current practices. The department also is responsible for issuing and renewing licenses and approving educational programs. The department also has the responsibility for promulgating administrative rules with advice from the board. In addition, the board can prepare a formal dissenting opinion if it strongly disagrees with any proposed rule change. The board has responsibility for the discipline of licensees, whereby four members of the profession and three public members decide whether to reprimand a licensee or to limit, suspend, or revoke a license, according to due process of law. The board may also fine a licensee and assess for the cost of investigating and prosecuting an investigative case.

Who Must Be Licensed (Section 452.03)

Under Section 452.03 of the Wisconsin Statutes, *it is illegal for a person to engage in the real estate business, to advertise, or to act temporarily as a real estate broker or sales-*

person without a real estate license. The penalty for acting as a broker or salesperson without a license or violating any other provision of the real estate law is a fine of up to $1,000 or up to six months' imprisonment or both (Section 4532.17).

In addition, a person engaged in the real estate business or acting as a real estate broker or salesperson *may not file a court suit to collect payment for such activities unless that person can prove that he or she was properly licensed at the time the activities or services in question were performed* (Section 452.20).

Generally, the Department of Regulation and Licensing and the Real Estate Board take the position that people who are physically present in Wisconsin when they negotiate the sale, rental, or exchange of real estate or a business must be licensed in Wisconsin. Negotiate includes showing Wisconsin property or placing your sign on a Wisconsin property.

However, a licensee of another state need not be licensed in Wisconsin to advertise the sale or rental of property in Wisconsin newspapers.

Nor must a licensee of another state be licensed in Wisconsin in order to send letters to prospective buyers, sellers, or renters in Wisconsin or call them on the telephone subject to the no-call law and lists.

Definitions

Real estate broker (Section 452.01[2]). A *real estate broker* is defined as any person who, while acting for another person for compensation or the promise of compensation, negotiates or attempts to negotiate a sale, exchange, purchase or rental of an interest or estate in real estate; sale, exchange, purchase or rental of any business, its goodwill, inventory, fixtures or an interest therein; or sale, exchange, or purchase of a time-share. (It includes a pattern of sales for one's own property or business.) Section 452.2(2) states that five sales in one year or ten sales in five years is presumptive evidence of a pattern of sales.

The word *person* as used throughout the license law refers to an individual, a partnership, a corporation, or a limited liability company.

Real estate salesperson (Section 452.01[7]). A *real estate salesperson* is defined as any person who is licensed under and associated with a supervising broker and who directly or indirectly represents that broker when performing any of the activities described under the definition of broker.

Time-share salesperson (Section 452.01[9]). A *time-share salesperson* is defined as any person who is employed by a licensed broker to sell, or offer, or attempt to negotiate an initial sale or purchase of a time-share, but who may not perform any other acts authorized to be performed by a broker or salesperson. A person desiring to act as a time-share salesperson must submit to the department an application for certificate of registration (Section 452.025[1]).

Apprentice salesperson (Section RL22). An *apprentice salesperson* is issued a one-year permit that allows him or her to perform some of the activities (discussed later in this chapter) of a real estate salesperson.

Cemetery brokers and salespeople (Section 452.02). Since November 1, 1991, the Real Estate Board no longer has any authority relating to the regulation of cemeteries and cemetery salespeople. A real estate broker or salesperson may negotiate an occasional sale of a cemetery lot for another person; however, if the broker or salesperson does so as an employee of a cemetery authority, the broker or salesperson must obtain a separate cemetery salesperson registration from the Wisconsin Department of Regulation and Licensing.

Mortgage bankers (DFI-Bkg Section RL40.03). A person is not able to participate as a mortgage banker, loan originator, or loan solicitor unless he or she has registered as such with the Wisconsin Department of Financial Institutions. The registrant is not required to take the real estate licensing examination. Licensees who receive a fee for finding or negotiating a mortgage would have to register as loan solicitors with the Wisconsin Department of Financial Institutions.

Exceptions (Section 452.01[3]). The real estate license law does not apply to the following nine categories:

1. Persons who purchase real estate for their own use or who sell, exchange, lease, rent, or otherwise dispose of their own real estate (note the exception under broker's definition)
2. Receivers, trustees, administrators, executors, guardians or persons appointed by or acting under the judgment or order for any court
3. Public officers while performing their official duties
4. Banks, savings and loans, and other designated financial institutions when transacting business within the scope of their corporate powers as provided by law
5. Credit unions or any licensed attorney who, incidental to the general practice of law, negotiates loans secured by real estate mortgages or encumbrances or transfers of real estate
6. Employees of persons engaged in the previously mentioned activities when such employees are engaged in the specific performance of their duties
7. Janitors, custodians, or other persons employed by an owner or a manager of a residential building who show apartments or accept lease applications
8. Persons who own rental properties, regardless of the number, and who act on their own behalf when renting these properties
9. Persons registered as mortgage bankers under Section 224.72 who do not engage in the activities of real estate brokers

THE WISCONSIN REAL ESTATE BOARD (SECTIONS 452.04, 15.07, AND 15.405[11])

Organization and Members

The Wisconsin Real Estate Board, as now constituted, was created in 1982. Seven members sit on the board, all of whom are appointed by the governor. The law requires that four of the board members be real estate brokers or salespeople licensed in Wisconsin and that three of the members be from the general public, not personally or by family or by business relationships be engaged in the practice of real estate. The members are paid $25 per day plus expenses when they are working for the board. Each board member serves for a four-year term; the appointments are staggered to avoid expirations occurring at the same time.

Duties and Powers

Each year, the board elects a chairperson, vice-chairperson, and secretary from its members. The board advises the department secretary on matters relating to real estate, especially on administrative rules, and it has the power to enforce such rules. Generally, these rules clarify the broader provisions of the law and describe more specific requirements for applicants and licensees.

The Department of Regulation and Licensing conducts examinations to determine the competency of real estate license applicants and prepares letters and bulletins for distribution to its licensees. The department also may authorize the revision of real estate study manuals and other research and educational projects for the benefit of its licensees and the protection of the public. The department, with the board's assistance, approves real estate contractual forms.

Roster of Brokers and Salespeople (Sections 440.035[4] and 452.12[4])

The department makes available *computer printouts of the names and addresses of all licensees in the state of Wisconsin* to the public for purchase at cost.

LICENSING PROCEDURE

Applications and Requirements (Section 452.09)

An application for a real estate license must be made on a form provided by the Wisconsin Department of Regulation and Licensing; applications are available on the department Web site. You may also download statutes and administrative rules there.

WEB LINK @

http://www.drl.state.wi.us

In addition to the application, every applicant must

- be at least 18 years old;
- provide proof of competency as reasonably may be required by the department;
- provide information on the business or occupation engaged in by the applicant for two years preceding application;
- pass the appropriate licensing examination;
- furnish proof of having completed the appropriate educational requirement as a condition to receiving the license;
- provide information on the location from which real estate business will be conducted and how this place of business will be designated, (Post Office address is not allowed); and
- furnish any additional information required by the department.

Before receiving a new license, applicants who previously were licensed may be asked to show proof that they did not engage in real estate activities during the time their licenses were expired.

Broker-Employer's Duty to Check Licensure of Employees (Section RL17)

Section RL17 states that a broker-employer shall, prior to employing a licensee and at the beginning of each biennial licensure period, determine that each licensee employed by the broker is properly licensed. A broker-employer may not employ an unlicensed person or a person who has failed to file the notice of employment required under Section RL17.04 or the transfer application required by Section RL17.05 to engage in real estate practice for the broker-employer.

Education Requirements (Section RL25)

Each applicant for an original salesperson's license must submit to the department proof of attendance at 72 classroom hours of educational programs approved by the department. Applicants may choose to take either classroom education or distance education to fulfill the educational requirements for prelicensing as well as continuing education.

Distance education focuses on the fact that neither an instructor nor a proctor is physically present with the student. The student may undertake instruction by using a paper, electronic, or audiovisual medium without an instructor or proctor present to take attendance or supervise the presentation of the instruction. The school is required to address various criteria including how it will provide a reasonable opportunity for student self-evaluation of mastery. The department may waive the educational requirement with proof that the applicant has received ten semester-hour credits in real estate or real estate-related law courses at an accredited institution of higher education.

Each applicant for an original broker's license must submit to the department proof of attendance at an additional 36 classroom hours of educational programs approved by the department.

The department may waive the educational requirement with proof that the applicant has received 20 semester-hour credits in real estate or real estate-related law courses at an accredited institution of higher education, or proof that the applicant is licensed to practice law in Wisconsin. Educational programs must be completed before taking the licensing examination.

Continuing-Education Requirements (Section 452.12[5])

All licensees, except those initially licensed during the current two-year licensure period, are required to attend up to 12 classroom hours of approved educational programs during each biennial renewal period as a condition of renewal. The continuing-education requirement is determined by the Wisconsin Department of Regulation and Licensing in conjunction with the recommendation of the Wisconsin Real Estate Board. In lieu of classroom education, a licensee may take and pass a test-out examination conducted by the department prior to July 1 of the second year of each biennium.

Examinations (Section 452.09[3])

The Wisconsin real estate licensing examinations for brokers and salespeople are administered by Promissor. The salesperson exam consists of 140 questions and is primarily state-specific and transaction based. The salesperson exam focuses on state law, the rules and regulations enforced by the Wisconsin Real Estate Board, and selected approved forms required for use by real estate licensees. The broker's exam focus is similar to the salesperson's exam and includes 100 questions. A score of 75 percent or better is required to pass the salesperson's and broker's examinations.

Licensing Corporations and Partnerships (Section 452.12[2])

A corporation, partnership, or limited liability company that applies for a real estate broker's license, entitled "business entity license," must have at least one officer or member who has a real estate broker's license. The application for a partnership license must be verified by two members of the partnership; an application for a corporate license must be signed by the president and secretary of the corporation. An application for a limited liability company license must be verified by two members of the limited liability company.

A corporation applying for a broker's license must give the department a list of the names and addresses of the officers and directors. In addition, every officer or member of the firm who wishes to engage in real estate activities must hold a real estate license. The department may require information on every officer and member of the firm, including their names, addresses, and previous businesses.

Fees (Sections 440.05 and 440.08)

The following fees are applicable to Wisconsin licensees:

- Issuance of an original salesperson license $53
- Issuance of an original broker license $53
- Renewal fee for a salesperson license $83
- Renewal fee for a broker license $128
- Renewal fee for a business entity license $56
- Penalty for renewing after the expiration date $25
- Transfer to a new employing broker $10

Issuing a License

An applicant who has passed the appropriate real estate license examination and has complied with the necessary requirements will be granted a license by the department. The license authorizes the new licensee to engage in the activities of a real estate broker or salesperson as described in the license law. Every license shows the name and address of the licensee. Both a wall license and a pocket license are issued to all licensees. Licenses are sent directly to the applicant.

Licensing Nonresidents (Sections RL25.025, RL25.035 and 452.11)

Nonresidents who apply for a license to engage in real estate activities in Wisconsin must fulfill all of the requirements that apply to a resident. Nonresident brokers do not have to maintain an active place of business in the state in which they are licensed and are allowed to employ brokers, salespeople, or time-share salespeople in Wisconsin. It is important to emphasize that an out-of-state applicant who has held an active real estate salesperson's license in another state within the two-year period prior to filing an application for an original salesperson's license may satisfy the 72-hour prelicensing educational requirement by attending 13 hours of the 72-hour salesperson class at a school approved by the Wisconsin Department of Regulation and Licensing. The applicant must also have completed 59 hours of education related to the 72-hour program at any school. The applicant is required to pass just the state specific portion of the salesperson exam (40 questions).

An out-of-state applicant who has held an active real estate broker's license in another state within the two-year period prior to filing an application for an original real estate broker's license may satisfy the 36-hour prelicensing educational requirement by attending 3 hours of the 36-hour broker's class at a school approved by the Wisconsin Department of Regulation and Licensing. The applicant must also have completed 33 hours of education related to the 36-hour program at any school. The applicant is required to pass a reciprocal broker's exam consisting of 70 questions rather than the 100-question broker's exam for in-state applicants.

Irrevocable consent. Before any license can be issued to an applicant, *the applicant or licensee and every resident licensee who becomes a nonresident must file an irrevocable consent form with the department.* This consent provides that actions brought against the out-of-state licensee in connection with real estate transactions in Wisconsin may be initiated in any Wisconsin court of competent jurisdiction. Notice of such suits may be served on the Wisconsin Department of

Regulation and Licensing, which will send a duplicate copy to the nonresident licensee. The consent also stipulates that the court's ruling on any suit will be binding on the nonresident licensee.

GENERAL OPERATION OF A REAL ESTATE BUSINESS

Place of Business

The department considers the address on a broker's license as the broker's *principal place of business*. The broker must conduct business only under the name and at the address indicated on his or her license unless the broker sends a notice of additional trade names to the department. A broker can work out of his or her home. It is unlawful for a broker to allow a salesperson to use the broker's license and operate a real estate business in the broker's name if the broker has no control or only nominal control of the business.

Branch Office (Sections 452.12; RL17.02; RL17.10)

A broker may establish one or more branch offices, as defined by Wisconsin regulations. All business transacted in the branch office may be performed by the broker-employer or under the direct supervision of a full-time broker-manager. Branch office managers are no longer required in Wisconsin, but the broker must still provide adequate guidance and supervision for all salespeople at the branch offices.

Change of Address (Section RL23)

The department must be notified of any change in a licensee's address within 30 days of the change. In such a case, the licensee may make the change on the license or may request a new license and pay a $10 fee. Failure to report a change of address constitutes grounds for disciplinary action.

License Renewal

Wisconsin real estate licenses are renewed on a biennial basis. Licensees should return the application for renewal in the fall of every even-numbered year following licensure. Any licensee who has failed to file an application to renew his or her license by January 1 must cease real estate activities until a new license is issued. Licenses may be renewed after the expiration date if the renewal application is accompanied by a late penalty of $25.

Termination of Employment (Section RL17.06)

A salesperson may be licensed under only one broker at a time. When a salesperson is discharged or terminated for any reason, the salesperson must send a notice of termination to the department within ten days after the termination of employment.

A salesperson who has terminated employment with a broker may not engage in any real estate activities until a transfer application has been filed with or mailed to the department. When transferring to a new broker-employer, a salesperson must submit the transfer form with a $10 fee. The license should not be submitted with the form and the fee. The transfer form will register the name of the new broker with the Wisconsin Department of Regulation and Licensing. A form will be sent to the salesperson, with a copy for his or her new broker-employer, stating the name of his or her registered broker-employer. The salesperson can begin working for the new broker as soon as the transfer form is completed and mailed. If the salesperson does not receive the registration slip, he or she should check with the department to be sure it received the transfer form.

Apprentice Salesperson's Activities (Section RL22)

Wisconsin regulations severely limit the real estate activities that may be performed by an apprentice salesperson under a temporary license. During the first six months, an apprentice salesperson is not permitted to secure any listing or offer to purchase unless accompanied by a licensed salesperson or broker. All contracts negotiated by the apprentice must be inspected by the employing broker before they are considered legally binding on the parties. Apprentices are never permitted to conduct closings, advertise property, or collect commissions on sales. Wisconsin brokers are charged with instructing apprentices in real estate activities for a minimum number of hours each week.

Delivery of Contracts (Chapter RL15)

Wisconsin brokers or salespeople must deliver a copy of every listing agreement, lease, offer to purchase, and closing statement to all parties connected with these transactions at the time such documents are signed.

Section RL15.04 states that a broker must retain for at least three years exact and complete copies of all listing contracts, offers to purchase, leases, closing statements, deposit receipts, canceled checks, trust account records, and other documents or correspondence received or prepared by the broker in connection with any transaction. The retention period runs from the date of closing of the transaction or, if the transaction has not been consummated, from the date of listing.

Care and Handling of Funds (Chapter RL18)

All funds entrusted to a broker in connection with a real estate transaction must be placed in a special trust account that the broker maintains for this purpose in a Wisconsin bank, savings bank, or credit union that is authorized to do business in Wisconsin. The law requires that client funds from sales transactions, such as earnest money or other money, be held in interest-bearing common trust accounts. The law defines client funds as all down payments, earnest money deposits, or other money related to a conveyance of sale, exchange, and option to buy of real estate that is received by a broker, salesperson, or time-share salesperson on behalf of the broker's, salesperson's, or time-share salesperson's principal, or any other person. Promissory notes are not included in the definition of client funds. Nonclient funds include property management and transactions involving leases.

The interest earned on interest-bearing trust accounts related to client funds will be paid annually by the depository institution to the Wisconsin Department of Administration to assist in the implementation of Wisconsin's program for aiding the homeless.

A broker may establish more than one trust-fund account. The only time a broker must keep a trust account and maintain records is when the broker has real estate trust funds in his or her possession.

The broker must inform the department of the name of the financial institution and the account number under which these funds are deposited. The broker also must notify the department of any changes in this information. The broker is held personally responsible for all funds while they are in his or her possession. In general, only the broker can withdraw or deposit funds into a trust account although other persons may sign trust-account checks or share drafts if certain requirements are met.

Funds must be deposited within 48 hours of receipt by the broker or salesperson. If money is received prior to a holiday or nonbusiness day, money may be deposited within the next two business days. In a few instances, earnest-money deposits will take the form of government bonds, stocks, or other nondepositable funds. Section RL18 states that nondepositable payments (with the exception of promissory notes) may not be held by a broker as a down payment; nondepositable payments must be held by some other party, subject to an escrow agreement prepared by the parties or an attorney.

Entrusted funds may never be commingled with a real estate licensee's personal funds. A broker is prohibited from depositing in the account any funds that were not received in connection with a real estate transaction for which the broker is acting as agent, except for one or two minor exceptions to the rule. However, a broker may deposit a sum not to exceed $300 from his or her personal funds that is specifically identified and deposited to cover service charges relating to the trust account.

The broker is required to remove commissions, fees, and reimbursable expenses from the trust account within 24 hours after the transaction is consummated or terminated or after the commissions or fees are earned in accordance with the contract involved.

There are four specific rule requirements:

1. Brokers may have more than one interest-bearing trust account for client funds.
2. Brokers may authorize other persons to sign trust-account checks provided the person is 18 years of age.
3. Brokers must transfer earnest money to a listing broker no later than 30 days after they receive it, unless they have obtained definitive information from the depository institution that a check has not cleared and within 24 hours after receiving notice of the check clearing the account.
4. Brokers have ten days to increase their personal funds in a trust account to cover a shortage of funds needed to pay service charges.

Record Keeping (Chapter RL18)

A broker is required to keep specific records regarding deposits and disbursements of entrusted funds. The broker must have a set of checks and deposit slips for the trust account that indicate the broker's business name and address and clearly identify the account as a real estate trust account. Checks drawn on this account must be identified as to the specific transactions and be retained by the broker along with any voided checks. The broker also must keep a duplicate deposit receipt that shows the source of each deposit and the date and place it was made.

In addition, the broker must keep a record book of itemized deposits and disbursements of entrusted funds. For all funds received, the record book (called a *journal*) must include the date, the names of the parties, and the amount. For all disbursements, the journal must include the date, the payee, the check number, and the amount. A running balance must be recorded for each day in which receipts or disbursements are entered in the journal.

Each broker also must keep an *individual trust ledger* sheet for each transaction, noting the details of the transaction and any entrusted funds taken in or paid out by the broker. For funds received, the ledger must include the names of the parties to a transaction, the date, and the amount. For disbursements, the date, the payee, the check number, and the amount must be recorded.

A real estate trust-fund account generally must be balanced monthly. All related records must be kept up to date, and a bank reconciliation must be prepared. The reconciliation then must be compared to the journal and the ledger. Departmental auditors or other representatives may examine and audit the broker's trust-fund account when they deem it necessary.

The rules state that if brokers have their trust-account records computerized, they must make a backup copy of them on any day in which entries are made. The backup copy must be on a medium that is separate from that on which the source documents reside. Brokers must also be able to immediately print out computer records and make them available to the Department of Regulation and Licensing when requested.

Commissions

As noted earlier, a person must hold a real estate license to collect a commission for engaging in real estate activities. In addition, Section 452.19 of the Wisconsin Statutes makes it illegal for a licensee to split a fee with someone who does not have a real estate license.

Licensees' Obligations to the General Public (Section RL24)

The department has adopted a comprehensive code of ethics. Copies of real estate statutes and rules, which include the code of ethics, may be obtained by writing to the following address:

Wisconsin Department of Regulation and Licensing
Bureau of Direct Licensing and Real Estate
PO Box 8935
Madison, WI 53708

Current rules relating to the practice of real estate in Wisconsin cost $5.28, which includes tax and handling. As stated above, you may download the statutes and rules on the department Web site.

WEB LINK

@

http://www.drl.state.wi.us

Legal Advice by Licensees (Section RL16)

As discussed in Chapter 7, Wisconsin brokers and salespeople may prepare approved preprinted documents relating to real estate transactions. However, a licensee may prepare documents only for transactions in which he or she is acting as a broker, an agent, or a principal. At no time may a licensee charge a fee for preparing those documents or attempt to explain any of the legal implications of the documents to any party to the transaction.

Advertising (Chapter RL24)

Regulations regarding advertising in real estate are covered in Section 100.18 of the statutes and enforced by the Wisconsin Department of Agriculture, Trade and Consumer Protection. This law includes a section that is meant to protect consumers against unfair, deceptive, false, and misleading practices by merchants. It is reasonably clear that the broker is considered a merchant in a transaction involving real estate. However, the 1995 Wisconsin Act 179, which became effective on

April 18, 1996, exempts real estate licensees from provisions in S. 100.18 of the Wisconsin Statutes relating to representations made while engaged in real estate practice. The exemption does not apply when a licensee knows that a representation is untrue, deceptive, or misleading. This act also states that no attorney fees may be recovered from a person licensed under Chapter 452, Wisconsin Statutes, while that person is engaged in real estate practice.

Section RL24.04 requires licensees to present a true picture when advertising or making representations to the public. Licensees may not advertise without disclosing the licensee's name or permit any person associated with the licensee to use individual names or telephone numbers unless such person's connection with the licensee is obvious in the ad.

For sale signs. Section 86.19 of the Wisconsin Statutes prohibits the placing of real estate signs within the right-of-way of any street or highway. Statutes and rules also control the placing of signs along, but off, the right-of-way. This control is accomplished by a permit process administered by the Wisconsin Department of Transportation District Maintenance Offices. Real estate signs are exempt from the permit process if they meet certain requirements relating to size, location, and lighting. Additionally, municipalities in the state have either limited the use of signs or prohibited them altogether.

Suspension or Revocation of a License (Section 452.14)

The department may investigate the actions of any licensee who is suspected of performing one or more prohibited acts while engaging in real estate activities. The investigation may be initiated solely by the department, or it may be prompted by the written complaint of any person claiming to have been injured or defrauded by the actions of a real estate licensee. A licensee may be disciplined for any of the following 15 acts:

1. Making a material misstatement
2. Making a substantial misrepresentation
3. Making false promises
4. Pursuing a continued course of misrepresentation through agents, salespeople, or advertising
5. Acting for more than one party in a transaction without informing all parties
6. Accepting a commission or referral fee as a salesperson from any person except the employer
7. Representing or attempting to represent a broker other than his or her employer, without the express knowledge and consent of the employer
8. Failing to account for or pay out any monies belonging to others that have come into the licensee's possession
9. Displaying any conduct that demonstrates incompetency
10. Paying or offering to pay a commission to anyone who does not hold a real estate license
11. Intentionally encouraging or discouraging any person from purchasing or renting real estate in a particular area on the basis of race
12. Being guilty of any other conduct that constitutes improper, fraudulent, or dishonest dealing
13. Violating any provision of Section 452 of the Wisconsin Statutes or of the department's rules and regulations

14. Failing to use current forms approved by the department
15. Treating any person unequally solely because of sex, race, color, disability, religion, sexual orientation, national origin, ancestry, marital status, lawful source of income, age, or familial status or in any other unlawful manner

In addition to the above discipline, the board may assess a forfeiture of not more than $1,000 for each violation and require additional education or training.

Right to a Hearing

The department cannot suspend or revoke a license of any licensee without offering the licensee a right to a public hearing. At least ten days before the hearing, the board must send written notice of the time and place of the hearing to the applicant or licensee and to his or her attorney.

A real estate broker or salesperson who is notified that his or her license is suspended or revoked immediately must forward the license to the department. A broker's license issued to a corporation, partnership, limited liability company, or limited liability partnership may be suspended if a licensed officer, partner, director, or member commits an action sufficient to cause suspension or revocation.

Restraining Orders (Section 440.21)

If the department feels that a person is acting without a license and that this activity might be injurious to the public interest, the department may petition the circuit court for a temporary restraining order or injunction against a licensee in lieu of a hearing.

Review (Section 227)

A person whose real estate license has been limited, suspended, or revoked, or who has been reprimanded by the board; or who has been otherwise disciplined (forfeiture, costs) has a right to request a review by the circuit court of the county in which the licensee resides. The court will review the proceedings at which the disciplinary action took place.

Reissue of Licenses (Section 452.15)

A licensee whose license is revoked or denied may not reapply for licensure until the expiration of a period determined in each case by the board, or in the case of a second offense of racial discrimination, not less than five years from the date the revocation became finally effective. The salesperson's exam covers most of the material discussed in this chapter.

QUESTIONS

1. Which of the following persons must have a real estate broker's license in order to transact business?
   a. Wilfred Shannon, who owns a six-flat and personally manages the building, collects rent, and shows the apartments to prospective tenants
   b. Leslie Albers, who negotiates the sale of entire businesses, including their stock, equipment, and buildings, for a promised fee
   c. Frank Drew, superintendent of a large apartment building, who shows apartments to prospective tenants as part of his regular duties
   d. Wanda Sutton, who has her father's written authority to negotiate the sale of and to convey a residence he owns

2. The Wisconsin Real Estate Board is composed of
   a. five members who are real estate brokers licensed in Wisconsin.
   b. six members who are real estate brokers licensed in Wisconsin.
   c. four members who are real estate brokers or salespeople licensed in Wisconsin and three public members.
   d. seven members who are real estate brokers or salespeople licensed in Wisconsin and three public members.

3. Applicants for a real estate salesperson's license must
   a. be at least 19 years of age.
   b. complete 30 credits in real estate before being issued a license.
   c. be at least 21 years of age.
   d. complete the appropriate educational requirement prior to taking the licensing exam.

4. Wisconsin real estate law requires that persons applying for a broker's license must attend how many classroom hours of educational programs approved by the department?
   a. 45
   b. 90
   c. 72
   d. 108

5. Which of the following statements regarding the licensing of corporations and partnerships as real estate brokers is *TRUE*?
   a. All the officers or partners must qualify as brokers and pass the required written examination.
   b. The corporation's or partnership's license is in effect only as long as the designated broker is associated with the firm.
   c. Any partner or officer of a licensed corporation may engage in brokerage activities.
   d. The applicant corporation or partnership must file an irrevocable consent agreement with the commission.

6. Which statement does *NOT* correctly describe a branch office?
   a. A branch office must operate under the same name as the parent office.
   b. A branch office must have a manager who is a licensed real estate broker.
   c. A broker may establish no more than ten branch offices.
   d. All business transacted in the branch office must be performed in the name of the broker-employer.

7. When a salesperson is discharged or terminated for any reason, the supervising broker
   a. must send a letter of release to the department.
   b. must send a communication to the salesperson's last known residence informing the salesperson that his or her license has been returned to the board.
   c. must state whether the person was competent.
   d. is not responsible for informing the department of the discharge or termination.

8. An earnest-money deposit received by the broker must be
   a. placed in the broker's business account.
   b. given to the seller within 24 hours.
   c. kept in an office safe with proper records maintained by the broker.
   d. deposited in a special trust account within 48 hours after the broker receives it.

9. Salesperson Omar Kent is unhappy with the terms of his association with the Sara Holmes Realty Company and has decided to associate with Jerry Curtis at Curtis Homes. What must be done before Kent can begin selling for Curtis?
   a. Sara Holmes must send Kent's pocket license to Curtis.
   b. Curtis must notify the department of the change.
   c. Kent must file a transfer application form with the department.
   d. Sara Holmes must return Kent's pocket license to the commission.

10. Which is *NOT* cause for the revocation of a real estate license in Wisconsin?
   a. Paying a commission to a person who does not hold a real estate license
   b. Selling cemetery plots without holding a Wisconsin real estate license
   c. Posting a For Sale sign without the consent of the owner
   d. Representing anyone other than a salesperson's supervising broker without the consent of that broker

11. Which statement correctly describes what an apprentice salesperson cannot do during an apprenticeship?
   a. The apprentice can conduct a closing.
   b. The apprentice can negotiate a contract without the direct supervision of a licensed salesperson or broker.
   c. The apprentice can collect commissions on sales.
   d. The apprentice can advertise property.

12. Which describes the Wisconsin continuing-education requirement?
   a. Applies only to salespeople
   b. Applies only to brokers
   c. Requires all licensees to complete up to 20 hours in approved education programs during each biennial renewal period
   d. Applies to salespeople and brokers

13. Which statement is *TRUE* regarding real estate licenses in Wisconsin?
   a. They must be renewed by December 31 of each year following licensure.
   b. They must be renewed by December 31 of every even-numbered year following licensure.
   c. They must be renewed by January 31 of every odd-numbered year following licensure.
   d. They entitle the holder to negotiate a loan secured by real estate.

14. Which does *NOT* correctly describe what a corporation must do in order to receive a license?
   a. Have one officer or member who has a broker's license
   b. Submit a statement from the corporation president and secretary swearing to the competency of the applicant
   c. Give the department a list of names and addresses of the officers and directors
   d. Prove that every officer of the corporation who will engage in real estate activity for the firm holds a broker's license

15. In order to keep proper records of all real estate transaction funds, a broker must
   a. keep a permanent record book of all deposits and withdrawals, including dates, names, and amounts of receipts and all disbursements.
   b. keep a separate trust account for each account and not commingle the funds of any two accounts.
   c. place all deposits in a business account.
   d. balance the trust-fund account on a daily basis.

16. Which is *TRUE* of a broker under Wisconsin law?
   a. Must maintain a copy of all closing statements for two years from the date of closing
   b. May explain the legal implications of a contract to any party
   c. May not advertise services as free
   d. Must maintain a definite address in the state

17. Which statement is *TRUE* of Wisconsin real estate licensees?
   a. They must deliver a copy of every contract to the involved parties.
   b. They may, after collecting the fee from the principal, split this fee with any person who has been instrumental in the successful completion of the sale.
   c. They may charge a fee for preparing listing contracts.
   d. They may explain the legal implications of a document to any party.

18. A broker may deposit a sum of money not to exceed a certain amount from his or her personal funds that is specifically identified and deposited to cover service charges relating to the trust account. The amount of money is
   a. $100.
   b. $300.
   c. $200.
   d. $400.

19. Which of the following persons would *NOT* have to have a real estate license in order to transact business?
   a. A business opportunity broker
   b. A time-share broker
   c. A real estate salesperson
   d. A time-share salesperson

20. Which is *TRUE* of a nonresident broker?
   a. Must maintain an active place of business in the state in which the person is licensed
   b. May employ brokers in Wisconsin
   c. Must file with the department an irrevocable consent form
   d. May not employ time-share salespeople in Wisconsin

21. A broker having to increase his or her personal funds in a trust account to cover a shortage of funds needed to pay service charges must do so within
   a. 24 hours.
   b. 5 business days.
   c. 48 years.
   d. 10 business days.

22. A broker must retain exact and complete copies of all documents and correspondence received or prepared by the broker in any transaction for
   a. 1 year.
   b. 6 years.
   c. 3 years.
   d. 10 years.

23. You listed a property on May 1, 2003. The seller accepted an offer to purchase on June 2, 2003, and the transaction closed on August 1, 2003. Which statement correctly describes your responsibility for holding the listing contract?
   a. You should retain a copy of the listing contract until May 1, 2006.
   b. You should retain a copy of the listing contract until June 1, 2006.
   c. You should retain a copy of the listing contract until August 1, 2006.
   d. You should retain a copy of the listing contract until June 1, 2007.

24. You are considering placing your real estate sign within the right-of-way of your county highway, but you are not sure whether you need a permit. You should contact the
   a. Wisconsin Department of Transportation.
   b. Wisconsin Department of Natural Resources.
   c. Wisconsin Department of Regulation and Licensing.
   d. Wisconsin Real Estate Board.

25. Which statement does *NOT* correctly describe Section 100.18 of the Wisconsin Statutes?
   a. An attorney may recover his or her fees from a person licensed under Section 452, Wisconsin Statutes, while that person is engaged in real estate practice.
   b. Real estate licensees are exempted from provisions of the statute if they did not know that a representation was untrue, deceptive, or misleading.
   c. An attorney may not recover his or her fees from a person licensed under Section 452, Wisconsin Statutes, while that person is engaged in real estate practice.
   d. The exemption under this statute does not apply when a licensee knows that a representation is untrue, deceptive, or misleading.

Real Estate Financing

MORTGAGES

Wisconsin is a *lien-theory state* with regard to mortgages. According to this theory, a mortgage creates a lien on real property but does not convey title to the property to the mortgagee (lender).

Mortgage Loan Instruments

Two instruments—the mortgage and the note—are executed in connection with a mortgage loan. The mortgage conveys an interest in the real estate to the lender as security for the debt, while the mortgage note is a promise to repay the debt. Mortgages are the most common form of loan instruments in Wisconsin. *Trust deeds* are used in Wisconsin as security for mortgage bond issues for major construction projects only where substantial sums of money are involved.

In Wisconsin, mortgage agreements completed by Wisconsin brokers must be made on forms approved by the Wisconsin Department of Regulation and Licensing or the Wisconsin State Bar Association. If the department's approval is withdrawn, the form no longer can be used. Several mortgage document forms have been prepared by the State Bar Association and approved by the department for use by real estate brokers in Wisconsin. An attorney should prepare or at least review a mortgage before it is executed. The most commonly used form is Form 6-L.

Mortgage Foreclosure

Most mortgages are foreclosed under *judicial foreclosure by sale*. Nonjudicial foreclosure under a power-of-sale clause is permitted in Wisconsin but is seldom used. *Strict foreclosure* is not allowed when a mortgage is foreclosed. It is, however, used for land contracts.

The Wisconsin Statutes prescribe the process to be followed in foreclosing mortgages. Generally one or two processes are followed. The first allows the borrower 12 months after the entry of a foreclosure judgment to redeem the property (pay off the lender), and if there is not redemption, the sheriff sells the property at an auction. If the property does not sell for enough to completely pay off the lender, the lender is entitled to a judgment against the borrower for the balance due. This is called a deficiency judgment. The second method reduces the redemption period to six months, but the lender is not entitled to a deficiency judgment regardless of what the property sells for at the sheriff's sale.

In addition to the procedures previously discussed, a defaulted Wisconsin borrower may settle with the lender on a voluntary, out-of-court basis. If the two parties come to an agreement, the lender may execute a satisfaction of mortgage to the borrower. When the satisfaction is recorded along with a deed to the property executed by the borrower to the lender, the title passes to the lender and the borrower is released from his or her debt. When the parties close out a defaulted mortgage in this manner, Wisconsin courts place a heavy burden of responsibility on the lender to ensure fair treatment of the creditor. If a suit is filed, the borrower may be granted the right to redeem the property if he or she can prove unfair treatment.

Redemption

A defaulted Wisconsin borrower has the *equitable right of redemption prior to the sale.* Wisconsin statutes allow a *one-year redemption period from the time the foreclosure judgment is entered* (at least 20 days after the action is begun). There is *no statutory redemption (period) after the sale.* Some mortgages, such as those that contain a waiver of deficiency judgment and give the lender the right to appoint a receiver, allow only a six-month equitable redemption period.

Wisconsin Mortgage Provisions

A mortgage generally places several obligations on a mortgagor (borrower). For example, they must keep the premises insured and name the lender as an additional insured; they must pay the real estate taxes before they become delinquent; and they may not commit waste (take any action that diminishes the value of the premises). Failure to comply with these requirements constitutes a default under the terms of the mortgage and may permit the lender to foreclose on the mortgage even though the monthly payments required in the note have been made in a timely fashion.

Assignment of Mortgage

In Wisconsin, a mortgage may be sold by a lender to a third party, called an *assignee.* The lender should execute an assignment of mortgage form (usually State Bar Form 14), which should be recorded in the office of the register of deeds in the county in which the land is located. The *assignee has exactly the same rights that the original lender had in relation to the borrower.* An assignee should insist that a lender sign his or her name on the back of the mortgage note. This prevents the lender from claiming payments that might be paid to the lender by the borrower. *The assignee should notify the borrower in writing to make payments directly to the assignee.*

Usury

The nine main features of the Wisconsin usury law that relate to mortgage credit are:

1. Residential mortgage loans covering first-lien mortgages on one-family to four-family dwellings used by borrowers as their principal places of residence can continue to be made without regard to an interest-rate ceiling.
2. A lender may charge a prepayment penalty on a fixed-rate mortgage loan equal to 60 days' interest if that loan is prepaid during the first five loan years.
3. Existing Wisconsin law requiring the refund of unearned interest on prepayment of a mortgage loan is retained; however, for purposes of computing this refund, interest does not include such items as loan-commitment fees and separate charges for services incidental to the loan paid to third parties.
4. A late-payment charge may be imposed by a lender, which is not to exceed 5 percent of the unpaid amount of any installment not paid on or before the 15th day after its due date.
5. All depository lenders are required to pay 5.25 percent interest on escrows for payment of taxes or insurance on loans originated after January 31, 1983.
6. The residential mortgage lending of the usury law does not apply to FHA-insured or VA-guaranteed mortgage loans or loans made to corporations.
7. Lenders violating the residential mortgage usury laws may be liable to a borrower for $500 plus actual damages, costs, and reasonable attorney fees; however, this liability does not apply to cases of unintentional mistakes corrected by the lender on demand.
8. Section 138.056 of the new usury statutes provides for a greatly expanded framework for Wisconsin lenders to make variable-rate mortgage loans.
9. The new Wisconsin law specifically rejects the federal rate ceiling preemption statute enacted in April 1980. However, under the operation of Wisconsin's new law, the need for the federal preemption is eliminated.

Prepayment

In Wisconsin, prepayment penalties may be charged on conventional loans and land contracts but not on FHA or VA loans. Also, some FHA or VA loans are generally assumable.

Wisconsin State Veterans Home-Loan Programs

Wisconsin is one of five states in the country to have a first-mortgage home-loan program for veterans. A law passed in 1974 allowed the state and the Wisconsin Department of Veterans Affairs (WDVA) to create funds by issuing bonds. The funds provided by these bonds are available for the purchase or construction of private housing with a minimal down payment. A first-mortgage loan, with an annual percentage rate determined by the cost of bonds sold to finance the program, is obtained through a local lending agency. The loan first must be approved by the WDVA.

Loans are available for the purchase of existing housing (including condominiums) and for the construction of a home as well as the acquisition of land for the construction of a home. The maximum first-mortgage home loan is 95 percent of the total cost. The minimum down payment is 5 percent of the total cost, with a maximum repayment term of 30 years. The 5 percent down payment, as well as the closing costs, must be made by the veteran with the veteran's own unborrowed funds, although gifted funds as well as loans secured by veteran's assets are acceptable. Wisconsin Statute 45.74(7) provides for a maximum mortgage amount which can be obtained from the WDVA. There no longer are maximum income limits on WDVA home loans.

Eligibility is limited to Wisconsin veterans or any other eligible person. The borrower is required to be a resident of Wisconsin, and the home must be located in Wisconsin. A veteran or any other eligible person must contact a county veterans service officer to obtain a certificate of eligibility prior to making application for a loan. The home must be occupied by the veteran and his or her family as their principal residence and must be adequately insured for the term of the loan. If mortgage cancellation insurance is used, it must be obtained at the veteran's expense.

Because of a number of recent and pending changes in state and federal law, this first-mortgage program is changing rapidly. Licensees should consult lenders in their area who are authorized to originate loans for the WDVA to check current requirements for eligibility for these loans. For more information on the program, call 1-800-947-8387, or log on to this Web site:

WEB LINK

http://www.dva.state.wi.us.

Veterans Home Improvement Loan Program (HILP)

Wisconsin veterans also are eligible for a home improvement loan of up to $25,000 at a 5.85 annual percentage rate. The general conditions relating to this program are similar in many respects to the first-mortgage home-loan program.

Wisconsin Home Program

Created by the legislature in April 1982, this program is designed to help middle-income and low-income people purchase homes by lowering the interest rate that they must pay. This is accomplished by diverting investors' money from other financial instruments to home loans.

Funds for the program are produced by bonds sold by the Wisconsin Housing and Economic Development Authority (WHEDA). Investors buy the bonds because their interest is exempt from federal tax. The bonds, in turn, are able to carry a lower interest rate.

To obtain a loan under the program, buyers must contact a lender authorized to make loans in the program, including banks, savings banks, credit unions, and mortgage banks.

WHEDA uses its funds to buy loans from the lenders and guarantee repayment. The authority repays bondholders with the payments from the homebuyers. WHEDA administers the program.

Homebuyers are required to make a 5 percent down payment on the loans. Loan terms range from 15 to 30 years. In addition, limits are imposed on the buyer's income and the home's cost. Annual gross income cannot exceed approximately 90 percent of the median income in the buyer's home county. Loans also are available for the purchase of homes in a target area or homes that are part of a rehabilitation project. A target area is either in chronic economic distress or has been designated by HUD as eligible for the program. The price of a home cannot exceed a maximum price, which varies from county to county. For more information on the program, call 1-800-334-6873 or log on to this Web site:

WEB LINK

http://www.wheda.com.

Wisconsin Home Improvement Loan Program

This program, administered by WHEDA, was designed to enable low-income and moderate-income homeowners to repair and upgrade their properties and install energy-conserving improvements. The WHEDA program provides FHA-insured home improvement loans at below-market interest rates through participating lending institutions.

The financing for these lower-interest-rate home improvement loans is through the sale of tax-exempt bonds. To apply for a loan, a borrower goes to a participating lending institution, that processes the loan and closes it in the lender's name. Loans are originated and closed by participating lenders at the interest rate set by the Housing and Neighborhood Conservation Program (HNCP) and are sent to WHEDA for certification and purchase. WHEDA then sends funds to the lender for disbursement to the borrower. The lender's responsibility ends with the disbursement of the proceeds of the loan; servicing is WHEDA's responsibility. For more information, call the HNCP at 1-800-334-6873.

Financing Legislation

Consumer protection in financing arrangements within Wisconsin is provided by the federal Truth-in-Lending Act, which applies to real estate transactions, and by the Wisconsin Consumer Act and its amendment, Chapter 428 of the Wisconsin Statutes.

The Wisconsin Consumer Act is aimed primarily at the regulation of consumer-credit financing of durable goods such as household appliances. *However, the act does include both real and personal property in its definition of a consumer-credit transaction.* Real estate licensees should be aware of the act's possible effect on real estate sales, especially on land contract sales. Two exemptions to the Wisconsin Consumer Act deal with real estate. The first exempts consumer-credit transactions in which the amount financed or the base price is more than $25,000. The second, added by amendment in 1973, exempts first-mortgage loans in which the amount financed is $25,000 or less and the interest rate is 12 percent or less. In other words, the provisions of the consumer act apply only to junior mortgage loans of $25,000 or less. Although most Wisconsin real estate transactions are exempt from the consumer act, the act may have a significant effect on transactions involving land contracts. This effect will be discussed later in this chapter. You may visit the following Web site to learn more about the act and Chapter 428 of the Wisconsin statutes:

WEB LINK

http://www.legis.state.WI.US/rsb/statues.html.

LAND CONTRACTS

The land contract is often used in financing real estate in Wisconsin.

Recording the Land Contract

To protect his or her interests, the buyer in a land contract sale *should record the contract with the register of deeds in the county in which the land is located.* Recording fees usually are paid by the buyer. As with a mortgage, the land contract must be acknowledged properly. No witnesses are necessary for recording or for the validity of the contract. If the property is the sellers' homestead, both spouses must sign. The signers' names should be typed or printed under their signatures, and the name of the person who drafted the instrument must be indicated clearly on the contract.

Land Contract Forms

Only forms approved by the Wisconsin Department of Regulation and Licensing or the Wisconsin State Bar Association may be used by brokers for land contracts in Wisconsin. State Bar Form 11 is designated as the approved form in transactions that are not subject to the Wisconsin Consumer Act. In cases where a land contract is or may be subject to the Consumer Act, State Bar Form 10 should be used.

Impact of the Wisconsin Consumer Act on Land Contracts

Although the Wisconsin Consumer Act does not mention land contracts specifically under its provisions, it may be applicable under certain circumstances. If a seller under a land contract is in the business of regularly advertising property "to induce a consumer transaction," he or she may be under the dictates of the Consumer Act. The act may

- prevent the buyer from using his or her equity interest in the parcel as security in the purchase of another parcel;
- prevent the seller from denying the buyer prepayment privileges;
- prohibit balloon payments; and
- undercut the seller's usual land contract remedies in case of default by limiting the use of acceleration clauses.

Assignment of a Land Contract

Nonassignment clauses prohibit the transfer of the buyer's interest without the seller's consent and are included in the approved land contract forms in Wisconsin. If there is no such clause in a land contract or if the seller consents, the buyer may transfer his or her interest in the real estate to another. The assignment *should be signed by the parties, acknowledged, and recorded.* Assignment of a land contract should be treated in the same manner as any other real estate transaction.

Foreclosure of a Land Contract

Under a land contract containing an acceleration clause, a seller may sue a buyer for the money owed and may obtain a money judgment if the buyer defaults on even one installment. Although acceleration clauses may be prohibited in land contract transactions that are covered by the Wisconsin Consumer Act, many land contract sales are not covered by the act.

A seller under a land contract also may sue the defaulted borrower for judicial foreclosure. As with a mortgage, the seller may sue the borrower in court to obtain a judgment against the borrower for the entire sum of the loan balance.

Because land contract foreclosures are not governed by statute, but rather by common law and principles of equity, the judge has a great deal of discretion in setting the amount of time granted to the purchaser for redemption. The court will consider such things as how much equity the purchasers have, whether they have abandoned the property, and whether they have a history of defaults. This period is usually shorter than the one-year mortgage redemption period. After the redemption period, the property is sold by the sheriff at public auction. If the proceeds from the sale are insufficient to meet the unpaid debt, the seller may apply for a deficiency judgment against the borrower.

In Wisconsin, a land contract also may be foreclosed by strict foreclosure. Under this procedure, the seller sues for foreclosure in court in the manner previously described. However, if the borrower fails to reclaim the property at the end of the redemption period, the seller *receives title to the property rather than having the property sold at auction. In this case, the vendor cannot obtain a deficiency judgment against the vendee.*

Because land contracts may have a shorter redemption period than mortgages, and in the case of strict foreclosure, the seller/lender regains title to the property, land contracts usually offer sellers certain advantages over mortgages.

QUESTIONS

1. With regard to mortgage loans, Wisconsin is what type of state?
   a. Lien theory
   b. Title theory
   c. Intermediate theory
   d. Combination of lien theory and title theory
2. The general remedy on a defaulted mortgage is
   a. a nonjudicial foreclosure.
   b. strict foreclosure.
   c. judicial foreclosure by sale.
   d. general foreclosure.
3. The Wisconsin usury law provides that the maximum interest rate, including points, that may be charged an individual on a real estate loan is
   a. 12 percent.
   b. 10 percent.
   c. 14 percent.
   d. unlimited.
4. In Wisconsin, the maximum veterans first-mortgage home loan is what percentage of the total cost?
   a. 90 percent
   b. 95 percent
   c. 70 percent
   d. 100 percent
5. In Wisconsin, mortgage agreements and land contracts may be made only
   a. where the interest is to be paid in monthly installments.
   b. where substantial sums of money are involved.
   c. on forms approved by the Wisconsin Department of Regulation and Licensing or the Wisconsin State Bar Association.
   d. during business hours.
6. Strict foreclosure is prohibited in Wisconsin
   a. when a land contract is involved.
   b. at all times.
   c. when the interest is more than 12 percent.
   d. when a mortgage is involved.
7. Which statement does *NOT* correctly describe an aspect of a land contract?
   a. Buyers in a land contract sale should record the contract with the registrar of deeds.
   b. State Bar Form 10 is designated as the approved form in transactions that are not subject to the Wisconsin Consumer Act.
   c. A seller under a land contract may sue the defaulted borrower for judicial foreclosure.
   d. A land contract may be foreclosed by strict foreclosure.
8. Which statement does *NOT* correctly describe the Wisconsin Consumer Act?
   a. The act may cover land contracts.
   b. The act may prevent the seller in a land contract from denying the buyer prepayment privileges.
   c. The act may not prohibit balloon payments.
   d. The act may undercut the seller's usual land contract remedies in case of default by limiting the use of acceleration clauses.

CHAPTER 12

Leases

LEASEHOLD ESTATES

Wisconsin recognizes four types of leasehold estates: *estate for years*, *periodic tenancy*, *tenancy at will*, and *tenancy at sufferance*. Tenancy at sufferance is referred to as a *holdover tenancy* in Wisconsin.

Statute of Frauds

The Wisconsin Statute of Frauds, as it applies to leases, requires that *all leases for more than a year be in writing*. A lease for one year or less may be made orally and still be valid.

Lease Forms

Forms for the lease of real property are no longer approved by the Wisconsin Department of Regulation and Licensing. Section RL16.03(1)(e) allows real estate licensees to use leases prepared by the broker entering into the agreement, the broker attorney, or the landlord. Section RL16.04(2) states that a licensee may, when acting as an agent, use lease forms that have been drafted by the principal to the transaction or an attorney and have been approved by the licensee's client. The rule also states that the lease forms shall identify the drafter.

Recording the Lease

A *lease for more than one year is legally a conveyance* under Section 706 of the Wisconsin Statutes. A lease, therefore, must meet the same requirements as a deed in order to be enforceable. A lease *should be recorded* to protect the interests of the parties involved and *to be valid against the claims of third parties without notice*, but short term leases, even if for a term of over one year, are rarely recorded. Ground leases are almost always recorded. The lease must include all the terms and conditions of the agreement. *It must be signed by the parties, must identify the parties, and must offer a reasonably definite description of the land. All material terms of the lease, the amount of rent, and the commencement and expiration of the lease must be included.* The rights and duties of landlords and tenants are set forth in the Wisconsin Statutes.

Any special provisions not included in the statutes that are agreed on by both parties may be written into the lease. Witnesses and acknowledgment are not essential to the validity of a lease in Wisconsin. A lease, however, must be acknowledged if it is to be recorded. Nonstandard clauses should be separately negotiated and reduced to writing in a separate document.

Termination of Leaseholds

An estate for years *terminates automatically at the end of the lease term* without advance notice from either the lessor or the lessee. A periodic tenancy and a tenancy at will may be terminated by giving at least *28 days' notice in writing* (Section 704.19). The Wisconsin Statutes require that the termination date set in the notice coincides with the end of the rent-paying period. The rules apply to both the lessor and lessee. In general, notice can be given more than 28 days in advance. An agreement between the lessor and lessee to terminate prior to the normal date or without statutory notice may be oral or written. However, if notice of termination is given more than one year before the normal date, it must be in writing. All tenancies may be terminated by mutual consent of the parties.

BREACH OF LEASE (SECTION 704)

Breach by Tenant

When a tenant fails to meet the terms specified and required in a lease, various remedies are available to the landlord. If, for example, a tenant remains in possession of the leased premises after the end of a tenancy without the landlord's consent, the landlord *may collect double the amount of the daily rent for the number of days the tenant remains in possession and remove the tenant.*

If a tenant vacates the premises before the end of the tenancy without paying the agreed-upon rent, the landlord *may recover the rent plus damages*. However, the landlord is required to minimize damages by making a reasonable effort to rent the premises after the tenant leaves.

If a month-to-month or week-to-week periodic tenant fails to pay rent, the landlord may give him or her a *5-day notice to pay or vacate or a 14-day notice to vacate.* If the tenant fails to pay within the 5-day pay-or-vacate period, the tenancy is terminated and the landlord may begin eviction proceedings. The tenant may not pay after the pay-or-vacate period has expired. Where the 14-day notice to vacate applies, the tenant cannot cure the default by paying rent.

Where a periodic tenant commits waste or breaches a lease *in any way other than nonpayment of rent*, the landlord *may give a 14-day notice to vacate*. For a year-to-year tenant or a tenant under a lease for one year or less, the landlord *may give a 5-day fix-or-vacate notice on the first violation of any lease term and a 14-day vacate notice on a second violation within a year*. For a tenant who has a lease for more than one year, the landlord *may give a 30-day notice*. *A landlord is prohibited from terminating a tenant in retaliation for the tenant's reporting of housing code violations.*

Notice. A landlord may (1) *deliver* notice personally or through the person in charge of the property; (2) *send* notice by registered mail or another delivery service; or (3) *post* notice in a conspicuous place on the premises and mail the notice.

Breach by Landlord

When a landlord fails to furnish the specified services required in a lease, such as adequate heat, *the tenant may sue for damages.* Where the breach is serious enough to interfere with the tenant's enjoyment of the premises, the tenant *may move out and not be liable for further rent.* This provision applies only if the damages to the premises or the inconveniences suffered are caused by the landlord rather than by the tenant's own negligence.

In Wisconsin, a landlord may include an *exculpatory clause* in a lease, which provides that the landlord *is not liable for certain specified conditions*, which might include damage caused by bursting water pipes, floods, or a leaky roof. This clause relieves the landlord of responsibility only for the specified conditions. Section AG134.08 places heavy restrictions on the use of an exculpatory clause in a lease.

Destruction of the Premises

If a property is destroyed or partially damaged by fire, the elements, or any conditions hazardous to a tenant's health, and if the damage is not repaired immediately, *the tenant may vacate the premises and not be liable for rent.* If a tenant moves because of the hardship caused by the inconvenience of the repairs, *the tenant is not liable for the rent so long as the premises are unhabitable or untenable.* This provision applies only if the damage was not caused by the negligence of the tenant.

Automatic Extension Clauses

Automatic renewal or extension clauses in residential leases are unenforceable against a tenant unless the landlord gives at least 15, but not more than 30, days' reminder notice of this lease provision to the tenant.

Eviction

A landlord may institute eviction proceedings by serving and *filing summons* and a *written complaint* in the court of the county in which the premises are located. The sheriff of the county enforces any eviction rulings.

TYPES OF LEASES

The basic types of lease agreements—*gross leases, net leases, and percentage leases*—are used in Wisconsin. A percentage-lease arrangement may be included as part of the terms of a gross or net lease.

Commercial and Farm Leases

Because commercial and farm leases usually involve a contractual relationship extending over many years, they are much more complicated to prepare and negotiate than most leases. Farm leases vary substantially depending on what the lessor and lessee are furnishing to the farm operation besides land and labor and on what type of risk each party is willing to take. *Commercial leases* generally center on *flexible rental terms* to protect the lessor and lessee through the use of *percentage leases*. The lessor requires the lessee to provide adequate information that reflects sales and maximum utilization of the facilities. Payment of taxes and insurance is among the many considerations to be negotiated in a commercial lease. Commercial leases may contain tenant options for renewing the leases or for outright purchase, as well as for allowing for the leasing of a portion of a building, the balance of which may be retained by the landlord or leased to other tenants.

Residential Rental Practices Code

The Residential Rental Practices Code (AG134, Wis. Adm. Code) is the product of an extensive investigation into problems between landlords and tenants by the staff of the Department of Agriculture, Trade, and Consumer Protection, performed at the request of the legislature.

The code is limited to problems that were documented during the department's investigation. It is intended to promote fair business practices in the rental of housing as well as to help ensure that landlords and tenants approach rental-agreement negotiations on equal terms so that informed rental-housing choices can be made.

AG134 does not, however, alter legal precedents or existing statutory law embodied in Section 704, Wisconsin Statutes, which is the basic law regulating landlord-tenant relations. Rather, it supplements and clarifies existing law in several respects, while at the same time addressing issues and business practices that are subject to Wisconsin's Unfair Trade Practices Act (S. 100.20, Wis. Stats.).

Included among the key provisions of the Residential Rental Practices Code are the following three:

1. When a security deposit is required, the code establishes specific elements of a mutual check-in procedure in order to objectively document pre-existing damages. It requires landlords to provide tenants with a notice informing the tenants they have the right to request a description of any physical damages charged against the previous tenant's security deposit. This description is to be provided before a security deposit is accepted or at the same time as notice to the previous tenant, whichever occurs later. The amount of the charges and the identity of the previous tenant need not be disclosed. If damages have been repaired, this can be noted in connection with the damage description. In addition, the tenant must be given no less than seven days in which to inspect and document other pre-existing conditions.
2. Security deposits, less any amounts withheld by the landlord, must be returned in person or by mail to the last known address of the tenant within 21 days after surrender of the premises or double the security deposit amount is due the tenant.
3. Where any deduction is made from the security deposit, the tenant must be provided with an itemized statement describing each item of damages or claim against the deposit and the amount withheld as reasonable compensation for each claim. A landlord is prohibited from intentionally falsifying any security deposit claim. For example, where a tenant's failure to clean certain portions of the premises is serious to the extent that it represents abuse, waste, or neglect, the rule does not prohibit reasonable deductions from the security deposit as compensation for necessary cleaning at the conclusion of tenancy. However, routine across-the-board deductions for cleaning or carpet shampooing, unrelated to any abuse, waste, or neglect by the tenant, are prohibited in the absence of a clear and separately negotiated written agreement, entered into at the time of initial rental.

The Wisconsin Department of Agriculture, Trade, and Consumer Protection Division publishes a booklet entitled *Landlords and Tenants—The Wisconsin Way*. This publication provides the exact language of Section 704 (1977 edition, Wis. Stats.) and AG134. It also contains an extensive explanation of the provisions of AG134 and how it complements existing law.

Copies of this publication are available from:

Wisconsin Department of Agriculture
Trade and Consumer Protection
2811 Agriculture Drive
PO Box 8911
Madison, WI 53708-8911
Phone: (608) 224-4960 (Madison), Milwaukee (414) 266-1235 or
1-800-422-7128

Copies are $10 if mailed; $8 if purchased locally.

QUESTIONS

1. Which of the following statements does *NOT* correctly describe a specific lease?
   a. A lease for more than one year is legally a conveyance.
   b. A lease should be recorded to protect the interests of the parties involved.
   c. Wisconsin licensees must use a department-approved form for an apartment lease.
   d. A lease for one year or less may be made orally and still be enforceable.

2. If a week-to-week periodic tenant fails to pay rent, the landlord may give him or her a
   a. 5-day notice to pay or vacate.
   b. 10-day notice to pay or vacate.
   c. 15-day notice to pay or vacate.
   d. 20-day notice to pay or vacate.

3. A tenant has a month-to-month tenancy in an apartment building. When the tenant failed to pay the rent for the month of June, the landlord gave the tenant a 14-day notice to vacate. The tenant
   a. may pay the rent and continue to live in the apartment building.
   b. must vacate immediately after the 14 days are up.
   c. may take the landlord to court.
   d. may ignore the notice to vacate.

4. Which statement does *NOT* correctly describe the Residential Rental Practices Code?
   a. The code is AG134 Wisconsin Administrative Code.
   b. The code is intended to promote fair business practices in the rental of housing.
   c. The code alters legal precedents embodied in Section 704, Wisconsin Statutes.
   d. The code clarifies existing law.

5. You are renting an apartment from a landlord who requires a security deposit. As part of the check-in procedure, the landlord is required to provide you with
   a. a description of any physical damages charged against the previous tenant's security deposit.
   b. the amount of damages charged against the previous tenant's security deposit.
   c. the name of the previous tenant.
   d. no less than three days in which to inspect and document pre-existing conditions.

6. Security deposits, less any amounts withheld by a landlord, must be returned in person or by mail to the last known address of the tenant within how many days after surrender of the premises?
   a. 7
   b. 21
   c. 14
   d. 28

7. Which of the following statements does *NOT* correctly describe the current status of forms for the lease of real property in Wisconsin?
   a. Real estate licensees may use commercially available lease forms, provided that the client approves of the forms.
   b. Real estate licensees must use lease forms approved by the Wisconsin Department of Regulation and Licensing.
   c. A real estate licensee acting as a principal may use forms that have been drafted by the licensee.
   d. Forms for the lease of real property are no longer approved by the Wisconsin Department of Regulation and Licensing.

CHAPTER 13

Land-Use Controls and Property Development

■ PLAN COMMISSION AND ZONING BOARD OF ADJUSTMENT

Land use in Wisconsin is planned and controlled by *local plan commissions and other local public agencies* in cities, towns, and villages. These plan commissions deal with the preparation of the master plan for an area. They *hold hearings* and are involved in the preparation of *zoning ordinances* and *zoning amendments*. There are no such plan commissions in Wisconsin counties. County planning functions are carried out by either the county park commission or a zoning committee of the county board.

In Wisconsin cities, the plan commission consists of seven members, including the mayor, the city engineer, the president of the park board, an alderperson, and three citizens. The *zoning board of adjustment* is common to both city and rural zoning. The board of adjustment *hears appeals from actions of the building inspector or other zoning administrators and has powers to grant use variances*. The board may, under a particular zoning ordinance, *grant special-use permits for exceptional uses*.

■ ZONING

All Wisconsin towns (under certain conditions), counties, villages, and cities have zoning powers. In addition, villages and fourth-class cities have power to zone one and one-half miles beyond their corporate limits. *Larger cities can exercise extraterritorial power up to three miles outside their limits*. This power can be exercised only if a specific procedure is followed: The town board for the outlying area must appoint three persons to join the three citizen members of the village or city plan commission. If the majority of the six approve extraterritorial zoning, they can recommend that it be adopted by the village or city governing board. The extraterritorial power is negative law in that the proposed zoning can be defeated, but new zoning cannot be dictated by the large municipality.

Wisconsin's Smart Growth Law

Wisconsin's Smart Growth law provides a more tangible definition of a comprehensive land-use plan. The comprehensive definition applies uniformly to all counties, cities, villages, towns, and regional planning commissions in Wisconsin (local governmental units). The plan is aimed at providing the framework for unified land-use planning and regulation in Wisconsin. It is also an attempt to help local officials more effectively determine the impact of their decisions on their communities.

Under the Smart Growth Law, all local governmental units must develop and implement a comprehensive plan by 2010. The comprehensive plan is required to include the following minimum elements:

1. an issues and opportunities element;
2. a housing element;
3. a transportation element;
4. a utilities and community facilities element;
5. an agricultural, natural, and cultural resources element;
6. an economic development element;
7. an intergovernmental cooperation element;
8. a land use element; and
9. an implementation element.

If a local governmental unit begins a comprehensive plan, it may qualify for state planning grants to help defray part of the costs.

Benefits that the Smart Growth law provides to the real estate industry include:

1. greater certainty in the development process; and
2. incentives for communities to promote higher densities and more affordable housing.

For more information on this program, visit *www.smartgrowth.org*.

Subdivision Regulations

Wisconsin's Subdivision Code is covered in Chapter 236 of the Wisconsin Statutes. All land in the state is subject to the code. However, the state regulations govern only where *five or more lots of one and one-half acres or less in an area are created within a period of five years for the purpose of sale or building development.* Chapter 236 does not apply where the parcels are larger than one and one-half acres or where four lots or fewer are created. Local units of government, however, are authorized to adopt more stringent regulations and certain municipalities have done so. In those cases where more stringent controls have not been adopted, Section 236.34 permits the use of a *certified survey map for four or fewer parcels* to provide greater accuracy in real estate descriptions.

Subdivision plats. *Copies of all subdivision plats must be sent to the Wisconsin Department of Commerce for review.* In a case where the land borders on a state trunk highway, the director submits copies of the plat to the Department of

Transportation for review. The director also sends copies to the Department of Health for review where the subdivision is not to be served by a public sewer. The county also may review the plat, and if the land is located in an unincorporated town, the plat also must be reviewed by the town board. *The final plat will not be accepted for the public records by the register of deeds until all of these public bodies are satisfied with the plat.* Any subdivider or agent who offers subdivided land for sale knowing that the final plat has not obtained final approval and/or been recorded is subject to a fine of $500 or imprisonment for up to six months or both.

Out-of-State Unimproved Properties or Subdivision Lots

No filing of any kind must be made with the Real Estate Board or the Department of Regulation and Licensing for marketing out-of-state subdivision lots. Any person who physically markets such lots in Wisconsin, even owners who are involved in a pattern of sales of their own properties, must have a Wisconsin real estate license or utilize the services of a Wisconsin licensee. Such licensees must observe all usual statutory and rule requirements and especially pay attention to requirements relating to full disclosure, approved contractual forms, and real estate trust funds.

Shoreland Zoning

The Wisconsin shoreland zoning laws were adopted in 1966. Their objectives include

- furthering the maintenance of healthful conditions;
- preventing and controlling water pollution;
- protecting spawning grounds, fish, and aquatic life;
- controlling building sites, placement of structures, and land uses; and
- preserving shore cover and natural beauty.

The 1966 laws require zoning of all land in unincorporated areas (outside city or village limits) *within 1,000 feet of a lake, pond, or flowage and all land within 300 feet of a river or stream or to the landward side of a flood plain,* whichever distance is greater. The law provides that county ordinance implement shoreland zoning, but if the county fails to adopt an ordinance that meets reasonable minimum standards, the Wisconsin Department of Natural Resources (DNR) may adopt a zoning ordinance that applies to the county. However, if a town has a zoning ordinance that is more restrictive than that adopted by the county, the more restrictive provisions remain in effect. It should be noted that it is very difficult to obtain a permit to place almost any permanent object closer than within 75 feet of water.

In Wisconsin, shoreland areas are subject to zoning regulations that include

- minimum standards for water supply and waste disposal;
- tree-cutting regulations;
- setbacks for structures from highways and navigable waters;
- minimum lot sizes;
- grading controls;
- lagooning and dredging regulations; and
- subdivision regulations.

Farmland Preservation Act (Chapter 91 of the Wisconsin Statutes)

The Farmland Preservation Act *provides an income tax credit to Wisconsin residents who own at least the minimum lot size as specified by their local exclusive agricultural zoning ordinance.*

The farmland must either *be zoned for exclusive agricultural use or be subject to a farmland-preservation agreement*. In addition, the farmland must have produced at least $6,000 in gross farm profits during the year preceding application for a farmland-preservation agreement or a total of at least $18,000 of gross farm profits during the three years preceding application. A farmland-preservation agreement refers to a restrictive covenant, evidenced by an instrument, whereby the owner and the state agree to hold jointly *the right to develop the land* except as may be expressly reserved in the instrument. Such an agreement also may contain a covenant running with the land for a term of years *not to develop* except as expressly reserved in the instrument. If the owner violates the agreement, the owner will be responsible for paying back taxes plus interest and penalties. Land covered by a farmland-preservation agreement may be sold, but the buyer takes title subject to the agreement.

Building Code

A state Uniform Building Code for single-family homes and duplexes went into effect June 1, 1980. It sets minimum standards for structure, heating, ventilation, and fire safety of conventional and manufactured housing. The code, still in use, specifies everything from the types of fasteners to be used in homebuilding to mandatory installation of smoke detectors. The code allows for innovative building techniques by specifying how a building ultimately must perform, rather than exactly how it must be built.

Wisconsin Environmental Policy Act

The Wisconsin Environmental Policy Act (WEPA Chapter 273 and Chapter 274 of the Wisconsin Statutes) became effective in April 1972. It is patterned after the National Environmental Policy Act, which became effective in January 1970.

The Wisconsin Environmental Policy Act (WEPA) *requires each state agency to prepare a detailed statement concerning the environmental effects of any proposed action that could significantly affect the quality of the environment* and to obtain the comments of any other agency that may have jurisdiction or special expertise with respect to the environmental impact of the proposed action. When a course of action involves unresolved conflicts in the use of resources, WEPA requires state agencies to study, develop, and describe appropriate alternatives. *State agencies also are required to initiate and utilize ecological information in the planning and development of resource-oriented projects.*

In Wisconsin, real estate licensees who engage in land development also are subject to environmental controls. Chapter 273 of the Wisconsin Statutes gives the Wisconsin Department of Natural Resources the power to grant permits to develop land on statutory approval. The DNR may require developers *to submit environmental impact statements if the area to be developed is more than 40 acres or if the cost of the project exceeds $25,000.*

QUESTIONS

1. Larger cities in Wisconsin have been given power to zone how many miles beyond their corporate limits?
   a. 1½ miles
   b. 3 miles
   c. 2 miles
   d. 5 miles
2. Which of the following statements does *NOT* correctly describe the zoning board of adjustment?
   a. The board may have the power to grant special-use permits.
   b. The board is common to both city and rural zones.
   c. The board hears appeals from actions of the building inspector.
   d. The board may change the zoning on a parcel of land.
3. In Wisconsin cities, the plan commission consists of how many members, including the mayor?
   a. 7 members
   b. 5 members
   c. 6 members
   d. 4 members
4. Copies of all subdivision plats must be sent for review to the
   a. director of the Department of Regulation and Licensing.
   b. Department of Commerce.
   c. director of the Department of Labor, Industry, and Human Relations.
   d. executive secretary of the Real Estate Board.
5. Which statement is *NOT* an objective of Wisconsin shoreland zoning law?
   a. Furthering the maintenance of healthful conditions
   b. Minimizing business interruptions
   c. Preventing and controlling water pollution
   d. Preserving shore cover and natural beauty
6. Which statement is *TRUE* of a farmland-preservation agreement?
   a. It provides an income tax credit to anyone who owns farmland in Wisconsin.
   b. It provides an income tax credit to anyone who owns at least 35 acres of farmland in Wisconsin.
   c. It requires that farmland be zoned for conservation.
   d. It may contain a covenant for a term of years not to develop land except as expressly reserved in the agreement.
7. Under the Smart Growth law, all local governmental units must develop and implement a comprehensive plan by
   a. 2008.
   b. 2009.
   c. 2010.
   d. 2011.

Fair Housing and Ethical Practices

PROHIBITED ACTIVITIES

Just like the federal fair housing laws, Wisconsin law prohibits a variety of activities when they are based on race, color, sex, sexual orientation, disability, religion, national origin, marital status, lawful source of income, age, ancestry, or familial status. These activities include the following:

- Refusing to sell, rent, finance, or contract to construct housing or refusing to negotiate or discuss the terms thereof
- Refusing to permit inspection or exacting different or more stringent price, terms or conditions for sale, lease, financing, or rental of housing
- Refusing to finance or sell an unimproved residential lot or to construct a home or residence upon such lot
- Advertising in a manner that indicates discrimination by a preference or limitation
- For a person in the business of insuring against hazards, refusing to enter into, or exacting different terms, conditions, or privileges with respect to, a contract of insurance against hazards to a dwelling
- Refusing to renew a lease, causing the eviction of a tenant from rental housing, or engaging in the harassment of a tenant
- Discriminating in the providing of privileges, services, or facilities that are available in connection with housing
- Falsely representing that housing is unavailable for inspection, rental, or sale
- Denying access to, or membership participation in, a multiple-listing service or other real estate service

- Coercing, intimidating, threatening, or interfering with a person in the exercise or enjoyment of, or on account of his or her having exercised or enjoyed a right granted or protected under Section 106.50 of the Wisconsin Statutes, or with a person who has aided or encouraged another person in the exercise or enjoyment of a right granted or protected under the law
- In making unavailable any of the following transactions, or discriminating in the terms or conditions of such transactions for a person whose business includes engaging in residential real estate-related transactions:
  - The making or purchasing of loans or the provision of other financial assistance for purchasing, constructing, improving, repairing, or maintaining housing, or the making or purchasing of loans on the provision of other financial assistance secured by residential real estate
  - Selling, brokering, or appraising residential real property
  - Otherwise making unavailable or denying housing

Protected Classes under Wisconsin Fair Housing Law

Wisconsin's Fair Housing Law includes two protected classes:

1. *Family status* that is broadly defined to cover households with children, the pregnancy of a member of a household, custody and visitation situations, guardianships, households shared by relatives, and single individuals.
2. *Disability* that includes
   a. physical or mental impairment, including any physical disability or developmental disability, which substantially limits one or more life activities;
   b. a record of having such an impairment; and
   c. being regarded as having such an impairment.

The law also states that disability does not include the current illegal use of a controlled substance, unless the individual is participating in a supervised drug rehabilitation program.

Wisconsin's Fair Housing law also includes several categories not covered under the federal fair housing law. They include the following four classes:

1. *Sexual orientation* is defined as having a preference for heterosexuality, homosexuality, or bisexuality; having a history of such a preference; or being identified with such a preference
2. *Lawful source of income*, including but not limited to moneys received from public assistance, pension, and Supplementary Security Income
3. *Marital status*, including being married, separated, divorced, widowed, or single
4. *Age*, including people 40 years of age or older

Disability

Section 106.50 also provides various requirements related to persons with disabilities including the following six:

1. Prohibiting discrimination in the sale, rental, or availability of housing and in the terms, conditions, privileges, services, rules, or facilities with respect to housing, against any buyer or renter because of a disability of
   a. that buyer or renter;
   b. a person residing in or intending to reside in that housing after it is sold, rented, or made available; and
   c. any person associated with the buyer or renter.

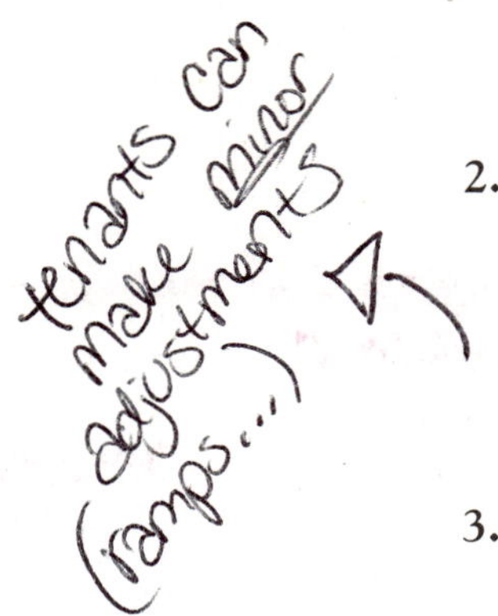

2. Prohibiting landlords from refusing to permit, at the expense of the person with a disability, the reasonable modification of existing housing if the modification may be necessary to afford the person full enjoyment of the housing. The law provides guidance to landlords for renters to restore modified housing to its prior condition and for escrowing funds to cover the cost of the restorations.
3. Prohibiting landlords from refusing to make reasonable accommodations in rules, policies, practices, or services that are associated with the housing, when accommodations may be necessary to afford the person equal opportunity to use and enjoy housing, unless the accommodation would impose an undue hardship on the owner of the housing.
4. Requiring newly constructed multifamily housing to be designed and constructed in a manner that ensures internal and external accessibility. The law specifies the guidelines to be used in determining accessibility and for granting variances and waivers when it is impractical to design and construct the housing to be accessible. Multifamily housing is defined as housing consisting of three or more dwelling units, if the housing has one or more elevators; and grade-level dwelling units in housing consisting of three or more dwelling units if the housing has no elevators. With respect to external accessibility, the law requires at least an accessible entrance for each building that is on an accessible route; any other extras that are at grade level must be accessible to the greatest extent feasible.
5. With respect to interior accessibility, the law specifies that public and common use areas must be accessible to persons with disabilities; interior and exterior doors, interior passages, kitchens, and bathrooms must be sufficiently wide for maneuverability by persons with disabilities who use wheelchairs, and switches and controls must be located in accessible locations. Also, bathroom walls must be sufficiently reinforced to allow later addition of grab bars and other aids. Unlike federal law, state law also requires landlords to provide, upon the request of a renter and without cost to a renter, lever door handles and appliance controls. As noted above, state law applies to newly constructed multifamily housing consisting of three or more units, whereas federal accessibility requirements apply only to multifamily housing with four units or more.
6. Requiring specified types of existing multifamily housing undergoing remodeling to meet accessibility requirements similar to the requirements for newly constructed housing, the extent of the requirements depending on how extensively the housing is being remodeled.

Exemptions

Wisconsin Fair Housing Law (Section 106.50) provides the following four exemptions to the prohibitions against discrimination:

1. *Tenancy would present direct threat:* Housing need not be made available to an individual whose tenancy would constitute a direct threat to the safety of other tenants or persons employed on the property or whose tenancy would result in substantial physical damage to the property of others, provided that the risk of direct threat or damage cannot be eliminated or sufficiently reduced through reasonable accommodations. Any claim that an individual's tenancy poses a direct threat or a substantial risk of harm or damage must be evidenced by behavior on the part of the individual who caused

harm or damage, that directly threatened harm or damage, or that caused a reasonable fear of harm or damage on the part of another.

2. *Housing for older persons:* It is permissible to discriminate based on age or familial status with respect to *housing for older persons*, defined under the state fair housing law as any of the following:
   a. housing provided under state or federal program that is specifically designed and operated to assist elderly persons as defined in the state or federal program
   b. housing intended for, and solely occupied by persons *62 years of age or older* or intended and operated for occupancy by at least one person 55 years of age or older per unit
   c. housing intended for occupancy by persons 55 years of age or older must meet the following two conditions:
      (1) at least 80 percent of the dwelling units are occupied by at least one person 55 years of age or older
      (2) policies and procedures are adhered to that demonstrate an intent by the owner or manager to provide housing for persons 55 years of age or older
3. *Housing for people with disabilities:* It is permissible to discriminate on the basis of disability by developing housing designed specifically for persons with disabilities and granting preference to persons with disabilities in regard to such housing.
4. *Occupancy standards:* It is not discrimination based on familial status to comply with any reasonable federal, state, or local government restrictions relating to the maximum number of occupants permitted to occupy a housing unit, but a local restriction that produces a disparate impact could be discriminatory and a violation of state or federal law.

Resolution of Complaints

Administrative enforcement. A complaint alleging housing discrimination must be filed with the Equal Rights Division (ERD) of the Wisconsin Department of Workforce Development no more than one year after the alleged discrimination occurred or terminated. The law also specifies the type of notice of the complaint to the respondent and requires the ERD to advise the complainant of various time limits that apply to administrative proceedings, the right to elect to take the case to circuit court once a finding of probable cause has been issued by the ERD, and the right to bring a private action in circuit court in lieu of proceeding administratively.

Determination of probable cause: conciliation. The state law permits the ERD to attempt conciliation of the case during the investigation period up until the ERD either issues a finding of probable cause or dismisses the claim due to lack of probable cause.

If at the conclusion of the investigation of the allegations, the ERD determines that probable cause exists to believe that discrimination has occurred or is about to occur, the ERD is required to immediately issue a charge on behalf of the aggrieved person.

Election of forum: prosecution of charge. Once a charge has been issued by the ERD, the complainant, respondent, and any aggrieved person on whose behalf the complaint was filed may elect to have the claim decided in an administrative proceeding or to bring a civil action in circuit court. The election must be made no later than 20 days after the receipt of the charge.

It is important to note that some differences exist between federal law and Wisconsin law with respect to processing claims. Under federal law, once a charge is issued by HUD, proceedings before the administrative law judge are prosecuted by an attorney from HUD at no cost to the aggrieved person. Any aggrieved person is permitted to intervene as a party in the proceeding and hire his or her own attorney; however, it is the primary responsibility of HUD to pursue the charge on behalf of the complainant.

By contrast, state law does not require the Wisconsin Department of Workforce Development to provide legal representation on administrative proceedings or, upon election, in circuit court. Although the claimant in an administrative proceeding is not required to hire an attorney, the claimant has the burden of proceeding on his or her own behalf. No legal representation is provided if the claimant elects to take the claim to circuit court.

Since the enactment of the 1988 Fair Housing Amendments and corresponding federal regulation, it has been the position of HUD that in order for a state's fair housing law to be certified as substantially equivalent to federal law (thereby entitling the state to referral of cases from HUD and some federal financial assistance in processing cases), the state must provide a means by which a claimant can pursue a claim without having to procure his or her own legal counsel. Thus, Wisconsin is not currently certified as substantially equivalent to federal law.

Penalties. Under Section 106.50 of the Wisconsin Statutes, the ERD may impose any of the following four penalties for violation of the Wisconsin Fair Housing Law:

1. Any economic and noneconomic damages suffered by the aggrieved person, regardless of whether he or she intervened in the action, but not including punitive damages
2. Any injunctive or other equitable relief
3. Costs and attorney fees to the prevailing plaintiff
4. A civil penalty in the amount of up to $10,000 for a first offense, up to $25,000 for a second offense within a five-year period, and up to $50,000 for a third or subsequent offense during a seven-year period

Time limitations. The ERD is required to commence proceeding within 30 days of receiving a housing complaint and complete the investigation within 100 days after receiving the complaint. The ERD must make final administrative disposition of the complaint within one year after receiving the complaint. If the ERD is unable to comply with the time limitation relating to investigation and administrative disposition of the complaint, it must notify the complainant and respondent, in writing, of the reasons for doing so.

Appeal. Under the Wisconsin Fair Housing Law, an order of an ERD hearing examiner will be appealable directly to the circuit court.

Civil actions. Section 106.50 of the Wisconsin Statutes authorizes persons alleging violations of the Wisconsin Fair Housing Law to bring a private action in circuit court.

In addition to court awards of costs, damages, and injunctive relief, a court may award up to $10,000 for the first offense, up to $25,000 for the second offense within a five-year period, and up to $50,000 for a third or subsequent offense during a seven-year period.

Local equal opportunity ordinances. Section 66.1011 of the Wisconsin Statutes authorizes local governments to enact fair housing ordinances consistent with, or providing more protection than, the state law. The statute adds all protected classes under the state law to the list of classes that may be offered protection under local ordinances. The statute also authorizes local ordinances to permit any party to elect either an administrative hearing or an option in civil court once a finding has been made by the administrative body that there is probable cause to believe that a violation of the ordinance has occurred.

Referral of discrimination to the Wisconsin Department of Regulation and Licensing. If the ERD finds probable cause to believe that an act of discrimination has been or is being committed by a person who is licensed by the Department of Regulation and Licensing (DRL), ERD is required to notify DRL of its findings and is required to file a complaint with DRL together with a request that the agency initiate proceedings to suspend or revoke the person's license or take other, less restrictive disciplinary action.

QUESTIONS

1. Municipalities in Wisconsin
   a. may be prevented by referendum from considering antidiscrimination ordinances.
   b. may enact antidiscrimination ordinances, so long as they do not go beyond the present state law.
   c. may be prevented by referendum from considering antidiscrimination ordinances.
   d. may enact antidiscrimination ordinances that are more comprehensive than state law.
2. The Wisconsin Fair Housing Law is primarily enforced by the
   a. Department of Justice.
   b. Department of Agriculture, Trade, and Consumer Protection.
   c. Department of Regulation and Licensing.
   d. Department of Workforce Development.
3. The statute of limitations in Wisconsin for investigating administrative proceedings on a fair housing complaint is
   a. 30 days after the alleged discriminatory housing practice.
   b. 90 days after the alleged discriminatory housing practice.
   c. 180 days after the alleged discriminatory housing practice.
   d. one year after the alleged discriminatory housing practice.
4. Which is *NOT* a protected class under the Wisconsin Fair Housing Law?
   a. Race
   b. Political beliefs
   c. Sexual orientation
   d. Marital status
5. Wisconsin Fair Housing Law covers
   a. just single-family homes.
   b. three or more units.
   c. four or more units.
   d. all housing units.
6. Wisconsin law specifies accessibility guidelines for the disabled for the development of multifamily housing. Multifamily housing for this purpose is defined as
   a. two or more dwelling units.
   b. three or more dwelling units.
   c. four or more dwelling units.
   d. eight or more dwelling units.
7. It is permissible in Wisconsin to discriminate in housing on the basis of
   a. age.
   b. lawful source of income.
   c. marital status.
   d. political beliefs.
8. Who of the following would not be considered to have a disability under Wisconsin law?
   a. A person with a split personality disorder who cannot hold down a full-time job
   b. A deaf person
   c. A blind person
   d. A person currently addicted to cocaine
9. All of the following are subject to the age provisions of the Wisconsin Fair Housing laws *EXCEPT*
   a. Bain, the owner of a three-unit apartment building who is living in one unit while renting out the other two units.
   b. Roarke, who is renting out his single-family home.
   c. Tyler, who is renting out units in her six-unit apartment building to people 62 years of age or older.
   d. Killmer, the owner of a four-unit apartment building who is living in one unit while renting out the other three units.
10. Under Wisconsin law, family status includes those
    a. living with a dependent senior citizen.
    b. who are pregnant.
    c. living alone.
    d. living with a senior citizen who is disabled.

11. Palmer rents an apartment to Mayer, a blind person. If Mayer alters the unit to accommodate his blindness, Palmer can
    a. report Mayer to the district attorney for misuse of property.
    b. require Mayer to pay a penalty for making alterations in the unit.
    c. require Mayer to restore the unit to its original condition (except for normal wear and tear).
    d. immediately evict Mayer.

12. Walker has filed a complaint regarding a housing violation with the Wisconsin Department of Workforce Development (DWD). DWD will have to complete the investigation within
    a. 30 days after receiving the complaint.
    b. 60 days after receiving the complaint.
    c. 100 days after receiving the complaint.
    d. one year after receiving the complaint.

Closing the Real Estate Transaction

In Wisconsin, most real estate transactions are closed in the office of the lending institution that is financing the sale or in the office of a title insurance company. In those cases where no lending institution or title insurance company is involved, closings generally are held at an attorney's office or at the office of the real estate broker. The seller's attorney is responsible for all details of the transaction that concern the title to the property, such as preparing the deed and making sure that any prior liens have been paid. The buyer's attorney makes the necessary disbursements of the buyer's checks.

BROKER'S ROLE AT THE CLOSING

The broker's role at closing will vary depending on the involvement of attorneys, lenders, and title companies. While the listing contract does not require the broker to do so, the broker has historically assumed the responsibility for the preparation of that part of the closing statement that deals with the relationship of the buyer and the seller. If a lender is involved, that lender will take the broker's information and add to it their charges and submit a complete closing statement to the parties. If no attorney or lender is involved, the broker will arrange the closing time and ensure everyone's attendance. The broker will also then bank the transaction, cutting checks and seeing to the payoff of all encumbrances. When a title company is involved in the closing, typically that company will assume most of the responsibilities of the broker and the lender. In that case, the broker will simply see to the collection of his or her commission and perhaps review the closing statement.

EVIDENCE OF TITLE

In Wisconsin, the seller is required to furnish and pay for satisfactory evidence of title in the form of either an abstract of title or title insurance. Title insurance is generally used in most real estate transactions. The buyer is responsible for examining the title to the real estate that is being purchased.

The buyer generally has his or her own attorney examine the title and pays the attorney's fees. However, less reliance is being placed on the title searches made by attorneys. As discussed in Chapter 9, most lenders are requiring the buyer to obtain a title insurance commitment as of the date of sale to protect the lender's interests.

In addition to this mortgage title insurance policy, the buyer's attorney usually will recommend that the buyer purchase an owner's title insurance policy to protect the buyer's interest as well. The title insurance company's decision to issue a policy generally is based on an abstract of title, prepared for this purchase by a professional abstractor.

As additional protection, most lenders also will require buyers to have a licensed surveyor prepare a survey of the real estate being purchased.

CLOSING PROBLEM

The following closing problem uses the procedures involved in an actual real estate transaction in Wisconsin. The data given in this problem were used to complete the listing contract reproduced in Chapter 2, as well as the offer to purchase that appears in Chapter 7. The student is advised to study these examples after reading the closing problem.

Data Describing the Real Estate Transaction

John James, a salesperson for Newhouse Realty, which is a member of the local REALTORS® multiple-listing service, secured a four-month exclusive listing on September 13, 2009, from George and Martha Carter. The listing was for their home at 1400 Regas Lane, Madison, Wisconsin. The legal description is Lot 2, Block 4, of the Fairmont Subdivision, NW 1/4 of Section 8, T9N, R7E, Dane County, Wisconsin. The Carters agreed to include the refrigerator, washer, dryer, carpeting, drapes, and drapery rods in the total selling price of $249,900. The Carters will give occupancy on the date of closing. James has agreed to hold at least one open house and to list the property with a multiple-listing service. The Carters have completed a sellers' condition report on the same day of the listing. The sellers have consented to the dual agency as described in the listing contract, and the Carters have agreed to pay a commission of 6 percent.

First Federal Bank of Madison holds a mortgage on the Carters' property with an unpaid balance of $176,650 as of September 1. The monthly payment, including interest, is $998.29; interest is charged at the rate of 5 percent per annum; and the final payment is to be made within 13 years. The bank has indicated that this mortgage may be assumed by a qualified buyer at the same rate of interest.

On November 15, 2009, salesperson James obtained an offer from Jay and Linda Jones to purchase the property for $248,000. The offer was made on the basis of the buyers' assumption of the balance of the existing mortgage and the balance of the selling price being paid in cash at closing. Possession was desired as of the date of closing, which was to be no later than December 15, 2009. The Joneses paid earnest money of $2,000, with another $2,000 to be paid on acceptance of the offer. The offer was accepted by the Carters on November 15, 2009. The Joneses received a copy of the sellers' condition report prior to buyers signing the offer to purchase. The buyers would like the washer and dryer. Real estate taxes for 2009 have not been paid yet. They must be prorated and credited to the buyers who will actually pay the taxes when they come due. Taxes for 2009 were $6,250. The sellers' assumable mortgage must be prorated and credited to the buyers on the closing statement. The Carters paid $518 for an owners' title insurance policy. The Carters are to pay the transfer tax appropriate for the transaction.

James made arrangements for the sellers' water to be read on the day of closing and billed accordingly on the closing statement. The water bill is $80. The broker's commission, as agreed to in the listing contract, is 6 percent of the selling price.

The buyers in this transaction are responsible for the $12 recording fee charged for filing the deed. They agree to pay the lender a 1 percent assumption fee on the remaining balance of the loan and reimburse the lender for the $15 credit report. The buyers also need a title insurance mortgage policy that costs $75. Their attorney's fee is $300. The buyers' expenses are not figured on the closing statement.

Completing the Closing Statements

Complete the blank closing statements on page 176 using the data outlined above. Prorate all expenses using the actual number of days in a month and 365 days in a year and round off calculations (where applicable).

After completing the closing statement, check your answers against the forms in the Answer Key on pages 239 and 240. An explanation of the closing statement follows this section.

Computing the prorations and charges. Following are illustrations of the various steps in computing the prorations and other amounts included in the closing statement.

1. Closing date: December 15, 2009
2. Commission 6 percent × $248,000 = $14,880
3. Assumed mortgage principal and interest: The unpaid balance of the seller's mortgage is $176,650 as of September 1 (the listing was taken September 13, 2009). Because the sale was closed on December 15, three more payments were made by the sellers and the balance reduced as follows:

Date		*Balance*		
September 1		$176,650.00		
$176,650.00 × 0.05	=	$8,832.50	=	Annual interest
$8,832.50 ÷ 365	=	$24.20	=	Interest per day
$24.1986 × 30	=	$725.96	=	Interest for September

$948.29 – $725.96	=	$222.33	= Principal to deduct from balance
$176,650 – $222.33	=	$176,427.67	= (October 1 balance)
October 1		$176,427.67	
$176,427.67 × 0.05	=	$8,821.38	= Annual interest
$8,821.38 ÷ 365	=	$24.17	= Interest per Day
$24.17 × 31	=	$749.27	= Interest for October
$948.29 – $749.27	=	$199.02	= Principal to deduct from balance
$176,427.69 – $199.02	=	$176,228.67	= (November 1 balance)
November 1		$176,228.67	
$176,228.67 × 0.05	=	$8,811.43	= Annual interest
$8,811.43 ÷ 365	=	$24.14	= Interest per Day
$24.14 × 30	=	$724.20	= Interest for November
$948.29 – $724.20	=	$224.09	= Principal to deduct from balance
$176,228.67 – $224.09	=	$176,004.58	= (December 1 balance)
December 1		$176,004.58	
$176,004.58 × 0.05	=	$8,800.23	= Annual interest
$8,800.23 ÷ 365	=	$24.11	= Interest per Day
$24.11 × 14	=	$337.54	= Interest owed by seller

$176,004.53 (Principal) + $337.54 (Interest) = $176,342.07 Credit to buyers on closing statement

Because the buyers agreed to assume the seller's remaining mortgage debt, the balance of the principal remaining is credited to them, as is the interest accrued on that principal while the sellers had possession of the property during part of December.

Estimated real estate taxes for 2009: $6,250 (estimate based on 2004 tax)

$6,250 ÷ 365 days = $17.12 per day

Earned period from January 1, 2009 to and including December 14, 2009 = 348 days

$17.12 × 348 = $5,957.76 Credit to buyers on closing statement.

SAMPLE CLOSING STATEMENTS AND EXPLANATION

The sample buyer's and seller's closing statements found in Figure 15.1 and Figure 15.2 are based on the sale of a home as follows. After completing the closing statements, go to pages 239 and 240 in the Answer Key to check your work.

Buyer's Closing Statement

The agreed-on sales price was $248,000, and the buyer made an earnest-money payment of $4,000. These are placed on lines 1 and 2 of the form (see Figure 15.1). The earnest money is a credit to the buyers.

The property was sold to the buyers subject to a mortgage that the buyers assumed and agreed to pay. The unpaid balance as of the date of closing is placed as a credit on line 4.

You should write the local treasurer's office and ask for any delinquent property taxes. You should also ask for a breakdown of the tax bills paid for the prior year. The treasurer's office also will tell you if there are any deferred taxes. All replies should be in writing. If you find delinquent taxes, you should request a letter showing the interest due. Any delinquent tax paid on or after the first of any month will include an interest charge for the entire month.

Line 6 would be used only if the buyers were buying the property subject to a mortgage and the mortgage holder had been collecting money regularly from the sellers in order to pay the taxes or insurance premiums when they came due. Any of the sellers' money in the possession of the mortgage holder would be shown as "due seller" on line 6.

Taxes were not delinquent in the sample problem. If the taxes had been delinquent and if the buyers had assumed and agreed to pay them, the amount of delinquent taxes as of the date of closing would be shown as a credit to the buyers on line 7.

Prior to the closing, you should check the parcel number and assessed value with either the assessor or the clerk in your municipality. You can check the current year's taxes with the local treasurer's office. If these offices do not have the information, they will direct you to the proper source. For most of the year, when no recent new improvements have been added, taxes are prorated on the basis of the net general tax for the previous year; however, later in the year, you should take into account possible higher current-year assessed values and mill-rate changes as known.

The expected taxes for the year 2009 were prorated through the day prior to closing based on the amount of tax for 2009 and a calendar year of 365 days. Taxes in 2008 were $6,250. The sellers owned the property 348 days in 2009 and are paying that proportionate part of the year's taxes. This is shown as a credit to the buyers on line 8.

When writing to the local treasurer's office, you should also inquire about unpaid special assessments and future special assessments. Be careful that you know what they are for and the exact amount, if available, it will take to pay them in full. It is a good policy, especially where recent special assessments are suspected, to check with the engineering department or the clerk's office in your municipality to get preliminary figures for any such work being done. These figures can be used as a basis of an escrow pending completion of the work and determination of the actual cost. Sidewalk repairs and tree removal are common special assessments on older properties, while sewer, water, and street curb and gutter are common in newer areas.

FIGURE 15.1

Sample Buyer's Closing Statement

FORM 930-B Buyer's Closing Statement

Wisconsin Legal Blank Co., Inc.
Milwaukee, WI

BROKER

BUYER'S CLOSING STATEMENT

Property Location ______

Seller(s) ______ Address ______

Buyer(s) ______ Address ______

Sale Contract Date ______ Closing Date ______ Closed At ______

BUYER'S SETTLEMENT WITH BROKER	DUE SELLER	CREDIT BUYER
1. Purchase Price		
2. Earnest Money		
3. Downpayment		
4. Mortgages (Assumed by Buyer)		
5. Land Contracts (Assumed by Buyer)		
6. Trust Funds Due Seller by Mortgagee		
7. Delinquent Taxes (if Assumed) for Years		
8. Seller's Share of Taxes: for ______ Prorated from ______ through ______ Last Year's Taxes ______ Prorated Basis @ $ ______ Per ______		
9. Special Assessments Assumed by Buyer		
10. Rent Prorated (list below)		
11. LP Gas/Fuel Oil and Other Items on Premises		
12. Recording Fees		
13. Transfer Fees		
14.		
15.		
16.		
17.		
18.		
Totals		

19. Daily Use and Occupancy Charge is $ ______
20. Date of Vacating Property ______
21. Escrow: ______
22. ______
23. ______

Less Credit to Buyer ______

Less: Mortgage or Land Contract Executed by Buyer to Seller ______

Balance Due Seller ______

TENANT'S NAME	MONTHLY RENTAL	DUE DATE	PAID UP TO	PRORATED AMOUNT

THIS STATEMENT IS ACCEPTED AS CORRECT ______, 20______

______ Buyer ______ Seller

______ Buyer ______ Seller

Source: Published with permission, Wisconsin Legal Blank Company, Inc. Line numbers have been added by the publisher for use in this textbook

There were no special assessments against the property. If there were unpaid special assessments that were to be paid by the sellers under the purchase agreement, and if they were assumed by the buyers as of the date of closing, they would be shown as a credit to the buyers on line 9. This approach can provide additional financing for a buyer. Assume that a property has a special assessment against it for $500 payable in five yearly installments. By assuming the special assessment that the seller would otherwise have to pay, the buyer is immediately credited with the payment of $500 on the purchase price, but the buyer actually will have five years in which to pay the money. The buyer will have to pay interest to the municipality, but often it will be at no higher rate than the buyer is paying on other borrowed money.

There is no tenant in the house. Therefore, you do not have to account for rental income. In the case of rented property, written approval of the tenants should be obtained prior to transferring security deposits on the closing statement. In addition, rents should be prorated between the parties. If the closing is taking place prior to the next rent-paying date, the buyer, of course, will collect the rent for the next rental period. If the closing is on or after the rent-paying date, the seller should collect the rent and give the buyer credit on the statement. Let's suppose for illustrative purposes that there is a tenant in another house who will not be moving until May 30. The tenant is paying rent at the rate of $100 per month in advance. The tenant pays the seller the April rent on April 1; the house is purchased on April 15. The rent for the last half of the month belongs to the buyer, so he or she would be credited with $50 on line 10. Fuel oil is shown on line 11. It is best to arrange with the seller to have the tank filled and charge the purchaser for a full tank on the closing statement. However, if the seller is opposed to having the tank filled, it may be prorated. You should call the oil company to determine the tank capacity, type of oil used, and cost per gallon. You should then have the gauge on the tank read to determine the amount in the tank and to compute the credit due the seller. Some oil companies will read the tank and calculate this for you. You should check with the buyer before you ask the seller to fill the tank.

In some cases, additional instruments have to be recorded to show clear title in the seller before the buyer will accept his or her deed. The cost of recording instruments for this purpose is the responsibility of the seller. As a matter of convenience, occasionally, the instruments are recorded by the buyer. When this happens, the buyer is credited for the recording fees on line 12.

If a land contract is being recorded, the Wisconsin Real Estate Transfer Return form must be completed by the vendor for submission at the time the contract is recorded; the Wisconsin transfer fee is paid at that time. It must be signed by both the buyer and the seller, setting forth the value of the ownership interest transferred by the land contract. When the contract has been paid off, the deed is offered for recording. Because the fee is imposed by law on the seller, but in practice the deed will be recorded by the buyer or the buyer's attorney and the fee paid by the buyer, the buyer will receive credit for the amount of the fee on the closing.

The totals show that the sellers are entitled to a total payment of $248,000 for the property and that the buyers have received credit for $186,299.83 of that amount. The buyers still owe $61,700.17, which they must pay before they receive the deed.

The balance due to sellers will be made up of a check for or cash of $61,700.17. The seller's closing statement showing the broker's settlement with the sellers is completed as follows.

Seller's Closing Statement

This form (see Figure 15.2) shows the amount that a broker has received for a seller (a buyer's down payment), the balance due from the buyer, and the deductions of the amounts that are owed by the seller to the broker. It also shows the net balance due the seller.

In the sample problem, the cash balance due from the buyers to the sellers at the closing is shown as due the sellers on line 1. It is $61,700.17.

The buyers' down payment of $4,000, which has been held by the broker in his trust account, is shown on line 2.

Often as a matter of convenience for the seller, the broker as agent orders and is billed for and pays the cost of the abstract extension or title insurance that shows the title in the seller's name. This is an expense that is the responsibility of the seller. The $518 charge for providing the owner's title insurance policy is shown as a charge to the sellers on line 4.

The $744 transfer fee is shown as a charge on line 6.

The seller has agreed to pay for the attorney's fee of $300 for preparation of the deed and this is shown as a charge on line 7.

Any advances that the broker has properly made for the sellers and any payments to be made for the sellers at the closing, such as the balance of the existing mortgage due or delinquent taxes, are charged to the sellers on lines 8–11.

Line 12 could be used for an occupancy escrow if called for by the contract; however, in this problem, occupancy was given to the buyers on the date of closing.

The broker's commission (6 percent × $248,000 sales price) is charged to the sellers on line 13.

Any extra services performed by the broker for which he or she can properly make additional charges are shown on lines 14–16. The broker has made arrangements for the sellers' water meter to be read on the day of closing. The water bill is $80. The water bill charge is shown on line 15.

The "total charges against seller" are $16,522.00, and the net balance of $49,148.17 is due the sellers.

FIGURE 15.2

Sample Seller's Closing Statement

FORM 930-S Seller's Closing Statement

Wisconsin Legal Blank Co., Inc.
Milwaukee, WI

BROKER

SELLER'S CLOSING STATEMENT

Property Location ______

Seller(s) ______ Address ______

Buyer(s) ______ Address ______

Sale Contract ______ Date Closing ______ Date Closed At ______

BROKER'S SETTLEMENT WITH SELLER	CHARGES AGAINST SELLER	DUE SELLER
1. Check/Cash Received from Buyer		
2. Earnest Money Deposit and Downpayment		
3. Total Due Seller Before Disbursements		
4. Abstract/Title Policy		
5. Recording Fees		
6. Transfer Fee		
7. Attorney's Fees Paid To:		
8. Mortgage or Land Contract Payoffs		
9. Delinquent Taxes (if Assumed) for Years		
10. Seller's Share of Taxes: for ______ Prorated from ______ to ______ Last Year's Taxes ______ Prorated Basis @ $ ______ Per ______		
11. Special Assessments		
12. Other Advances		
13. Commission		
14. Services (Itemize)		
15.		
16.		
17.		
18.		
19.		
20.		

21. Daily Use and Occupancy Charge is $______
22. Date of Vacating Property ______
23. Escrow: ______

Total Charges Against Seller ______

Balance to be Paid Seller ______

THIS STATEMENT IS ACCEPTED AS CORRECT ______, 20______

______ Broker ______ Seller

By ______ ______ Seller

Source: Published with permission, Wisconsin Legal Blank Company, Inc. Line numbers have been added by the publisher for use in this textbook

QUESTIONS

1. At the closing, the seller's broker usually does *NOT*
   a. ensure that the parties appear at the designated time and place.
   b. prepare the closing statement.
   c. collect his or her commission.
   d. prepare the deed.
2. In the closing statement for a real estate transaction, the earnest money deposit is charged as a
   a. credit to the seller.
   b. credit to the buyer.
   c. charge due the buyer.
   d. charge due the seller.
3. In order to protect their interests, many lenders in Wisconsin require a borrower to
   a. have an environmental survey made on the real estate involved.
   b. obtain an owner's title insurance policy.
   c. obtain a title insurance commitment as of the date of the offer to purchase.
   d. obtain a title insurance commitment as of the date of the sale.
4. The person responsible for furnishing and paying for satisfactory title evidence in Wisconsin real estate transactions is the
   a. seller's attorney.
   b. seller.
   c. buyer.
   d. buyer's broker.

Use your completed closing statements in Figure 15.1 and Figure 15.2 to answer Question 5 through Question 9.

5. The amount due from the buyers at the closing is
   a. $57,699.06.
   b. $61,700.17.
   c. $4,000.00.
   d. $5,958.87.
6. The unpaid principal of the assumed mortgage is:
   a. $176,650.00.
   b. $176,228.59.
   c. $176,427.67.
   d. $176,004.53.
7. At the closing, the sellers will receive
   a. $18,802.00.
   b. $49,148.17.
   c. $61,699.06.
   d. $65,699.06.
8. The sellers' expenses in the transaction include
   a. a title insurance policy.
   b. prorated insurance.
   c. special assessment taxes.
   d. prorated rents.
9. The broker's commission in this transaction is
   a. based on 7 percent of the list price.
   b. $14,880.00.
   c. $17,360.00.
   d. $17,493.00.
10. Real estate taxes are prorated through the
    a. day prior to closing.
    b. day of closing.
    c. day after closing.
    d. second day after closing.

Summary of Wisconsin Statutes and Administrative Rules Relating to the Practice of Real Estate

SUMMARY OF WISCONSIN STATUTES

Section 23.32 Wetlands

This statute states that the Department of Natural Resources will prepare, or cause to be prepared, maps that at a minimum identify as accurately as is practical the individual wetlands in the state that have an area of five acres or more. The statute defines wetlands as an area where water is at, near, or above the land surface long enough to be capable of supporting aquatic or hydrophytic vegetation and that has soils indicative of wet conditions.

Section 66.432 Equal Opportunity Law

Equal opportunity in housing is stated to be a matter of statewide concern. The protected classes are identified; you may find them in both the listing contract and the offer to purchase. The statute also states that cities, villages, towns, or counties may enact their own equal housing ordinances provided that they are as protective as the state statute. Municipalities may also enact an ordinance that is more comprehensive than the state statute.

Section 70.043 Mobile Homes

A mobile home is considered to be real property if it is connected to utilities and is set upon a foundation on land that is owned by the mobile home owner. A mobile home is set upon a foundation if it is off its wheels and is set upon some other support. A mobile home is considered to be personal property if the land on which it is located is not owned by the mobile home owner or if the mobile home is not set upon a foundation or connected to utilities.

Section 70.095 Assessment Roll; Time-Share Property

A time-share instrument must provide a method for allocating real property taxes among the time-share owners. Only one entry is to be made on the assessment roll for each time-share property, which entry is to consist of the cumulative real property value of all time-share interests in the unit.

Sections 74.15 and 74.47 Real Property Taxes

Section 74.15 states that if there is no valid written agreement between the buyer and seller regarding how taxes will be prorated, the seller shall pay to the buyer an amount equal to one-twelfth of the taxes assessed for the previous calendar year, including the month in which the conveyance is made if it occurs after the 15th day of the month.

Section 74.47 states that a monthly interest charge of 1 percent will be added to each tax installment that is not paid by the January 31 due date. The county board or city council also may impose an additional penalty of ½ percent per month on any delinquent real estate taxes or special assessments.

Sections 77.22 and 77.27 Taxation and Transfer Fee

Wisconsin does not require a documentary stamp tax, but the state does impose a real estate transfer fee on all conveyances of real estate. The fee is $0.30 per $100 of the value of the property or fraction thereof. For example, if the value of the property sold is $30,000, the fee is $90. If the value is $30,050, the fee is $90.30. The sale price is rounded up to the next $100 so the $30,050 becomes $30,100 multiplied by 0.003. The fee applies to the full sale price of the property regardless of any liens or encumbrances that may stand against the property. In addition, the transfer fee must be paid by the seller (grantor) at the time a land contract is recorded even though the deed will be recorded later. For example, the transfer fee would be $149.70 on a property sold for $49,000 even though there might be a $30,000 mortgage assumed by the buyer.

The transfer fee must be paid by the seller (grantor) to the register of deeds at the time the deed is recorded. A Wisconsin Real Estate Transfer Return form must be submitted at the time the fee is paid and must show the value of the property.

Section 77.27 states that any person who intentionally falsifies value on a transfer fee return required to be filed may be fined not more than $1,000, or imprisoned in the county jail for not more than one year, or both.

Section 87.30 Flood Plain Zoning

All flood plains in Wisconsin are now or soon will be subject to zoning. The Wisconsin Department of Natural Resources will adopt zoning for any flood plain for which a county, city, or village does not adopt zoning. Any citizen of the state may bring action in court to force the removal of any structure, fill, or development placed in a flood plain in violation of any ordinance, and the one who placed it there may be fined up to $50 per day until it is removed.

Chapter 91 Farmland Preservation

The Farmland Preservation Act provides an income tax credit to Wisconsin residents who own at least the minimum lot size as specified by their exclusive agricultural ordinance. The farmland must either be zoned for exclusive agricultural use or be subject to a farmland-preservation agreement. In addition, the farmland must have produced at least $6,000 in gross farm profits during the year preceding application for a farmland preservation agreement or a total of at least $18,000 of gross farm profits during the three years preceding application. A farmland-preservation agreement refers to a restrictive covenant, evidenced by an instrument, whereby the owner and the state agree to hold jointly the right to develop the land except as may be expressly reserved in the instrument. Such an agreement also may contain a covenant running with the land for a term of years not to develop except as expressly reserved in the instrument. If the owner violates the agreement, the owner will be responsible for paying back taxes plus interest and penalties.

Land covered by a farmland-preservation agreement may be sold by the buyer who takes title subject to the agreement. If the owner or a successor in title of the land upon which a farmland preservation agreement has been recorded changes the use of land to a prohibited use, the successor will be subject to a civil penalty not to exceed twice the value of the land as established at the time of the application.

Section 106.50 Equal Rights and Fair Housing

It is the policy of the state to declare discrimination in the sale or rental of housing unlawful. The statute identifies protected classes that may be found in the listing contract or offer to purchase. The statute covers single-family status or housing residences that are owner-occupied. The statute does allow all discrimination on the basis of age, or family status with respect to housing for older persons, or housing specifically for persons with disabilities.

The statute states that people with disabilities must be allowed to make reasonable modification to existing housing, provided that it is at the expense of the person with disabilities. The law also provides that the tenant with disabilities must restore the housing to its original use upon expiration of the occupancy.

The law also states that it is discriminatory for a landlord to refuse to rent to a tenant because that tenant keeps a life support animal. However, an owner renting owner-occupied housing does not have to rent to a person with a life support animal if the owner, or a member of the owner's immediate family occupying that housing, can present to the prospective tenant a certificate signed by a physician stating that the owner or family member is allergic to the type of animal the individual possesses.

The Equal Rights Division of the Wisconsin Department of Workforce Development investigates complaints filed in writing not later than one year after the alleged discrimination occurred or terminated.

This statute is summarized in Chapter 14 of this book.

Chapter 236 Platting Subdivisions

All land in Wisconsin is subject to this statute. However, the state regulations govern only situations where five or more lots of one and one-half acres or less in area are created within a period of five years for the purpose of sale and building development. Section 236 does not apply where the parcels are larger than one and one-half acres or where four lots or fewer are created. Local units of government, however, are authorized to adopt more stringent regulations and certain municipalities have done so. In those cases where more stringent controls have not been adopted, Section 236.34 permits the use of a certified survey map for four or fewer parcels to provide greater accuracy in real estate descriptions.

Section 240.10 Real Estate Agency Contracts and Fraud

The Wisconsin Statute of Frauds stipulates that in order for a listing to be valid it must: (1) be in writing; (2) state the rate or exact amount of commission to be earned by the broker; (3) specify a definite termination date for the agreement; (4) state the price of the real estate and the terms of the sale; (5) include a description that specifically identifies the property; (6) name the broker; and (7) bear the signature of the person who is to pay the broker's commission. Under the Statute of Frauds, an oral listing agreement is unenforceable.

According to the statute, a buyer or agency agreement does not need to describe the property.

Contracts to pay a commission for a leasing agreement for a term exceeding three years are also covered in this statute.

Chapter 254 Lead Hazard Reduction

This statute is summarized in Chapter 1 of this book.

Chapter 406 Bulk Transfer

A bulk transfer is the sale of a business as a whole, including all fixtures, merchandise, and chattels. When an agent sells a business, he or she is frequently selling merchandise and chattels rather than real estate. This statute protects creditors of a business being sold by stating that the buyer must require the seller to furnish a list and schedule of the seller's existing creditors. The buyer must preserve the list and schedule of the property for six months following the transfer. Responsibility for the accuracy of the list and schedule rests on the seller. In addition, any bulk transfer subject to this section, except one made by auction sale, is ineffective against any creditor or the seller unless, at least 10 days before the buyer takes possession of the goods or pays the major part of the purchase price, whichever happens first, the buyer gives notice of the transfer to the persons specified in the list of creditors.

Regulation DFI—Banking 40.03 Negotiating and Finding a Loan

This regulation defines loan originators, loan solicitors, and mortgage bankers, and it specifies when they must register as such with the state.

Chapter 452 Real Estate Practice

Chapter 10 of this book provides a summary of this statute.

Chapter 703 Condominiums

This statute is summarized in Chapter 4 of this book.

Chapter 706 Conveyances and Homesteads

This statute is summarized in Chapters 3 and 7 of this book.

Section 707 Time-Share Ownership

This statute states that a disclosure statement must be given to the purchaser of a time-share prior to transferring the title. The purchaser has five days to cancel the contract, in writing, without penalty after the disclosure has been delivered.

Prior to the sale of any time-shares in a project, the developers must establish an escrow account and designate an escrow agent for the purpose of protecting the deposits of purchasers. The escrow agents must be independent of the developer. In addition, the developer as well as any affiliated of the developer, or any officer, director, subsidiary, or employee of the developer, may not serve as the escrow agent. The statute identifies the responsibilities of the escrow agent including the obligation to retain for five years all affidavits requesting the release of the escrowed deposit received by the developer or the buyer in the case of cancellation. Until the deposit can be released from escrow, an amount equal to 50 percent of the deposit must be deposited in an escrow account under an escrow agreement.

Chapter 709 Disclosure by Owners of Residential Property

This statute is summarized in Chapter 1 of this book.

Chapter 710 Property Provisions for Aliens and Corporations

This statute states that no more than 640 acres of land in Wisconsin may be purchased or held by nonresident aliens or a foreign-based corporation. The statute does, however, allow for the ownership of more than 640 acres in certain situations, such as an exploration mining lease. Interests exceeding 640 acres must generally be divested within four years. The penalty for failure to report to the Secretary of Agriculture, Trade, and Consumer Protection, is not less than $500 nor more than $5,000.

Chapter 766 Property Rights of Married Persons

The Wisconsin Marital Property Act is summarized in Chapters 3 and 7 of this book.

SUMMARY OF ADMINISTRATIVE RULES

RL15 Documents and Records

A broker or salesperson must promptly provide an exact and complete copy of any document used in real estate practice to any person who has signed the document. In addition, the listing broker or the broker's designee is required to prepare an accurate closing statement and provide complete copies for the appropriate parties. The broker must also retain exact and complete records of all documents and correspondence for at least three years from the date of closing of the transaction or from the date of listing if the transaction has not been consummated.

RL16 Contractual Forms

RL16 is summarized in Chapter 7 of this book. A licensee may not make a separate charge for completing an approved form in connection with a transaction. A licensee may use a preprepared addendum or other attached pages of provisions provided these pages are incorporated by language into the contract. A preprepared addendum that alters or supplants the printed provisions of an approved form must be drafted by an attorney who is identified on the addendum. Other requirements for this type of situation are presented in RL16.

RL17 Licensure and Supervision of Employees

RL17 is summarized in Chapter 10 of this book. RL17 states that a broker who is employed by a broker-employer may also engage in real estate practice in his own name if he obtains written approval from the broker-employer and avoids conflicts of interest with his or her employment by the broker-employer. It is also important to emphasize that a salesperson may engage in real estate practice only when employed by a broker.

RL18 Trust Accounts

RL18 is summarized in Chapter 10 of this book.

RL23 Change of Name, Address, Trade Name

A licensee who changes the name appearing on his or her current license must notify the Wisconsin Department of Regulation and Licensing in writing within 30 days after the change of name. The 30-day period also applies to the licensee's changing of the address that appears on his or her license.

Additionally, a licensed broker, before doing business under any trade name, must notify the Wisconsin Department of Regulation and Licensing in writing of the trade name change.

RL24 on Conduct

RL24 on conduct and ethical practices is discussed in Chapter 1 of this book.

Finally, a broker may not engage in real estate activities under a different form of business organization until a new license has been issued.

RL40 Real Estate Agent as Loan Solicitor

A real estate licensee who finds a loan for a person is not required to register as a loan solicitor if the licensee does not receive a commission, money, or other thing of value from any person for finding the loan.

COMM10 Underground Storage Tanks

This rule covers groundwater protection for small farm and residential motor fuel Underground Storage Tanks (USTs) and heating oil USTs. It specifically covers farm and residential UST systems of 1,100 gallons or less capacity used for storing motor fuel for noncommercial purposes; and UST systems used for storing heating oil for consumptive use on the premises. All USTs must be registered with the Wisconsin Department of Commerce.

New and replacement UST systems must comply with performance standards except that spill and overfill equipment is not required for heating oil UST systems of 4,000 gallons or less capacity. In addition, vent whistles must be provided for heating oil UST systems of 4,000 gallons or less capacity.

ATCP134 Residential Rental Practices

Whenever a security deposit is required, the landlord must, upon acceptance of the deposit, inform the tenant that the tenant may inspect the dwelling unit and notify the landlord of any damages or defects that existed before the beginning of the tenancy. The tenant must be given at least seven days after the beginning of tenancy for the inspection and notification. The tenant must also be furnished with a written itemized description of any physical damages or defects for which deductions from the previous tenant's security deposit were made.

The landlord must return all security deposits less any amounts withheld within 21 days after surrender of the premises. Security deposits may be withheld only for tenant damage, waste, or neglect of premises or the nonpayment of rent or utilities. If any portion of a security deposit is withheld, the landlord must deliver or mail to the tenant a written statement accounting for all amounts withheld.

A landlord may not enter a dwelling unit during tenancy without advance notice of at least 12 hours and at reasonable times unless the tenant agrees to a shorter time period. A landlord may not confiscate a tenant's personal property unless that property was abandoned.

COMM67 Rental Weatherization Requirements

This rule is summarized in Chapter 8 of this book.

NR116 Flood Plains

This rule is summarized in Chapter 13 of this book.

APPENDIX B Test-Taking Tips: Real Estate License Examination Review

Wisconsin Real Estate: Practice & Law is designed to help you prepare for a career in real estate. But before opening a brokerage office or a salesperson's listing book, you have to obtain a license for which you must pass an examination, a test of what you have learned about real estate laws, principles, and practices.

The Wisconsin real estate licensing examination is administered and prepared by an independent testing service, Promissor. A number of states subscribe to Promissor's service. In each state, the program is adapted to local real estate laws and practices and the individual priorities of the state's licensing agency.

Wisconsin examinees are now taking the exam by computer. Taking the Promissor examination by computer is simple; neither computer experience nor typing skills are required for taking the test that will require you to use fewer than 12 keys on the keyboard. Upon being seated at the computer terminal, you will be prompted to confirm your name, identification number, and the examination for which you are registered.

An introduction to the computer and keyboard will appear on the screen prior to your starting the exam. The time allowed for this introduction will not count as part of your exam time.

The introduction will include a sample screen display telling you to press A, B, C, or D to select your answer or to press ? to mark for a later review. You then could press enter to record your answer before moving on to the next question. You may change your answer as often as you like before pressing enter. It is important to note that during the examination, the time remaining for your examination will be displayed at the top of the screen and updated as you record your answers. After you have answered every question in the examination, if you have time remaining, you will be given the opportunity to review all of the questions in the examination. You also will have the choice of reviewing only those questions that you marked for review or of ending your examination and seeing your results. You may change your answers during the review options. You may repeat the review options as time allows.

It is important to emphasize that candidates taking the Real Estate Salesperson combined examination will be presented with the national and state questions in a single test session in which the questions appear in random order.

TOPIC AREAS ON THE EXAM

Broker's Examination

The Wisconsin real estate broker's exam consists of 100 multiple-choice questions. The exam tests the knowledge and skills required for real estate brokers licensed in Wisconsin. The content outline for the broker exam has been approved by the Wisconsin Department of Regulation and Licensing. Questions for the broker's exam are drawn from the following six areas:

1. Real estate practice. Your knowledge of Chapter 452 of the Wisconsin Statutes regarding real estate practice as well as S. 703.33 and Chapter RL17 and RL23 is examined. There are 19 questions on the topic.

2. Trust accounts. Your knowledge of Chapter 18 is tested. There are 12 questions on this topic.

3. Conduct and ethical practices for real estate licensees. Your knowledge of Chapter RL24 is plumbed. There are 22 questions on this topic.

4. Approved forms and legal advice. Your knowledge of Chapter RL16 is ascertained. There are 6 questions on this topic.

5. Drafting and supervision knowledge. An understanding of selected approved forms, issues related to forms, and the broker's obligation to furnish copies and maintain records is examined. There are 37 questions on this topic.

6. Miscellaneous. Your knowledge of Wisconsin fair housing law and federal lead-based paint law is tested. There are 4 questions on this topic.

The broker's exam lasts 3.25 hours and includes several questions based on a story problem that is built around a listing contract and offer to purchase.

Out-of-state applicants are required to take the entire 100-question state-specific exam.

Salesperson's Examination

Questions for the salesperson's exam are drawn from the following ten major areas:

1. Ownership and transfer of property. Your knowledge of the characteristics affecting the acquisition and transfer of real estate is tested. Included is an understanding of classes of property, encumbrances, types of ownership, and the various types of deeds. Title insurance, types of title, and conveyances of real property are also covered. There are 14 questions on this topic.

2. Land use controls and regulations. How well you know the kinds of restrictions that can be put on property use, including public restrictions such as zoning ordinances and private restrictions such as deed restrictions, is tested. There are 5 questions on this topic.

3. Valuing and financing property and calculations. A knowledge of the financial aspects of real property transfer including financial alternatives such as fixed and adjustable rate mortgages is examined. This section also includes questions on the comparative market analysis, definitions of value, and basic mathematical skills such as prorations and calculation of property tax payments. There are 20 questions on this topic.

4. Law of agency. Your understanding of what agency is, how it is created and terminated, and the distinction between various kinds of agency relationships is plumbed. Included is a knowledge of duties, responsibilities, and legal obligation of an agent toward a principal and other parties as well as the various types of agency contracts required for use by licensees in Wisconsin. There are 32 questions on this topic.

5. Disclosures. Your knowledge of the types of disclosure required by owners in a real estate transaction is tested. There are 13 questions on this topic.

6. Contract law and approved forms. How well you understand approved forms and legal advice as well as the various types of offers to purchase used in a Wisconsin real estate transaction is evaluated. There are 22 questions on this topic.

7. Business ethics. Your knowledge of the conduct and ethical practices for which real estate licensees are responsible in Wisconsin is examined. There are 14 questions on this topic.

8. Fair housing. Your comprehension of Wisconsin fair housing law and local equal opportunities as well as providing services for the disabled is ascertained. There are 6 questions on this topic.

9. Federal antitrust law. Your familiarity with price fixing and group boycotts is tested. There are 2 questions on this topic.

10. Miscellaneous. Your knowledge of trust accounts, fee splitting, licensure, supervision of employees, leases, and rental residential practices is plumbed. There are 12 questions on this topic.

The salesperson exam consists of 140 questions that are primarily state specific and transaction based. The content of the exam has been approved by the Wisconsin Department of Regulation and Licensing. Candidates are allowed 4 hours to complete the exam.

Like the broker's exam, this exam includes some questions based on a story problem that is built around a listing contract, offer to purchase, and closing statement. Also, salesperson applicants are expected to complete basic problems in real estate mathematics related to such topics as commissions and prorations. Note that only nonprogrammable calculators that are silent, operate on batteries, have no paper tape printing capabilities, and have no keyboard containing the alphabet will be permitted.

Sample questions. The questions on the exam are not set up to trick you. You will, however, encounter several exam questions that are more complex than the majority. Such questions are usually in a situational (story) format. You must read each question carefully to know exactly what is being asked before you begin to formulate your answer. Examples of some of the questions that seem to be the most difficult for examinees are illustrated in this section. These include questions with superfluous facts; questions asking for synthesis of facts; questions asking for reading comprehension, multistep math and value judgments; and best-answer questions.

Exam questions frequently contain superfluous facts that are not needed to answer the questions. For example:

> *The Koepkes paid $200,000 for their home five years ago and made a $10,000 down payment. Their monthly payments, including interest at 7 percent, amounted to $997.50. The interest portion of their last payment was $875. What was their approximate loan balance before their last payment?*

The only facts you need to answer this question are the amount of the last interest payment and the rate of interest. To solve the problem, you simply multiply the amount of the monthly interest, $875, by 12. You then divide the result by the interest rate, .07, to get the approximate loan balance of $150,000.

Another type of question you will find on the test asks you to take facts that you have learned separately and synthesize that information to answer the question. For example:

> *Twelve years ago, the Zieglers, parents of two children, retired and left Madison, Wisconsin, taking up residence in Alabama along the Gulf Coast. They decided to keep their Madison residence, which they owned as tenants in common, and to rent it to friends. Mae Ziegler died suddenly, leaving no will. Alabama law provides that when a wife dies intestate, a widower receives a life estate in all real property owned by his wife at death. Paul will inherit which of the following interests in the Madison home?*
>
> a. In severalty due to the right of survivorship
> b. A life estate
> c. One-half of the interest
> d. The entire estate

The correct answer is d. To answer this question, you need to know: (1) that rights of survivorship do not apply to a tenancy in common; (2) that Wisconsin property is probated in Wisconsin in accordance with Wisconsin law; (3) that the laws of descent apply because the wife died intestate; (4) what the laws of descent are in Wisconsin; and (5) how to combine numerically the real estate interest held before and after the wife's death.

The third type of question you may find on the test requires you to read each word extremely carefully for comprehension. For example:

> *Closing of a transaction for a residential property is set for April 19, 2004. Seller has a three-year insurance policy that expires June 25, 2005. Seller has prepaid a three-year premium of $1,665. Buyer is to take over the policy as of the date of closing. The amount credited to the buyer at closing is:*
>
> a. $555.00
> b. $608.97
> c. $693.75
> d. None of the above

The answer here is d because the prorated amount of the prepaid insurance would be debited to the buyer.

Another type of question that frequently appears on the Promissor exam is the multistep math question. For example:

> *Karen Valentine bought a house at exactly the appraised value. She negotiated a loan through Prairieville Savings and Loan Association at 75 percent of the appraised value. The interest rate was 9 percent. The first month's interest was $405. What was the selling price of the property?*

To answer this question, you must first multiply $405 by 12 to get the annual interest of $4,860. You then divide $4,860 by the interest rate, 0.09, to get the loan amount of $54,000. Next, you divide $54,000 by 0.75 to find the appraised value of $72,000, which is the same as the purchase price.

TAKING THE LICENSE EXAMINATION

For best results, you should go through the entire examination first and answer those questions you are certain about, leaving the doubtful ones for last. This way you at least will avoid missing a question you know through lack of time. After you have answered all the questions you know for certain, return to the remaining questions. If you are unable to arrive at an answer the second time through, guess. There is no penalty for guessing.

One of the most important assets in taking an examination is to remain relaxed. If you are nervous, your mind may not function as well as it should and you might have difficulty with the material. If you are prepared and have an adequate knowledge of the subject, you should be able to complete the examination successfully.

APPENDIX C

Sample Salesperson Examination

1. According to law, a trade fixture is
   a. a fixture.
   b. an easement.
   c. personalty.
   d. a license.

2. A copy of the WB-1 listing contract must be
   a. given to the insurance agent upon closing.
   b. left with the seller upon signature.
   c. delivered to the seller upon approval of the broker employer.
   d. given to the seller at closing.

3. According to Wisconsin Fair Housing Law, which of the following is *NOT* a protected class?
   a. Marital status
   b. Political beliefs
   c. Sexual orientation
   d. Lawful source of income

4. The real estate broker's responsibility to keep the principal informed of all of the facts that could affect a transaction is the duty of
   a. care.
   b. disclosure.
   c. obedience.
   d. accounting.

5. The relationship of a broker to his or her client is that of a(n)
   a. trustee.
   b. subagent.
   c. fiduciary.
   d. attorney in fact.

6. Statements by a real estate licensee exaggerating the benefits of a property are called
   a. polishing.
   b. puffing.
   c. prospecting.
   d. marketing.

7. A broker is permitted to represent both the seller and the buyer in the same transaction when
   a. the principals are not aware of such action.
   b. the broker is a subagent rather than the agent of the seller.
   c. commissions are collected from both parties.
   d. both parties have been informed and agree to the dual representation.

8. According to Wisconsin law, a lead hazard is any substance, surface, or object that contains lead and that, due to its condition, location, or nature may contribute to the lead poisoning or lead exposure of a child under
   a. 6 years of age.
   b. 8 years of age.
   c. 10 years of age.
   d. 12 years of age.

9. As an agent for the seller, a real estate broker can
   a. guarantee a prospective buyer that the seller will accept an offer at the listed price and terms.
   b. solicit an offer to purchase the property from a prospective buyer.
   c. advise a prospective buyer of the best manner of taking title to the property.
   d. change the terms of the listing contract on behalf of the seller.

10. A seller has listed her home with a broker for $190,000, and the broker tells a prospective buyer to submit a low offer because the seller is desperate to sell. The buyer offers $166,000 and the seller accepts it. In this situation
    a. the broker has violated his agency relationship with the seller.
    b. the broker was unethical, but the seller did get to sell her property.
    c. the broker acted properly to obtain a quick offer on the property.
    d. any broker is authorized to encourage such bids for the property.

11. When Broker Howard was told by his principal not to advertise her property in the XYZ newspaper, which was out of the area, Broker Howard complied because he
    a. had never advertised in the XYZ newspaper anyway.
    b. must obey the lawful instructions of his principal.
    c. was not intending to advertise the property at all.
    d. is allowed to advertise only in local newspapers.

12. A landowner subdivides his acreage and offers the lots for sale. Broker Easley tells the landowner that she can sell the lots. After Broker Easley sells some of the lots, the landowner refuses to pay her a commission. Broker Easley can
    a. report the landowner to the real estate licensing authorities.
    b. file a lien against the landowner's remaining lots.
    c. sue the landowner for breach of contract.
    d. do nothing at all.

13. You are a Wisconsin real estate broker in the process of moving to a new home. You must notify the Wisconsin Department of Regulation and Licensing of your change of address within
    a. 5 days of the change.
    b. 10 days of the change.
    c. 30 days of the change.
    d. 90 days of the change.

14. A broker who is the agent of the buyer should do which of the following?
    a. Disclose to the seller that the buyer is a minority person
    b. Disclose to the seller the maximum price the buyer is willing to pay
    c. Present to the seller only offers that are acceptable
    d. Advise the buyer if the listing price of the seller's house is realistic

15. A salesperson sells a buyer a property listed by another brokerage firm in the MLS. The salesperson has been working with the buyer for many months but does not have an agency contract with the buyer. This salesperson has fiduciary obligations to
    a. the seller.
    b. the buyer.
    c. no one.
    d. the public.

16. Mr. Miles' house has been listed for sale for more than one year, and he is very anxious to move into a retirement condominium. A salesperson, who is a subagent of the seller, tells a prospective buyer to make a low offer because the salesperson is sure that the seller will accept it. Regarding the salesperson's conduct, which of the following would *NOT* be *TRUE*?
    a. The salesperson acted appropriately to get the seller's property sold.
    b. The salesperson violated the fiduciary to the seller.
    c. The salesperson's conduct could indicate that he or she is working for the buyer.
    d. The salesperson should not assume that an anxious seller will accept a lower offer.

17. You are a Wisconsin real estate salesperson who has been terminated by your broker. You must send a notice of termination to the Wisconsin Department of Regulation and Licensing within
    a. 3 days after the termination of employment.
    b. 5 days after the termination of employment.
    c. 10 days after the termination of employment.
    d. 30 days after termination of employment.

18. Which would *NOT* need to be licensed when acting for another person in the sale or lease of real estate?
    a. One who is personally representing a dealer in real estate
    b. Anyone acting under a power of attorney
    c. A relative of the party
    d. A next-door neighbor

19. The amount of commission due to a salesperson is determined by
    a. state law.
    b. the local real estate board.
    c. mutual agreement.
    d. court decree.

20. Broker J was accused of violating antitrust laws. She was probably accused of
    a. not having an equal housing opportunity sign in her office window.
    b. undisclosed dual agencies.
    c. allocation of customers or price fixing.
    d. dealing in unlicensed exchange services.

21. A salesperson may advertise a property for sale only if he or she
    a. personally listed the property.
    b. uses the employing broker's name in the advertisement.
    c. personally pays for the advertisement.
    d. is a member of the local real estate board.

22. A real estate salesperson who is an independent contractor receives
    a. a monthly salary or hourly wage.
    b. company-provided health insurance.
    c. a company-provided automobile.
    d. negotiated commissions on transactions.

23. Which is *NOT* required of a broker in order for that broker to collect a commission on the sale of a property? That he or she
    a. had a valid real estate broker's license.
    b. was a procuring cause.
    c. was employed to perform that activity.
    d. belonged to a real estate board.

24. A broker lists a property for sale at $100,000 with a 5 percent commission, and he later obtains a verbal offer to purchase the property from a prospective buyer. The seller indicates to the broker that the offer would be acceptable if it were submitted in writing. Before it can be put in writing, the buyer backs out and revokes the verbal offer. In this situation the broker would be entitled to
    a. a commission of $5,000.
    b. only a partial commission.
    c. no commission.
    d. the normal rate of commission.

25. You listed a property on August 1, 2009. The seller accepted an offer to purchase on September 4, 2009, and the transaction closed on November 21, 2009. According to Wisconsin laws, which of the following statements correctly describes your responsibility for holding the listing contract?
    a. You should retain a copy of the listing contract until August 1, 2009.
    b. You should retain a copy of the listing contract until September 4, 2009.
    c. You should retain a copy of the listing contract until November 21, 2012.
    d. You should retain a copy of the listing contract until August 1, 2012.

26. Which is prohibited under the antitrust laws?
    a. Property management companies standardizing management fees
    b. A broker chooses to list only properties above $200,000
    c. A real estate company refuses to cooperate with a broker because of the fees that broker charges
    d. A broker deciding whether to join MLS

27. A licensed salesperson may receive compensation or commission from
    a. only the employing broker.
    b. the principal.
    c. any broker.
    d. a landlord.

28. The type of listing agreement that provided for the payment of a commission to the broker even though the owner makes the sale without the aid of the broker is called a(n)
    a. exclusive-right-to-sell listing.
    b. open listing.
    c. exclusive-agency listing.
    d. option listing.

29. A Wisconsin real estate salesperson received an earnest money deposit on a home for which he or she drafted an offer to purchase. The salesperson should deposit the earnest money in his or her broker's trust account within
    a. 12 hours of receipt.
    b. 24 hours of receipt.
    c. 48 hours of receipt.
    d. 72 hours of receipt.

30. A property owner signed a 90-day listing agreement with a broker. The owner was killed in an accident before the listing expired. Now the listing is
    a. binding on the owner's spouse for the remainder of the 90 days.
    b. still in effect as the owner's intention was clearly defined.
    c. binding only if the broker can produce offers to purchase the property.
    d. terminated automatically upon the death of the principal.

31. A broker who represents a seller under an exclusive listing receives two offers for the property at the same time, one from one of his or her salespeople and one from a salesperson of a cooperating broker. What should the broker do?
    a. Submit the offer from his or her salesperson first
    b. Submit the offer from the other salesperson first
    c. Submit the higher offer first
    d. Submit both offers at the same time

32. What is the difference between a general and a specific lien?
    a. A general lien cannot be enforced in court, while a specific lien can be enforced.
    b. A specific lien is held by one person, while a general lien is held by at least two persons.
    c. A general lien covers all of the debtor's property, while a specific lien covers only a certain piece of real property.
    d. A specific lien covers real estate, while a general lien covers personal property.

33. A home valued at $168,500 has just had a 70 percent mortgage loan placed on it. The interest rate is 11.25 percent. The monthly payment is $1,292.22 including principal and interest. What will the principal balance of the mortgage loan be after the next monthly payment?
    a. $117.560.28
    b. $117,763.56
    c. $117,913.56
    d. $117,950.00

34. The effective gross income from an office building is $73,500 and the annual operating expenses total $52,300. If the owner expects to receive an 11 percent return on his investment, what is the value of the building?
    a. $125,800
    b. $192,727
    c. $474,454
    d. $668,181

35. The amount of land for a rural homestead in Wisconsin is defined as not less than one-quarter acre and not more than how many acres?
    a. 5 acres
    b. 10 acres
    c. 20 acres
    d. 40 acres

36. The commission on the sale of a house is $4,410. Five percent of the commission goes to the multiple-listing service. Twenty-five percent goes to the broker who listed the property. Of the remainder, the broker whose salesperson completed the transaction gets 45 percent, and the salesperson receives the balance. How much does the salesperson who made the sale receive?

    a. $1,102.50
    b. $1,697.85
    c. $1,728.85
    d. $2,425.50

37. J owned the fee simple title to a vacant lot adjacent to a hospital and was persuaded to make a gift of the lot. She had her attorney prepare a deed that conveyed the ownership of the lot to the hospital "so long as it is used for medical purposes." After the completion of the gift, the hospital will own a

    a. life estate.
    b. tenancy for years.
    c. fee simple determinable.
    d. periodic tenancy.

38. S and N bought a store building and took title as joint tenants. N died testate. S now owns the store

    a. as a joint tenant with rights of survivorship.
    b. in severalty.
    c. as a tenant in common with N's heirs.
    d. in trust.

39. A parcel of vacant land has an assessed valuation of $274,550. If the assessment is 85 percent of market value, what is the market value?

    a. $315,732.50
    b. $320,000.00
    c. $323,000.00
    d. $1,830,333.33

40. A Wisconsin real estate salesperson has been asked by his or her cousin to critique an offer to purchase prepared by another broker. The salesperson should

    a. critique the offer to purchase but may not charge a fee.
    b. critique the offer to purchase but must charge a fee.
    c. not critique the offer to purchase because he or she is related to the party requesting his or her services.
    d. not critique the offer to purchase because he or she is neither acting as an agent nor as a party to the transaction.

41. Ensor lives in an apartment building. The land and structures are owned by a corporation, with one mortgage loan covering the entire property. Like the other residents, Ensor owns stock in the corporation and has a lease to his apartment. This type of ownership is called a

    a. condominium.
    b. planned unit development.
    c. time-share.
    d. cooperative.

42. J and S are next-door neighbors. S tells J that he can store his camper in her yard for a few weeks until she needs the space. S did not charge J rent for the use of her yard. S has given J a(n):

    a. easement appurtenant.
    b. easement by necessity.
    c. estate in land.
    d. license.

43. Wisconsin salespersons may *NOT* use which forms?

    a. Listing contracts
    b. Land contracts
    c. Offer to purchase
    d. Bill of sale

44. An unlicensed landlord renting out her own apartment

    a. must use forms drafted by an attorney.
    b. must use forms approved by the Wisconsin Department of Regulation and Licensing.
    c. may use nonapproved forms.
    d. must use forms approved by the Apartment Owners Association.

45. A statutory right that a family has in its residence is called
    a. entirety.
    b. survivorship.
    c. curtesy.
    d. homestead.

46. If the amount realized at a sheriff's sale as part of a mortgage foreclosure is more than the amount of the indebtedness and expenses, then the excess belongs to the
    a. mortgagor.
    b. mortgagee.
    c. sheriff's office.
    d. county.

47. A house in Wisconsin is sold for $102,090. The buyer has a mortgage for $81,672. How much must the seller pay as a real estate transfer fee when the deed is recorded?
    a. $245.10
    b. $306.00
    c. $306.27
    d. $306.30

48. Your neighbors use your driveway to reach their garage on their property. Your attorney explains that the ownership of the neighbor's real estate includes an easement appurtenant giving them the driveway right. Your property is the
    a. leasehold interest.
    b. dominant tenement.
    c. servient tenement.
    d. license property.

49. If the borrower paid $189.06 interest last month on a $27,500 loan, what is the interest rate?
    a. 7½ percent
    b. 7¾ percent
    c. 8¼ percent
    d. 8½ percent

50. The clause in a trust deed or mortgage that permits the lender to declare the entire unpaid balance immediately due and payable upon default is the
    a. judgment clause.
    b. escalator clause.
    c. forfeiture clause.
    d. acceleration clause.

51. Nonresident aliens of the United States may own no more than
    a. 40 acres of land in Wisconsin.
    b. 60 acres of land in Wisconsin.
    c. 240 acres of land in Wisconsin.
    d. 640 acres of land in Wisconsin.

52. Property purchased five years ago was assessed for tax purposes at 50 percent of market value. At that time, the tax rate was $4.90 per $100 of assessed valuation. Today, the taxes have increased by $637. How much has the market value of the property increased?
    a. $3,121.30
    b. $6,242.60
    c. $13,000.00
    d. $26,000.00

53. L conveys the ownership of his house to his mother and stipulates that upon her death he will recapture the ownership. The interest L has in the ownership is a
    a. remainder estate.
    b. curtesy estate.
    c. legal life estate.
    d. reversion estate.

54. The pledging of property as security for payment of a loan is
    a. disintermediation.
    b. equity.
    c. hypothecation.
    d. subordination.

55. When real estate is sold under an installment land contract and the buyer takes possession of the property, the legal title
    a. is subject to a purchase-money mortgage.
    b. must be transferred to a land trust.
    c. is kept by the seller until the purchase price is paid according to the contract.
    d. is transferred to the buyer.

56. A method of sealing off disintegrating asbestos is called
    a. capping.
    b. encapsulation.
    c. containment.
    d. contamination closure.

57. Forms prepared by government agencies for use in programming administered by the government may be used by
   a. salespersons only.
   b. brokers only.
   c. either brokers or salespersons.
   d. neither brokers nor salespersons.

58. Assume that the listing and selling brokers split the commission evenly. What is the sales price of a house if the listing broker received $2,593.50 and the total commission rate is 6½ percent?
   a. $88,400
   b. $79,800
   c. $76,200
   d. $39,900

59. Contractual forms for the sale, purchase, or rental of real estate or a business opportunity located in another state may be used by
   a. salespersons only.
   b. brokers only.
   c. either brokers or salespersons.
   d. neither brokers nor salespersons.

60. A licensee may *NOT* alter an approved exclusive-right-to-sell listing contract to create
   a. an exclusive agency listing.
   b. an open listing.
   c. a net listing.
   d. All of the above

61. Which of the following is *NOT* an example of police power?
   a. Zoning ordinances
   b. Building codes
   c. Restrictive covenants
   d. City planning requirements

62. A nonresident alien purchased 1,000 acres of land in Wisconsin. The alien will have to divest excess acres of land within
   a. one year.
   b. two years.
   c. three years.
   d. four years.

63. Which does *NOT* correctly describe the Bulk Transfer Law in Wisconsin?
   a. The transferee must require the transferor to furnish a list of the transferor's creditors.
   b. The parties must prepare a schedule of the property transferred which is sufficient to identify it.
   c. The list of creditors must be signed and sworn to or affirmed by the transferors or the transferor's agent.
   d. Responsibility for the completeness and accuracy of the list of creditors rests on the transferee.

64. Any bulk transfer subject to S.406 except by an auction sale is ineffective against any creditor of the transferors unless the transferee gives notice of the transfer at *LEAST*
   a. 3 days before taking possession of the goods or pays the major part of the purchase price.
   b. 5 days before taking possession of the goods or pays the major part of the purchase price.
   c. 10 days before taking possession of the goods or pays the major part of the purchase price.
   d. 30 days before taking possession of the goods or pays the major part of the purchase price.

65. According to Wisconsin law, a licensee may use a preprepared addendum that supplants or alters the printed provisions of an approved form if the addendum
   a. has been drafted by the principal.
   b. has been drafted by the broker who is identified on the addendum.
   c. has been drafted by the salesperson who is identified on the addendum.
   d. is drafted by an attorney who is identified on the addendum.

66. In Wisconsin, a reasonably competent and diligent inspection of real estate improved with a structure requires
   a. the operation of mechanical equipment.
   b. the opening of panels for access to mechanical systems.
   c. the moving of furniture.
   d. None of the above

67. A vacant lot that measures 100 feet wide by 125 feet deep is listed at a price of $250 per front foot. The broker will collect an 8 percent commission on the sale. If the lot sells for the full asking price, how much is the broker's fee?
   a. $2,500
   b. $2,000
   c. $1,500
   d. $1,250

68. An appraiser is responsible for
   a. finding value.
   b. computing value.
   c. determining value.
   d. estimating value.

69. The sales comparison approach to value would be most important when estimating the value of a(n)
   a. existing residence.
   b. apartment building.
   c. retail location.
   d. new residence.

70. In Wisconsin, a net listing is
   a. approved for use by real estate licensees.
   b. approved only in residential transactions.
   c. approved only in commercial transactions.
   d. prohibited.

71. The primary intent of zoning ordinances is to:
   a. ensure the health, safety, and welfare of the community.
   b. demonstrate the police power of the state.
   c. limit the amount and types of businesses in a given area.
   d. protect residential neighborhoods from commercial encroachment.

72. The condemnation of private property for public use is made possible by the right of
   a. police power.
   b. escheat.
   c. eminent domain.
   d. confiscation.

73. For the past 30 years, the Laceys have operated a neighborhood grocery store. Last week the city council passed a zoning ordinance that prohibits packaged food sales in the area where the Lacey's grocery store is located. The store is now an example of a(n)
   a. illegal enterprise.
   b. nonconforming use.
   c. violation of the zoning laws.
   d. variance of the zoning laws.

74. You are a Wisconsin broker who has just entered into a listing contract with a homeowner. You should leave a copy of the listing contract with the seller
   a. because it will make the seller more comfortable.
   b. because it is a good business procedure.
   c. if the seller asks for a copy.
   d. because it is required by administrative rule.

75. According to Chapter ATCP134, a security deposit means the total of all payments and deposits given by a tenant to the landlord as security for the performance of the tenants' obligations and includes all rent payments in excess of
   a. 15 days prepaid rent.
   b. 1 month.
   c. 3 months.
   d. 6 months.

76. A building is valued at $215,000 and contains four apartments that rent for $470 each per month. The owner estimates that the net operating income is 65 percent of the gross rental receipts. What is the capitalization rate?
   a. 3.7 percent
   b. 6.8 percent
   c. 10.5 percent
   d. 14.2 percent

77. Nonresident brokers in Wisconsin must
   a. file an irrevocable consent form with the Wisconsin Department of Regulation and Licensing.
   b. not employ brokers in Wisconsin.
   c. maintain an active place of business in the state in which they are licensed.
   d. not employ salespeople in Wisconsin.

78. A prospective buyer who is African American inquires about the availability of a home in a predominately white residential neighborhood. What should the broker say to the prospect?
   a. "You wouldn't want to live in this area because the neighbors are trying to protect the integrity of the area."
   b. "I'd be happy to show you homes in other areas where African American people are welcome."
   c. "The residents here have expressed a desire to keep the area homogeneous with no minorities."
   d. "I'll be pleased to show you any houses you're interested in."

79. Exact and complete copies of the Residential Offer to Purchase must be promptly
   a. filed with the Wisconsin Department of Regulation and Licensing.
   b. filed with the Wisconsin Real Estate Board.
   c. distributed to the proper parties of the contract.
   d. filed with the Wisconsin REALTORS® Association.

80. Broker P listed the K's property for sale under an exclusive-right-to-sell agreement. Today, one of P's salespeople, T, obtained an offer to purchase the property along with a certified check for 5 percent of the purchase price as earnest money. What should T do with the earnest money check?
   a. Give it to the Ks
   b. Hold it until the closing
   c. Deposit the money in his trust account
   d. Give the money to P for deposit in the trust account

81. Which of the following would *NOT* be an example of client funds in Wisconsin?
   a. A down payment related to the purchase of a home
   b. An earnest money deposit related to the sale of a duplex
   c. An earnest money deposit related to the exchange of an income property
   d. Promissory notes

82. The broker enters into a listing agreement with a seller in which the seller will receive $12,000 from the sale of a lot and the broker will receive any sale proceeds over this amount. This type of listing is a(n)
   a. gross listing.
   b. legal and ethical way to ensure that the broker is compensated.
   c. exclusive agency.
   d. net listing.

83. The practice of channeling families with children away from other buildings into an apartment building where other families with children reside is
   a. most practical.
   b. blockbusting.
   c. redlining.
   d. steering.

84. If a seller needs to net $50,000 after the sale, how much must the real estate sell for if the selling costs include a 7 percent commission and $1,200 in other expenses?
   a. $54,700.00
   b. $54,963.44
   c. $55,053.76
   d. $55,633.25

85. In Wisconsin, the purchaser of a rental property can accept the responsibility for bringing the building into compliance by signing a stipulation requiring that a certificate of compliance be obtained within
   a. 90 days after transfer.
   b. 6 months after transfer.
   c. 1 year after transfer.
   d. 2 years after transfer.

86. Under an exclusive-agency listing, the listing broker would *NOT* be entitled to a commission if the
   a. broker sells the property.
   b. property is sold through another broker.
   c. property is sold through the multiple-listing service.
   d. seller sells the property to a neighbor across the street who has his or her property listed with another broker.

87. The gross rent multiplier is used as a guideline for estimating value based on the
   a. ratio of the gross rents to the net rents after expenses.
   b. proportion of rents due to the actual rents collected.
   c. capitalization of the annual gross rental income.
   d. relationship of the sales prices to the rental income.

88. When a security deposit is required in Wisconsin, the landlord is required to provide tenants with a notice concerning the description of any physical damages charged against the previous tenants' security deposit. In addition, the tenant must be given no less than
   a. 48 hours in which to inspect and document other pre-existing conditions.
   b. 5 days in which to inspect and document other pre-existing conditions.
   c. 7 days in which to inspect and document other pre-existing conditions.
   d. 21 days in which to inspect and document other pre-existing conditions.

89. A and B are joint tenants. B sells his interest to C. What is the relationship of A and C?
   a. They are joint tenants.
   b. They are tenants in common.
   c. There can be no relationship because B cannot sell to C.
   d. A owns a 2/3 interest and C owns a 1/3 interest.

90. The listing broker or broker's designees must ensure that a complete copy of the Buyer's Closing Statement is delivered to the buyer
   a. within 24 hours after the closing.
   b. within 5 days after the closing.
   c. within 30 days after the closing.
   d. at the time of closing.

91. If, upon the receipt of a Residential Offer to Purchase his or her property under certain conditions, the seller makes a counter-offer, the prospective buyer is
   a. bound by his or her original offer.
   b. bound to accept the counteroffer.
   c. bound by whichever offer is lower.
   d. relieved of his or her original offer.

92. Which handles the interest earned on a client funds account?
   a. Wisconsin Department of Revenue
   b. Wisconsin Department of Regulation and Licensing
   c. Wisconsin Department of Administration
   d. Wisconsin Real Estate Board

93. An option to buy
   a. requires the optionee to complete the purchase.
   b. gives the optionee an easement on the property.
   c. keeps the offer open for a specified time.
   d. makes the seller liable for a commission.

94. When a prospective buyer makes a written purchase offer that the seller accepts, then the
   a. buyer may take possession of the real estate.
   b. seller grants the buyer ownership rights.
   c. buyer receives legal title to the property.
   d. buyer receives equitable title to the property.

95. Which of the following does an appraiser use in the income approach?
   a. Equalization
   b. Depreciation
   c. Appreciation
   d. Capitalization

96. A house for sale was advertised: "Fine executive home in an exclusive neighborhood, suitable for an older couple, near St. Mary's Church." All of the following are *TRUE, EXCEPT*
   a. this is descriptive of the property for sale and is a good ad.
   b. an exclusive neighborhood could be interpreted to mean that minorities are not welcome.
   c. it appears that families with children are not welcome.
   d. the neighborhood could appear to be undesirable for people who do not follow the same religion as St. Mary's Church.

97. A bilateral contract is one in which
   a. only one of the parties is obligated to act.
   b. the promise of one party is given in exchange for the promise of the other party.
   c. something is to be done by only one party.
   d. a restriction is placed in the contract by one party to limit the performance by the other.

98. A broker may authorize other persons to sign real estate trust account checks. However, the person who signs must be at *LEAST*
   a. 18 years of age.
   b. 21 years of age.
   c. 25 years of age.
   d. 30 years of age.

99. The restrictive covenant in a condominium complex prohibits pets. A prospective buyer with a physical disability relies on an animal to assist him. Which statement is *TRUE*?
   a. The condominium has the right to establish this private restriction if it chooses.
   b. This restriction is unenforceable only if the animal is used to assist people with visual impairments.
   c. This restriction is unenforceable when any person with a disability uses the animal for assistance.
   d. The condominium can waive the enforcement of the covenant only if there are suitable accommodations in the complex for the animal.

100. A Wisconsin broker is required to remove commissions from the trust account within
   a. 12 hours after the transaction is consummated or terminated.
   b. 24 hours after the transaction is consummated or terminated.
   c. 48 hours after the transaction is consummated or terminated.
   d. 72 hours after the transaction is consummated or terminated.

101. The law that requires real estate contracts to be in writing to be enforceable is the
   a. law of descent and distribution.
   b. statute of frauds.
   c. parol evidence rule.
   d. statute of limitations.

102. When a salesperson represents that minorities are moving into the area to get homeowners to sell their properties, this activity is
   a. panic selling.
   b. steering.
   c. discriminatory advertising.
   d. legal as long as it is true.

103. The Americans with Disabilities Act requires that
   a. all real estate is free of barriers to people with disabilities.
   b. all employers adopt nondiscriminatory employment practices.
   c. reasonable accommodations be provided to people with disabilities.
   d. the existing premises must be remodeled regardless of the cost involved.

104. Which is illegal?
   a. Refusing to lend money to a minority person who has poor credit
   b. Refusing to allow families with children to live in a housing development intended exclusively for people over 62
   c. Refusing to hire an otherwise qualified person because he cares for his wife who has a disability
   d. Refusing to rent to a person who has been convicted of distributing cocaine

105. Any subdivider or agent who offers subdivided land in Wisconsin for sale knowing that the final plat has not been recorded is subject to a fine of
   a. $300 or imprisonment for up to 30 days or both.
   b. $500 or imprisonment for up to 6 months or both.
   c. $1,000 or imprisonment for up to 1 year or both.
   d. $5,000 or imprisonment for up to 2 years or both.

106. Two salespeople working for the same broker obtained offers on a property listed with their firm. The first offer was obtained early in the day. The second offer for a higher purchase price was obtained later in the afternoon. The broker presented the first offer to the seller that evening. The broker did not inform the seller about the second offer so that the seller could make a decision about the first offer. Which statement is *TRUE?*

a. The broker's actions are permissible provided the commission is split between the two salespeople.
b. After the first offer was received, the broker should have told the salespeople that no additional offers would be accepted until the seller decided on the offer.
c. The broker has no authority to withhold any offers from the seller.
d. The broker was smart to protect the seller from getting into a negotiating battle over two offers.

107. Deed restrictions are a means by which

a. local zoning laws are enforced.
b. the planning commission controls developers.
c. municipalities enforce building restrictions.
d. grantors control the future use of the ownership.

108. Which of the following would be considered to be legal?

a. Charging a family with children a higher security deposit than is charged to adults
b. Requiring a person with a disability to establish an escrow account for the costs to restore a property after it has been modified
c. Picturing only white people in a brochure as the "happy residents" in a housing development
d. Refusing to sell a house to a person who has a history of mental illness

109. Which of the following statements correctly describes the responsibility of licensees with regard to confidentiality of offers?

a. A licensee may not disclose the existence of other offers on a property.
b. A licensee may disclose the terms of the offer on a property.
c. A licensee may not disclose the existence of a right of first refusal.
d. A licensee may disclose the existence of the other offers on a property.

110. Under RL24.07 a licensee must disclose

a. all material adverse facts that the broker knows and that the party does not know or cannot discover through reasonably diligent observation.
b. the amount of the commission.
c. the existence of other offers.
d. how long a property has been on the market.

111. A broker has an exclusive-right-to-sell listing on a building. The owner is out of town when the broker gets an offer from a buyer to purchase the building providing the seller agrees to take a purchase-money mortgage. The buyer must have a commitment from the seller before the seller is scheduled to return to the city. Under these circumstances the

a. broker may enter into a binding agreement on behalf of the seller.
b. broker may collect commission even if the transaction falls through because of the seller's absence from the city.
c. buyer is obligated to keep the offer open until the seller returns.
d. broker must obtain the signature of the seller to effect a contract.

112. On Monday, the seller offers to sell his vacant lot to the buyer for $72,000. On Tuesday, the buyer counter-offers to buy for $70,000. On Friday, the buyer withdraws the counter-offer and accepts the original offer of $72,000. Under these conditions there is

a. a valid agreement because the buyer accepted the seller's offer exactly as it was made.
b. not a valid agreement because the buyer's counter-offer was a rejection of the seller's offer and, once it was rejected, it cannot be accepted later.
c. a valid agreement because the buyer accepted before the seller advised the buyer that the offer was withdrawn.
d. not a valid agreement because the seller's offer was not accepted within 72 hours.

113. Which is a variance?

a. An exception to a zoning ordinance
b. A court order prohibiting certain activities
c. A reversion of ownership
d. A nullification of an easement

114. Which statement correctly describes Wisconsin Fair Housing Law?

a. One may discriminate in the sale or rental of an owner-occupied single-family residence.
b. One may discriminate in the rental of rooms or apartments in an owner-occupied one-family to four-family building.
c. One may discriminate in the sale of an owner-occupied single-family residence if a broker is not used.
d. One may not discriminate in the sale or rental of an owner-occupied single-family residence.

115. The broker receives an earnest-money deposit with a written offer to purchase that includes a ten-day acceptance clause. On the fifth day, before the offer is accepted, the buyer notifies the broker that she is withdrawing the offer and demands the return of the earnest-money deposit. In this situation the

a. buyer cannot withdraw the offer because it must be held open for the full ten days.
b. buyer has the right to revoke the offer at any time until it is accepted and recover the earnest money.
c. seller and the broker have the right to each retain one-half of the deposit.
d. broker declares the deposit forfeited and retains it for his services.

116. The Real Estate Settlement Procedures Act (RESPA) applies to the activities of

a. licensed real estate brokers when selling commercial and office buildings.
b. licensed securities salespeople when selling limited partnership interests.
c. lenders financing the purchase of a borrower's residence.
d. Fannie Mae and Freddie Mac when purchasing residential mortgages.

117. A small office building sold for $949,000 and the broker received a commission of $54,990. What was the broker's commission rate?

a. 5.8 percent
b. 6.2 percent
c. 7 percent
d. 11.3 percent

118. The purpose of a mortgage is to

a. provide security for the loan.
b. convey title of the property to the lender.
c. restrict the borrower's use of the property.
d. create a lien on the property.

119. Fannie Mae

a. makes FHA loans.
b. buys FHA loans.
c. services FHA loans.
d. insures FHA loans.

120. The Real Estate Settlement Procedures Act (RESPA) provides that
   a. all real estate purchasers must receive their closing statements.
   b. real estate advertisements must include the annual percentage rate, including all charges.
   c. the borrower must be given an estimate of the closing costs before the time of the closing.
   d. real estate syndicates must comply with the disclosure of "blue sky" laws.

121. Which of the following forms would require the sellers to sign twice in order for the contract to become binding?
   a. Amendment to Offer to Purchase
   b. Multiple Counter-Proposal
   c. Notice Relating to Offer to Purchase
   d. Counter-Offer

122. Regulation Z applies to
   a. business loans.
   b. real estate sales agreements.
   c. commercial loans under $10,000.
   d. personal credit transactions under $25,000.

123. As an entity operating in the secondary mortgage market, the Federal Home Loan Mortgage Corporation was established to assist the
   a. Federal Housing Administration.
   b. Federal National Mortgage Association.
   c. federal savings and loans.
   d. federal banks.

124. Fannie Mae, Ginnie Mae, and Freddie Mac have in common the purpose of
   a. originating residential mortgage loans.
   b. purchasing existing mortgage loans.
   c. insuring residential mortgage loans.
   d. guaranteeing existing mortgage loans.

125. The *BEST* assurance of good title that a real estate purchaser can obtain is a
   a. valid warranty deed signed by the seller.
   b. valid quitclaim deed signed by seller.
   c. policy of title insurance.
   d. certificate of title.

126. A defect or a cloud on the title may be cured by
   a. obtaining quitclaim deeds from all interested parties.
   b. bringing an action to register title.
   c. paying cash for the property at closing.
   d. obtaining title insurance.

The following story problem is used to answer Question 127 through Question 140, which follow this narrative.

Data Describing the Real Estate Transaction

Joe Dannen, a salesperson for Quality Realty, which is a member of the local REALTORS® multiple-listing service, secured a four-month exclusive-right-to-sell listing on November 14, 2009, from Jack and Mary Nelson. The listing was for their home at 2901 Newman Street, Madison, WI 53705. The legal description is Lot 8, Block 3, of the Olympia Subdivision SW 1/4 of Section 6, T9N, R7E, Dane County, Wisconsin. The Nelsons agreed to include the refrigerator, washer, and dryer in the purchase price of $156,000. The Nelsons will give occupancy at closing. Dannen has agreed to hold at least two open houses, to advertise in the local newspaper, and to list the property with a multiple-listing service. The Nelsons have consented to designated agency as described in the listing contract, and they have agreed to pay a commission of 6 percent.

The Nelsons have paid off the mortgage on their house. The house measured 40 feet by 60 feet on the exterior. It was a two-story with a detached garage. The lot was 100 feet by 140 feet. The assessed value of the property was $120,000 for the improvements, and $30,000 for the land, with a tax rate of $30 per thousand.

The Nelsons have been negotiating with a friend, Bill Tankel, who may be interested in buying the property. The Nelsons would like Tankel excluded from the contract until November 21, so if Bill decided to buy the Nelsons' home during that time, the Nelsons would not owe Dannen for a commission. The sellers signed a Real Estate Condition Report on November 14.

The sellers would like to occupy the property for three days after closing and agreed to pay $100 per day. The sellers owed $500 in delinquent taxes, which they were to pay at closing.

The sellers would not allow any buyers to photograph or videotape their property.

On November 22, 2009, Dannen obtained an offer from Jay and Linda Norris to purchase the property for $153,000. The Norrises lived at 4226 Adderly Avenue, Milwaukee, Wisconsin. The offer called for $1,000 in earnest money in the form of a check with additional earnest money of $2,000 to be paid on acceptance of the offer. The offer is contingent upon the buyers obtaining a first mortgage within 30 days for not less than $122,400 at an interest rate of not more than 7¾ percent for a term of not less than 30 years.

The Norrises' offer must be accepted and returned to them by November 24. They wanted to close on December 21, 2009. The buyers wanted title insurance as evidence of title. The buyers did not want the sellers to remain in the house after closing.

The sellers countered the offer on November 23 for $154,000 with acceptance by November 24. The counter-offer was signed by the sellers on November 23. The counter-offer was presented to the buyers on November 24.

The title insurance policy costs $425 and the recording fees for the seller were $12. Subsequent to the counter-offer's acceptance by the buyers, the buyers asked the sellers to hold the closing on December 23, 2009. Both the buyers and the sellers signed the amendment to the contract on December 9. Dannen made arrangements for the seller's water bill to be read on the day of closing and billed accordingly on the closing statement. The water bill was $90.

127. According to the listing contract, which statement is *TRUE*?

a. The broker will receive a 6 percent commission on the sale of the house.
b. The buyer is to pay delinquent taxes of $500.
c. The roof leaks.
d. Buyers may videotape the property.

128. Which statement is *TRUE* regarding the sellers?

a. They will not consent to designated agency.
b. They will include the dryer.
c. They are asking $154,000.
d. They will give occupancy at closing.

129. The listing contract does *NOT*

a. provide the broker to use MLS.
b. require the broker to hold at least two open houses.
c. list any prospective buyer as excluded from the agency agreement.
d. expire at midnight of March 16, 2010.

130. According to the listing contract, if the sellers do not want buyers to videotape their property, this type of information will be placed on line(s)

a. 10–14.
b. 30–32.
c. 36–38.
d. 242–250.

131. According to the listing contract, the seller owes delinquent taxes of
    a. $100.
    b. $500.
    c. $1,200.
    d. $3,000.

132. According to the offer to purchase, which statement is *TRUE*?
    a. The property is being purchased by Jack and Mary Nelson.
    b. Legally, it is described as Lot 3, Block 3, of the Olympia subdivision, SW 1/4 of Section 6, T9N, R7E, Dane County, Wisconsin.
    c. It is being sold by Jay and Linda Norris.
    d. It is being purchased for a sales price of $154,000.

133. According to the offer to purchase, the amount of earnest money is
    a. $1,000.
    b. $2,000.
    c. $3,000.
    d. $4,000.

134. The offer to purchase was to be accepted by
    a. November 22, 2009.
    b. November 23, 2009.
    c. November 24, 2009.
    d. December 9, 2009.

135. According to the accepted offer to purchase, if the premises are damaged in the amount of $6,200 before the closing
    a. sellers may back out of the transaction.
    b. buyers may back out of the transaction.
    c. buyers must go through with the transaction and the seller's insurance will pay for the damage.
    d. buyers and sellers do none of the above.

136. According to the accepted offer to purchase, the sellers
    a. must provide an abstract.
    b. must provide title insurance.
    c. have their choice of either abstract or title insurance.
    d. must do none of the above.

137. The amount due from the buyers at closing is
    a. $4,389.04.
    b. $7,389.04.
    c. $146,610.96.
    d. $154,000.00.

138. At the closing, the sellers will receive
    a. $10,729.00.
    b. $138,881.96.
    c. $146,610.96.
    d. $147,910.06.

139. The amount of the tax proration is
    a. $4,376.71.
    b. $4,389.04.
    c. $4,401.37.
    d. $4,413.70.

140. The amount of the transfer fee is
    a. $94.80.
    b. $413.10
    c. $444.00.
    d. $462.00.

The following pages contain forms related to the story problem for which you will be responsible on the salesperson and broker licensing exam. You may fill out each form and then compare it to the completed form to determine your understanding of each contract. You will not have to fill out any of the forms on the licensing exam. However, you will be asked questions regarding your understanding of the forms.

FIGURE A

Blank WB-1 Listing Contract—Exclusive Right to Sell

Approved by Wisconsin Department of Regulation and Licensing
1-1-08 (Optional Use Date) 7-1-08 (Mandatory Use Date)

Wisconsin Legal Blank Co., Inc.
Milwaukee, Wisconsin

WB-1 RESIDENTIAL LISTING CONTRACT - EXCLUSIVE RIGHT TO SELL

page 1 of 5

SELLER GIVES BROKER THE EXCLUSIVE RIGHT TO SELL THE PROPERTY ON THE FOLLOWING TERMS:

■ **PROPERTY DESCRIPTION:** Street address is: ______________ ______________ in the ______________ of ______________, County of ______________, Wisconsin. Insert additional description, if any, at lines 242-250 or attach as an addendum per lines 251-254.

■ **LIST PRICE:** ______________ Dollars ($ ______________).

■ **INCLUDED IN LIST PRICE:** Seller is including in the list price the Property, all Fixtures not excluded on lines 11-14, and the following items: ______________.

■ **NOT INCLUDED IN LIST PRICE:** CAUTION: Identify Fixtures to be excluded by Seller or which are rented and will continue to be owned by the lessor. (See lines 199-210): ______________.

■ **MARKETING:** Seller authorizes and Broker agrees to use reasonable efforts to procure a buyer for the Property. Seller agrees that Broker may market Seller's personal property identified on lines 7-9 during the term of this Listing. Broker's marketing may include: ______________.

Broker may advertise the following special financing and incentives offered by Seller: ______________. Seller has a duty to cooperate with Broker's marketing efforts. See lines 74-80 regarding Broker's role as marketing agent and Seller's duty to notify Broker of any potential buyer known to Seller. Seller agrees that Broker may market other properties during the term of this Listing.

■ **OCCUPANCY:** Unless otherwise provided, Seller agrees to give buyer occupancy of the Property at time of closing and to have the Property in broom swept condition and free of all debris and personal property except for personal property belonging to current tenants, sold to buyer or left with buyer's consent.

■ **COOPERATION, ACCESS TO PROPERTY OR OFFER PRESENTATION:** The parties agree that Broker will work and cooperate with other brokers in marketing the Property, including brokers from other firms acting as subagents (agents from other companies engaged by Broker - See lines 138-141) and brokers representing buyers. Cooperation includes providing access to the Property for showing purposes and presenting offers and other proposals from these brokers to Seller. Note any brokers with whom Broker shall not cooperate, any brokers or buyers who shall not be allowed to attend showings, and the specific terms of offers which should not be submitted to Seller: ______________.

CAUTION: Limiting Broker's cooperation with other brokers may reduce the marketability of the Property.

■ **EXCLUSIONS:** All persons who may acquire an interest in the Property as a Protected Buyer under a prior listing contract are excluded from this Listing to the extent of the prior broker's legal rights, unless otherwise agreed to in writing. Within seven days of the date of this Listing, Seller agrees to deliver to Broker a written list of all such prospective buyers. The following other buyers are excluded from this Listing until ______________ [INSERT DATE]: ______________. These other buyers are no longer excluded from this Listing after the specified date unless, on or before the specified date, Seller has either accepted an offer from the buyer or sold the Property to the buyer.

■ **COMMISSION:** Broker's commission shall be ______________.

Seller shall pay Broker's commission, which shall be earned, if, during the term of this Listing:

1) Seller sells or accepts an offer which creates an enforceable contract for the sale of all or any part of the Property;
2) Seller grants an option to purchase all or any part of the Property which is subsequently exercised;
3) Seller exchanges or enters into a binding exchange agreement on all or any part of the Property;
4) A transaction occurs which causes an effective change in ownership or control of all or any part of the Property; or
5) A buyer is procured for the Property by Broker, by Seller, or by any other person, at no less than the price and on substantially the same terms set forth in this Listing and in the standard provisions of the current WB-11 RESIDENTIAL OFFER TO PURCHASE, even if Seller does not accept this buyer's offer. (See lines 215-218 regarding procurement.)

A percentage commission, if applicable, shall be calculated based on the purchase price if commission is earned under 1) or 2) above, or calculated based on the list price under 3), 4) or 5). A percentage commission shall be calculated on the fair market value of the Property exchanged under 3) if the exchange involves less than the entire Property or on the fair market value of the Property to which an effective change in ownership or control takes place, under 4) if the transaction involves less than the entire Property.

Once earned, Broker's commission is due and payable in full at the earlier of closing or the date set for closing, unless otherwise agreed in writing. Broker's commission shall be earned if, during the term of the Listing, one owner of the Property sells, conveys, exchanges or options an interest in all or any part of the Property to another owner, except by divorce judgment.

NOTE: A sale, option, exchange or procurement of a buyer for a portion of the Property does not terminate the Listing as to any remaining Property.

■ **COMPENSATION TO OTHERS:** Broker offers the following commission to cooperating brokers: ______________ ______________. (Exceptions if any): ______________.

FIGURE A (CONTINUED)

Blank WB-1 Listing Contract—Exclusive Right to Sell

Wisconsin Legal Blank Co., Inc.
Milwaukee, Wisconsin

■ **EXTENSION OF LISTING:** The Listing term is extended for a period of one year as to any Protected Buyer. Upon receipt of a written request from Seller or a broker who has listed the Property, Broker agrees to promptly deliver to Seller a written list of those buyers known by Broker to whom the extension period applies. Should this Listing be terminated by Seller prior to the expiration of the term stated in this Listing, this Listing shall be extended for Protected Buyers, on the same terms, for one year after the Listing is terminated.

■ **TERMINATION OF LISTING:** Neither Seller nor Broker has the legal right to unilaterally terminate this Listing absent a material breach of contract by the other party. Seller understands that the parties to the Listing are Seller and the Broker (firm). Agents (salespersons) for Broker (firm) do not have the authority to enter into a mutual agreement to terminate the Listing, amend the commission amount or shorten the term of this Listing, without the written consent of the agent(s)' supervising broker. Seller and Broker agree that any termination of this Listing by either party before the date stated on line 259 shall be indicated to the other party in writing and shall not be effective until delivered to the other Party in accordance with lines 193-198. CAUTION: Early termination of this Listing may be a breach of contract, causing the terminating party to potentially be liable for damages.

■ **SELLER COOPERATION WITH MARKETING EFFORTS:** Seller agrees to cooperate with Broker in Broker's marketing efforts and to provide Broker with all records, documents and other material in Seller's possession or control which are required in connection with the sale. Seller authorizes Broker to do those acts reasonably necessary to effect a sale and Seller agrees to cooperate fully with these efforts which may include use of a multiple listing service, Internet advertising or a lockbox system on Property. Seller shall promptly notify Broker in writing of any potential buyers with whom Seller negotiates during the term of this Listing and shall promptly refer all persons making inquiries concerning the Property to Broker.

■ **LEASED PROPERTY:** If Property is currently leased and lease(s) will extend beyond closing, Seller shall assign Seller's rights under the lease(s) and transfer all security deposits and prepaid rents (subject to agreed upon prorations) thereunder to buyer at closing. Seller acknowledges that Seller remains liable under the lease(s) unless released by tenants. CAUTION: Seller should consider obtaining an indemnification agreement from buyer for liabilities under the lease(s) unless released by tenants.

■ **BROKER DISCLOSURE TO CLIENTS:**

UNDER WISCONSIN LAW, A BROKER OWES CERTAIN DUTIES TO ALL PARTIES TO A TRANSACTION:

(a) The duty to provide brokerage services to you fairly and honestly.
(b) The duty to exercise reasonable skill and care in providing brokerage services to you.
(c) The duty to provide you with accurate information about market conditions within a reasonable time if you request it, unless disclosure of the information is prohibited by law.
(d) The duty to disclose to you in writing certain material adverse facts about a property, unless disclosure of the information is prohibited by law. (See Lines 211-214)
(e) The duty to protect your confidentiality. Unless the law requires it, the broker will not disclose your confidential information or the confidential information of other parties. (See Lines 147-163)
(f) The duty to safeguard trust funds and other property the broker holds.
(g) The duty, when negotiating, to present contract proposals in an objective and unbiased manner and disclose the advantages and disadvantages of the proposals.

■ **BECAUSE YOU HAVE ENTERED INTO AN AGENCY AGREEMENT WITH A BROKER, YOU ARE THE BROKER'S CLIENT. A BROKER OWES ADDITIONAL DUTIES TO A CLIENT:**

(a) The broker will provide, at your request, information and advice on real estate matters that affect your transaction, unless you release the broker from this duty.
(b) The broker must provide you with all material facts affecting the transaction, not just adverse facts.
(c) The broker will fulfill the broker's obligations under the agency agreement and fulfill your lawful requests that are within the scope of the agency agreement.
(d) The broker will negotiate for you, unless you release the broker from this duty.
(e) The broker will not place the broker's interests ahead of your interests. The broker will not, unless required by law, give information or advice to other parties who are not the broker's clients, if giving the information or advice is contrary to your interests.
(f) If you become involved in a transaction in which another party is also the broker's client (a "multiple representation relationship"), different duties may apply.

■ **MULTIPLE REPRESENTATION RELATIONSHIPS AND DESIGNATED AGENCY:**

■ A multiple representation relationship exists if a broker has an agency agreement with more than one client who is a party in the same transaction. In a multiple representation relationship, if all of the broker's clients in the transaction consent, the broker may provide services to the clients through designated agency.

■ Designated agency means that different salespersons employed by the broker will negotiate on behalf of you and the other client or clients in the transaction, and the broker's duties will remain the same. Each salesperson will provide

FIGURE A (CONTINUED)

Blank WB-1 Listing Contract—Exclusive Right to Sell

Wisconsin Legal Blank Co., Inc.
Milwaukee, Wisconsin
page 3 of 5, WB-1

information, opinions, and advice to the client for whom the salesperson is negotiating, to assist the client in the negotiations. Each client will be able to receive information, opinions, and advice that will assist the client, even if the information, opinions, or advice gives the client advantages in the negotiations over the broker's other clients. A salesperson will not reveal any of your confidential information to another party unless required to do so by law.

■ If a designated agency relationship is not in effect you may authorize or reject a multiple representation relationship. If you authorize a multiple representation relationship the broker may provide brokerage services to more than one client in a transaction but neither the broker nor any of the broker's salespersons may assist any client with information, opinions, and advice which may favor the interests of one client over any other client. If you do not consent to a multiple representation relationship the broker will not be allowed to provide brokerage services to more than one client in the transaction.

INITIAL ONLY ONE OF THE THREE LINES BELOW:

_______I consent to designated agency.

_______I consent to multiple representation relationships, but I do not consent to designated agency.

_______I reject multiple representation relationships.

NOTE: YOU MAY WITHDRAW YOUR CONSENT TO DESIGNATED AGENCY OR TO MULTIPLE REPRESENTATION RELATIONSHIPS BY WRITTEN NOTICE TO THE BROKER AT ANY TIME. YOUR BROKER IS REQUIRED TO DISCLOSE TO YOU IN YOUR AGENCY AGREEMENT THE COMMISSION OR FEES THAT YOU MAY OWE TO YOUR BROKER. IF YOU HAVE ANY QUESTIONS ABOUT THE COMMISSION OR FEES THAT YOU MAY OWE BASED UPON THE TYPE OF AGENCY RELATIONSHIP YOU SELECT WITH YOUR BROKER YOU SHOULD ASK YOUR BROKER BEFORE SIGNING THE AGENCY AGREEMENT.

■ **SUBAGENCY:** The broker may, with your authorization in the agency agreement, engage other brokers who assist your broker by providing brokerage services for your benefit. A subagent will not put the subagent's own interests ahead of your interests. A subagent will not, unless required by law, provide advice or opinions to other parties if doing so is contrary to your interests.

PLEASE REVIEW THIS INFORMATION CAREFULLY. A broker or salesperson can answer your questions about brokerage services, but if you need legal advice, tax advice, or a professional home inspection, contact an attorney, tax advisor, or home inspector. This disclosure is required by section 452.135 of the Wisconsin statutes and is for information only. It is a plain language summary of a broker's duties to you under section 452.133 (2) of the Wisconsin statutes.

■ **CONFIDENTIALITY NOTICE TO CLIENTS:** Broker will keep confidential any information given to Broker in confidence, or any information obtained by Broker that he or she knows a reasonable person would want to be kept confidential, unless the information must be disclosed by law or you authorize Broker to disclose particular information. Broker shall continue to keep the information confidential after Broker is no longer providing brokerage services to you.

The following information is required to be disclosed by law:

1) Material adverse facts, as defined in section 452.01 (5g) of the Wisconsin statutes (lines 211-214).
2) Any facts known by the Broker that contradict any information included in a written inspection report on the property or real estate that is the subject of the transaction.

To ensure that the Broker is aware of what specific information you consider confidential, you may list that information below (see lines 158-160). At a later time, you may also provide the Broker with other information you consider to be confidential.

CONFIDENTIAL INFORMATION: ____

____

____.

NON-CONFIDENTIAL INFORMATION (The following may be disclosed by Broker):____

____

____.

■ **REAL ESTATE CONDITION REPORT:** Seller agrees to complete the real estate condition report provided by Broker to the best of Seller's knowledge. Seller agrees to amend the report should Seller learn of any defect(s) after completion of the report but before acceptance of a buyer's offer to purchase. Seller authorizes Broker to distribute the report to all interested parties and agents inquiring about the Property. Seller acknowledges that Broker has a duty to disclose all material adverse facts as required by law.

■ **SELLER REPRESENTATIONS REGARDING DEFECTS:** Seller represents to Broker that as of the date of this Listing, Seller has no notice or knowledge of any defects affecting the Property other than those noted on the real estate condition report.

WARNING: IF SELLER REPRESENTATIONS ARE INCORRECT OR INCOMPLETE, SELLER MAY BE LIABLE FOR DAMAGES AND COSTS.

■ **OPEN HOUSE AND SHOWING RESPONSIBILITIES:** Seller is aware that there is a potential risk of injury, damage and/or theft involving persons attending an "individual showing" or an "open house." Seller accepts responsibility for preparing the Property to minimize the likelihood of injury, damage and/or loss of personal property. Seller agrees to hold Broker harmless for any losses or liability resulting from personal injury, property damage, or theft occurring during "individual showings" or "open houses" other than those caused by Broker's negligence or intentional wrongdoing. Seller acknowledges that individual showings and open houses may be conducted by licensees other than Broker, that appraisers and inspectors may conduct appraisals and inspections without being accompanied by Broker or other licensees, and that buyers or licensees may be present at all inspections and testing and may photograph or videotape Property unless otherwise provided for in additional provisions at lines 242-250 or in an addendum per lines 251-254.

FIGURE A (CONTINUED)

Blank WB-1 Listing Contract—Exclusive Right to Sell

Wisconsin Legal Blank Co., Inc.
Milwaukee, Wisconsin

■ **DEFINITIONS:**

ADVERSE FACT: An "adverse fact" means any of the following:
(a) A condition or occurrence that is generally recognized by a competent licensee as doing any of the following:
1) Significantly and adversely affecting the value of the Property;
2) significantly reducing the structural integrity of improvements to real estate; or
3) presenting a significant health risk to occupants of the Property.
(b) Information that indicates that a party to a transaction is not able to or does not intend to meet his or her obligations under a contract or agreement made concerning the transaction.

DEADLINES - DAYS: Deadlines expressed as a number of "days" from an event are calculated by excluding the day the event occurred and by counting subsequent calendar days.

DELIVERY: Delivery of documents or written notices related to this Listing may only be accomplished by:
1) giving the document or written notice personally to the party;
2) depositing the document or written notice postage or fees prepaid or charged to an account in the U.S. Mail or a commercial delivery system, addressed to the party, at the party's address (See lines 265, 271 and 277.);
3) electronically transmitting the document or written notice to the party's fax number (See lines 267, 273 and 279.); and,
4) as otherwise agreed in additional provisions on lines 242-250 or in an addendum to this Listing.

FIXTURES: A "fixture" is an item of property which is physically attached to or so closely associated with land or buildings so as to be treated as part of the real estate, including, without limitation, physically attached items not easily removable without damage to the premises, items specifically adapted to the premises, and items customarily treated as fixtures, including, but not limited to, all: garden bulbs; plants; shrubs and trees; screen and storm doors and windows; electric lighting fixtures; window shades; curtain and traverse rods; blinds and shutters; central heating and cooling units and attached equipment; water heaters and treatment systems; sump pumps; attached or fitted floor coverings; awnings; attached antennas, garage door openers and remote controls; installed security systems; central vacuum systems and accessories; in-ground sprinkler systems and component parts; built-in appliances; ceiling fans; fences; storage buildings on permanent foundations and docks/piers on permanent foundations.

CAUTION: Exclude any Fixtures to be retained by Seller or which are rented (e.g., water softener or other water conditioning systems, home entertainment and satellite dish components, L.P. tanks, etc.) on lines 11-14 and in the offer to purchase.

MATERIAL ADVERSE FACT: A "material adverse fact" means an adverse fact that a party indicates is of such significance, or that is generally recognized by a competent licensee as being of such significance to a reasonable party, that it affects or would affect the party's decision to enter into a contract or agreement concerning a transaction or affects or would affect the party's decision about the terms of such a contract or agreement.

PROCURE: A buyer is procured when, during the term of the Listing, an enforceable contract of sale is entered into between the Seller and the buyer or when a ready, willing and able buyer submits to the Seller or the Listing Broker a written offer at the price and on substantially the terms specified in this Listing. A buyer is ready, willing and able when the buyer submitting the written offer has the ability to complete the buyer's obligations under the written offer. (See lines 46-49)

PROPERTY: Unless otherwise stated, "Property", means the real estate described at lines 2-4.

PROTECTED BUYER: Means a buyer who personally, or through any person acting for such buyer: 1) delivers to Seller or Broker a written offer to purchase, exchange or option on the Property during the term of this Listing; 2) negotiates directly with Seller by discussing with Seller the potential terms upon which buyer might acquire an interest in the Property; or 3) attends an individual showing of the Property or discusses with Broker or cooperating brokers the potential terms upon which buyer might acquire an interest in the Property, but only if Broker delivers the buyer's name to Seller, in writing, no later than three days after the expiration of the Listing. The requirement in 3), to deliver the buyer's name to Seller in writing, may be fulfilled as follows: a) If the Listing is effective only as to certain individuals who are identified in the Listing, by the identification of the individuals in the Listing; or, b) if a buyer has requested that the buyer's identity remain confidential, by delivery of a written notice identifying the broker with whom the buyer negotiated and the date(s) of any showings or other negotiations.

■ **FAIR HOUSING: Seller and Broker agree that they will not discriminate against any prospective buyer on account of race, color, sex, sexual orientation as defined in Wisconsin Statutes, Section 111.32 (13m), disability, religion, national origin, marital status, lawful source of income, age, ancestry, familial status, or in any other unlawful manner.**

■ **EARNEST MONEY:** If Broker holds trust funds in connection with the transaction, they shall be retained by Broker in Broker's trust account. Broker may refuse to hold earnest money or other trust funds. Should Broker hold the earnest money, Seller authorizes Broker to disburse the earnest money as directed in a written earnest money disbursement agreement signed by or on behalf of all parties having an interest in the trust funds. If the transaction fails to close and the earnest money is disbursed to Seller, then upon disbursement to Seller the earnest money shall be paid first to reimburse Broker for cash advances made by Broker on behalf of Seller and one half of the balance, but not in excess of the agreed commission, shall be paid to Broker as Broker's full commission in connection with said purchase transaction and the balance shall belong to Seller. This payment to Broker shall not terminate this Listing.

FIGURE A (CONTINUED)

Blank WB-1 Listing Contract—Exclusive Right to Sell

Wisconsin Legal Blank Co., Inc.
Milwaukee, Wisconsin

■ **ADDITIONAL PROVISIONS:** ______________________________

■ **ADDENDA:** The attached addenda ______________________________ is/are made part of this Listing.

■ **NOTICE ABOUT SEX OFFENDER REGISTRY:** You may obtain information about the sex offender registry and persons registered with the registry by contacting the Wisconsin Department of Corrections on the Internet at http://www.widocoffenders.org or by telephone at (608)240-5830.

■ **TERM OF THE CONTRACT:** From the __________ day of __________, ______, up to and including midnight of the __________ day of __________, ______.

■ **READING/RECEIPT: BY SIGNING BELOW, SELLER ACKNOWLEDGES RECEIPT OF A COPY OF THIS LISTING CONTRACT AND THAT HE/SHE HAS READ ALL FIVE PAGES AS WELL AS ANY ADDENDA AND ANY OTHER DOCUMENTS INCORPORATED INTO THE LISTING.**

(x)______________ ______________ ______________
Seller's Signature ▲ Print Name Here: ▲ Date ▲

______________ ______________
Seller's Address ▲ Seller's Phone # ▲

______________ ______________
Seller's Fax # ▲ `Seller's E-Mail Address ▲

(x)______________ ______________ ______________
Seller's Signature ▲ Print Name Here: ▲ Date ▲

______________ ______________
Seller's Address ▲ Seller's Phone # ▲

______________ ______________
Seller's Fax # ▲ `Seller's E-Mail Address ▲

(x)______________ ______________ ______________ ______________
Agent for Broker ▲ Print Name Here ▲ Broker/Firm Name ▲ Date ▲

______________ ______________
Broker/Firm Address ▲ Broker/Firm Phone # ▲

______________ ______________
Broker/Firm Fax # ▲ Broker/Firm E-Mail Address ▲

FIGURE B

Completed WB-1 Listing Contract—Exclusive Right to Sell

Approved by Wisconsin Department of Regulation and Licensing
1-1-08 (Optional Use Date) 7-1-08 (Mandatory Use Date)

Wisconsin Legal Blank Co., Inc.
Milwaukee, Wisconsin

WB-1 RESIDENTIAL LISTING CONTRACT - EXCLUSIVE RIGHT TO SELL

SELLER GIVES BROKER THE EXCLUSIVE RIGHT TO SELL THE PROPERTY ON THE FOLLOWING TERMS:

■ **PROPERTY DESCRIPTION:** Street address is: 2901 Newman St. ____________ in the City of Madison, County of Dane, Wisconsin. Insert additional description, if any, at lines 242-250 or attach as an addendum per lines 251-254.

■ **LIST PRICE:** One hundred fifty-six thousand and 00/100 Dollars ($ 156,000.00).

■ **INCLUDED IN LIST PRICE:** Seller is including in the list price the Property, all Fixtures not excluded on lines 11-14, and the following items: washer, dryer, and refrigerator.

■ **NOT INCLUDED IN LIST PRICE:** CAUTION: Identify Fixtures to be excluded by Seller or which are rented and will continue to be owned by the lessor. (See lines 199-210): ____________.

■ **MARKETING:** Seller authorizes and Broker agrees to use reasonable efforts to procure a buyer for the Property. Seller agrees that Broker may market Seller's personal property identified on lines 7-9 during the term of this Listing. Broker's marketing may include: holding at least two open houses, advertise in local newspaper, use MLS. Broker may advertise the following special financing and incentives offered by Seller: ____________. Seller has a duty to cooperate with Broker's marketing efforts. See lines 74-80 regarding Broker's role as marketing agent and Seller's duty to notify Broker of any potential buyer known to Seller. Seller agrees that Broker may market other properties during the term of this Listing.

■ **OCCUPANCY:** Unless otherwise provided, Seller agrees to give buyer occupancy of the Property at time of closing and to have the Property in broom swept condition and free of all debris and personal property except for personal property belonging to current tenants, sold to buyer or left with buyer's consent.

■ **COOPERATION, ACCESS TO PROPERTY OR OFFER PRESENTATION:** The parties agree that Broker will work and cooperate with other brokers in marketing the Property, including brokers from other firms acting as subagents (agents from other companies engaged by Broker - See lines 138-141) and brokers representing buyers. Cooperation includes providing access to the Property for showing purposes and presenting offers and other proposals from these brokers to Seller. Note any brokers with whom Broker shall not cooperate, any brokers or buyers who shall not be allowed to attend showings, and the specific terms of offers which should not be submitted to Seller: None.

CAUTION: Limiting Broker's cooperation with other brokers may reduce the marketability of the Property.

■ **EXCLUSIONS:** All persons who may acquire an interest in the Property as a Protected Buyer under a prior listing contract are excluded from this Listing to the extent of the prior broker's legal rights, unless otherwise agreed to in writing. Within seven days of the date of this Listing, Seller agrees to deliver to Broker a written list of all such prospective buyers. The following other buyers are excluded from this Listing until November 21, 2009 [INSERT DATE]: Bill Tankel. These other buyers are no longer excluded from this Listing after the specified date unless, on or before the specified date, Seller has either accepted an offer from the buyer or sold the Property to the buyer.

■ **COMMISSION:** Broker's commission shall be 6%.

Seller shall pay Broker's commission, which shall be earned, if, during the term of this Listing:

1) Seller sells or accepts an offer which creates an enforceable contract for the sale of all or any part of the Property;
2) Seller grants an option to purchase all or any part of the Property which is subsequently exercised;
3) Seller exchanges or enters into a binding exchange agreement on all or any part of the Property;
4) A transaction occurs which causes an effective change in ownership or control of all or any part of the Property; or
5) A buyer is procured for the Property by Broker, by Seller, or by any other person, at no less than the price and on substantially the same terms set forth in this Listing and in the standard provisions of the current WB-11 RESIDENTIAL OFFER TO PURCHASE, even if Seller does not accept this buyer's offer. (See lines 215-218 regarding procurement.)

A percentage commission, if applicable, shall be calculated based on the purchase price if commission is earned under 1) or 2) above, or calculated based on the list price under 3), 4) or 5). A percentage commission shall be calculated on the fair market value of the Property exchanged under 3) if the exchange involves less than the entire Property or on the fair market value of the Property to which an effective change in ownership or control takes place, under 4) if the transaction involves less than the entire Property.

Once earned, Broker's commission is due and payable in full at the earlier of closing or the date set for closing, unless otherwise agreed in writing. Broker's commission shall be earned if, during the term of the Listing, one owner of the Property sells, conveys, exchanges or options an interest in all or any part of the Property to another owner, except by divorce judgment.

NOTE: A sale, option, exchange or procurement of a buyer for a portion of the Property does not terminate the Listing as to any remaining Property.

■ **COMPENSATION TO OTHERS:** Broker offers the following commission to cooperating brokers: ____________. (Exceptions if any): ____________.

FIGURE B (CONTINUED)

Completed WB-1 Listing Contract—Exclusive Right to Sell

Wisconsin Legal Blank Co., Inc.
Milwaukee, Wisconsin

page 2 of 5, WB-1

■ **EXTENSION OF LISTING:** The Listing term is extended for a period of one year as to any Protected Buyer. Upon receipt of a written request from Seller or a broker who has listed the Property, Broker agrees to promptly deliver to Seller a written list of those buyers known by Broker to whom the extension period applies. Should this Listing be terminated by Seller prior to the expiration of the term stated in this Listing, this Listing shall be extended for Protected Buyers, on the same terms, for one year after the Listing is terminated.

■ **TERMINATION OF LISTING:** Neither Seller nor Broker has the legal right to unilaterally terminate this Listing absent a material breach of contract by the other party. Seller understands that the parties to the Listing are Seller and the Broker (firm). Agents (salespersons) for Broker (firm) do not have the authority to enter into a mutual agreement to terminate the Listing, amend the commission amount or shorten the term of this Listing, without the written consent of the agent(s)' supervising broker. Seller and Broker agree that any termination of this Listing by either party before the date stated on line 259 shall be indicated to the other party in writing and shall not be effective until delivered to the other Party in accordance with lines 193-198. CAUTION: Early termination of this Listing may be a breach of contract, causing the terminating party to potentially be liable for damages.

■ **SELLER COOPERATION WITH MARKETING EFFORTS:** Seller agrees to cooperate with Broker in Broker's marketing efforts and to provide Broker with all records, documents and other material in Seller's possession or control which are required in connection with the sale. Seller authorizes Broker to do those acts reasonably necessary to effect a sale and Seller agrees to cooperate fully with these efforts which may include use of a multiple listing service, Internet advertising or a lockbox system on Property. Seller shall promptly notify Broker in writing of any potential buyers with whom Seller negotiates during the term of this Listing and shall promptly refer all persons making inquiries concerning the Property to Broker.

■ **LEASED PROPERTY:** If Property is currently leased and lease(s) will extend beyond closing, Seller shall assign Seller's rights under the lease(s) and transfer all security deposits and prepaid rents (subject to agreed upon prorations) thereunder to buyer at closing. Seller acknowledges that Seller remains liable under the lease(s) unless released by tenants. CAUTION: Seller should consider obtaining an indemnification agreement from buyer for liabilities under the lease(s) unless released by tenants.

■ **BROKER DISCLOSURE TO CLIENTS:**

UNDER WISCONSIN LAW, A BROKER OWES CERTAIN DUTIES TO ALL PARTIES TO A TRANSACTION:

(a) The duty to provide brokerage services to you fairly and honestly.
(b) The duty to exercise reasonable skill and care in providing brokerage services to you.
(c) The duty to provide you with accurate information about market conditions within a reasonable time if you request it, unless disclosure of the information is prohibited by law.
(d) The duty to disclose to you in writing certain material adverse facts about a property, unless disclosure of the information is prohibited by law. (See Lines 211-214)
(e) The duty to protect your confidentiality. Unless the law requires it, the broker will not disclose your confidential information or the confidential information of other parties. (See Lines 147-163)
(f) The duty to safeguard trust funds and other property the broker holds.
(g) The duty, when negotiating, to present contract proposals in an objective and unbiased manner and disclose the advantages and disadvantages of the proposals.

■ **BECAUSE YOU HAVE ENTERED INTO AN AGENCY AGREEMENT WITH A BROKER, YOU ARE THE BROKER'S CLIENT. A BROKER OWES ADDITIONAL DUTIES TO A CLIENT:**

(a) The broker will provide, at your request, information and advice on real estate matters that affect your transaction, unless you release the broker from this duty.
(b) The broker must provide you with all material facts affecting the transaction, not just adverse facts.
(c) The broker will fulfill the broker's obligations under the agency agreement and fulfill your lawful requests that are within the scope of the agency agreement.
(d) The broker will negotiate for you, unless you release the broker from this duty.
(e) The broker will not place the broker's interests ahead of your interests. The broker will not, unless required by law, give information or advice to other parties who are not the broker's clients, if giving the information or advice is contrary to your interests.
(f) If you become involved in a transaction in which another party is also the broker's client (a "multiple representation relationship"), different duties may apply.

■ **MULTIPLE REPRESENTATION RELATIONSHIPS AND DESIGNATED AGENCY:**

■ A multiple representation relationship exists if a broker has an agency agreement with more than one client who is a party in the same transaction. In a multiple representation relationship, if all of the broker's clients in the transaction consent, the broker may provide services to the clients through designated agency.

■ Designated agency means that different salespersons employed by the broker will negotiate on behalf of you and the other client or clients in the transaction, and the broker's duties will remain the same. Each salesperson will provide

FIGURE B (CONTINUED)

Completed WB-1 Listing Contract—Exclusive Right to Sell

Wisconsin Legal Blank Co., Inc.
Milwaukee, Wisconsin
page 3 of 5, WB-1

information, opinions, and advice to the client for whom the salesperson is negotiating, to assist the client in the negotiations. Each client will be able to receive information, opinions, and advice that will assist the client, even if the information, opinions, or advice gives the client advantages in the negotiations over the broker's other clients. A salesperson will not reveal any of your confidential information to another party unless required to do so by law.

■ If a designated agency relationship is not in effect you may authorize or reject a multiple representation relationship. If you authorize a multiple representation relationship the broker may provide brokerage services to more than one client in a transaction but neither the broker nor any of the broker's salespersons may assist any client with information, opinions, and advice which may favor the interests of one client over any other client. If you do not consent to a multiple representation relationship the broker will not be allowed to provide brokerage services to more than one client in the transaction.

INITIAL ONLY ONE OF THE THREE LINES BELOW:

_______I consent to designated agency.

_______I consent to multiple representation relationships, but I do not consent to designated agency.

_______I reject multiple representation relationships.

NOTE: YOU MAY WITHDRAW YOUR CONSENT TO DESIGNATED AGENCY OR TO MULTIPLE REPRESENTATION RELATIONSHIPS BY WRITTEN NOTICE TO THE BROKER AT ANY TIME. YOUR BROKER IS REQUIRED TO DISCLOSE TO YOU IN YOUR AGENCY AGREEMENT THE COMMISSION OR FEES THAT YOU MAY OWE TO YOUR BROKER. IF YOU HAVE ANY QUESTIONS ABOUT THE COMMISSION OR FEES THAT YOU MAY OWE BASED UPON THE TYPE OF AGENCY RELATIONSHIP YOU SELECT WITH YOUR BROKER YOU SHOULD ASK YOUR BROKER BEFORE SIGNING THE AGENCY AGREEMENT.

■ **SUBAGENCY:** The broker may, with your authorization in the agency agreement, engage other brokers who assist your broker by providing brokerage services for your benefit. A subagent will not put the subagent's own interests ahead of your interests. A subagent will not, unless required by law, provide advice or opinions to other parties if doing so is contrary to your interests.

PLEASE REVIEW THIS INFORMATION CAREFULLY. A broker or salesperson can answer your questions about brokerage services, but if you need legal advice, tax advice, or a professional home inspection, contact an attorney, tax advisor, or home inspector. This disclosure is required by section 452.135 of the Wisconsin statutes and is for information only. It is a plain language summary of a broker's duties to you under section 452.133 (2) of the Wisconsin statutes.

■ **CONFIDENTIALITY NOTICE TO CLIENTS:** Broker will keep confidential any information given to Broker in confidence, or any information obtained by Broker that he or she knows a reasonable person would want to be kept confidential, unless the information must be disclosed by law or you authorize Broker to disclose particular information. Broker shall continue to keep the information confidential after Broker is no longer providing brokerage services to you.

The following information is required to be disclosed by law:

1) Material adverse facts, as defined in section 452.01 (5g) of the Wisconsin statutes (lines 211-214).
2) Any facts known by the Broker that contradict any information included in a written inspection report on the property or real estate that is the subject of the transaction.

To ensure that the Broker is aware of what specific information you consider confidential, you may list that information below (see lines 158-160). At a later time, you may also provide the Broker with other information you consider to be confidential.

CONFIDENTIAL INFORMATION: ______________________________

NON-CONFIDENTIAL INFORMATION (The following may be disclosed by Broker): ______________________________

■ **REAL ESTATE CONDITION REPORT:** Seller agrees to complete the real estate condition report provided by Broker to the best of Seller's knowledge. Seller agrees to amend the report should Seller learn of any defect(s) after completion of the report but before acceptance of a buyer's offer to purchase. Seller authorizes Broker to distribute the report to all interested parties and agents inquiring about the Property. Seller acknowledges that Broker has a duty to disclose all material adverse facts as required by law.

■ **SELLER REPRESENTATIONS REGARDING DEFECTS:** Seller represents to Broker that as of the date of this Listing, Seller has no notice or knowledge of any defects affecting the Property other than those noted on the real estate condition report.

WARNING: IF SELLER REPRESENTATIONS ARE INCORRECT OR INCOMPLETE, SELLER MAY BE LIABLE FOR DAMAGES AND COSTS.

■ **OPEN HOUSE AND SHOWING RESPONSIBILITIES:** Seller is aware that there is a potential risk of injury, damage and/or theft involving persons attending an "individual showing" or an "open house." Seller accepts responsibility for preparing the Property to minimize the likelihood of injury, damage and/or loss of personal property. Seller agrees to hold Broker harmless for any losses or liability resulting from personal injury, property damage, or theft occurring during "individual showings" or "open houses" other than those caused by Broker's negligence or intentional wrongdoing. Seller acknowledges that individual showings and open houses may be conducted by licensees other than Broker, that appraisers and inspectors may conduct appraisals and inspections without being accompanied by Broker or other licensees, and that buyers or licensees may be present at all inspections and testing and may photograph or videotape Property unless otherwise provided for in additional provisions at lines 242-250 or in an addendum per lines 251-254.

FIGURE B (CONTINUED)

Completed WB-1 Listing Contract—Exclusive Right to Sell

Wisconsin Legal Blank Co., Inc.
Milwaukee, Wisconsin

■ **DEFINITIONS:**

ADVERSE FACT: An "adverse fact" means any of the following:

(a) A condition or occurrence that is generally recognized by a competent licensee as doing any of the following:

1) Significantly and adversely affecting the value of the Property;

2) significantly reducing the structural integrity of improvements to real estate; or

3) presenting a significant health risk to occupants of the Property.

(b) Information that indicates that a party to a transaction is not able to or does not intend to meet his or her obligations under a contract or agreement made concerning the transaction.

DEADLINES – DAYS: Deadlines expressed as a number of "days" from an event are calculated by excluding the day the event occurred and by counting subsequent calendar days.

DELIVERY: Delivery of documents or written notices related to this Listing may only be accomplished by:
1) giving the document or written notice personally to the party;
2) depositing the document or written notice postage or fees prepaid or charged to an account in the U.S. Mail or a commercial delivery system, addressed to the party, at the party's address (See lines 265, 271 and 277.);
3) electronically transmitting the document or written notice to the party's fax number (See lines 267, 273 and 279.); and,
4) as otherwise agreed in additional provisions on lines 242-250 or in an addendum to this Listing.

FIXTURES: A "fixture" is an item of property which is physically attached to or so closely associated with land or buildings so as to be treated as part of the real estate, including, without limitation, physically attached items not easily removable without damage to the premises, items specifically adapted to the premises, and items customarily treated as fixtures, including, but not limited to, all: garden bulbs; plants; shrubs and trees; screen and storm doors and windows; electric lighting fixtures; window shades; curtain and traverse rods; blinds and shutters; central heating and cooling units and attached equipment; water heaters and treatment systems; sump pumps; attached or fitted floor coverings; awnings; attached antennas, garage door openers and remote controls; installed security systems; central vacuum systems and accessories; in-ground sprinkler systems and component parts; built-in appliances; ceiling fans; fences; storage buildings on permanent foundations and docks/piers on permanent foundations.

CAUTION: Exclude any Fixtures to be retained by Seller or which are rented (e.g., water softener or other water conditioning systems, home entertainment and satellite dish components, L.P. tanks, etc.) on lines 11-14 and in the offer to purchase.

MATERIAL ADVERSE FACT: A "material adverse fact" means an adverse fact that a party indicates is of such significance, or that is generally recognized by a competent licensee as being of such significance to a reasonable party, that it affects or would affect the party's decision to enter into a contract or agreement concerning a transaction or affects or would affect the party's decision about the terms of such a contract or agreement.

PROCURE: A buyer is procured when, during the term of the Listing, an enforceable contract of sale is entered into between the Seller and the buyer or when a ready, willing and able buyer submits to the Seller or the Listing Broker a written offer at the price and on substantially the terms specified in this Listing. A buyer is ready, willing and able when the buyer submitting the written offer has the ability to complete the buyer's obligations under the written offer. (See lines 46-49)

PROPERTY: Unless otherwise stated, "Property", means the real estate described at lines 2-4.

PROTECTED BUYER: Means a buyer who personally, or through any person acting for such buyer: 1) delivers to Seller or Broker a written offer to purchase, exchange or option on the Property during the term of this Listing; 2) negotiates directly with Seller by discussing with Seller the potential terms upon which buyer might acquire an interest in the Property; or 3) attends an individual showing of the Property or discusses with Broker or cooperating brokers the potential terms upon which buyer might acquire an interest in the Property, but only if Broker delivers the buyer's name to Seller, in writing, no later than three days after the expiration of the Listing. The requirement in 3), to deliver the buyer's name to Seller in writing, may be fulfilled as follows: a) If the Listing is effective only as to certain individuals who are identified in the Listing, by the identification of the individuals in the Listing; or, b) if a buyer has requested that the buyer's identity remain confidential, by delivery of a written notice identifying the broker with whom the buyer negotiated and the date(s) of any showings or other negotiations.

■ **FAIR HOUSING: Seller and Broker agree that they will not discriminate against any prospective buyer on account of race, color, sex, sexual orientation as defined in Wisconsin Statutes, Section 111.32 (13m), disability, religion, national origin, marital status, lawful source of income, age, ancestry, familial status, or in any other unlawful manner.**

■ **EARNEST MONEY:** If Broker holds trust funds in connection with the transaction, they shall be retained by Broker in Broker's trust account. Broker may refuse to hold earnest money or other trust funds. Should Broker hold the earnest money, Seller authorizes Broker to disburse the earnest money as directed in a written earnest money disbursement agreement signed by or on behalf of all parties having an interest in the trust funds. If the transaction fails to close and the earnest money is disbursed to Seller, then upon disbursement to Seller the earnest money shall be paid first to reimburse Broker for cash advances made by Broker on behalf of Seller and one half of the balance, but not in excess of the agreed commission, shall be paid to Broker as Broker's full commission in connection with said purchase transaction and the balance shall belong to Seller. This payment to Broker shall not terminate this Listing.

FIGURE B (CONTINUED)

Completed WB-1 Listing Contract—Exclusive Right to Sell

Wisconsin Legal Blank Co., Inc.
Milwaukee, Wisconsin

page 5 of 5, WB-1

■ **ADDITIONAL PROVISIONS:** Seller will not allow any buyers to photgraph of videotape their property.

Legal description is: Lot 8, Block 8 of the Olympia Subdivision, SW 1/4 of Section 6, T9N, RTE, Dane County, Wisconsin

■ **ADDENDA:** The attached addenda N/A ______ is/are made part of this Listing.

■ **NOTICE ABOUT SEX OFFENDER REGISTRY:** You may obtain information about the sex offender registry and persons registered with the registry by contacting the Wisconsin Department of Corrections on the Internet at http://www.widocoffenders.org or by telephone at (608)240-5830.

■ **TERM OF THE CONTRACT:** From the ______ day of ______, ______, up to and including midnight of the ______ day of ______, ______.

■ **READING/RECEIPT: BY SIGNING BELOW, SELLER ACKNOWLEDGES RECEIPT OF A COPY OF THIS LISTING CONTRACT AND THAT HE/SHE HAS READ ALL FIVE PAGES AS WELL AS ANY ADDENDA AND ANY OTHER DOCUMENTS INCORPORATED INTO THE LISTING.**

(x)______ Seller's Signature ▲ | Jack Nelson Print Name Here: ▲ | Nov. 14, 2009 Date ▲

______ Seller's Address ▲ | ______ Seller's Phone # ▲

______ Seller's Fax # ▲ | ______ `Seller's E-Mail Address ▲

(x)______ Seller's Signature ▲ | Mary Nelson Print Name Here: ▲ | Nov. 14, 2009 Date ▲

______ Seller's Address ▲ | ______ Seller's Phone # ▲

______ Seller's Fax # ▲ | ______ `Seller's E-Mail Address ▲

(x)______ Agent for Broker ▲ | ______ Print Name Here ▲ | Joe Dannen Broker/Firm Name ▲ | ______ Date ▲

______ Broker/Firm Address ▲ | ______ Broker/Firm Phone # ▲

______ Broker/Firm Fax # ▲ | ______ Broker/Firm E-Mail Address ▲

FIGURE C

Blank WB-11 Residential Offer to Purchase

Approved by Wisconsin Department of Regulation and Licensing
4-1-99 (Optional Use Date)
11-1-99 (Mandatory Use Date)

Wisconsin Legal Blank Co., Inc.
Milwaukee, Wis.

WB-11 RESIDENTIAL OFFER TO PURCHASE

Page 1 of 5

BROKER DRAFTING THIS OFFER ON ________________ [DATE] IS (AGENT OF SELLER) (AGENT OF BUYER) (DUAL AGENT) STRIKE TWO

GENERAL PROVISIONS The Buyer, ______________________________, offers to purchase the Property known as [Street Address] ______________________________ ____________ in the ____________ of ______________________, County of ______________________ Wisconsin (Insert additional description, if any, at lines 180 - 186, 317 - 320 or attach as an addendum per line 316), on the following terms:

■ PURCHASE PRICE: ______________________________ ______________________________ Dollars ($______________________).

■ EARNEST MONEY of $____________________ accompanies this Offer and earnest money of $____________________ will be paid within ________ days of acceptance.

■ THE BALANCE OF PURCHASE PRICE will be paid in cash or equivalent at closing unless otherwise provided below.

■ ADDITIONAL ITEMS INCLUDED IN PURCHASE PRICE: Seller shall include in the purchase price and transfer, free and clear of encumbrances, all fixtures, as defined at lines 124 - 132 and as may be on the Property on the date of this Offer, unless excluded at lines 15 - 16, and the following additional items: ______________________________ ______________________________

■ ITEMS NOT INCLUDED IN THE PURCHASE PRICE: ______________________________ ______________________________

ACCEPTANCE Acceptance occurs when all Buyers and Sellers have signed an identical copy of the Offer, including signatures on separate but identical copies of the Offer. ***CAUTION: Deadlines in the Offer are commonly calculated from acceptance. Consider whether short term deadlines running from acceptance provide adequate time for both binding acceptance and performance.***

BINDING ACCEPTANCE This Offer is binding upon both Parties only if a copy of the accepted Offer is delivered to Buyer on or before ______________________. ***CAUTION: This Offer may be withdrawn prior to delivery of the accepted Offer.***

DELIVERY OF DOCUMENTS AND WRITTEN NOTICES Unless otherwise stated in this Offer, delivery of documents and written notices to a Party shall be effective only when accomplished by one of the methods specified at lines 24 - 33.

(1) By depositing the document or written notice postage or fees prepaid in the U.S. Mail or fees prepaid or charged to an account with a commercial delivery service, addressed either to the Party, or to the Party's recipient for delivery designated at lines 27 or 29 (if any) for delivery to the Party's delivery address at lines 28 or 30.

Seller's recipient for delivery (optional): ______________________________

Seller's delivery address: ______________________________

Buyer's recipient for delivery (optional): ______________________________

Buyer's delivery address: ______________________________

(2) By giving the document or written notice personally to the Party, or the Party's recipient for delivery if an individual is designated at lines 27 or 29.

(3) By fax transmission of the document or written notice to the following telephone number:

Buyer: (________)______________________ Seller: (________)______________________

OCCUPANCY Occupancy of the entire Property shall be given to Buyer at time of closing unless otherwise provided in this Offer (lines 293 through 297). At time of Buyer's occupancy, Property shall be free of all debris and personal property except for personal property belonging to current tenants, or that sold to Buyer or left with Buyer's consent. Occupancy shall be given subject to tenant's rights, if any.

LEASED PROPERTY If Property is currently leased and lease(s) extend beyond closing, Seller shall assign Seller's rights under said lease(s) and transfer all security deposits and prepaid rents thereunder to Buyer at closing. The terms of the (written) (oral) STRIKE ONE lease(s), if any, are ______________________________.

RENTAL WEATHERIZATION This transaction (is) (is not) STRIKE ONE exempt from State of Wisconsin Rental Weatherization Standards (Wis. Admin. Code Comm 67). If not exempt, (Buyer) (Seller) STRIKE ONE will be responsible for compliance, including all costs. If Seller is responsible for compliance, Seller shall provide a Certificate of Compliance at closing.

PLACE OF CLOSING This transaction is to be closed at the place designated by Buyer's mortgagee or ______________ ______________ no later than ______________________, __________ unless another date or place is agreed to in writing.

CLOSING PRORATIONS The following items shall be prorated at closing: real estate taxes, rents, water and sewer use charges, garbage pick-up and other private and municipal charges, property owner's association assessments, fuel and ______________ ______________________. Any income, taxes or expenses shall accrue to Seller, and be prorated, through the day prior to closing. Net general real estate taxes shall be prorated based on (the net general real estate taxes for the current year, if known, otherwise on the net general real estate taxes for the preceding year) (______________________________ ______________________________). STRIKE AND COMPLETE AS APPLICABLE

CAUTION: If proration on the basis of net general real estate taxes is not acceptable (for example, completed/pending reassessment, changing mill rate, lottery credits), insert estimated annual tax or other formula for proration.

PROPERTY CONDITION PROVISIONS

■ PROPERTY CONDITION REPRESENTATIONS: Seller represents to Buyer that as of the date of acceptance Seller has no notice or knowledge of conditions affecting the Property or transaction (see below) other than those identified in Seller's Real Estate Condition Report dated ________________, which was received by Buyer prior to Buyer signing this Offer and which is made a part of this Offer by reference COMPLETE DATE OR STRIKE AS APPLICABLE and ______________________________ ______________________________ INSERT CONDITIONS NOT ALREADY INCLUDED IN THE CONDITION REPORT.

FIGURE C (CONTINUED)

Blank WB-11 Residential Offer to Purchase

■ A "condition affecting the Property or transaction" is defined as follows:

(a) planned or commenced public improvements which may result in special assessments or otherwise materially affect the Property or the present use of the Property;

(b) completed or pending reassessment of the Property for property tax purposes;

(c) government agency or court order requiring repair, alteration or correction of any existing condition;

(d) construction or remodeling on Property for which required state or local permits had not been obtained;

(e) any land division involving the subject Property, for which required state or local approvals had not been obtained;

(f) violation of applicable state or local smoke detector laws; ***NOTE: State law requires operating smoke detectors on all levels of all residential properties.***

(g) any portion of the Property being in a 100 year floodplain, a wetland or a shoreland zoning area under local, state or federal laws;

(h) that a structure on the Property is designated as an historic building or that any part of Property is in an historic district;

(i) structural inadequacies which if not repaired will significantly shorten the expected normal life of the Property;

(j) mechanical systems inadequate for the present use of the Property;

(k) insect or animal infestation of the Property;

(l) conditions constituting a significant health or safety hazard for occupants of Property; ***Note: Specific federal lead paint disclosure requirements must be complied with in the sale of most residential properties built before 1978.***

(m) underground or aboveground storage tanks on the Property for storage of flammable or combustible liquids including but not limited to gasoline and heating oil which are currently or which were previously located on the Property; ***NOTE: Wis. Adm. Code, Chapter Comm 10 contains registration and operation rules for such underground and aboveground storage tanks.***

(n) material violations of environmental laws or other laws or agreements regulating the use of the Property;

(o) high voltage electric (100 KV or greater) or steel natural gas transmission lines located on but not directly serving the Property;

(p) other conditions or occurrences which would significantly reduce the value of the Property to a reasonable person with knowledge of the nature and scope of the condition or occurrence.

■ REAL ESTATE CONDITION REPORT: Wisconsin law requires owners of property which includes 1-4 dwelling units to provide buyers with a Real Estate Condition Report. Excluded from this requirement are sales of property that has never been inhabited, sales exempt from the real estate transfer fee, and sales by certain court-appointed fiduciaries, (for example, personal representatives who have never occupied the Property). The form of the Report is found in Wis. Stat. § 709.03. The law provides: "709.02 Disclosure . . . the owner of the property shall furnish, not later than 10 days after acceptance of the contract of sale . . . , to the prospective buyer of the property a completed copy of the report . . . A prospective buyer who does not receive a report within the 10 days may, within 2 business days after the end of that 10 day period, rescind the contract of sale . . . by delivering a written notice of rescission to the owner or the owner's agent." Buyer may also have certain rescission rights if a Real Estate Condition Report disclosing defects is furnished before expiration of the 10 days, but after the Offer is submitted to Seller. Buyer should review the report form or consult with an attorney for additional information regarding these rescission rights.

■ PROPERTY DIMENSIONS AND SURVEYS: Buyer acknowledges that any land, building or room dimensions, or total acreage or building square footage figures, provided to Buyer by Seller or by a broker, may be approximate because of rounding or other reasons, unless verified by survey or other means. Buyer also acknowledges that there are various formulas used to calculate total square footage of buildings and that total square footage figures will vary dependent upon the formula used. ***CAUTION: Buyer should verify total square footage formula, total square footage/acreage figures, land, building or room dimensions, if material.***

■ INSPECTIONS: Seller agrees to allow Buyer's inspectors reasonable access to the Property upon reasonable notice if the inspections are reasonably necessary to satisfy the contingencies in this Offer. Buyer agrees to promptly provide copies of all such inspection reports to Seller, and to listing broker if Property is listed. Furthermore, Buyer agrees to promptly restore the Property to its original condition after Buyer's inspections are completed, unless otherwise agreed with Seller. An "inspection" is defined as an observation of the Property which does not include testing of the Property, other than testing for leaking carbon monoxide, or testing for leaking LP gas or natural gas used as a fuel source, which are hereby authorized.

■ TESTING: Except as otherwise provided, Seller's authorization for inspections does not authorize Buyer to conduct testing of the Property. A "test" is defined as the taking of samples of materials such as soils, water, air or building materials from the Property and the laboratory or other analysis of these materials. If Buyer requires testing, testing contingencies must be specifically provided for at lines 180 - 186, 317 - 320 or in an addendum per line 316. Note: Any contingency authorizing such tests should specify the areas of the Property to be tested, the purpose of the test, (e.g., to determine if environmental contamination is present), any limitations on Buyer's testing and any other material terms of the contingency (e.g., Buyer's obligation to return the Property to its original condition). Seller acknowledges that certain inspections or tests may detect environmental pollution which may be required to be reported to the Wisconsin Department of Natural Resources.

■ PRE-CLOSING INSPECTION: At a reasonable time, pre-approved by Seller or Seller's agent, within 3 days before closing, Buyer shall have the right to inspect the Property to determine that there has been no significant change in the condition of the Property, except for ordinary wear and tear and changes approved by Buyer, and that any defects Seller has elected to cure have been repaired in a good and workmanlike manner.

■ PROPERTY DAMAGE BETWEEN ACCEPTANCE AND CLOSING: Seller shall maintain the Property until the earlier of closing or occupancy of Buyer in materially the same condition as of the date of acceptance of this Offer, except for ordinary wear and tear. If, prior to closing, the Property is damaged in an amount of not more than five per cent (5%) of the selling price, Seller shall be obligated to repair the Property and restore it to the same condition that it was on the day of this Offer. If the damage shall exceed such sum, Seller shall promptly notify Buyer in writing of the damage and this Offer may be canceled at option of Buyer. Should Buyer elect to carry out this Offer despite such damage, Buyer shall be entitled to the insurance proceeds relating to the damage to the Property, plus a credit towards the purchase price equal to the amount of Seller's deductible on such policy. However, if this sale is financed by a land contract or a mortgage to Seller, the insurance proceeds shall be held in trust for the sole purpose of restoring the Property.

FIXTURES A "Fixture" is defined as an item of property which is physically attached to or so closely associated with land or improvements so as to be treated as part of the real estate, including, without limitation, physically attached items not easily removable without damage to the Property, items specifically adapted to the Property, and items customarily treated as fixtures, including, but not limited to, all: garden bulbs; plants; shrubs and trees; screen and storm doors and windows; electric lighting fixtures; window shades; curtain and traverse rods; blinds and shutters; central heating and cooling units and attached equipment; water heaters and softeners; sump pumps; attached or fitted floor coverings; awnings; attached antennas, satellite dishes and component parts; garage door openers and remote controls; installed security systems; central vacuum systems and accessories; in-ground sprinkler systems and component parts; built-in appliances; ceiling fans; fences; storage buildings on permanent foundations and docks/piers on permanent foundations. ***NOTE: The terms of the Offer will determine what items are included/excluded. Address rented fixtures (e.g., water softeners), if any.***

FIGURE C (CONTINUED)

Blank WB-11 Residential Offer to Purchase

Wisconsin Legal Blank Co., Inc.

PROPERTY ADDRESS: ____ [page 3 of 5, WB-11]

TIME IS OF THE ESSENCE "Time is of the Essence" as to: (1) earnest money payment(s); (2) binding acceptance; (3) occupancy; (4) date of closing; (5) contingency deadlines STRIKE AS APPLICABLE and all other dates and deadlines in this Offer except: ____. If "Time is of the Essence" applies to a date or deadline, failure to perform by the exact date or deadline is a breach of contract. If "Time is of the Essence" does not apply to a date or deadline, then performance within a reasonable time of the date or deadline is allowed before a breach occurs.

DATES AND DEADLINES Deadlines expressed as a number of "days" from an event, such as acceptance, are calculated by excluding the day the event occurred and by counting subsequent calendar days. The deadline expires at midnight on the last day. Deadlines expressed as a specific number of "business days" exclude Saturdays, Sundays, any legal public holiday under Wisconsin or Federal law, and other day designated by the President such that the postal service does not receive registered mail or make regular deliveries on that day. Deadlines expressed as a specific number of "hours" from the occurrence of an event, such as receipt of a notice, are calculated from the exact time of the event, and by counting 24 hours per calendar day. Deadlines expressed as a specific day of the calendar year or as the day of a specific event, such as closing, expire at midnight of that day.

THE FINANCING CONTINGENCY PROVISIONS AT LINES 149 - 163 ARE A PART OF THIS OFFER IF LINE 149 IS MARKED, SUCH AS WITH AN "X". THEY ARE NOT PART OF THIS OFFER IF LINE 149 IS MARKED N/A OR IS NOT MARKED.

☐ **FINANCING CONTINGENCY:** This Offer is contingent upon Buyer being able to obtain a ____________ INSERT LOAN PROGRAM OR SOURCE first mortgage loan commitment as described below, within ______ days of acceptance of this Offer. The financing selected shall be in an amount of not less than $____________ for a term of not less than ______ years, amortized over not less than ______ years. Initial monthly payments of principal and interest shall not exceed $____________. Monthly payments may also include 1/12th of the estimated net annual real estate taxes, hazard insurance premiums, and private mortgage insurance premiums. The mortgage may not include a prepayment premium. Buyer agrees to pay a loan fee not to exceed ______% of the loan. (Loan fee refers to discount points and/or loan origination fee, but DOES NOT include Buyer's other closing costs.) If the purchase price under this Offer is modified, the financed amount, unless otherwise provided, shall be adjusted to the same percentage of the purchase price as in this contingency and the monthly payments shall be adjusted as necessary to maintain the term and amortization stated above. **CHECK AND COMPLETE APPLICABLE FINANCING PROVISION AT LINE 159 OR 160.**

☐ **FIXED RATE FINANCING:** The annual rate of interest shall not exceed ______%.

☐ **ADJUSTABLE RATE FINANCING:** The initial annual interest rate shall not exceed ______%. The initial interest rate shall be fixed for ______ months, at which time the interest rate may be increased not more than ______% per year. The maximum interest rate during the mortgage term shall not exceed ______%. Monthly payments of principal and interest may be adjusted to reflect interest changes.

LOAN COMMITMENT: Buyer agrees to pay all customary financing costs (including closing fees), to apply for financing promptly, and to provide evidence of application promptly upon request by Seller. If Buyer qualifies for the financing described in this Offer or other financing acceptable to Buyer, Buyer agrees to deliver to Seller a copy of the written loan commitment no later than the deadline for loan commitment at line 150. **Buyer's delivery of a copy of any written loan commitment to Seller (even if subject to conditions) shall satisfy the Buyer's financing contingency unless accompanied by a notice of unacceptability.** ***CAUTION: BUYER, BUYER'S LENDER AND AGENTS OF BUYER OR SELLER SHOULD NOT DELIVER A LOAN COMMITMENT TO SELLER WITHOUT BUYER'S PRIOR APPROVAL OR UNLESS ACCOMPANIED BY A NOTICE OF UNACCEPTABILITY.***

SELLER TERMINATION RIGHTS: If Buyer does not make timely delivery of said commitment, Seller may terminate this Offer if Seller delivers a written notice of termination to Buyer prior to Seller's actual receipt of a copy of Buyer's written loan commitment.

FINANCING UNAVAILABILITY: If financing is not available on the terms stated in this Offer (and Buyer has not already delivered an acceptable loan commitment for other financing to Seller), Buyer shall promptly deliver written notice to Seller of same including copies of lender(s)' rejection letter(s) or other evidence of unavailability. Unless a specific loan source is named in this Offer, Seller shall then have 10 days to give Buyer written notice of Seller's decision to finance this transaction on the same terms set forth in this Offer, and this Offer shall remain in full force and effect, with the time for closing extended accordingly. If Seller's notice is not timely given, this Offer shall be null and void. Buyer authorizes Seller to obtain any credit information reasonably appropriate to determine Buyer's credit worthiness for Seller financing.

ADDITIONAL PROVISIONS/CONTINGENCIES ____

TITLE EVIDENCE

■ CONVEYANCE OF TITLE: **Upon payment of the purchase price, Seller shall convey the Property by warranty deed (or other conveyance as provided herein)** free and clear of all liens and encumbrances, except: municipal and zoning ordinances and agreements entered under them, recorded easements for the distribution of utility and municipal services, recorded building and use restrictions and covenants, general taxes levied in the year of closing and ____ (provided none of the foregoing prohibit present use of the Property), which constitutes merchantable title for purposes of this transaction. Seller further agrees to complete and execute the documents necessary to record the conveyance. ***WARNING: Municipal and zoning ordinances, recorded building and use restrictions, covenants and easements may prohibit certain improvements or uses and therefore should be reviewed, particularly if Buyer contemplates making improvements to Property or a use other than the current use.***

■ FORM OF TITLE EVIDENCE: Seller shall give evidence of title in the form of an owner's policy of title insurance in the amount of the purchase price on a current ALTA form issued by an insurer licensed to write title insurance in Wisconsin. ***CAUTION: IF TITLE EVIDENCE WILL BE GIVEN BY ABSTRACT, STRIKE TITLE INSURANCE PROVISIONS AND INSERT ABSTRACT PROVISIONS.***

FIGURE C (CONTINUED)

Blank WB-11 Residential Offer to Purchase

[page 4 of 5, WB-11]

■ PROVISION OF MERCHANTABLE TITLE: Seller shall pay all costs of providing title evidence. For purposes of closing, title evidence shall be acceptable if the commitment for the required title insurance is delivered to Buyer's attorney or Buyer not less than 3 business days before closing, showing title to the Property as of a date no more than 15 days before delivery of such title evidence to be merchantable, subject only to liens which will be paid out of the proceeds of closing and standard title insurance requirements and exceptions, as appropriate. ***CAUTION: BUYER SHOULD CONSIDER UPDATING THE EFFECTIVE DATE OF THE TITLE COMMITMENT PRIOR TO CLOSING OR A "GAP ENDORSEMENT" WHICH WOULD INSURE OVER LIENS FILED BETWEEN THE EFFECTIVE DATE OF THE COMMITMENT AND THE DATE THE DEED IS RECORDED.***

■ TITLE ACCEPTABLE FOR CLOSING: If title is not acceptable for closing, Buyer shall notify Seller in writing of objections to title by the time set for closing. In such event, Seller shall have a reasonable time, but not exceeding 15 days, to remove the objections, and the time for closing shall be extended as necessary for this purpose. In the event that Seller is unable to remove said objections, Buyer shall have 5 days from receipt of notice thereof, to deliver written notice waiving the objections, and the time for closing shall be extended accordingly. If Buyer does not waive the objections, this Offer shall be null and void. Providing title evidence acceptable for closing does not extinguish Seller's obligations to give merchantable title to Buyer.

■ SPECIAL ASSESSMENTS: Special assessments, if any, for work actually commenced or levied prior to date of this Offer shall be paid by Seller no later than closing. All other special assessments shall be paid by Buyer. ***CAUTION: Consider a special agreement if area assessments, property owner's association assessments or other expenses are contemplated.*** "Other expenses" are one-time charges or ongoing use fees for public improvements (other than those resulting in special assessments) relating to curb, gutter, street, sidewalk, sanitary and stormwater and storm sewer (including all sewer mains and hook-up and interceptor charges), parks, street lighting and street trees, and impact fees for other public facilities, as defined in Wis. Stat. §66.55(1)(c) & (f).

DELIVERY/RECEIPT Unless otherwise stated in this Offer, any signed document transmitted by facsimile machine (fax) shall be treated in all manner and respects as an original document and the signature of any Party upon a document transmitted by fax shall be considered an original signature. Personal delivery to, or actual receipt by, any named Buyer or Seller constitutes personal delivery to, or actual receipt by Buyer or Seller Once received, a notice cannot be withdrawn by the Party delivering the notice without the consent of the Party receiving the notice. A Party may not unilaterally reinstate a contingency after a notice of a contingency waiver has been received by the other Party. **The delivery/receipt provisions in this Offer may be modified when appropriate (e.g., when mail delivery is not desirable (see lines 24 - 30) or when a party will not be personally available to receive a notice (see line 286)).** Buyer and Seller authorize the agents of Buyer and Seller to distribute copies of the Offer to Buyer's lender, appraisers, title insurance companies and any other settlement service providers for the transaction as defined by the Real Estate Settlement Procedures Act (RESPA).

DEFAULT Seller and Buyer each have the legal duty to use good faith and due diligence in completing the terms and conditions of this Offer. A material failure to perform any obligation under this Offer is a default which may subject the defaulting party to liability for damages or other legal remedies.

If Buyer defaults, Seller may:
(1) sue for specific performance and request the earnest money as partial payment of the purchase price; or
(2) terminate the Offer and have the option to: (a) request the earnest money as liquidated damages; or (b) direct Broker to return the earnest money and have the option to sue for actual damages.

If Seller defaults, Buyer may:
(1) sue for specific performance; or
(2) terminate the Offer and request the return of the earnest money, sue for actual damages, or both.

In addition, the Parties may seek any other remedies available in law or equity.

The Parties understand that the availability of any judicial remedy will depend upon the circumstances of the situation and the discretion of the courts. If either Party defaults, the Parties may renegotiate the Offer or seek nonjudicial dispute resolution instead of the remedies outlined above. By agreeing to binding arbitration, the Parties may lose the right to litigate in a court of law those disputes covered by the arbitration agreement.

NOTE: IF ACCEPTED, THIS OFFER CAN CREATE A LEGALLY ENFORCEABLE CONTRACT. BOTH PARTIES SHOULD READ THIS DOCUMENT CAREFULLY. BROKERS MAY PROVIDE A GENERAL EXPLANATION OF THE PROVISIONS OF THE OFFER BUT ARE PROHIBITED BY LAW FROM GIVING ADVICE OR OPINIONS CONCERNING YOUR LEGAL RIGHTS UNDER THIS OFFER OR HOW TITLE SHOULD BE TAKEN AT CLOSING. AN ATTORNEY SHOULD BE CONSULTED IF LEGAL ADVICE IS NEEDED.

EARNEST MONEY

■ HELD BY: Unless otherwise agreed, earnest money shall be paid to and held in the trust account of the listing broker (buyer's agent if Property is not listed or Seller's account if no broker is involved), until applied to purchase price or otherwise disbursed as provided in the Offer. ***CAUTION: Should persons other than a broker hold earnest money, an escrow agreement should be drafted by the Parties or an attorney. If someone other than Buyer makes payment of earnest money, consider a special disbursement agreement.***

■ DISBURSEMENT: If negotiations do not result in an accepted offer, the earnest money shall be promptly disbursed (after clearance from payor's depository institution if earnest money is paid by check) to the person(s) who paid the earnest money. At closing, earnest money shall be disbursed according to the closing statement. If this Offer does not close, the earnest money shall be disbursed according to a written disbursement agreement signed by all Parties to this Offer (Note: Wis. Adm. Code s. RL 18.09(1)(b) provides that an offer to purchase is not a written disbursement agreement pursuant to which the broker may disburse). If said disbursement agreement has not been delivered to broker within 60 days after the date set for closing, broker may disburse the earnest money: (1) as directed by an attorney who has reviewed the transaction and does not represent Buyer or Seller; (2) into a court hearing a lawsuit involving the earnest money and all Parties to this Offer; (3) as directed by court order; or (4) any other disbursement required or allowed by law. Broker may retain legal services to direct disbursement per (1) or to file an interpleader action per (2) and broker may deduct from the earnest money any costs and reasonable attorneys fees, not to exceed $250, prior to disbursement.

■ LEGAL RIGHTS/ACTION: Broker's disbursement of earnest money does not determine the legal rights of the Parties in relation to this Offer. Buyer's or Seller's legal right to earnest money cannot be determined by broker. At least 30 days prior to disbursement per (1) or (4) above, broker shall send Buyer and Seller notice of the disbursement by certified mail. If Buyer or Seller disagree with broker's proposed disbursement, a lawsuit may be filed to obtain a court order regarding disbursement. Small Claims Court has jurisdiction over all earnest money disputes arising out of the sale of residential property with 1-4 dwelling units and certain other earnest money disputes. Buyer and Seller should consider consulting attorneys regarding their legal rights under this Offer in case of a dispute. Both Parties agree to hold the broker harmless from any liability for good faith disbursement of earnest money in accordance with this Offer or applicable Department of Regulation and Licensing regulations concerning earnest money. See Wis. Adm. Code Ch. RL 18.

ENTIRE CONTRACT This Offer, including any amendments to it, contains the entire agreement of the Buyer and Seller regarding the transaction. All prior negotiations and discussions have been merged into this Offer. This agreement binds and inures to the benefit of the Parties to this Offer and their successors in interest.

FIGURE C (CONTINUED)

Blank WB-11 Residential Offer to Purchase

Wisconsin Legal Blank Co., Inc.

PROPERTY ADDRESS: ______________________________ [page 5 of 5, WB-11]

OPTIONAL PROVISIONS: THE PROVISIONS ON LINES 278 THROUGH 316 ARE A PART OF THIS OFFER IF MARKED, SUCH AS WITH AN "X". THEY ARE NOT PART OF THIS OFFER IF MARKED N/A OR ARE LEFT BLANK (EXCEPT AS PROVIDED AT LINES 280 - 281).

☐ **SALE OF BUYER'S PROPERTY CONTINGENCY:** This Offer is contingent upon the sale and closing of Buyer's property located at ______________________________, no later than ______________. Seller may keep Seller's Property on the market for sale and accept secondary offers. **If this contingency is made a part of this Offer, lines 282 - 286 are also a part of this offer unless marked N/A at line 282 or otherwise deleted.**

☐ **CONTINUED MARKETING:** If Seller accepts a bona fide secondary offer, Seller may give written notice to Buyer of acceptance. If Buyer does not deliver to Seller a written waiver of sale of Buyer's property contingency and ______________________________ **[INSERT OTHER REQUIREMENTS, IF ANY (e.g., PAYMENT OF ADDITIONAL EARNEST MONEY, WAIVER OF ALL CONTINGENCIES, OR PROVIDING EVIDENCE OF SALE OR BRIDGE LOAN, etc.)]** within ________ hours of Buyer's actual receipt of said notice, this Offer shall be null and void.

☐ **SECONDARY OFFER:** This Offer is secondary to a prior accepted offer. This Offer shall become primary upon delivery of written notice to Buyer that this Offer is primary. Unless otherwise provided, Seller is not obligated to give Buyer notice prior to any deadline, nor is any particular secondary buyer given the right to be made primary ahead of other secondary buyers. Buyer may declare this Offer null and void by delivering written notice of withdrawal to Seller prior to delivery of Seller's notice that this Offer is primary. Buyer may not deliver notice of withdrawal earlier than ________ days after acceptance of this Offer. All other Offer deadlines which are run from acceptance shall run from the time this Offer becomes primary.

☐ **PRE/POST CLOSING OCCUPANCY:** Occupancy of ______________________________ shall be given to Buyer on ______________ at ________ am/pm. (Seller)(Buyer) STRIKE ONE shall pay an occupancy charge of $________ per day or partial day of pre/post-closing occupancy. Payment shall be due at the beginning of the occupancy period. Any unearned post closing occupancy fee (shall)(shall not) STRIKE ONE be refunded based on actual occupancy.

CAUTION: Consider a special agreement regarding occupancy escrow, insurance, utilities, maintenance, keys, etc.

☐ **INSPECTION CONTINGENCY:** This Offer is contingent upon a Wisconsin registered home inspector performing a home inspection of the Property, and an inspection, by a qualified independent inspector, of ______________________________ which discloses no defects as defined below. This contingency shall be deemed satisfied unless Buyer, within ________ days of acceptance, delivers to Seller, and to listing broker if Property is listed, a copy of the inspector's written inspection report(s) and a written notice listing the defect(s) identified in the inspection report(s) to which Buyer objects. ***CAUTION: A proposed amendment will not satisfy this notice requirement.*** Buyer shall order the inspection and be responsible for all costs of inspection, including any inspections required by lender or as follow-up inspections to the home inspection. **Note: This contingency only authorizes inspections, not testing. (See lines 97 - 110.)**

■ RIGHT TO CURE: Seller (shall) (shall not) STRIKE ONE have a right to cure the defects. (Seller shall have a right to cure if no choice is indicated.) If Seller has right to cure, Seller may satisfy this contingency by: (1) delivering a written notice within 10 days of receipt of Buyer's notice of Seller's election to cure defects, (2) curing the defects in a good and workmanlike manner and (3) delivering to Buyer a written report detailing the work done no later than 3 days prior to closing. This Offer shall be null and void if Buyer makes timely delivery of the above notice and report and: (1) Seller does not have a right to cure or (2) Seller has a right to cure but: a) Seller delivers notice that Seller will not cure or b) Seller does not timely deliver the notice of election to cure.

■ "DEFECT" DEFINED: For the purposes of this contingency, a defect is defined as a structural, mechanical or other condition that would have a significant adverse effect on the value of the Property; that would significantly impair the health or safety of future occupants of the Property; or that if not repaired, removed or replaced would significantly shorten or have a significant adverse effect on the expected normal life of the Property. Defects do not include structural, mechanical or other conditions the nature and extent of which Buyer had actual knowledge or written notice before signing this Offer.

☐ **ADDENDA:** The attached ______________________________ is/are made part of this Offer.

ADDITIONAL PROVISIONS/CONTINGENCIES ______________________________

This Offer was drafted on ______________ [date] by [Licensee and firm] ______________________________.

(x)______________________________ ______________ ________
Buyer's Signature ▲ Print Name Here: ▶ Social Security No. or FEIN ▲ (Optional) Date ▲

(x)______________________________ ______________ ________
Buyer's Signature ▲ Print Name Here: ▶ Social Security No. or FEIN ▲ (Optional) Date ▲

EARNEST MONEY RECEIPT Broker acknowledges receipt of earnest money as per line 8 of the above Offer. **(See lines 247 - 271.)**

______________________________ Broker (By) ______________________________

SELLER ACCEPTS THIS OFFER. THE WARRANTIES, REPRESENTATIONS AND COVENANTS MADE IN THIS OFFER SURVIVE CLOSING AND THE CONVEYANCE OF THE PROPERTY. SELLER AGREES TO CONVEY THE PROPERTY ON THE TERMS AND CONDITIONS AS SET FORTH HEREIN AND ACKNOWLEDGES RECEIPT OF A COPY OF THIS OFFER.

(x)______________________________ ______________ ________
Seller's Signature ▲ Print Name Here: ▶ Social Security No. or FEIN ▲ (Optional) Date ▲

(x)______________________________ ______________ ________
Seller's Signature ▲ Print Name Here: ▶ Social Security No. or FEIN ▲ (Optional) Date ▲

This Offer was presented to Seller by ______________ on ______________, ________, at ________ a.m./p.m.

THIS OFFER IS REJECTED ________ ________ THIS OFFER IS COUNTERED [See attached counter] ________ ________
Seller Initials ▲ Date ▲ Seller Initials ▲ Date ▲

FIGURE D

Completed WB-11 Residential Offer to Purchase

Approved by Wisconsin Department of Regulation and Licensing
4-1-99 (Optional Use Date)
11-1-99 (Mandatory Use Date)

WB-11 RESIDENTIAL OFFER TO PURCHASE

Wisconsin Legal Blank Co., Inc.
Milwaukee, Wis.

Page 1 of 5

BROKER DRAFTING THIS OFFER ON Nov. 14, 2009 **[DATE] IS (AGENT OF SELLER) (AGENT OF BUYER) (DUAL AGENT)** STRIKE TWO

GENERAL PROVISIONS The Buyer, Jay and Linda Norris, offers to purchase the Property known as [Street Address] 2901 Newman Street in the City of Madison, County of Dane Wisconsin (Insert additional description, if any, at lines 180 - 186, 317 - 320 or attach as an addendum per line 316), on the following terms:

■ PURCHASE PRICE: One hundred fifty-three thousand and no/100-- Dollars ($ 153,000.00).

■ EARNEST MONEY of $ 1,000.00 accompanies this Offer and earnest money of $ 2,000.00 will be paid within upon xxxxxx acceptance.

■ THE BALANCE OF PURCHASE PRICE will be paid in cash or equivalent at closing unless otherwise provided below.

■ ADDITIONAL ITEMS INCLUDED IN PURCHASE PRICE: Seller shall include in the purchase price and transfer, free and clear of encumbrances, all fixtures, as defined at lines 124 - 132 and as may be on the Property on the date of this Offer, unless excluded at lines 15 - 16, and the following additional items: washer, dryer, and refrigerator

■ ITEMS NOT INCLUDED IN THE PURCHASE PRICE: ______

ACCEPTANCE Acceptance occurs when all Buyers and Sellers have signed an identical copy of the Offer, including signatures on separate but identical copies of the Offer. ***CAUTION: Deadlines in the Offer are commonly calculated from acceptance. Consider whether short term deadlines running from acceptance provide adequate time for both binding acceptance and performance.***

BINDING ACCEPTANCE This Offer is binding upon both Parties only if a copy of the accepted Offer is delivered to Buyer on or before Nov. 24, 2005. ***CAUTION: This Offer may be withdrawn prior to delivery of the accepted Offer.***

DELIVERY OF DOCUMENTS AND WRITTEN NOTICES Unless otherwise stated in this Offer, delivery of documents and written notices to a Party shall be effective only when accomplished by one of the methods specified at lines 24 - 33.

(1) By depositing the document or written notice postage or fees prepaid in the U.S. Mail or fees prepaid or charged to an account with a commercial delivery service, addressed either to the Party, or to the Party's recipient for delivery designated at lines 27 or 29 (if any) for delivery to the Party's delivery address at lines 28 or 30.

Seller's recipient for delivery (optional): Jack or Mary Nelson

Seller's delivery address: 2901 Newman Street, Madison, Wisconsin

Buyer's recipient for delivery (optional): Jay or Linda Norris

Buyer's delivery address: 4226 Adderly Avenue, Milwaukee, Wisconsin

(2) By giving the document or written notice personally to the Party, or the Party's recipient for delivery if an individual is designated at lines 27 or 29.

(3) By fax transmission of the document or written notice to the following telephone number:

Buyer: (______) ______ Seller: (______) ______

OCCUPANCY Occupancy of the entire Property shall be given to Buyer at time of closing unless otherwise provided in this Offer (lines 293 through 297). At time of Buyer's occupancy, Property shall be free of all debris and personal property except for personal property belonging to current tenants, or that sold to Buyer or left with Buyer's consent. Occupancy shall be given subject to tenant's rights, if any.

LEASED PROPERTY If Property is currently leased and lease(s) extend beyond closing, Seller shall assign Seller's rights under said lease(s) and transfer all security deposits and prepaid rents thereunder to Buyer at closing. The terms of the (written) (oral) STRIKE ONE lease(s), if any, are ______.

RENTAL WEATHERIZATION This transaction (is) (is not) STRIKE ONE exempt from State of Wisconsin Rental Weatherization Standards (Wis. Admin. Code Comm 67). If not exempt, (Buyer) (Seller) STRIKE ONE will be responsible for compliance, including all costs. If Seller is responsible for compliance, Seller shall provide a Certificate of Compliance at closing.

PLACE OF CLOSING This transaction is to be closed at the place designated by Buyer's mortgagee or National Title ______ no later than December 21, 2009 unless another date or place is agreed to in writing.

CLOSING PRORATIONS The following items shall be prorated at closing: real estate taxes, rents, water and sewer use charges, garbage pick-up and other private and municipal charges, property owner's association assessments, fuel and ______. Any income, taxes or expenses shall accrue to Seller, and be prorated, through the day prior to closing. Net general real estate taxes shall be prorated based on (the net general real estate taxes for the current year, if known, otherwise on the net general real estate taxes for the preceding year) (latest known mill rate latest known assessed value). STRIKE AND COMPLETE AS APPLICABLE

CAUTION: If proration on the basis of net general real estate taxes is not acceptable (for example, completed/pending reassessment, changing mill rate, lottery credits), insert estimated annual tax or other formula for proration.

PROPERTY CONDITION PROVISIONS

■ PROPERTY CONDITION REPRESENTATIONS: Seller represents to Buyer that as of the date of acceptance Seller has no notice or knowledge of conditions affecting the Property or transaction (see below) other than those identified in Seller's Real Estate Condition Report dated Nov. 14, 2009, which was received by Buyer prior to Buyer signing this Offer and which is made a part of this Offer by reference COMPLETE DATE OR STRIKE AS APPLICABLE and ______ INSERT CONDITIONS NOT ALREADY INCLUDED IN THE CONDITION REPORT.

FIGURE D (CONTINUED)

Completed WB-11 Residential Offer to Purchase

[page 2 of 5, WB-11]

■ A "condition affecting the Property or transaction" is defined as follows:

(a) planned or commenced public improvements which may result in special assessments or otherwise materially affect the Property or the present use of the Property;

(b) completed or pending reassessment of the Property for property tax purposes;

(c) government agency or court order requiring repair, alteration or correction of any existing condition;

(d) construction or remodeling on Property for which required state or local permits had not been obtained;

(e) any land division involving the subject Property, for which required state or local approvals had not been obtained;

(f) violation of applicable state or local smoke detector laws; ***NOTE: State law requires operating smoke detectors on all levels of all residential properties.***

(g) any portion of the Property being in a 100 year floodplain, a wetland or a shoreland zoning area under local, state or federal laws;

(h) that a structure on the Property is designated as an historic building or that any part of Property is in an historic district;

(i) structural inadequacies which if not repaired will significantly shorten the expected normal life of the Property;

(j) mechanical systems inadequate for the present use of the Property;

(k) insect or animal infestation of the Property;

(l) conditions constituting a significant health or safety hazard for occupants of Property; ***Note: Specific federal lead paint disclosure requirements must be complied with in the sale of most residential properties built before 1978.***

(m) underground or aboveground storage tanks on the Property for storage of flammable or combustible liquids including but not limited to gasoline and heating oil which are currently or which were previously located on the Property; ***NOTE: Wis. Adm. Code, Chapter Comm 10 contains registration and operation rules for such underground and aboveground storage tanks.***

(n) material violations of environmental laws or other laws or agreements regulating the use of the Property;

(o) high voltage electric (100 KV or greater) or steel natural gas transmission lines located on but not directly serving the Property;

(p) other conditions or occurrences which would significantly reduce the value of the Property to a reasonable person with knowledge of the nature and scope of the condition or occurrence.

■ REAL ESTATE CONDITION REPORT: Wisconsin law requires owners of property which includes 1-4 dwelling units to provide buyers with a Real Estate Condition Report. Excluded from this requirement are sales of property that has never been inhabited, sales exempt from the real estate transfer fee, and sales by certain court-appointed fiduciaries, (for example, personal representatives who have never occupied the Property). The form of the Report is found in Wis. Stat. § 709.03. The law provides: "709.02 Disclosure . . . the owner of the property shall furnish, not later than 10 days after acceptance of the contract of sale . . . , to the prospective buyer of the property a completed copy of the report . . . A prospective buyer who does not receive a report within the 10 days may, within 2 business days after the end of that 10 day period, rescind the contract of sale . . . by delivering a written notice of rescission to the owner or the owner's agent." Buyer may also have certain rescission rights if a Real Estate Condition Report disclosing defects is furnished before expiration of the 10 days, but after the Offer is submitted to Seller. Buyer should review the report form or consult with an attorney for additional information regarding these rescission rights.

■ PROPERTY DIMENSIONS AND SURVEYS: Buyer acknowledges that any land, building or room dimensions, or total acreage or building square footage figures, provided to Buyer by Seller or by a broker, may be approximate because of rounding or other reasons, unless verified by survey or other means. Buyer also acknowledges that there are various formulas used to calculate total square footage of buildings and that total square footage figures will vary dependent upon the formula used. ***CAUTION: Buyer should verify total square footage formula, total square footage/acreage figures, land, building or room dimensions, if material.***

■ INSPECTIONS: Seller agrees to allow Buyer's inspectors reasonable access to the Property upon reasonable notice if the inspections are reasonably necessary to satisfy the contingencies in this Offer. Buyer agrees to promptly provide copies of all such inspection reports to Seller, and to listing broker if Property is listed. Furthermore, Buyer agrees to promptly restore the Property to its original condition after Buyer's inspections are completed, unless otherwise agreed with Seller. An "inspection" is defined as an observation of the Property which does not include testing of the Property, other than testing for leaking carbon monoxide, or testing for leaking LP gas or natural gas used as a fuel source, which are hereby authorized.

■ TESTING: Except as otherwise provided, Seller's authorization for inspections does not authorize Buyer to conduct testing of the Property. A "test" is defined as the taking of samples of materials such as soils, water, air or building materials from the Property and the laboratory or other analysis of these materials. If Buyer requires testing, testing contingencies must be specifically provided for at lines 180 - 186, 317 - 320 or in an addendum per line 316. Note: Any contingency authorizing such tests should specify the areas of the Property to be tested, the purpose of the test, (e.g., to determine if environmental contamination is present), any limitations on Buyer's testing and any other material terms of the contingency (e.g., Buyer's obligation to return the Property to its original condition). Seller acknowledges that certain inspections or tests may detect environmental pollution which may be required to be reported to the Wisconsin Department of Natural Resources.

■ PRE-CLOSING INSPECTION: At a reasonable time, pre-approved by Seller or Seller's agent, within 3 days before closing, Buyer shall have the right to inspect the Property to determine that there has been no significant change in the condition of the Property, except for ordinary wear and tear and changes approved by Buyer, and that any defects Seller has elected to cure have been repaired in a good and workmanlike manner.

■ PROPERTY DAMAGE BETWEEN ACCEPTANCE AND CLOSING: Seller shall maintain the Property until the earlier of closing or occupancy of Buyer in materially the same condition as of the date of acceptance of this Offer, except for ordinary wear and tear. If, prior to closing, the Property is damaged in an amount of not more than five per cent (5%) of the selling price, Seller shall be obligated to repair the Property and restore it to the same condition that it was on the day of this Offer. If the damage shall exceed such sum, Seller shall promptly notify Buyer in writing of the damage and this Offer may be canceled at option of Buyer. Should Buyer elect to carry out this Offer despite such damage, Buyer shall be entitled to the insurance proceeds relating to the damage to the Property, plus a credit towards the purchase price equal to the amount of Seller's deductible on such policy. However, if this sale is financed by a land contract or a mortgage to Seller, the insurance proceeds shall be held in trust for the sole purpose of restoring the Property.

FIXTURES A "Fixture" is defined as an item of property which is physically attached to or so closely associated with land or improvements so as to be treated as part of the real estate, including, without limitation, physically attached items not easily removable without damage to the Property, items specifically adapted to the Property, and items customarily treated as fixtures, including, but not limited to, all: garden bulbs; plants; shrubs and trees; screen and storm doors and windows; electric lighting fixtures; window shades; curtain and traverse rods; blinds and shutters; central heating and cooling units and attached equipment; water heaters and softeners; sump pumps; attached or fitted floor coverings; awnings; attached antennas, satellite dishes and component parts; garage door openers and remote controls; installed security systems; central vacuum systems and accessories; in-ground sprinkler systems and component parts; built-in appliances; ceiling fans; fences; storage buildings on permanent foundations and docks/piers on permanent foundations. ***NOTE: The terms of the Offer will determine what items are included/excluded. Address rented fixtures (e.g., water softeners), if any.***

FIGURE D (CONTINUED)

Completed WB-11 Residential Offer to Purchase

PROPERTY ADDRESS: ______ [page 3 of 5, WB-11]

TIME IS OF THE ESSENCE "Time is of the Essence" as to: (1) earnest money payment(s); (2) binding acceptance; (3) occupancy; (4) date of closing; (5) contingency deadlines STRIKE AS APPLICABLE and all other dates and deadlines in this Offer except: ______ ______. If "Time is of the Essence" applies to a date or deadline, failure to perform by the exact date or deadline is a breach of contract. If "Time is of the Essence" does not apply to a date or deadline, then performance within a reasonable time of the date or deadline is allowed before a breach occurs.

DATES AND DEADLINES Deadlines expressed as a number of "days" from an event, such as acceptance, are calculated by excluding the day the event occurred and by counting subsequent calendar days. The deadline expires at midnight on the last day. Deadlines expressed as a specific number of "business days" exclude Saturdays, Sundays, any legal public holiday under Wisconsin or Federal law, and other day designated by the President such that the postal service does not receive registered mail or make regular deliveries on that day. Deadlines expressed as a specific number of "hours" from the occurrence of an event, such as receipt of a notice, are calculated from the exact time of the event, and by counting 24 hours per calendar day. Deadlines expressed as a specific day of the calendar year or as the day of a specific event, such as closing, expire at midnight of that day.

THE FINANCING CONTINGENCY PROVISIONS AT LINES 149 - 163 ARE A PART OF THIS OFFER IF LINE 149 IS MARKED, SUCH AS WITH AN "X". THEY ARE NOT PART OF THIS OFFER IF LINE 149 IS MARKED N/A OR IS NOT MARKED.

☐ **FINANCING CONTINGENCY:** This Offer is contingent upon Buyer being able to obtain a ______ INSERT LOAN PROGRAM OR SOURCE first mortgage loan commitment as described below, within ______ days of acceptance of this Offer. The financing selected shall be in an amount of not less than $______ for a term of not less than ______ years, amortized over not less than ______ years. Initial monthly payments of principal and interest shall not exceed $______. Monthly payments may also include 1/12th of the estimated net annual real estate taxes, hazard insurance premiums, and private mortgage insurance premiums. The mortgage may not include a prepayment premium. Buyer agrees to pay a loan fee not to exceed ______% of the loan. (Loan fee refers to discount points and/or loan origination fee, but DOES NOT include Buyer's other closing costs.) If the purchase price under this Offer is modified, the financed amount, unless otherwise provided, shall be adjusted to the same percentage of the purchase price as in this contingency and the monthly payments shall be adjusted as necessary to maintain the term and amortization stated above. **CHECK AND COMPLETE APPLICABLE FINANCING PROVISION AT LINE 159 OR 160.**

☐ **FIXED RATE FINANCING:** The annual rate of interest shall not exceed ______%.

☐ **ADJUSTABLE RATE FINANCING:** The initial annual interest rate shall not exceed ______%. The initial interest rate shall be fixed for ______ months, at which time the interest rate may be increased not more than ______% per year. The maximum interest rate during the mortgage term shall not exceed ______%. Monthly payments of principal and interest may be adjusted to reflect interest changes.

LOAN COMMITMENT: Buyer agrees to pay all customary financing costs (including closing fees), to apply for financing promptly, and to provide evidence of application promptly upon request by Seller. If Buyer qualifies for the financing described in this Offer or other financing acceptable to Buyer, Buyer agrees to deliver to Seller a copy of the written loan commitment no later than the deadline for loan commitment at line 150. **Buyer's delivery of a copy of any written loan commitment to Seller (even if subject to conditions) shall satisfy the Buyer's financing contingency unless accompanied by a notice of unacceptability. *CAUTION: BUYER, BUYER'S LENDER AND AGENTS OF BUYER OR SELLER SHOULD NOT DELIVER A LOAN COMMITMENT TO SELLER WITHOUT BUYER'S PRIOR APPROVAL OR UNLESS ACCOMPANIED BY A NOTICE OF UNACCEPTABILITY.***

SELLER TERMINATION RIGHTS: If Buyer does not make timely delivery of said commitment, Seller may terminate this Offer if Seller delivers a written notice of termination to Buyer prior to Seller's actual receipt of a copy of Buyer's written loan commitment.

FINANCING UNAVAILABILITY: If financing is not available on the terms stated in this Offer (and Buyer has not already delivered an acceptable loan commitment for other financing to Seller), Buyer shall promptly deliver written notice to Seller of same including copies of lender(s)' rejection letter(s) or other evidence of unavailability. Unless a specific loan source is named in this Offer, Seller shall then have 10 days to give Buyer written notice of Seller's decision to finance this transaction on the same terms set forth in this Offer, and this Offer shall remain in full force and effect, with the time for closing extended accordingly. If Seller's notice is not timely given, this Offer shall be null and void. Buyer authorizes Seller to obtain any credit information reasonably appropriate to determine Buyer's credit worthiness for Seller financing.

ADDITIONAL PROVISIONS/CONTINGENCIES ______

TITLE EVIDENCE

■ CONVEYANCE OF TITLE: **Upon payment of the purchase price, Seller shall convey the Property by warranty deed (or other conveyance as provided herein)** free and clear of all liens and encumbrances, except: municipal and zoning ordinances and agreements entered under them, recorded easements for the distribution of utility and municipal services, recorded building and use restrictions and covenants, general taxes levied in the year of closing and ______ ______ (provided none of the foregoing prohibit present use of the Property), which constitutes merchantable title for purposes of this transaction. Seller further agrees to complete and execute the documents necessary to record the conveyance. ***WARNING: Municipal and zoning ordinances, recorded building and use restrictions, covenants and easements may prohibit certain improvements or uses and therefore should be reviewed, particularly if Buyer contemplates making improvements to Property or a use other than the current use.***

■ FORM OF TITLE EVIDENCE: Seller shall give evidence of title in the form of an owner's policy of title insurance in the amount of the purchase price on a current ALTA form issued by an insurer licensed to write title insurance in Wisconsin. ***CAUTION: IF TITLE EVIDENCE WILL BE GIVEN BY ABSTRACT, STRIKE TITLE INSURANCE PROVISIONS AND INSERT ABSTRACT PROVISIONS.***

FIGURE D (CONTINUED)

Completed WB-11 Residential Offer to Purchase

[page 4 of 5, WB-11]

■ PROVISION OF MERCHANTABLE TITLE: Seller shall pay all costs of providing title evidence. For purposes of closing, title evidence shall be acceptable if the commitment for the required title insurance is delivered to Buyer's attorney or Buyer not less than 3 business days before closing, showing title to the Property as of a date no more than 15 days before delivery of such title evidence to be merchantable, subject only to liens which will be paid out of the proceeds of closing and standard title insurance requirements and exceptions, as appropriate. ***CAUTION: BUYER SHOULD CONSIDER UPDATING THE EFFECTIVE DATE OF THE TITLE COMMITMENT PRIOR TO CLOSING OR A "GAP ENDORSEMENT" WHICH WOULD INSURE OVER LIENS FILED BETWEEN THE EFFECTIVE DATE OF THE COMMITMENT AND THE DATE THE DEED IS RECORDED.***

■ TITLE ACCEPTABLE FOR CLOSING: If title is not acceptable for closing, Buyer shall notify Seller in writing of objections to title by the time set for closing. In such event, Seller shall have a reasonable time, but not exceeding 15 days, to remove the objections, and the time for closing shall be extended as necessary for this purpose. In the event that Seller is unable to remove said objections, Buyer shall have 5 days from receipt of notice thereof, to deliver written notice waiving the objections, and the time for closing shall be extended accordingly. If Buyer does not waive the objections, this Offer shall be null and void. Providing title evidence acceptable for closing does not extinguish Seller's obligations to give merchantable title to Buyer.

■ SPECIAL ASSESSMENTS: Special assessments, if any, for work actually commenced or levied prior to date of this Offer shall be paid by Seller no later than closing. All other special assessments shall be paid by Buyer. ***CAUTION: Consider a special agreement if area assessments, property owner's association assessments or other expenses are contemplated.*** "Other expenses" are one-time charges or ongoing use fees for public improvements (other than those resulting in special assessments) relating to curb, gutter, street, sidewalk, sanitary and stormwater and storm sewer (including all sewer mains and hook-up and interceptor charges), parks, street lighting and street trees, and impact fees for other public facilities, as defined in Wis. Stat. §66.55(1)(c) & (f).

DELIVERY/RECEIPT Unless otherwise stated in this Offer, any signed document transmitted by facsimile machine (fax) shall be treated in all manner and respects as an original document and the signature of any Party upon a document transmitted by fax shall be considered an original signature. Personal delivery to, or actual receipt by, any named Buyer or Seller constitutes personal delivery to, or actual receipt by Buyer or Seller Once received, a notice cannot be withdrawn by the Party delivering the notice without the consent of the Party receiving the notice. A Party may not unilaterally reinstate a contingency after a notice of a contingency waiver has been received by the other Party. **The delivery/receipt provisions in this Offer may be modified when appropriate (e.g., when mail delivery is not desirable (see lines 24 - 30) or when a party will not be personally available to receive a notice (see line 286)).** Buyer and Seller authorize the agents of Buyer and Seller to distribute copies of the Offer to Buyer's lender, appraisers, title insurance companies and any other settlement service providers for the transaction as defined by the Real Estate Settlement Procedures Act (RESPA).

DEFAULT Seller and Buyer each have the legal duty to use good faith and due diligence in completing the terms and conditions of this Offer. A material failure to perform any obligation under this Offer is a default which may subject the defaulting party to liability for damages or other legal remedies.

If Buyer defaults, Seller may:

(1) sue for specific performance and request the earnest money as partial payment of the purchase price; or

(2) terminate the Offer and have the option to: (a) request the earnest money as liquidated damages; or (b) direct Broker to return the earnest money and have the option to sue for actual damages.

If Seller defaults, Buyer may:

(1) sue for specific performance; or

(2) terminate the Offer and request the return of the earnest money, sue for actual damages, or both.

In addition, the Parties may seek any other remedies available in law or equity.

The Parties understand that the availability of any judicial remedy will depend upon the circumstances of the situation and the discretion of the courts. If either Party defaults, the Parties may renegotiate the Offer or seek nonjudicial dispute resolution instead of the remedies outlined above. By agreeing to binding arbitration, the Parties may lose the right to litigate in a court of law those disputes covered by the arbitration agreement.

NOTE: IF ACCEPTED, THIS OFFER CAN CREATE A LEGALLY ENFORCEABLE CONTRACT. BOTH PARTIES SHOULD READ THIS DOCUMENT CAREFULLY. BROKERS MAY PROVIDE A GENERAL EXPLANATION OF THE PROVISIONS OF THE OFFER BUT ARE PROHIBITED BY LAW FROM GIVING ADVICE OR OPINIONS CONCERNING YOUR LEGAL RIGHTS UNDER THIS OFFER OR HOW TITLE SHOULD BE TAKEN AT CLOSING. AN ATTORNEY SHOULD BE CONSULTED IF LEGAL ADVICE IS NEEDED.

EARNEST MONEY

■ HELD BY: Unless otherwise agreed, earnest money shall be paid to and held in the trust account of the listing broker (buyer's agent if Property is not listed or Seller's account if no broker is involved), until applied to purchase price or otherwise disbursed as provided in the Offer. ***CAUTION: Should persons other than a broker hold earnest money, an escrow agreement should be drafted by the Parties or an attorney. If someone other than Buyer makes payment of earnest money, consider a special disbursement agreement.***

■ DISBURSEMENT: If negotiations do not result in an accepted offer, the earnest money shall be promptly disbursed (after clearance from payor's depository institution if earnest money is paid by check) to the person(s) who paid the earnest money. At closing, earnest money shall be disbursed according to the closing statement. If this Offer does not close, the earnest money shall be disbursed according to a written disbursement agreement signed by all Parties to this Offer (Note: Wis. Adm. Code s. RL 18.09(1)(b) provides that an offer to purchase is not a written disbursement agreement pursuant to which the broker may disburse). If said disbursement agreement has not been delivered to broker within 60 days after the date set for closing, broker may disburse the earnest money: (1) as directed by an attorney who has reviewed the transaction and does not represent Buyer or Seller; (2) into a court hearing a lawsuit involving the earnest money and all Parties to this Offer; (3) as directed by court order; or (4) any other disbursement required or allowed by law. Broker may retain legal services to direct disbursement per (1) or to file an interpleader action per (2) and broker may deduct from the earnest money any costs and reasonable attorneys fees, not to exceed $250, prior to disbursement.

■ LEGAL RIGHTS/ACTION: Broker's disbursement of earnest money does not determine the legal rights of the Parties in relation to this Offer. Buyer's or Seller's legal right to earnest money cannot be determined by broker. At least 30 days prior to disbursement per (1) or (4) above, broker shall send Buyer and Seller notice of the disbursement by certified mail. If Buyer or Seller disagree with broker's proposed disbursement, a lawsuit may be filed to obtain a court order regarding disbursement. Small Claims Court has jurisdiction over all earnest money disputes arising out of the sale of residential property with 1-4 dwelling units and certain other earnest money disputes. Buyer and Seller should consider consulting attorneys regarding their legal rights under this Offer in case of a dispute. Both Parties agree to hold the broker harmless from any liability for good faith disbursement of earnest money in accordance with this Offer or applicable Department of Regulation and Licensing regulations concerning earnest money. See Wis. Adm. Code Ch. RL 18.

ENTIRE CONTRACT This Offer, including any amendments to it, contains the entire agreement of the Buyer and Seller regarding the transaction. All prior negotiations and discussions have been merged into this Offer. This agreement binds and inures to the benefit of the Parties to this Offer and their successors in interest.

FIGURE D (CONTINUED)

Completed WB-11 Residential Offer to Purchase

Wisconsin Legal Blank Co., Inc.

PROPERTY ADDRESS: 2901 Newman Street, Madison, Wisconsin [page 5 of 5, WB-11]

OPTIONAL PROVISIONS: THE PROVISIONS ON LINES 278 THROUGH 316 ARE A PART OF THIS OFFER IF MARKED, SUCH AS WITH AN "X". THEY ARE NOT PART OF THIS OFFER IF MARKED N/A OR ARE LEFT BLANK (EXCEPT AS PROVIDED AT LINES 280 - 281).

n/a **SALE OF BUYER'S PROPERTY CONTINGENCY:** This Offer is contingent upon the sale and closing of Buyer's property located at ________________, no later than ________________. Seller may keep Seller's Property on the market for sale and accept secondary offers. **If this contingency is made a part of this Offer, lines 282 - 286 are also a part of this offer unless marked N/A at line 282 or otherwise deleted.**

n/a **CONTINUED MARKETING:** If Seller accepts a bona fide secondary offer, Seller may give written notice to Buyer of acceptance. If Buyer does not deliver to Seller a written waiver of sale of Buyer's property contingency and ________________ **[INSERT OTHER REQUIREMENTS, IF ANY (e.g., PAYMENT OF ADDITIONAL EARNEST MONEY, WAIVER OF ALL CONTINGENCIES, OR PROVIDING EVIDENCE OF SALE OR BRIDGE LOAN, etc.)]** within ________ hours of Buyer's actual receipt of said notice, this Offer shall be null and void.

n/a **SECONDARY OFFER:** This Offer is secondary to a prior accepted offer. This Offer shall become primary upon delivery of written notice to Buyer that this Offer is primary. Unless otherwise provided, Seller is not obligated to give Buyer notice prior to any deadline, nor is any particular secondary buyer given the right to be made primary ahead of other secondary buyers. Buyer may declare this Offer null and void by delivering written notice of withdrawal to Seller prior to delivery of Seller's notice that this Offer is primary. Buyer may not deliver notice of withdrawal earlier than ________ days after acceptance of this Offer. All other Offer deadlines which are run from acceptance shall run from the time this Offer becomes primary.

n/a **PRE/POST CLOSING OCCUPANCY:** Occupancy of ________________ shall be given to Buyer on ________________ at ________ am/pm. (Seller)(Buyer) [STRIKE ONE] shall pay an occupancy charge of $________ per day or partial day of pre/post-closing occupancy. Payment shall be due at the beginning of the occupancy period. Any unearned post closing occupancy fee (shall)(shall not) [STRIKE ONE] be refunded based on actual occupancy. ***CAUTION: Consider a special agreement regarding occupancy escrow, insurance, utilities, maintenance, keys, etc.***

n/a **INSPECTION CONTINGENCY:** This Offer is contingent upon a Wisconsin registered home inspector performing a home inspection of the Property, and an inspection, by a qualified independent inspector, of ________________ which discloses no defects as defined below. This contingency shall be deemed satisfied unless Buyer, within ________ days of acceptance, delivers to Seller, and to listing broker if Property is listed, a copy of the inspector's written inspection report(s) and a written notice listing the defect(s) identified in the inspection report(s) to which Buyer objects. ***CAUTION: A proposed amendment will not satisfy this notice requirement.*** Buyer shall order the inspection and be responsible for all costs of inspection, including any inspections required by lender or as follow-up inspections to the home inspection. **Note: This contingency only authorizes inspections, not testing. (See lines 97 - 110.)**

■ RIGHT TO CURE: Seller (shall) (shall not) [STRIKE ONE] have a right to cure the defects. (Seller shall have a right to cure if no choice is indicated.) If Seller has right to cure, Seller may satisfy this contingency by: (1) delivering a written notice within 10 days of receipt of Buyer's notice of Seller's election to cure defects, (2) curing the defects in a good and workmanlike manner and (3) delivering to Buyer a written report detailing the work done no later than 3 days prior to closing. This Offer shall be null and void if Buyer makes timely delivery of the above notice and report and: (1) Seller does not have a right to cure or (2) Seller has a right to cure but: a) Seller delivers notice that Seller will not cure or b) Seller does not timely deliver the notice of election to cure.

■ "DEFECT" DEFINED: For the purposes of this contingency, a defect is defined as a structural, mechanical or other condition that would have a significant adverse effect on the value of the Property; that would significantly impair the health or safety of future occupants of the Property; or that if not repaired, removed or replaced would significantly shorten or have a significant adverse effect on the expected normal life of the Property. Defects do not include structural, mechanical or other conditions the nature and extent of which Buyer had actual knowledge or written notice before signing this Offer.

n/a **ADDENDA:** The attached ________________ is/are made part of this Offer.

ADDITIONAL PROVISIONS/CONTINGENCIES ________________

This Offer was drafted on Nov. 22, 2009 [date] by [Licensee and firm] Joe Dannen, Quality Realty.

(x)________________ 452-63-9607 Nov. 22, 2009
Buyer's Signature ▲ Print Name Here: ▶ Jay Norris Social Security No. or FEIN ▲ (Optional) Date ▲

(x)________________ 425-08-9142 Nov. 22, 2009
Buyer's Signature ▲ Print Name Here: ▶ Linda Norris Social Security No. or FEIN ▲ (Optional) Date ▲

EARNEST MONEY RECEIPT Broker acknowledges receipt of earnest money as per line 8 of the above Offer. **(See lines 247 - 271.)**

________________ Broker (By) ________________

SELLER ACCEPTS THIS OFFER. THE WARRANTIES, REPRESENTATIONS AND COVENANTS MADE IN THIS OFFER SURVIVE CLOSING AND THE CONVEYANCE OF THE PROPERTY. SELLER AGREES TO CONVEY THE PROPERTY ON THE TERMS AND CONDITIONS AS SET FORTH HEREIN AND ACKNOWLEDGES RECEIPT OF A COPY OF THIS OFFER.

(x)________________
Seller's Signature ▲ Print Name Here: ▶ Social Security No. or FEIN ▲ (Optional) Date ▲

(x)________________
Seller's Signature ▲ Print Name Here: ▶ Social Security No. or FEIN ▲ (Optional) Date ▲

This Offer was presented to Seller by Joe Dannen on November 23, 2009, at 3:00 ~~a.m.~~/p.m.

THIS OFFER IS REJECTED ________ ________ THIS OFFER IS COUNTERED [See attached counter] JN MN Nov. 23, 2009
Seller Initials ▲ Date ▲ Seller Initials ▲ Date ▲

FIGURE E

Blank Counter-Offer

Approved by Wisconsin Department of Regulation and Licensing
7-1-99 (Optional Use Date) 1-1-00 (Mandatory Use Date)

Wisconsin Legal Blank Co., Inc.
Milwaukee, Wis.

WB-44 COUNTER-OFFER

Counter-Offer No. ________ by (Buyer/Seller) STRIKE ONE

The Offer to Purchase dated ____________________ and signed by Buyer, ____, for purchase of real estate at ____ is rejected and the following counter-offer is hereby made. **All terms and conditions remain the same as stated in the Offer to Purchase except the following: [CAUTION: This Counter-Offer does not include the terms or conditions in any other Counter-Offer unless incorporated by reference.]**

ANY WARRANTIES AND REPRESENTATIONS MADE IN THIS COUNTER-OFFER SURVIVE THE CLOSING OF THIS TRANSACTION. This Counter-Offer is binding upon Seller and Buyer only if a copy of the accepted Counter-Offer is delivered to the Party making the Counter-Offer on or before ____ (Time is of the essence). Delivery of the accepted Counter-Offer may be made in any manner specified in the Offer to Purchase, unless otherwise provided in this Counter-Offer. ***NOTE: The Party makng this Counter-Offer may withdraw the Counter-Offer prior to acceptance and delivery as provided at lines 33 to 36.***

This Counter-Offer was drafted by ____ on ______________.
Licensee and Firm ▲ Date ▲

________________________________ ________ ________________________________ ________
Signature of Party Making Counter-Offer ▲ Date ▲ Signature of Party Making Counter-Offer ▲ Date ▲

________________________________ ________ ________________________________ ________
Signature of Party Accepting Counter-Offer ▲ Date ▲ Signature of Party Accepting Counter-Offer ▲ Date ▲

This Counter-Offer was presented by ____ on ______________.
Licensee and Firm ▲ Date ▲

This Counter-Offer is **(rejected) (countered)** STRIKE ONE (Party's Initials) ______________ (Party's Initials) ______________

Note: Provisions from a previous Counter-Offer may be included by reproduction of the entire provision or incorporation be reference. Provisions incorporated by reference may be indicated in the subsequent Counter-Offer by specifying the number of the provision or the lines containing the provision. In transactions involving more than one Counter-Offer, the Counter-Offer referred to should be clearly specified. **NOTE: Number this Counter-Offer sequentially, e.g. Counter-Offer No. 1 by Seller, Counter-Offer No. 2 by Buyer, etc.** **ATTACH THIS COUNTER-OFFER TO THE OFFER TO PURCHASE-INSERT SOCIAL SECURITY NUMBERS OR FEIN ON OFFER.**

FIGURE F

Completed Counter-Offer

Approved by Wisconsin Department of Regulation and Licensing
7-1-99 (Optional Use Date) 1-1-00 (Mandatory Use Date)

Wisconsin Legal Blank Co., Inc.
Milwaukee, Wis.

WB-44 COUNTER-OFFER

Counter-Offer No. ________ by (Buyer/Seller) STRIKE ONE

The Offer to Purchase dated 11/22/09 and signed by Buyer, Jay and Linda Norris, for purchase of real estate at 2901 Newman Street, Madison, WI 53705 is rejected and the following counter-offer is hereby made. **All terms and conditions remain the same as stated in the Offer to Purchase except the following: [CAUTION: This Counter-Offer does not include the terms or conditions in any other Counter-Offer unless incorporated by reference.]**

The selling price is increased to $154,000 (One Hundred and Fifty-Four Thousand Dollars)

ANY WARRANTIES AND REPRESENTATIONS MADE IN THIS COUNTER-OFFER SURVIVE THE CLOSING OF THIS TRANSACTION. This Counter-Offer is binding upon Seller and Buyer only if a copy of the accepted Counter-Offer is delivered to the Party making the Counter-Offer on or before Nov. 24, 2009 (Time is of the essence). Delivery of the accepted Counter-Offer may be made in any manner specified in the Offer to Purchase, unless otherwise provided in this Counter-Offer. ***NOTE: The Party makng this Counter-Offer may withdraw the Counter-Offer prior to acceptance and delivery as provided at lines 33 to 36.***

This Counter-Offer was drafted by Joe Dannen, Quality Realty on 11/23/09
Licensee and Firm ▲ Date ▲

Jack Nelson	11/23/09	Mary Nelson	11/23/09
Signature of Party Making Counter-Offer ▲	Date ▲	Signature of Party Making Counter-Offer ▲	Date ▲
Jay Norris	11/24/09	Linda Norris	11/24/09
Signature of Party Accepting Counter-Offer ▲	Date ▲	Signature of Party Accepting Counter-Offer ▲	Date ▲

This Counter-Offer was presented by Joe Dannen, Quality Realty on 11/24/09
Licensee and Firm ▲ Date ▲

This Counter-Offer is **(rejected) (countered)** STRIKE ONE (Party's Initials) ________ (Party's Initials) ________

Note: Provisions from a previous Counter-Offer may be included by reproduction of the entire provision or incorporation be reference. Provisions incorporated by reference may be indicated in the subsequent Counter-Offer by specifying the number of the provision or the lines containing the provision. In transactions involving more than one Counter-Offer, the Counter-Offer referred to should be clearly specified. **NOTE: Number this Counter-Offer sequentially, e.g. Counter-Offer No. 1 by Seller, Counter-Offer No. 2 by Buyer, etc.**

ATTACH THIS COUNTER-OFFER TO THE OFFER TO PURCHASE-INSERT SOCIAL SECURITY NUMBERS OR FEIN ON OFFER.

FIGURE G

Blank WB-40 Amendment to Offer to Purchase

Approved by the Wisconsin Department of Regulation and Licensing
7-1-99 (Optional Use Date) 1-1-00 (Mandatory Use Date)

Wisconsin Legal Blank Co., Inc.
Milwaukee, Wis.

WB-40 AMENDMENT TO OFFER TO PURCHASE

Caution: Use A WB-40 Amendment If Both Parties Will Be Agreeing To Modify The Terms Of The Offer. Use A WB-41 Notice If A Party Is Giving A Notice Which Does Not Require The Other Party's Agreement.

Buyer and Seller agree to amend the Offer dated ____________, ______, and accepted ____________, ______, for the purchase and sale of real estate at ____ as follows:

( ) Closing date is changed from ____________ to ____________.

( ) Purchase price is changed from $____________ to $____________.

( ) Occupancy date is changed from ____________ to ____________.

( ) Occupancy charge is changed from $____________ to $____________.

( ) Other: ____

ALL OTHER TERMS OF THE OFFER TO PURCHASE AND ANY PRIOR AMENDMENTS REMAIN THE SAME.

This Amendment is binding upon Seller and Buyer only if a copy of the accepted Amendment is delivered to the Party offering the Amendment on or before ____________________ (Time is of the essence). Delivery of the accepted Amendment may be made in any manner specified in the Offer to Purchase, unless otherwise provided in this Amendment. ***NOTE: The Party offering this Amendment may withdraw the offered Amendment prior to acceptance and delivery as provided at lines 34 to 37.***

This Amendment was drafted by ____________________ on ____________.
Licensee and Firm ▲ Date ▲

This Amendment was presented by ____________________ on ____________.
Licensee and Firm ▲ Date ▲

____________________ ____________________
Buyer's Signature ▲ Date ▲ Buyer's Signature ▲ Date ▲

____________________ ____________________
Seller's Signature ▲ Date ▲ Seller's Signature ▲ Date ▲

NOTE: ATTACH THIS AMENDMENT TO THE OFFER TO PURCHASE.

FIGURE H

Completed WB-40 Amendment to Offer to Purchase

Approved by the Wisconsin Department of Regulation and Licensing
7-1-99 (Optional Use Date) 1-1-00 (Mandatory Use Date)

Wisconsin Legal Blank Co., Inc.
Milwaukee, Wis.

WB-40 AMENDMENT TO OFFER TO PURCHASE

Caution: Use A WB-40 Amendment If Both Parties Will Be Agreeing To Modify The Terms Of The Offer. Use A WB-41 Notice If A Party Is Giving A Notice Which Does Not Require The Other Party's Agreement.

Buyer and Seller agree to amend the Offer dated Nov. 22, 2009, and accepted Nov. 23, 2009, for the purchase and sale of real estate at ______________________________ as follows:

( ) Closing date is changed from Dec. 21, 2009 to Dec. 23, 2009.
( ) Purchase price is changed from $______ to $______.
( ) Occupancy date is changed from ______ to ______.
( ) Occupancy charge is changed from $______ to $______.
( ) Other: ______________________________

ALL OTHER TERMS OF THE OFFER TO PURCHASE AND ANY PRIOR AMENDMENTS REMAIN THE SAME.

This Amendment is binding upon Seller and Buyer only if a copy of the accepted Amendment is delivered to the Party offering the Amendment on or before Dec. 6, 2009 (Time is of the essence). Delivery of the accepted Amendment may be made in any manner specified in the Offer to Purchase, unless otherwise provided in this Amendment. ***NOTE: The Party offering this Amendment may withdraw the offered Amendment prior to acceptance and delivery as provided at lines 34 to 37.***

This Amendment was drafted by Joe Dannen, Quality Reality (Licensee and Firm ▲) on 11/23/09 (Date ▲).

This Amendment was presented by Joe Dannen, Quality Reality (Licensee and Firm ▲) on 11/23/09 (Date ▲).

Buyer's Signature ▲ Jay Norris	Date ▲ 12/09/09	Buyer's Signature ▲ Linda Norris	Date ▲ 12/09/09
Seller's Signature ▲ Jack Nelson	Date ▲ 12/09/09	Seller's Signature ▲ Mary Nelson	Date ▲ 12/09/09

NOTE: ATTACH THIS AMENDMENT TO THE OFFER TO PURCHASE.

FIGURE I

Blank WB-41 Notice Relating to Offer to Purchase

Approved by the Wisconsin Department of Regulation and Licensing
7-1-99 (Optional Use Date) 1-1-00 (Mandatory Use Date)

Wisconsin Legal Blank Co., Inc.
Milwaukee. Wis.

WB-41 NOTICE RELATING TO OFFER TO PURCHASE

Caution:* *Use A WB-41 Notice If A Party Is Giving A Notice Which Does Not Require The Other Party's Agreement. Use A WB-40 Amendment If Both Parties Will Be Agreeing to Modify The Terms Of The Offer.

This Notice by (Seller)(Buyer) STRIKE ONE relates to the Offer to Purchase dated ____________, ______, and accepted ____________, ______, for the purchase and sale of real estate at ____________________ ____________________.

(1) The following are no longer contingencies or conditions to the Offer to Purchase (Note: Attach supporting documents, if required): ____________________

(2) Notice is given that: ____________________

This Notice was drafted by ____________________ on ____________.
Licensee and Firm ▲ Date ▲

This Notice was delivered by ____________________ on ____________,
Date ▲

at ________ a.m./p.m. STRIKE ONE using the following method of delivery: ☐ mail, ☐ fax, ☐ personal delivery,
☐ other ____________________ CHECK AS APPLICABLE.

This Notice was presented by ____________________ on ____________, at ________
Licensee and Firm ▲ Date ▲ a.m./p.m. ▲

(x) ____________________ (x) ____________________
Signature of Party Giving Notice ▲ Date ▲ Signature of Party Giving Notice ▲ Date ▲

NOTE: ATTACH THIS NOTICE TO THE OFFER TO PURCHASE.

FIGURE J

Blank Buyer's Closing Statement

FORM 930-B Buyer's Closing Statement

Wisconsin Legal Blank Co., Inc.
Milwaukee, WI

BROKER

BUYER'S CLOSING STATEMENT

Property Location ____________________

Seller(s) ____________________ Address ____________________

Buyer(s) ____________________ Address ____________________

Sale Contract Date __________ Closing Date __________ Closed At ____________________

BUYER'S SETTLEMENT WITH BROKER	DUE SELLER	CREDIT BUYER
1. Purchase Price		
2. Earnest Money		
3. Downpayment		
4. Mortgages (Assumed by Buyer)		
5. Land Contracts (Assumed by Buyer)		
6. Trust Funds Due Seller by Mortgagee		
7. Delinquent Taxes (if Assumed) for Years		
8. Seller's Share of Taxes: for ______ Prorated from ______ through ______ Last Year's Taxes ______ Prorated Basis @ $ ______ Per ______		
9. Special Assessments Assumed by Buyer		
10. Rent Prorated (list below)		
11. LP Gas/Fuel Oil and Other Items on Premises		
12. Recording Fees		
13. Transfer Fees		
14.		
15.		
16.		
17.		
18.		
Totals		

19. Daily Use and Occupancy Charge is $__________
20. Date of Vacating Property __________
21. Escrow: __________
22. __________
23. __________

Less Credit to Buyer __________

Less: Mortgage or Land Contract Executed by Buyer to Seller __________

Balance Due Seller __________

TENANT'S NAME	MONTHLY RENTAL	DUE DATE	PAID UP TO	PRORATED AMOUNT

THIS STATEMENT IS ACCEPTED AS CORRECT ____________________, 20______

__________________ Buyer __________________ Seller

__________________ Buyer __________________ Seller

Source: Published with permission, Wisconsin Legal Blank Company, Inc. Line numbers have been added by the publisher for use in this textbook.

FIGURE K

Completed Buyer's Closing Statement

FORM 930-B Buyer's Closing Statement

Wisconsin Legal Blank Co., Inc.
Milwaukee, WI

BROKER

Quality Realty

BUYER'S CLOSING STATEMENT

Property Location 2901 Newman Street, Madison, WI 53705

Seller(s) Jack and Mary Nelson Address

Buyer(s) Jay and Linda Norris Address

Sale Contract Date 11/24/09 Closing Date 12/23/09 Closed At

BUYER'S SETTLEMENT WITH BROKER	DUE SELLER		CREDIT BUYER	
1. Purchase Price	$154,000	00		
2. Earnest Money			3,000	00
3. Downpayment				
4. Mortgages (Assumed by Buyer)				
5. Land Contracts (Assumed by Buyer)				
6. Trust Funds Due Seller by Mortgagee				
7. Delinquent Taxes (if Assumed) for Years				
8. Seller's Share of Taxes: for 2009 Prorated from 01/09 through 12/22/09 Last Year's Taxes $4,500.00 Prorated Basis @ $ $12.3287 Per 356 days			4,389	04
9. Special Assessments Assumed by Buyer				
10. Rent Prorated (list below)				
11. LP Gas/Fuel Oil and Other Items on Premises				
12. Recording Fees				
13. Transfer Fees				
14.				
15.				
16.				
17.				
18.				
Totals	$154,000	00	$7,389	04
Less Credit to Buyer	7,389	04		
Less: Mortgage or Land Contract Executed by Buyer to Seller				
Balance Due Seller	$146,610	96		

19. Daily Use and Occupancy Charge is $
20. Date of Vacating Property
21. Escrow:
22.
23.

TENANT'S NAME	MONTHLY RENTAL	DUE DATE	PAID UP TO	PRORATED AMOUNT

THIS STATEMENT IS ACCEPTED AS CORRECT ______, ______

______ Buyer ______ Seller

______ Buyer ______ Seller

Source: Published with permission, Wisconsin Legal Blank Company, Inc. Line numbers have been added by the publisher for use in this textbook.

FIGURE L

Blank Seller's Closing Statement

FORM 930-S Seller's Closing Statement

Wisconsin Legal Blank Co., Inc.
Milwaukee, WI

BROKER

SELLER'S CLOSING STATEMENT

Property Location ______

Seller(s) ______ Address ______

Buyer(s) ______ Address ______

Sale Contract ______ Date Closing ______ Date Closed At ______

BROKER'S SETTLEMENT WITH SELLER	CHARGES AGAINST SELLER	DUE SELLER
1. Check/Cash Received from Buyer		
2. Earnest Money Deposit and Downpayment		
3. Total Due Seller Before Disbursements		
4. Abstract/Title Policy		
5. Recording Fees		
6. Transfer Fee		
7. Attorney's Fees Paid To:		
8. Mortgage or Land Contract Payoffs		
9. Delinquent Taxes (if Assumed) for Years		
10. Seller's Share of Taxes: for ______ Prorated from ______ to ______ Last Year's Taxes ______ Prorated Basis @ $ ______ Per ______		
11. Special Assessments		
12. Other Advances		
13. Commission		
14. Services (Itemize)		
15.		
16.		
17.		
18.		
19.		
20.		

21. Daily Use and Occupancy Charge is $______
22. Date of Vacating Property ______
23. Escrow: ______

Total Charges Against Seller ______

Balance to be Paid Seller ______

THIS STATEMENT IS ACCEPTED AS CORRECT ______, 20______

______ Broker ______ Seller

By ______ ______ Seller

Source: Published with permission, Wisconsin Legal Blank Company, Inc. Line numbers have been added by the publisher for use in this textbook.

FIGURE M

Completed Seller's Closing Statement

FORM 930-S Seller's Closing Statement

Wisconsin Legal Blank Co., Inc.
Milwaukee, WI

BROKER

SELLER'S CLOSING STATEMENT

Property Location 2901 Newman Street, Madison, WI 53705

Seller(s) Jack and Mary Nelson Address

Buyer(s) Jay and Linda Norris Address

Sale Contract 11/24/09 Date Closing 12/23/09 Date Closed At

BROKER'S SETTLEMENT WITH SELLER	CHARGES AGAINST SELLER	DUE SELLER
1. Check/Cash Received from Buyer		146,610 96
2. Earnest Money Deposit and Downpayment		3,000 00
3. Total Due Seller Before Disbursements		149,610 96
4. Abstract/Title Policy	425 00	
5. Recording Fees	12 00	
6. Transfer Fee	462 00	
7. Attorney's Fees Paid To:		
8. Mortgage or Land Contract Payoffs		
9. Delinquent Taxes (if Assumed) for Years	500 00	
10. Seller's Share of Taxes: for ____ Prorated from ____ to ____ Last Year's Taxes ____ Prorated Basis @ $ ____ Per ____		
11. Special Assessments		
12. Other Advances		
13. Commission	9,240 00	
14. Services (Itemize)		
15. Water Meter Reading 12/23/09	90 00	
16.		
17.		
18.		
19.		
20.	10,729 00	

21. Daily Use and Occupancy Charge is $ ____
22. Date of Vacating Property ____
23. Escrow: ____

Total Charges Against Seller	10,729 00
Balance to be Paid Seller	$138,881 96

THIS STATEMENT IS ACCEPTED AS CORRECT ____________, 20____

____________ Broker ____________ Seller

By ____________ ____________ Seller

Source: Published with permission, Wisconsin Legal Blank Company, Inc. Line numbers have been added by the publisher for use in this textbook.

Answer Key: Chapter Questions

The following answers are given for questions in each chapter in order to help you make maximum use of the tests. If you did not answer a question correctly, study the course material until you understand the correct answer.

CHAPTER 1

1. b
2. d
3. c
4. d
5. c
6. d
7. d
8. b
9. b
10. d
11. c
12. c
13. c
14. b
15. d
16. c
17. c
18. b
19. d
20. c

CHAPTER 2

1. d
2. a
3. c
4. b
5. d
6. d
7. c
8. b
9. a
10. b
11. d
12. b
13. d
14. a
15. b
16. c
17. d
18. b
19. c
20. a
21. a
22. d
23. c
24. a
25. d
26. c
27. d
28. d
29. d
30. c
31. b
32. a
33. c
34. d
35. d
36. b
37. d
38. d
39. d
40. d
41. d
42. c
43. d
44. d
45. d
46. b

CHAPTER 3

1. c
2. a
3. c
4. c
5. c
6. c

CHAPTER 4

1. b
2. b
3. b
4. b
5. b
6. c
7. c
8. c
9. c
10. c
11. a
12. d
13. d
14. d

CHAPTER 5

1. d
2. b
3. b
4. c
5. c
6. d
7. a

CHAPTER 6

1. d
2. d
3. d
4. c
5. c
6. b
7. c
8. b
9. d
10. c
11. d
12. d

CHAPTER 7

1. d
2. c
3. a
4. a
5. a
6. b
7. b
8. b
9. c
10. b
11. c
12. d
13. b
14. b
15. d
16. a
17. c
18. b
19. a
20. a
21. a
22. b
23. c
24. d
25. b
26. c
27. c
28. d
29. c
30. d
31. a
32. d
33. d
34. b
35. b

CHAPTER 8

1. c
2. c
3. d
4. d
5. d
6. c
7. b
8. d
9. b
10. c
11. c

CHAPTER 9

1. c
2. a
3. d
4. b
5. a
6. a
7. c

CHAPTER 10

1. b
2. c
3. d
4. d
5. b
6. c
7. d
8. d
9. c
10. b
11. b
12. d
13. b
14. d
15. a
16. d
17. a
18. b
19. d
20. c
21. d
22. c
23. c
24. a
25. a

CHAPTER 11

1. a
2. c
3. d
4. b
5. c
6. d
7. b
8. c

CHAPTER 12

1. c
2. a
3. b
4. c
5. a
6. b
7. b

CHAPTER 13

1. b
2. d
3. a
4. b
5. b
6. d
7. c

CHAPTER 14

1. d
2. d
3. d
4. b
5. d
6. b
7. a
8. d
9. c
10. b
11. c
12. c

CHAPTER 15

1. d
2. b
3. d
4. b
5. b
6. a
7. b
8. a
9. b
10. a

FIGURE N

Completed Buyer's Closing Statement (from Chapter 15)

FORM 930-B Buyer's Closing Statement

Wisconsin Legal Blank Co., Inc.
Milwaukee, WI

BROKER

BUYER'S CLOSING STATEMENT

Property Location 1400 Regas Lane, Madison, WI 53705

Seller(s) George and Martha Carter Address

Buyer(s) Jay and Linda Jones Address

Sale Contract Date 11/15/09 Closing Date 12/15/09 Closed At

BUYER'S SETTLEMENT WITH BROKER	DUE SELLER		CREDIT BUYER	
1. Purchase Price	248,000	00		
2. Earnest Money			4,000	00
3. Downpayment				
4. Mortgages (Assumed by Buyer) Principal $176,004.53 Int. 337.54			176,342	07
5. Land Contracts (Assumed by Buyer)				
6. Trust Funds Due Seller by Mortgagee				
7. Delinquent Taxes (if Assumed) for Years				
8. Seller's Share of Taxes: for 2009 Prorated from 1/1/09 through 12/14/09 Last Year's Taxes $6,250.00 Prorated Basis @ $ 17.12 Per 348 days			5,957	76
9. Special Assessments Assumed by Buyer				
	5,957	76		
10. Rent Prorated (list below)				
11. LP Gas/Fuel Oil and Other Items on Premises				
12. Recording Fees				
13. Transfer Fees				
14.				
15.				
16.				
17.				
18.				
Totals	248,000	00	186,299	83
Less Credit to Buyer	186,299	83		
Less: Mortgage or Land Contract Executed by Buyer to Seller				
Balance Due Seller	61,700	17		

19. Daily Use and Occupancy Charge is $
20. Date of Vacating Property
21. Escrow:
22.
23.

TENANT'S NAME	MONTHLY RENTAL	DUE DATE	PAID UP TO	PRORATED AMOUNT

THIS STATEMENT IS ACCEPTED AS CORRECT ____________, ______

____________ Buyer ____________ Seller

____________ Buyer ____________ Seller

FIGURE O

Completed Seller's Closing Statement (from Chapter 15)

FORM 930-S Seller's Closing Statement

Wisconsin Legal Blank Co., Inc.
Milwaukee, WI

BROKER

SELLER'S CLOSING STATEMENT

Property Location 1400 Regas Lane, Madison, WI 53705

Seller(s) George and Martha Carter Address

Buyer(s) Jay and Linda Jones Address

Sale Contract 11/15/09 Date Closing 12/15/09 Date Closed At

	BROKER'S SETTLEMENT WITH SELLER	CHARGES AGAINST SELLER		DUE SELLER	
1.	Check/Cash Received from Buyer			61,700	17
2.	Earnest Money Deposit and Downpayment			4,000	00
3.	Total Due Seller Before Disbursements			65,700	17
4.	Abstract/Title Policy				
5.	Recording Fees	518	00		
6.	Transfer Fee $248,000 × .003	744	00		
7.	Attorney's Fees Paid To: Prepare Deed	300	00		
8.	Mortgage or Land Contract Payoffs				
9.	Delinquent Taxes (if Assumed) for Years				
10.	Seller's Share of Taxes: for ____ Prorated from ____ to ____ Last Year's Taxes ____ Prorated Basis @ $ ____ Per ____				
11.	Special Assessments				
12.	Other Advances				
13.	Commission $248,000 × .06	14,880	00		
14.	Services (Itemize)				
15.	Water Meter Reading 12/14/09	80	00		
16.					
17.					
18.					
19.					
20.					
	Total Charges Against Seller			16,522	00
	Balance to be Paid Seller			$46,148	17

21. Daily Use and Occupancy Charge is $

22. Date of Vacating Property

23. Escrow:

THIS STATEMENT IS ACCEPTED AS CORRECT ____________, 20____

____________ Broker ____________ Seller

By ____________ ____________ Seller

Answer Key: Sample Salesperson Exam

1. c
2. b
3. b
4. b
5. c
6. b
7. d
8. a
9. b
10. a
11. b
12. d
13. c
14. d
15. a
16. a
17. c
18. b
19. c
20. c
21. b
22. d
23. d
24. c
25. c
26. d
27. a
28. a
29. c
30. d
31. d
32. c
33. b
34. b
35. d
36. b
37. c
38. b
39. c
40. d
41. d
42. d
43. b
44. c
45. d
46. a
47. d
48. c
49. c
50. d
51. d
52. d
53. d
54. c
55. c
56. b
57. c
58. b
59. c
60. c
61. c
62. d
63. d
64. c
65. d
66. d
67. b
68. d
69. a
70. d
71. a
72. c
73. b
74. d
75. b
76. b
77. a
78. d
79. c
80. d
81. d
82. d
83. d
84. c
85. c
86. d
87. d
88. c
89. b
90. d
91. d
92. c
93. c
94. d
95. d
96. a
97. b
98. a
99. c
100. b
101. b
102. a
103. c
104. c
105. b
106. c
107. d
108. b
109. d
110. a
111. d
112. b
113. a
114. d
115. b
116. c
117. a
118. a
119. b
120. c
121. b
122. d
123. c
124. b
125. c
126. a
127. a
128. b
129. d
130. d
131. b
132. d
133. c
134. c
135. c
136. b
137. c
138. b
139. b
140. d

Index

T

U–V

W–Z